Public Regulation

MIT Press Series on the Regulation of Economic Activity

General Editor
Richard Schmalensee, MIT Sloan School of Management

1 *Freight Transport Regulation*, Ann F. Friedlaender and Richard H. Spady, 1981
2 *The SEC and the Public Interest*, Susan M. Phillips and J. Richard Zecher, 1981
3 *The Economics and Politics of Oil Price Regulation*, Joseph P. Kalt, 1981
4 *Studies in Public Regulation*, Gary Fromm, editor, 1981
5 *Incentives for Environmental Protection*, Thomas C. Schelling, editor, 1983
6 *United States Oil Pipeline Markets: Structure, Pricing, and Public Policy*, John A. Hansen, 1983
7 *Folded, Spindled, and Mutilated: Economic Analysis and U.S. v. IBM*, Franklin M. Fisher, John J. McGowan, and Joen E. Greenwood, 1983
8 *Targeting Economic Incentives for Environmental Protection*, Albert L. Nichols, 1984
9 *Deregulation and the New Airline Entrepreneurs*, John R. Meyer and Clinton V. Oster, Jr., with Marni Clippinger, Andrew McKey, Don H. Pickrell, John Strong, and C. Kurt Zorn, 1984
10 *Deregulating the Airlines*, Elizabeth E. Bailey, David R. Graham, and Daniel P. Kaplan, 1985
11 *The Gathering Crisis in Federal Deposit Insurance*, Edward J. Kane, 1985
12 *Perspectives on Safe and Sound Banking: Past, Present, and Future*, George J. Benston, Robert A. Eisenbeis, Paul M. Horvitz, Edward J. Kane, and George G. Kaufman, 1986
13 *The Economics of Public Utility Regulation*, Michael A. Crew and Paul R. Kleindorfer, 1987
14 *Public Regulation: New Perspectives on Institutions and Policies*, Elizabeth E. Bailey, editor, 1987

Public Regulation
New Perspectives on Institutions and Policies

edited by Elizabeth E. Bailey

The MIT Press
Cambridge, Massachusetts
London, England

© 1987 Massachusetts Institute of Technology

All rights reserved. No part of this book may be reproduced in any form by any electronic or mechanical means (including photocopying, recording, or information storage and retrieval) without permission in writing from the publisher.

This book was set in Times New Roman by Asco Trade Typesetting Ltd., Hong Kong, and printed and bound by Halliday Lithograph in the United States of America.

Library of Congress Cataloging-in-Publication Data

Public regulation.

  (MIT Press series on the regulation of economic activity; 14)
  "Essays ... presented at a conference on public regulation sponsored by Carnegie Mellon University"—Pref.
  Includes index.
  1. Trade regulation—United States—Congresses. 2. Trade regulation—Congresses.
I. Bailey, Elizabeth E. II. Carnegie Mellon University. III. Series.
HD3616.U47P83 1987   338.973   86-21302
ISBN 0-262-02258-3

Contents

List of Contributors	vii
Series Foreword	ix
Preface	xi

I
DESIGN AND FORMATION OF REGULATORY REGIMES

1
Information and Regulation — 3
David E. M. Sappington and Joseph E. Stiglitz

2
Judicial Review of Questions of Law and Policy — 45
Stephen G. Breyer

3
Modern Political Economy and the Study of Regulation — 73
Thomas Romer and Howard Rosenthal

4
The Regulatory Surge of the 1970s in Historical Perspective — 117
Elizabeth Sanders

II
ASSESSMENT OF REGULATORY PERFORMANCE — 151

5
General Equilibrium Analysis of Natural Gas Price Regulation — 153
Dale W. Jorgenson and Daniel T. Slesnick

6
Experimental Evaluation of the Contestable Markets Hypothesis — 191
Glenn W. Harrison

7
Risk Analysis and Relevance of Uncertainties in Nuclear Safety Decisions — 227
M. E. Paté-Cornell

8
Cartels That Vote: Agricultural Marketing Boards and Induced Voting Behavior 255
Jonathan Cave and Stephen W. Salant

9
An Assessment of the Efficiency Effects of U.S. Airline Deregulation via an International Comparison 285
Douglas W. Caves, Laurits R. Christensen, Michael W. Tretheway, and Robert J. Windle

10
Occupational Disease Remedies: The Asbestos Experience 321
Leslie I. Boden and Carol Adaire Jones

11
Industrywide Regulation and the Formation of Reputations: A Laboratory Analysis 347
Andrew F. Daughety and Robert Forsythe

Index 399

List of Contributors

Elizabeth E. Bailey
Graduate School of Industrial
 Administration
Carnegie Mellon University
Pittsburgh, PA

Leslie I. Boden
Boston University School of Public
 Health
Boston, MA

Stephen Breyer
United States Court of Appeals,
 First Circuit
Boston, MA

Jonathan Cave
The Rand Corporation
Santa Monica, CA

Douglas W. Caves
University of Wisconsin and
 Christensen Associates Inc.
Madison, WI

Laurits R. Christensen
University of Wisconsin and
 Christensen Associates, Inc.
Madison, WI

Andrew F. Daughety
Department of Economics
The University of Iowa
Iowa City, IA

Robert Forsythe
Department of Economics
The University of Iowa
Iowa City, IA

Glenn W. Harrison
Department of Economics
University of Western Ontario
London, Ontario, Canada

Carol Adaire Jones
The School of Natural Resources
University of Michigan
Ann Arbor, MI

Dale W. Jorgenson
Department of Economics
Harvard University
Cambridge, MA

M. E. Paté-Cornell
IE/EM Department
Stanford University
Stanford, CA

Thomas Romer
Graduate School of Industrial
 Administration
Carnegie Mellon University
Pittsburgh, PA

Howard Rosenthal
Graduate School of Industrial
 Administration
Carnegie Mellon University
Pittsburgh, PA

Stephen W. Salant
The Rand Corporation
Santa Monica, CA

Elizabeth Sanders
New School for Social Research
New York, NY

David E. M. Sappington
Bell Communications Research
Lincoln Park, NJ

Daniel T. Slesnick
Department of Economics
University of Texas
Austin, TX

Joseph E. Stiglitz
Department of Economics
Princeton University
Princeton, NJ

Michael W. Tretheway
Transportation Center
University of British Columbia
Vancouver, BC, Canada

Robert J. Windle
University of Wisconsin and
  Christensen Associates, Inc.
Madison, WI

Series Foreword

Government regulation of economic activity in the United States has grown dramatically in this century, radically transforming government-business relations. Economic regulation of prices and conditions of service was first applied to transportation and public utilities and was later extended to energy, health care, and other sectors. In the early 1970s explosive growth occurred in social regulation, focusing on workplace safety, environmental preservation, consumer protection, and related goals. Regulatory reform has occupied a prominent place on the agendas of recent administrations, and though considerable economic deregulation and other reform have occurred, the aims, methods, and results of many regulatory programs remain controversial.

The purpose of the MIT Press series, Regulation of Economic Activity, is to inform the ongoing debate on regulatory policy by making significant and relevant research available to both scholars and policymakers. Books in this series present new insights into individual agencies, programs, and regulated sectors, as well as the important economic, political, and administrative aspects of the regulatory process that cut across these boundaries.

This broad collection of essays, carefully assembled and edited by Elizabeth Bailey, is a sample of the best recent academic work on regulation. Its high quality reflects the important impact of the National Science Foundations' decade-long program on Regulation and Policy Analysis on a generation of scholars. The multifaceted and interdisciplinary nature of research on regulation is made clear here, as is the wide range of regulatory programs, problems, and issues that still confronts us despite the "Reagan Revolution." The essays collected here will be of interest to overlapping sets of specialists; the collection as a whole should be read by anyone interested in the state of the art in analysis of the design and performance of regulatory regimes and programs.

Richard Schmalensee

Preface

The essays in this volume were presented at a conference on public regulation sponsored by Carnegie Mellon University under a grant awarded by the National Science Foundation (NSF). The conference marked a decade of research funding by NSF's Regulation and Policy Analysis program. Sadly it also marked the end of its existence. Since there is not likely to be another occasion quite so auspicious as this one, I wish to thank Laurence Rosenberg of the NSF for his accomplishments in managing this program. Under his stewardship the program achieved several significant contributions of lasting importance.

First, the program nurtured a generation of scholars. It provided funds and an imprimatur of excellence for their research. It helped researchers, as graduate students and young professors, to believe that the phenomenon of regulation creates an extremely important and intellectually challenging area for research. It gave stature and excitement to such research.

Second, the program opened new frontiers of knowledge about regulation. It sponsored research that provided evidence for the mid-1970s' debate on banking regulation, on issues of consumer credit, on competition for financial services and the impact of technology. It funded research about efficient pricing in regulated industries, about productivity measurement, about the inefficiency of regulation in surface and air transportation, and thereby laid the framework for regulatory reform and deregulation. It also supported significant advances in knowledge about health and safety regulation, the measurement of costs and benefits in environmental regulation, and the political economy of regulation and its distributional aspects.

Third, the program sponsored a series of conferences that assembled about as influential and interesting a group as one could imagine of those who have thought about and, in many cases, practiced their ideas about regulation. The community included economists, lawyers, political scientists, and policymakers. The first such conference, organized by Gary Fromm, took place in 1977. The conference volume, *Studies in Public Regulation*, was subsequently published in this MIT Press series. Other conferences followed. In 1980 a small group of distinguished scholars was convened to consider the possibilities for further attracting social scientists to regulation research. This led to a 1982 conference on social science and regulatory policy, organized by Roger Noll, and to a 1983 conference on administrative law and political economy, organized by Susan Rose-Ackerman. The last NSF regulation conference, held in 1985, is represented by this volume.

As in the first conference, papers to be presented were selected in an open competition. A call was issued and more than 120 abstracts were received. These were reviewed by a steering committee of experts on public regulation. The committee discussed the merits of the leading candidates, so as to choose papers that would lend new perspectives on the formulation, analysis, and evaluation of regulatory institutions and policies. During the conference each paper was critiqued by an outstanding scholar in the field. After the conference each paper was sent to a referee who offered further suggestions for revisions. Decisions were then made about which papers were to be included in the proceedings volume.

The fine group of essays that constitutes this volume is a testimony to the importance, quality, and interdisciplinary nature of research on issues of regulation. The papers fit into two broad categories. The first category consists of papers that address the design and formulation of regulatory regimes. The papers portray vividly the collective (multistage, multiplayer) aspects of regulatory structure and decisions. David E. M. Sappington and Joseph E. Stiglitz review a new literature concerned with the interaction between regulators and regulated firms under imperfect information. The primary vehicle for analysis is the principal-agent model, familiar to readers of research on information economics. The authors do an excellent job in outlining the relation of informational problems to regulatory behaviors and in making the modern theoretical tools in this area accessible to the reader. Judge Stephen G. Breyer deals with the institutional capabilities of the independent agencies and the courts. He makes an important contribution to legal research with his argument that courts are beginning to be relied on for policy decisions, rather than for decisions pertaining to law, while the reverse is becoming true for agencies. Unfortunately such a division is likely to make matters worse because courts have a poorer information base than the agencies and a deeper legal expertise.

The last two papers in the section deal with formation (rather than design) of regulatory policy. Both are presented from the political science perspective. Thomas Romer and Howard Rosenthal survey the current base of theoretical and empirical research on policy formation, focusing particularly on optimization models. They offer the view that unidimensional (liberal-conservative) models of voting can be fruitfully applied to study the formation of regulatory policy. In contrast, Elizabeth Sanders offers a provocative essay where the intention is to describe the broad alliances that have historically stood behind the movement for regulation. The alliances are portrayed as issuing from an industrial core and an extractive periphery, which set the scene for decisions about regulation.

The second broad category of essays deals with methods for assessing the benefits and costs of regulation. The first three papers focus on the development of theory and methods. Dale W. Jorgenson and Daniel T. Slesnick offer an important applied econometric perspective on classical welfare economics. They develop creative and attractive computer-based tools for practical normative analysis within a general equilibrium framework, and then apply these tools to compare three regulatory policies of natural gas supply. Glenn W. Harrison reports on the design and results of a series of laboratory experiments aimed at testing the contestable markets hypothesis and finds that experiments offer support for the robustness of the theory. M. Elisabeth Paté-Cornell discusses the role of risk assessment in regulatory analysis. She outlines the joint role of engineering and economics in achieving resolution of problems in nuclear power industry regulation.

The final group of papers focuses on performance and effects of current regulatory and deregulatory policy. Jonathan A. K. Cave and Stephen W. Salant use game theory to study the operation and economic consequences of a voting mechanism used by firms that take part in an agricultural marketing cartel. The cartel operates with immunity from the antitrust laws. Their basic premise is that the operation of the voting mechanism leads to equilibrium outcomes that are not cartel joint-profit maximizing. Douglas W. Caves, Laurits R. Christensen, Robert J. Windle, and Michael W. Tretheway use modern cost-function analysis techniques to compare the productivity and unit-cost trends of U.S. and foreign air carriers before and after deregulation. Leslie I. Boden and Carol Adaire Jones address yet a third regulated sector, that of occupational health and safety. They analyze the asbestos problem and convey interesting empirical results. Andrew F. Daughety and Robert Forsythe use experiments to show that periods of active and extensive cooperation between firms (periods of regulation) have effects on behavior that persist beyond the period of formal cooperation (into periods of deregulation).

Overall, then, the volume addresses both how regulatory institutions and policies come about and whether these institutions and policies perform and work well. Many of the essays go beyond traditional tools used by regulatory researchers—we encounter here general equilibrium theory, experimental research methods, the integration of rational expectations and game theory tools with regulation, the use of new cost function techniques, and the introduction of probabilistic risk analysis. The papers combine these theoretical advances with rich empirical analyses. Clearly many of the leading scholars now doing research in the regulation area have made an investment in institutional knowledge; yet their research is based solidly on economic theory and other social science and law disciplines. This new and important perspective lends an exciting richness and freshness to this volume.

Much is owed the program participants and referees for the high quality of this volume. The group consisted of Elizabeth E. Bailey, Chair, Carnegie Mellon University; William F. Baxter, Stanford University; Ronald R. Braeutigam, Northwestern University; E. Gerald Corrigan, Federal Reserve Bank of New York; Robert W. Crandall, The Brookings Institution; Christopher C. DeMuth, Lexecon, Inc.; George C. Eads, University of Maryland; Morris P. Fiorina, Harvard University; Ann F. Friendleander, Massachusetts Institute of Technology; Benjamin M. Friedman, Harvard University; Dale W. Jorgenson, Harvard University; Paul L. Joskow, Massachusetts Institute of Technology; Lester B. Lave, Carnegie Mellon University; Michael E. Levine, University of Southern California; Paul W. MacAvoy, University of Rochester; Thomas G. Moore, Council of Economic Advisors; William A. Niskanen, The Cato Institution; Roger G. Noll, Stanford University; Thomas R. Palfrey, Carnegie Mellon University; John C. Panzar, Northwestern University; M. Elisabeth Paté-Cornell, Stanford University; Sam Peltzman, University of Chicago; William H. Riker, University of Rochester; Thomas Romer, Carnegie Mellon University; Susan Rose-Ackerman, Columbia University; Laurence C. Rosenberg, National Science Foundation; Howard Rosenthal, Carnegie Mellon University; Steven C. Salop, Georgetown University; Richard Schmalensee, Massachusetts Institute of Technology; Alan Schwartz, University of Southern California; David S. Sibley, Bell Communications; Vernon L. Smith, University of Arizona; A. Michael Spence, Harvard University; Barry R. Weingast, Washington University; and Robert D. Willig, Princeton University. Thanks are also due to Ann Grekila of Carnegie Mellon University, who did an exceptional job of conference planning and administration.

I

DESIGN AND FORMATION OF REGULATORY REGIMES

1

Information and Regulation

David E. M. Sappington and Joseph E. Stiglitz

Governments are involved in a large number of regulatory activities, from regulating utilities, to regulating financial institutions, to regulating automobile safety and setting emission standards. Regulations are but one means that the government has of attempting to elicit certain desired outcomes. To some extent, regulations represent a half-way house between methods that involve more direct controls (nationalization of an industry) and those that involve the use of more indirect control mechanisms (taxes and subsidies). The theme of this chapter is that central to an understanding of both the choice among these methods of control—and, when regulation is opted for, the design of the regulatory scheme—is an understanding of the problems posed by imperfect and costly information.

The discussion proceeds as follows. The first section contains an overview of the basic issues associated with government control. The analysis is broken down as follows. First, the reasons for government control are outlined. The essence of the information problems under consideration here is then described, and it is noted that the particular control problems on which we and the literature focus are properly viewed within the context of a broader range of control problems. The different control structures under taxation, regulation, and public enterprise are illustrated. The reasons that the structure and hierarchy of control are not inconsequential are then outlined. The role that franchise bidding can play in the regulatory arena is considered. We next examine the apparent duality between problems of optimal taxation, regulation, and monopoly pricing—a duality that if not properly treated, can given misleading results. The regulatory problem of rent extraction from an established firm is then outlined and thereby serves as an introduction to the second section of the chapter.

The second section focuses on regulation as a method of control. It begins with a formal statement of the regulator's problem of rent extraction. It identifies the problems caused for the regulator by imperfect information and reviews proposed methods for dealing with these problems. In particular, regulatory schemes that involve auditing, comparisons across firms, and comparisons over time are considered. An attempt is also made to relate the "new" models of regulation under imperfect information to the "classic" models of regulation (e.g., the analysis in Averch and Johnson 1982).

A caveat is in order before proceeding. We attempt to provide an evenhanded overview of the literature on the design of regulatory policy in the presence of limited information. But it is likely that we fail to cite some important references and manage to cite papers with which we are most familiar (e.g., our own) too often. We apologize in advance for any shortcomings on these two accounts. We also note at the outset two complementary surveys that are recommended. The one most closely related to ours is by Caillaud et. al. (1985). The other is an overview of the contracting literature by Hart and Holmstrom (1985).

Reasons for Government Control

As noted at the outset, government control is observed in at least three distinct forms: indirect control, regulation, and nationalization. Government action in one of these forms generally arises from a belief that markets do not always work well. One of the central results of modern economics is the fundamental theorem of welfare economics. The theorem establishes conditions under which competitive market allocations are Pareto efficient and under which Pareto-efficient allocations can be sustained by competitive markets. When these conditions fail to hold, markets will not, in general, be efficient. Thus, in principle, there is scope for government intervention.

Much of regulation is aimed at three broad classes of market failure:

1. *Imperfect competition.* Under a variety of circumstances the market will not be competitive. (What is required for economic efficiency is more than just rivalry; what is required is that firms be price takers, which they may not be, even when there are many firms in a market.) This is particularly relevant where there are large nonconvexities, giving rise to natural monopolies. This provides the motivation for government intervention in utilities.[1]

2. *Imperfect information.* The fundamental theorem of welfare economics assumes that there is perfect information. Recently Greenwald and Stiglitz (1986) have shown that when there is imperfect information, there is almost always scope for government intervention (even if the government is restricted to imposing commodity taxes and subsidies) which is Pareto improving. Imperfect information provides the basis of two broad sets of government regulatory activities: First, in insurance markets the likelihood

of the event occurring that is insured against is increased by the provision of insurance; to offset this, the insurer attempts to *regulate* the actions of the insured. Since the government, either implicitly or explicitly, is involved in a large number of insurance activities, it attempts to impose regulations that reduce the incidence of events that are insured against.[2] Second, consumer protection and worker protection legislation is largely based on the presumption that individuals cannot look after themselves as well as the government, largely because they are imperfectly informed and it is costly for them to gather information:

3. *Externalities.* Whenever there are externalities, competitive market solutions will be inefficient. Government regulations aimed at controlling pollution, for example, are directed at alleviating the problems posed by these externalities.

Critics of government activities suggest that even when the simple competitive model does not yield efficient outcomes, a broader interpretation of the competitive process will. For instance, in the case of externalities, there are incentives for individuals to get together to eliminate such inefficient outcomes. This assertion is loosely referred to as the Coase theorem. It ignores of course all the standard public good/free rider problems. Moreover it ignores the transactions costs involved in these private deliberations: the government can be thought of as the mechanism that has, indeed, been set up to deal with these externalities. Finally, in small group situations it ignores the bargaining problems and the inefficiencies that arise in bargaining under imperfect information.[3]

With perfect information the three approaches of regulation, nationalization, and control via tax/subsidy schemes are equivalent.[4] To see this, assume the government wishes to effect a particular outcome. It can either *induce* the private firms to do what the government would like them to do through taxes and subsidies, or it can, via the regulatory mechanism, *order* the firms to do what it wishes them to do. Alternatively, the government can carry out the task itself (with nationalization). Indeed, in some sense, regulation can be viewed simply as the imposition of a nonlinear tax/subsidy schedule, with large penalties being imposed for noncompliance with the orders of the regulator (sufficiently large that the regulated is always induced to voluntarily comply with the wishes of the regulator).[5] With perfect information none of the controversies about the efficiency of government control or its form would arise.

With imperfect information regulation, nationalization, and tax/subsidy schemes are not equivalent; and the form of regulation becomes of importance. Research to date has not delineated clearly the distinctions among these alternative control mechanisms. Our objective is to identify some of the salient differences. To see what is at issue, we focus our attention on the regulation of utilities, but it should be apparent how the analysis can be adapted to other regulatory contexts.

The information theoretic approach to these issues begins by attempting to delineate who knows what when, and who has the right to take what actions under various circumstances. The natural assumption is that those involved in production (i.e., in running the utility) have more information concerning (1) the technology of production (both current technology and the possibilities for technological improvements), (2) the demand structure for the commodity, and/or (3) relevant factor costs than do outside parties.[6] Others (the government, the regulator) may come to know about some of these variables, but only with a lag, and indeed, in a rapidly changing environment, the information that they acquire may be of only limited relevance to the current situation. It is this limited information that poses the central problem for the government. The government can only order the firm to do something that is feasible, but it may not know what is feasible. And even if it were to know what is feasible, what it would wish the firm to do depends on factor costs, technology, and consumer preferences, about which it may be less informed than the firm—for example, if the costs of reducing pollution are enormous, the government might not wish the firm to reduce its pollutant levels by very much; if the costs are insignificant, it may wish a large reduction. But if the government must rely on the firm to tell it what the costs are, what is the government to do? It cannot, in general, rely on the firm to tell it the truth—for instance, what manager of the firm would truthfully tell the government his reservation wage, or the opportunity cost of his time? Much of the detailed modeling we describe in the second section of this chapter is aimed at devising methods by which the firm is induced to reveal this information truthfully (although at a cost, often in the form of "distorted" behavior).

The information problems with which we are concerned arise because of the impact that they have on the government's attempt to control the firm and to "extract" rents from it. We now turn to consider directly the problem of control.

The Hierarchy of Control
The simplest model of control involves two parties: the party that establishes the controls (the principal) and the party that operates under

these controls (the agent). The simplest model of regulation, for example, considers the interaction between one regulator and a single firm. In fact, this is the type of model that has been afforded the vast majority of attention in the literature, as the review in the second section makes clear. In reality, however, the control problem is far more complicated.

Take, for instance, the case of regulation. And for simplicity, suppose that there is only a single firm in the economy and that this firm produces the sole commodity that is consumed by society. Thus with only a single market we need not be concerned with distinctions between partial and general equilibrium analyses. Even in this simple setting there are a host of control problems that are intricately intertwined.

In the traditional nineteenth-century model of such a firm, there was no division between ownership and management: the owner-manager took whatever actions were required to maximize his (expected) utility, and since little attention was paid to any disutility of effort, it was usually presumed that he simply maximized his (expected) profits or the (market) value of the firm.

It is now recognized that this provides an inadequate description of most modern corporations where ownership is widely held. The earlier naive models simply substituted the "board of directors" for the "owner" and ignored any problems the owner (or board of directors) faced in controlling the management. But the members of the board of directors (other than those who are part of management itself) usually have very limited information, both concerning what the management is doing, and what the firm's full opportunity set is—that is, they have limited information concerning technology, markets, and factor prices. These information limitations provide management with considerable discretion.[7]

But even this view, which emphasizes the distinction between owner-managed and nonowner-managed firms, does not provide a good description of corporations in which shares are widely held. For it is not apparent that shareholders can effectively exercise even the limited control associated with ownership. As has been repeatedly emphasized, good management is a public good: all shareholders benefit from having the firm run in a better way. There is, however, a cost to learning whether the current management is performing its job well (and of course to attempting to replace inadequate management). There is thus an incentive for each small shareholder to attempt to free ride on the management efforts of others.[8]

But shareholders are not the only ones affected by the actions of the firm. Debtors, though they do not share in large gains, will be adversely affected by large losses. The institutional structure by which one bank acts as the lead bank reduces the "free rider" problem, which in any case is much less than that for shareholders, since individual banks are likely to have large positions with particular firms. The threat of banks to cut off credit, and the explicitly specified rights of banks to intervene in the firm under stipulated conditions, enable the banks to exercise some indirect control over management. This suggests that the appropriate way to view a firm is as an agent for multiple principles.[9] And as is by now well known, the equilibrium to multiple-principal agent problems is not Pareto efficient (see Braverman and Stiglitz 1982, Bernheim and Whinston 1984, Arnott and Stiglitz 1985). This basic depiction of the simplest control structure within a firm is illustrated in figure 1.1.

Figure 1.1 also illustrates an additional problem of control within the regulated setting. When regulation is introduced, there is another "principal" who can exercise some control over the firm's activities. However, the effectiveness of the regulator's control is reduced by her limited information. For example, the regulated utility can claim that at current rates of return, capacity expansion is unprofitable; it can attempt to create a "crisis." The regulator may find it difficult to ascertain whether the crisis is real.

There is another important aspect of the control structure in a regulated setting. Generally, the regulator is either elected or appointed by an elected official. To ensure that the regulator is acting according to the interests of her constituency, she may be subject to a variety of controls. Thus, in practice, the regulator is most often both a principal (to the firm) and an agent (of her constituency, or the "government"). Note too that the judiciary often serves as an independent check on the activities of both the regulator and the firm.

Figure 1.2 illustrates the basic hierarchy of control under nationalization. It is still important for managers within the public enterprise to create incentive systems for their subordinates. Furthermore the judiciary will still exercise control over the activities of the enterprise. The distinctive element of nationalization is that the board of directors, rather than being elected by shareholders, is appointed by the government. Initially, this fact was interpreted to mean that no separate regulatory authority was needed, since it was generally assumed either that the firm acts according to the government's wishes or that effective control can be exercised via the board of directors.

More recently, discussions have correctly emphasized the similarity between nationalized and nonnationalized (including regulated) industries: the actions of the firm are still controlled by managers, who have

Information and Regulation 9

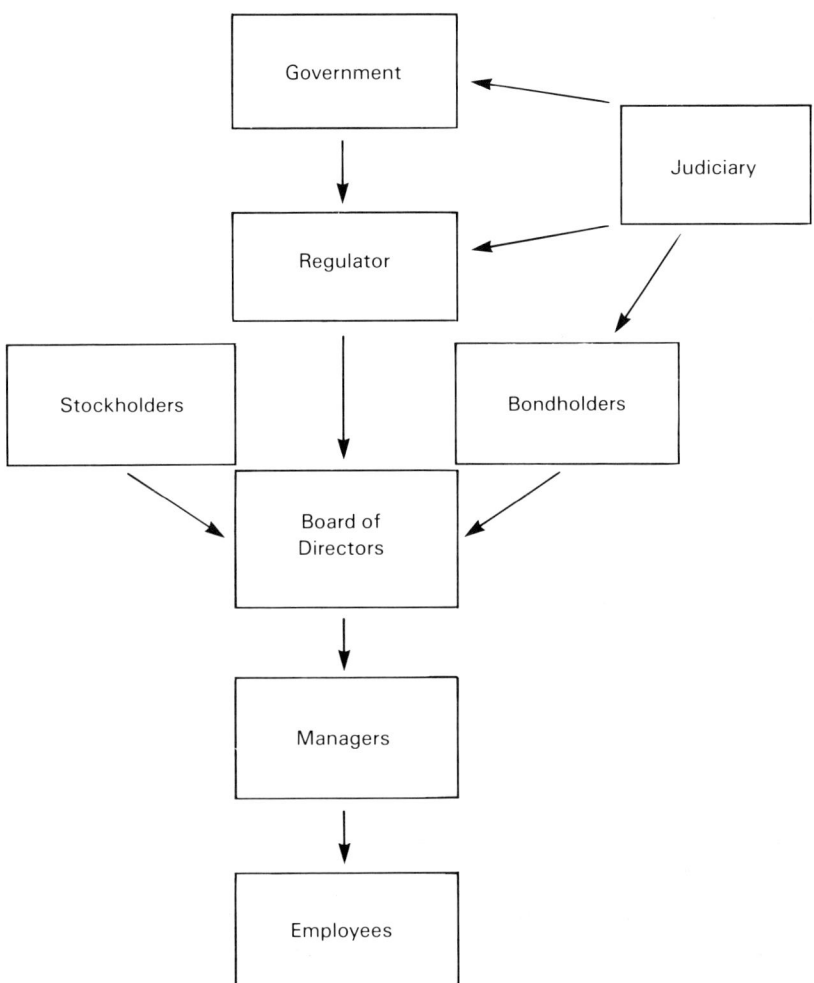

Figure 1.1 Control structure in a regulated setting

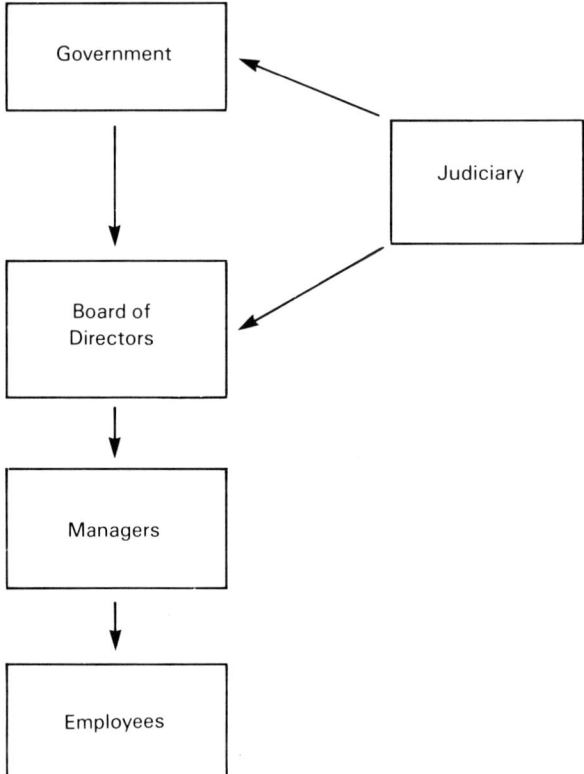

Figure 1.2 Control structure under nationalization

considerable discretion. In either case, the directors have an incentive problem in inducing the managers to undertake the desired actions and to reveal their private information, so that the directors can ascertain what actions should be undertaken.

But this is not the only problem. Often, the directors of an enterprise come to identify with the problems of the firm. Thus they see themselves as representing the interests of the firm—its workers and other members of the nationalized industry—within the government (e.g., in seeking greater government subsidies). Thus, in at least one country which has nationalized many industries, the focus of current concern is on the "socialization" of nationalized industries, trying to alter the behavior of the firm to pursue national objectives rather than private objectives.

Moreover the possibility of large government subsidies replaces the indirect control exercised by banks (and credit markets in general) by the indirect control exercised by political institutions. The differences in incentives (to management, or to the board of directors) should be apparent.[10]

Why Is Control Important?

We have proceeded in our discussion emphasizing the differences in the structure of control associated with different institutional structure.[11] At first glance it is not obvious why differences in firm behavior must necessarily be associated with differences in institutional structure. For instance, vertical integration need not have any effect on the behavior of either the upstream or downstream firm, if all contingencies are contracted for. That is, just as we argued for the equivalence between regulation and indirect control in the presence of perfection information, there is a similar equivalence, even in the presence of at least certain kinds of information imperfections, between a vertically integrated and a nonvertically integrated industry. So long as the set of observables remains unchanged, the same set of contracts for each of the actors can be designed. And with the same set of contracts, behavior of each of the actors will presumably be the same.

But contracts are never complete. Thus the debt contract allows the creditor to intervene in specified ways in specified circumstances, but it does not specify precisely what he will do—that is, what kinds of direct or indirect control mechanisms he will employ. (The reason that contracts are not fully specified should by now be obvious. For a detailed discussion, see Williamson 1975.) Because contracts are not complete, different institutional structures differ according to which party has "residual control," namely who can take what actions when unspecified contingencies arise and who has the right to intervene in the activities of others and under what circumstances. And because of incomplete contracting, it may not be possible for a principal who has the right to intervene to commit himself in advance not to intervene.

There remains, however, the question of why control is important. In the traditional competitive (Arrow-Debreu) model, control is not important; the manager of the firm simply maximizes the firm's market value. Any other manager would do precisely the same thing that the firm's current manager does. Indeed, the manager's beliefs about the likelihood of any given state of nature have no impact on the firm's actions.

In the Arrow-Debreu economy there is unanimity among all shareholders concerning what actions the firm should take. However, when there is not a complete set of Arrow-Debreu securities, there may be disagreements, both about whether the firm should maximize its stock market value, and what will be the consequences (e.g., for future market value) of any particular course of action.[12] Though these disagreements are of some theoretical interest, the disagreements between the interests of the debtors and creditors are undoubtedly of greater significance. In particular, the firm's shareholders are concerned only with those returns in the states of nature in which the firm does not go bankrupt, the firm's debtors only with the likelihood of bankruptcy, and the returns in the bankrupt states (which affect what can be recovered). There is a real conflict of interest, and as the probability of bankruptcy looms large, this conflict of interest becomes of sufficient importance that the debtors can no longer trust the manager: they wish to intervene, and the debt contract gives them the right to do so.

It is important to realize that in nationalized enterprises, the government stands in the position as a creditor, either losing the returns on its investment or being "forced" to extend further funds to the enterprise. (The issues are more complicated in regulated enterprises, where shareholders may not be allowed to retain profits from "good" decisions and where ratepayers may be "forced" to pay for "bad" decisions.)

But the government's involvement in these decisions is broader. We argued earlier that it is only under the highly idealized conditions of the Arrow-Debreu model that there would be complete congruence between the objectives of the firm and Pareto efficiency. Thus, in principle, the government might wish to intervene to alleviate some important observed inefficiency in the firm's behavior (e.g., the firm fails to take into account the cost to the government, in unemployment insurance, of closing a plant). In practice, the government seems equally likely to intervene for distributional reasons (e.g., to ensure that some remote areas obtain services at subsidized rates). In some cases the two are hard to distinguish (largely because of the informational concerns that are the central concern of this chapter). Is the government's attempt to reduce the prices paid by a certain class of consumers an attempt to restrict the exercise of monopoly power, or is it an attempt to subsidize that class of consumers?

Auctions as a Means of Control
It is precisely because of the difficulty of separating out these distributional questions from more narrowly defined efficiency issues that some economists have argued for a more limited role of government: the gains from efficiency enhancing interventions may be more than offset by the losses from efficiency decreasing interventions.

Let us assume, for the moment, that the government is simply concerned with efficiency issues; problems of distribution, it is frequently argued, are the proper province of taxation. Let us also assume that the government and potential producers share the same perfect information about consumers' preferences. For simplicity, also consider the case where the regulator's objective is to maximize some well-defined measure of consumers' welfare, such as consumers' surplus. Thus we are abstracting from any problems associated with controlling the regulator. (We will similarly abstract from the control problems within the firm.) Finally, suppose that there are a number of firms who have or can acquire technological information but that this information is unavailable to the regulator.

Auctions have been proposed as a means to render inconsequential the regulator's limited knowledge in this setting. Loeb and Magat (1979), for example, suggested that the regulator might grant a monopoly franchise and subsidize the monopolist for his output according to the magnitude of consumers' surplus generated. The subsidy ensures marginal cost pricing and least cost production. And, with sufficiently competitive bidding, the government can appropriate all monopoly rents. In as much, the regulator effects the outcome that she would have if she had perfect knowledge of the most efficient technology.

Of course for this scheme to perform as well as this analysis suggests, a number of conditions must be satisfied. In particular, there are a number of important institutional assumptions implicit in the theory. For example, unlimited subsidies are presumed feasible (and costless). If subsidies are not feasible (for political or other reasons), so that the firm's only income must be derived from its sales revenue, efficient pricing will not result unless the producing firm is able to price discriminate perfectly. Furthermore, when firms differ in their abilities to price discriminate, a firm may be willing to bid more for the franchise, not because it is a more efficient producer but because it has developed better methods of discrimination.

It is also important for this proposed auction scheme that the bidding be sufficiently competitive to eliminate all monopoly rents. In practice, it is costly for firms to prepare a bid (which entails determining the expected present discounted value of the profits associated with the monopoly franchise). And since these costs are generally sunk costs, only a small number of firms may bid for the monopoly rights.[13]

Thus, though it is true that the presence of technological information dispersed among many firms can help alleviate control problems that arise when the regulator's information is limited, auctions are not necessarily a panacea.

There are some circumstances under which, even in the absence of the ability to discriminate perfectly, an auction will yield efficient outcomes. Assume all individuals are identical and that only linear prices (i.e., a constant price per unit consumed) are feasible. Then an auction in which the government imposes a lower bound on the utility level of the consumers will yield Pareto-efficient outcomes, provided the utility level is set appropriately. The markups of price over marginal cost will not be uniform. Rather, they will correspond to Ramsey prices, after Frank Ramsey (1927).[14] In the simple case of independent demand curves, goods with inelastic demand will have proportionately higher markups.

This result follows from the duality between the optimal pricing problem of a monopolist and the problem of optimal taxation: the latter maximizes utility subject to a profit constraint, whereas the former maximizes profit subject to a utility constraint. The Lagrangian functions associated with these two problems have the same form, and for appropriately chosen values of the constraints yield identical solutions. But this result requires some critical assumptions, which we will return to shortly.

The Locus of Control

To this point, the analysis has largely been concerned with a partial equilibrium analysis. General equilibrium considerations also warrant attention, for they further complicate problems of control. To illustrate this point, consider a setting related to the setting of the preceding section. In particular, suppose there are a number of regulated markets in the economy, with one good produced in each market. Suppose also that the regulator in each market knows how consumer demand varies with the product's price in that market but lacks global demand information. The regulator is again presumed to have as her goal the maximization of consumers' surplus. Similarly, suppose that there are a large number of potential producers of each product who are perfectly informed about the costs of producing that one product but none of whom has global technological information. For simplicity, also assume that the firms in each sector are identical in their ability to price discriminate.

It is immediate from the preceding discussion that if the regulator in each sector is permitted to subsidize the producer under her jurisdiction—and if none of the other sources of market failure noted earlier arise—she can effect her most desired outcome within that sector through an auction. And even without subsidies, the most preferred price vector can be ensured if potential producers can sign binding contracts with consumers. This is accomplished by awarding the franchise to the firm that, with its signed contracts, generates the highest amount of consumer's surplus. Competition will eliminate any rents to the monopolist and will ensure that the least cost producer in each sector wins the franchise.[15]

If subsidies are not allowed, price will not equal marginal cost in each sector. It is apparent that this solution is not as desirable as the solution when subsidies are feasible. But given the restriction, the outcome is the same one that would arise under a system of direct control and full knowledge of technological possibilities.

More subtle questions arise if there are multiple products in each sector, but subsidies across sectors are still not allowed. Will the pattern of prices required to break even be Pareto efficient? This question seems similar to that posed earlier, where we argued that the duality between the optimal tax problem and the monopoly pricing problem ensured the efficiency of the pricing structure. But there we ignored the interactions between the regulated sector and the rest of the economy, interactions that would be taken into account with direct government control. We will show that there is less to this duality result than meets the eye in a general equilibrium analysis. The global optimum to the government's problem will take into account the impact of each firm's pricing decisions on (1) the tax revenues (and profits) generated elsewhere in the economy and (2) the prices of other commodities. The decentralized, partial equilibrium approach outlined earlier will not do so.

Thus, if coal is used as an input into electricity, a railroad monopoly would ignore the effect of its pricing structure on the price the utility has to charge to break even. Since price in that sector exceeds marginal cost, there are real welfare effects from this apparent pecuniary externality (see Ebrill and Slutsky 1985; McFarland 1985). Similarly, a change in the price of electricity may affect the demand for oil, and hence the revenues the government receives from the windfall profits tax.

There is an additional problem with this decentralized approach to regulation. The least cost producer of a single product is not necessarily the least cost producer of two or more products. Thus, when franchises are awarded on the basis of performance within a particular market, the producer that is globally most efficient may be overlooked, particularly if the franchises are not all awarded simultaneously.

It is also the case that in practice, the monopolist is usually granted a limited monopoly. Thus, being concerned with the entry of competitors (producing "related" products), the monopolist will choose prices with entry deterrence in mind. To illustrate, suppose that there is some "inefficient" technology for producing some commodity. The associated production cost puts a constraint on what the monopolist can charge for its output. If the demand for the product is very inelastic, the monopolist will have to charge less than the unconstrained Ramsey price. If the stand-alone technology has diminishing returns, the monopolist will consider only his residual demand curve (taking into account the amount supplied by others) in calculating the "Ramsey" prices. In as much, these prices may differ markedly from those the government would charge.

Of course all of these problems could be avoided if the monopoly franchise were defined "appropriately." In particular, if the entire economy were defined as the franchise, the distinction between the partial and general equilibrium approaches would disappear. But, for the proposed bidding schemes to operate well in this setting, there would have to be a number of firms with detailed *global* technological information. Clearly this is an unlikely possibility. For effective operation of the scheme, the government would also need to know global demand functions. Such knowledge is also unlikely. Indeed, one apparent reason for delegating authority to individual regulators within individual markets is to have them develop expertise and make informed judgments using that expertise. With limited abilities to acquire and process information, regulators cannot be expected to develop anything close to global expertise.

Thus some degree of decentralization is inevitable. But we have shown that even with complete information about local demand and cost structures, regulators will generally be unable to effect the outcome that is globally optimal.

Our analysis has suggested that defining the franchise appropriately is of critical importance. Even limiting ourselves to the static entry deterrence and residual demand problems, this is not an easy matter.[16] In a dynamic setting, awarding a broad franchise may result in "correct" prices today. But broad franchises imply that some new, more efficient technologies that develop may not be employed.

The duality between the standard optimal tax problem and the standard monopoly pricing problem will fail to hold for another reason when consumers differ and their characteristics are not completely known to the government or monopoly firm. Under such circumstances the government may employ nonlinear price schedules to allocate the burden of the fixed costs of the utility in an equitable manner. In setting its price structure, the government may know that some individuals are better able to pay than others but can only distinguish among them on the basis of, say, the quantity of electricity consumed. Formally, the set of Pareto-efficient discriminating pricing structures are those that maximize one group's utility subject to other groups attaining particular levels of utility, while ensuring that no group consumes the (price-quantity) "bundle" designed for a different group. These latter constraints are referred to as the self-selection constraints.[17]

The optimal pricing problem of the monopolist is not fully dual to the problem of Pareto-efficient taxation in this setting, for the monopolist is concerned only with maximizing revenue subject to the self-selection constraints. In particular, for indivduals who are inframarginal (i.e., who derive strictly positive consumer surplus from consuming the product), the monopolist is only concerned with how a change in pricing policy affects his demand and revenues, and not how it affects their utility.[18] Moreover, there are important situations where the government prefers a pooling outcome (where individuals' characteristics cannot be discerned from their consumption patterns), though a monopolist would always discriminate.[19]

It is thus apparent that the formal similarity between the government's pricing problem and that of the monopolist is just that: a formal similarity. The government would not in general simply wish to delegate the problem of pricing to a monopolist, even if it could capture the rents through an auction. Our analysis has shown that a monopolist would not behave as would the government if the government had access to the monopolist's information about technology and demand.

In practice, the problem faced by the government is that it neither knows the technology nor the demand structure. Thus it finds it difficult to ascertain what the marginal costs are, and hence what the implicit tax is on any particular service. The government also has difficulty determining the deadweight losses associated with any particular discriminatory pricing scheme. It knows that the monopolist need not be acting in the public interest, but it may now know how to take appropriate corrective action.

Rent Extraction from Established Firms

These important informational problems, as large as they may loom in political debates, have not played quite so central a role in recent literature on the regulatory problem. This literature has been more concerned with the problem of extracting rents from a utility in a partial equilibrium setting where there is an established firm, so that a "fair" auction of the franchise is not feasible. If the government attempts to extract too much rent from the firm, the firm may terminate operations. The government must make an inference concerning the technology but must extract the information through the standard method of framing the choices of the firm in such a way as to induce it to reveal its true characteristics, so the firm's behavior is distorted. The second section describes more formally how this is done, and identifies some important situations where the associated distortions are limited in magnitude.

Before presenting these results, several general observations are in order. First, this literature focuses on the rent-extraction problem, not the incentive problem of providing the manager with the appropriate impetus to work hard.[20] It focuses on imperfections of information relating to technology, rather than to factor prices. In fact, these informational problems are related: the regulator finds it difficult to know whether some factor (e.g., "management") is being paid more than its opportunity cost. Thus, observed inefficiencies may arise from an incompetent (but overpaid) management working as hard as they can, rather than a competent management sloughing off on the job. (Indeed, it is possible that it is often no more difficult to make good managerial decisions than to make bad managerial decisions. Since much of the effort involved in making better managerial decisions entail costs not borne by the manager himself (e.g., he hires a contractor to do some research), the importance of effort disutility is hard to ascertain).

Second, it will become apparent that the structure of the regulator's policy is highly dependent on what she knows, what she can monitor, and how quickly she can learn. We suspect that in the static environments underlying most of the models to be presented, the government would eventually learn most of the relevant aspects of technology, and thus the informational asymmetry would disappear. But in the real world, technologies (as well as demands and factor prices) are constantly changing. Thus the magnitude of the informational problem is related to how fast the environment changes and how fast the regulator learns.

Third, we turn to "revelation problems," where the regulated firm is induced to reveal his information by the choices he makes. The regulator also learns a considerable amount from auditing, namely from directly monitoring the actions or performance of the regulated. The design of optimal monitoring behavior would be the subject of a separate review.[21]

Some Simple Models of Regulator-Firm Interaction

In this section we focus on the implications of the recent literature on the economics of information for the direct interaction between a regulator and regulated firm(s). We attempt to describe a general framework within which existing work can be analyzed. We discuss the essential similarities and differences among the various models in the literature and also some important regulatory models not normally associated with that literature (e.g., the Averch-Johnson 1962 model). We close with a brief discussion of important issues that have been afforded relatively little attention in the literature. Though our formal review of the literature is slanted toward models that concern the regulation of public utilities, the basic insights of the literature apply more generally. Note also that the focus of the entire analysis here is on a small part of the entire hierarchy of control. This concerns the direct interaction between the regulator and the firm (figure 1.1). Furthermore the "firm" is treated as a "black box," and the assorted control problems within the firm are not addressed.

The central features of the models that we will discuss here are the following. First, the nature of the information asymmetry between regulator and firm is crucial. As noted earlier, what is known to each party at various points in time largely determines the properties of the optimal regulatory policy. Second, the policy tools available to the regulator and the costs of using them are of paramount importance. Bounds on penalties that the firm can be forced to bear and large (perhaps infinite) costs of auditing the firm's activities will severely limit the regulator's ability to influence the firm's decisions. Third, whether or not interaction between the regulator and firm is repeated will be shown to play a major role in shaping optimal regulatory policy. Fourth, the manner in which the regulator's strategy varies with the number of firms under her control will be considered.

A General Model

We begin with a description of a simple but fairly general model that allows us to consider in some detail the first two of these four features—the nature of the information asymmetry and the set of policy tools available to the regulator. The model thus presumes nonrepeated interaction between a regulator and single firm. We return later to discuss repeated play and multiple firms.

A common element of most principal-agent analyses is that the principal (here, the regulator) is the Stackleberg leader in the "game" played with the agent (here, the regulated firm). That is, the regulator specifies the terms of an incentive scheme before any other actions take place. Following the announcement of how the firm's compensation and the regulator's actions will depend on observable variables, the firm and then the regulator may alternate actions that influence the ultimate outcome of the regulatory process. Some models have each party undertake only one action. In other models it is important that the parties alternate actions, with both the regulator and firm undertaking at least two distinct moves. Both possibilities are incorporated in the general model we construct here.

Often the firm's initial action ($\mathbf{a}_1^F$) is simply some communication about its information ($\mathbf{I}^F$) to the regulator. Based on this communication and her own information ($\mathbf{I}^R$), the regulator undertakes an action ($\mathbf{a}_1^R$) according to the terms of the announced regulatory policy.[22] This action might include an audit of the firm's communication or a decision as to whether to allow the firm to continue operations. There is assumed to be an outcome ($\mathbf{Z}_1$) that is observed by both the regulator and firm following their initial actions. This outcome could include the firm's message to the regulator and/or the result of the regulator's audit of this report.

Next the firm undertakes a second action ($\mathbf{a}_2^F$). This action might be a production or pricing decision, for example. Then the regulator undertakes a second action ($\mathbf{a}_2^F$), which might represent an observation of industry performance, an audit of the firm's activities, and/or a payment to the firm. Following these actions, a second outcome ($\mathbf{Z}_2$) is commonly observed. This outcome might include realized prices and outputs, and/or the result of an audit of the firm's activities (e.g., realized costs). Note that all actions, outcomes, information sets, and so forth, may well be vectors.

The regulatory policy (**R**) consists of the regulator's actions and the payment schedule, $\tilde{P}(\cdot)$. This schedule specifies payments to the firm as a function of observable variables $\mathbf{Z}_1$, $\mathbf{Z}_2$, $\mathbf{a}_1^F$, and $\mathbf{a}_2^R$. Thus the firm's compensation can depend on its communications with the regulator, its performance, and the regulator's actions, for example. The regulatory policy is presumed chosen to maximize the regulator's expected utility given her initial information $\tilde{E}\{U^R(\cdot)|\mathbf{I}^R\}$. Here and throughout the ensuing analysis, E represents expectations over unknown variables. $U^R(\cdot)$ is the regulator's utility function. This function may have as arguments payments (P) to the firm, the regulator's actions ($\mathbf{a}_1^R$, $\mathbf{a}_2^R$), the firm's utility level (U^F), and the (vector of) outcome(s) of the regulatory process (**X**). Typically the regulator is regarded as acting to maximize the expected level of consumers' surplus or a weighted average of producers' and consumers' surplus.[23] The firm is generally thought to maximize its own expected profits.

Thus a fairly general representation of the regulator's problem (RP) is the following:

$$\underset{R}{\text{Maximize}} \quad E\{U^R(\mathbf{X}, P, \mathbf{a}_1^R, \mathbf{a}_2^R, U^F)|\mathbf{I}^R\}, \qquad (RP)$$

subject to

$$\mathbf{a}_1^F \in \underset{\mathbf{a}}{\operatorname{argmax}}\ E\{U^F(P, \mathbf{a}, \mathbf{a}_2^F)|\mathbf{H}_1^F\}, \tag{AS_1}$$

$$\mathbf{a}_2^F \in \underset{\mathbf{a}}{\operatorname{argmax}}\ E\{U^F(P, \mathbf{a}_1^F, \mathbf{a})|\mathbf{H}_2^F\}, \tag{AS_2}$$

$$E\{U^F(P, \mathbf{a}_1^F, \mathbf{a}_2^F)|H_1^F\} \geq \bar{U}^F, \quad i = 1, 2, \tag{$\mathbb{R}$}$$

$$\tilde{P} \in \hat{\mathbf{P}}, \tag{FP}$$

$$\mathbf{a}_i^s \in A_i^s, \quad i = 1, 2, \quad s = R, F, \tag{FA_i^s}$$

where

$$P = \tilde{P}(\mathbf{Z}_1, \mathbf{Z}_2),$$

$$\mathbf{Z}_1 = \tilde{\mathbf{Z}}_1(\mathbf{a}_1^F, \mathbf{a}_1^R, \mathbf{I}^F, \mathbf{I}^R),$$

$$\mathbf{Z}_2 = \tilde{\mathbf{Z}}_2(\mathbf{a}^F, \mathbf{a}^R, \mathbf{I}^F, \mathbf{I}^R),$$

$$\mathbf{X} = \tilde{\mathbf{X}}(\mathbf{a}^F, \mathbf{a}^R, \mathbf{I}^F, \mathbf{I}^R).$$

In the statement of (RP), $\mathbf{H}_i^F$, $i = 1, 2$, denotes the history of outcomes that are known to the firm at the time it undertakes action $\mathbf{a}_i^F$. Thus, for example, $\mathbf{H}_2^F = \{\mathbf{I}^F, \mathbf{R}, \mathbf{a}_1^F, \mathbf{Z}_1\}$. Also $\bar{U}^F$ is the reservation expected utility level of the firm.

The act-selection (AS) constraints in (RP) capture the fact that the firm chooses its actions to maximize its expected utility, given all available information. The individual rationality $(\mathbb{R})$ constraint guarantees that **R** promises the firm at least its reservation level of expected utility, so that the firm will not choose to employ its resources elsewhere.

The fourth constraint in (RP) defines feasible payment (FP) schedules. For example, upper bounds on rewards and lower bounds on penalties (e.g., bankruptcy limitations) may be imposed by appropriate specification of $\hat{\mathbf{P}}$, the set of feasible payment schedules. The (FA_i^s) constraints simply define the set of feasible actions $(\mathbf{a}_i^s)$ for both the regulator $(s = R)$ and the firm $(s = F)$. These constraints might, for example, structure communication between the firm and the regulator, and/or dictate that the regulator cannot expropriate the firm's assets.

Special Cases: Adverse Selection and Moral Hazard

Many models of regulation in the literature are special cases of (RP). These models differ only in the interpretation of actions, in the restrictions placed on payment schedules, and in the nature and timing of the information that becomes known to the regulator and firm. Before describing a few of these models, let us reiterate that problems of control only arise for the regulator if the firm's private information is better than her own and/or if she cannot costlessly observe the firm's actions. Absent these difficulties, the regulator can effect $\mathbf{a}_1^F$ and $\mathbf{a}_2^F$ to maximize her own expected utility (subject only to individual rationality concerns for the firm). This outcome is known as the first-best outcome. It is achieved in the presence of perfect information with a "forcing" contract. The regulator specifies the actions that she wants carried out and ensures the firm its reservation utility level if and only if these actions are carried out. Otherwise, the firm is penalized and is thereby "forced" to effect the desired behavior.

The dual concerns of private information and unobservable actions reflect two classes of problems. When the actions of the firm are unobservable and when the actions enter the firm's utility function in a nontrivial manner, a moral hazard problem is said to exist. For example, in Laffont and Tirole's (1986) model of public enterprise, personally costly effort supplied by the manager to reduce costs cannot be observed by the government. Here, a moral hazard problem exists because it is costly for the government to induce the manager to supply an "appropriate" level of effort.

A problem of adverse selection is said to exist when the firm has nontrivial information about its capabilities (e.g., its technology) that is not shared by the regulator. For example, in Baron and Myerson's (1982) model, the regulated firm knows its cost structure perfectly while the regulator does not.

When Is the First-Best Outcome Feasible?
It is important to note that the regulator may be able to achieve the first-best outcome even though problems of moral hazard and adverse selection are potentially present. This ideal outcome will be feasible if (1) the firm is risk-neutral toward monetary payoffs, (2) the regulator and firm share the same information initially (i.e., $\mathbf{I}^R = \mathbf{I}^F$ at the time when $\mathbf{R}$ is announced), (3) $\hat{\mathbf{P}}$ is unrestricted, and (4) the outcome ($\mathbf{X}$) of the regulatory process is observable. The first-best is effected in this scenario by equating the firm's compensation schedule with the regulator's utility function (i.e., $P = U^R(\cdot)$). Thus the expected payment to the firm is the expected level of the regulator's utility. In addition, to effect the desired distribution of rents, the firm is required to make a lump sum payment to the regulator prior to beginning production equal to the difference between its expected payoff under this scheme and its reservation utility level. Due to symmetric beliefs the regulator and firm will concur on the appropriate magnitude of this

lump sum payment (k). And because the firm is risk-neutral, it need be awarded no risk premium for undertaking this venture.

When the firm's objective function is made to coincide with the regulator's, it is apparent that the firm will act as the regulator would require it to if she shared the firm's private information. Thus any problems of moral hazard and/or adverse selection are avoided.[24] It is this intuition that underlines the subsidy scheme proposed by Loeb and Magat (1979). They note that if the firm is subsidized with the level of consumers' surplus it generates, the firm will effect marginal cost prices and engage in the socially optimal level of cost-reducing activities.

Aside from the important general equilibrium effects discussed in the first section, there are a number of other reasons why, in practice, it may not be possible to effect the first-best outcome. For one, the firm (or its investors) may have some aversion to risk. Second, the firm's information about its environment may be better than the regulator's information from the start of the regulatory regime. Third, the firm may not have the resources to make the requisite payment before demand and cost functions become known, and legal limitations on the firm's liability may allow the firm in some adverse circumstances to renege on the promised lump sum payment (k). In the presence of binding bankruptcy constraints of this sort, (i.e., when the definition of $\hat{\mathbf{P}}$ in (RP) places binding restrictions on the compensation schedule), it will no longer be optimal for the regulator to reward the firm according to the social objective (i.e., set $P = U^R(\cdot)$) and accept a payment less than k when the firm's profits are too low. Such a policy provides inappropriate incentives to the firm. Since it cannot be forced to bear the full "downside" risk from its activities, for example, the firm may well undertake actions that are too risky from the perspective of the regulator. (A more detailed discussion of this point is provided by Stiglitz and Weiss 1981.)[25] Furthermore the firm may be tempted to declare bankruptcy under circumstances where the net social surplus from continued production is positive. To counteract these tendencies, the regulator will effect a policy that induces an outcome different from the first-best outcome. The nature and intent of the distortions are analogous to those that will be introduced when the firm's information is initially better than the regulator's.[26] These distortions are described next.

When the firm's information about its environment is strictly better than the regulator's from the onset of the regulatory regime, the regulator's problem becomes more difficult. It is on this problem that much of the recent literature has focused. In this case the regulator must make the terms of the regulatory contract sufficiently attractive to the firm whatever its private information might be. (Technically, the individual rationality ($\mathbb{R}$) constraint in (RP) must be satisfied for all values of $\mathbf{I}^F$.) This will generally entail some rents for the firm under favorable circumstances (e.g., low costs or high productivity).

Auditing
Obviously the rents of the firm can generally be reduced if the regulator is able to verify directly the firm's private information through some costly investigation (e.g., an audit of the firm's costs). It is well known, for example, that if an unbounded penalty can be imposed on the firm when it is found to have falsely reported ($\mathbf{a}_1^F$) its private information, then a perfect audit of the firm's report ($\mathbf{a}_1^R$) need only be carried out with arbitrarily low probability to ensure the firm will always truthfully reveal its private knowledge.[27] Thus aside from the cost of obtaining this direct observation of the firm's private knowledge, the regulator can effect the first-best outcome.

Of course this conclusion may be sensitive to the quality of the audit. If the firm's compensation is based on the realization of an imperfect monitor of its private information, some risk is necessarily imposed on the firm. Thus the first-best outcome cannot be attained if the firm is averse to risk. If the firm is risk-neutral, though, an imperfect signal may allow the regulator to effect the first-best outcome. Necessary and sufficient conditions for this to be the case are recorded in Riordan and Sappington (1985b).[28] A sufficient (though not a necessary) condition is that the dimension of the signal space be at least as great as the dimension of the space of the firm's private information.

Bounds on penalties that the firm can be forced to bear following an unfavorable audit (like bankruptcy constraints) will also inhibit the regulator's ability to achieve the first-best outcome. Baron and Besanko (1984b) examine the regulator's optimal strategy when an imperfect monitor of the firm's costs is available to the regulator and when payments to the firm are bounded from below. Intuitively, to maximize expected surplus net of auditing costs the regulator will optimally investigate any report of costs above a critical level and impose the maximum feasible penalty on the firm if the audit and original report are sufficiently inconsistent.

When moral hazard complicates the incentive problem, the optimal use of imperfect cost information is a bit different. Laffont and Tirole (1986) examine a setting in which the firm's manager can reduce operating costs through the expenditure of effort. The disutility associated with such effort is common knowledge, though the level of effort expended is unobservable.

The manager also has private information about the marginal cost of production that would prevail in the absence of any cost-reducing effort. Thus the model incorporates both adverse selection and moral hazard problems. After production occurs, the regulator observes an informative signal about realized production costs.

To induce the manager to exert effort to reduce costs, the regulator must promise the manager a reward if realized costs are small relative to predicted costs. On the other hand, the manager must be rewarded for predicting that costs will be low; otherwise, incentives will exist to exaggerate cost projections. Laffont and Tirole demonstrate that the optimal incentive scheme is linear in the difference between predicted and realized costs. Payments increase more rapidly with this difference the smaller are predicted costs, providing the requisite incentive both to reveal truthfully cost estimates and to put forth the effort required to reduce costs.

Self-Selection

Absent access to an auditing technology, the regulator will generally have to rely on other policy instruments. Many studies have focused on the optimal use of prices, subsidies, and taxes to deal with the adverse selection problem. A large number of these studies have adopted the assumption that there is a single technological parameter (e.g., marginal cost of production) that is known to the firm, whereas the regulator only knows the statistical distribution of this parameter (e.g., see Baron and Myerson 1982).[29] Communication about this parameter between the regulator and firm is presumed costless. In terms of (RP) these models have $\mathbf{a}_1^F$ as a report by the firm to the regulator concerning its technological parameter, and $\mathbf{a}_1^R$ may be a decision by the regulator as to whether the firm's operations should be terminated. If the firm produces, $\mathbf{a}_2^F$ includes production by the firm at the regulated price, and $\mathbf{a}_2^R$ includes a verification of the firm's output and the payment of compensation to the firm. Thus the firm's compensation can depend on both its initial report to the regulator and other observable variables (e.g., its production level).[30] Most models of this type (with the aforementioned exceptions) presume the firm's costs cannot be observed by the regulator at any cost.

The solutions to models of this type have a number of common and central features. First, the firm is generally able to command rents from its superior information. Second, distortions in production decisions are generally effected. Third, firms with different information (e.g., costs) will generally be induced to behave differently (e.g., produce different levels of output). These features arise from a few fundamental considerations. For simplicity, these considerations are illustrated here, assuming that the sole information asymmetry concerns which of two possible values ($c_1 < c_2$) characterize the firm's two (constant) average production costs. Also the regulator's presumed objective is to maximize the expected level of consumers' surplus.

Ideally the regulator would have the firm with costs c_i produce output $Q(c_i)$ at price $p_i = c_i$, $i = 1, 2$, where $Q(\cdot)$ is the demand curve. Given a choice among these two prices, however, the firm with low costs will select p_2 and thereby earn rents. To induce the low-cost firm to choose the lower price, an additional payment of at least the magnitude of these rents must be promised the firm. Faced with this trade-off, it will be optimal for the regulator to reduce the rents that must be afforded the low-cost firm by raising p_2 above c_2, and thereby reducing the number of units of output on which the firm can exercise its cost advantage.[31] In extreme cases the optimal level of p_2 may be so high that the firm with high costs will not produce at all. But the more certain is the regulator that the firm's costs are c_2, and the smaller is the cost advantage of the lower cost firm (i.e., the smaller is $[c_2 - c_1]$), the closer to marginal cost c_2 will be the optimal price level p_2.[32]

Thus the optimal regulatory policy will induce the firm to set a lower price the lower are its costs so that ex post, the firm's true costs can generally be inferred from the price it has set. However, this "self-selection" only results because the regulator has made a binding commitment not to use against the firm the cost information that she will ultimately infer. We will return at the close of this section to consider how the optimal regulatory policy changes in the absence of such ability to precommit.

Distortions other than prices in excess of marginal cost will generally arise when the regulator's set of policy tools is more extensive. For example, if variable production costs are affected by observable fixed costs differentially according to the firm's technological parameter, the regulator will generally instruct the firm to operate with other than the cost-minimizing level of fixed costs (see Sappington 1983b).[33] And more generally, the regulator is likely to base the firm's final compensation on observable inputs and/or outputs that interact in a nontrivial manner with the source of the firm's private information. Doing so will generally distort the use and/or production of these inputs and/or outputs from efficient levels. And even if these variables of indirect interest can only be observed with some error and at some cost, the regulator is likely to incur the requisite costs provided the signal is sufficiently informative about the variable in question.[34]

Averch-Johnson

One form of input distortion that has received widespread attention in the regulatory literature is the overcapitalization bias considered by Averch and Johnson (A-J) (1962). The question of interest here is how their analysis is related to the general model described in (RP). There appear to be two crucial sources of information asymmetry in the A-J model. First, input prices (i.e., the cost of capital, r) are known to the firm but not the regulator. Second, the firm has superior information about the functional form of its technology. One might interpret the regulator's beliefs about r as having positive density on some interval $(r,\bar{r})$. The fact that the regulator always sets the allowed rate of return, s, in excess of the true cost of capital suggests that the regulator sets $s = \bar{r}$. Such a policy might be optimal if there are infinite costs associated with forcing the firm into bankruptcy. Baron and Taggart (1980) have also shown that the A-J regulatory policy can only be optimal if the regulator has no knowledge of the firm's cost structure. Otherwise, the optimal regulatory policy would employ the firm's choice of capital stock as an informative signal about its technology.[35]

A critical assumption in the A-J model is that r is exogenous. In fact the firm's cost of capital is likely to be sensitive to regulatory policy. One possibility is that if s is set below the current cost of capital, the firm's scale will be reduced (due to the difficulty in raising new capital), thereby reducing the firm's operating risk which in turn reduces the firm's cost of capital. A second possibility is that improved performance by the firm (e.g., reducing organizational "slack") will reduce its cost of capital. Thus the implicit assumption that the firm will go bankrupt if s is set below r may be an extreme one.

In practice, the regulator will also couple rate-of-return regulation with direct controls on the firm's choice of capital. Holmstrom's (1984) analysis suggests that these controls will be less stringent the less disparate are the objectives of the regulator and the firm and the more severe is the information asymmetry between the two parties.[36] When the firm's information is much better than the regulator's it is much better able to determine the socially optimal level of investment. Thus, provided its interest does not diverge too drastically from the social interests, the firm will be afforded greater freedom in selecting investments.

Repeated Interactions

To this point we have focused on models in which the interaction between the regulator and the firm is not repeated. In practice, regulation is most often an ongoing affair. Thus we turn to the question of how repeated interaction alters the conclusions derived from static models. Of central concern is how the firm will alter current behavior in order to influence future regulations when these regulations are based on current performance. Thus the main issue here is analogous to that faced in planning and labor settings. In the Soviet incentive problem (e.g., see Holmstrom 1982a; Loeb and Magat 1978; Weitzman 1976), when future production targets increase with current output, firms may intentionally operate below their capabilities. Similarly, if future piece rates are revised downward as output is produced more rapidly, workers will reduce current effort levels (see Stiglitz 1975).

To begin, note that there are conditions under which the conclusions of static models carry over exactly to their dynamic counterparts. For example, consider the adverse selection problem in which the regulator can costlessly commit herself to execute faithfully the terms of any regulatory policy announced at the outset of the regulatory regime. Furthermore suppose, for example, that the firm's cost structure (which it knows perfectly) is the same in every period, as is the regulator's imperfect information about these costs. Thus the regulator can never observe the firm's historic costs. Under these circumstances the optimal dynamic regulatory policy will be to institute the optimal single period policy in every period of the regulatory regime.[37] When the firm's costs are not perfectly correlated over time, the optimal dynamic regulatory policy will differ from its static counterpart, though the nature of the output distortions is the same in both.[38]

The severity of the information asymmetry about costs between regulator and firm may be of no consequence in repeated adverse selection problems if the regulator can observe the past performance of the firm. Sappington and Sibley (1985) propose a regulatory mechanism that guarantees that total surplus is maximized and that the firm is held to its reservation profit level in every period. The regulator is required only to know the firm's demand curve and discount rate and to be able to observe with a lag of one period (e.g., a year) the firm's historic expenditures (which the firm may manipulate strategically to exceed minimum possible production costs). She need have no knowledge of the firm's technology. The scheme awards the firm in each period the increment in consumers' surplus that its activities generate and imposes a tax equal to the difference between revenues and expenditures in the preceding period. The scheme is effective because it makes the objectives of the regulator and firm essentially coincidental.[39]

The ability to observe historic expenditures can ultimately render inconsequential even more severe forms of information asymmetry between regulator and firm. Vogelsang and Finsinger (1979) explore the case in which the regulator has virtually no information about the technology or demand structure of a multiproduct monopoly firm.[40] They propose an elegantly simple scheme that induces the firm to set prices that converge to their Ramsey levels. The scheme constrains a Laspeyre's index of the firm's prices in each period not to exceed the realized expenditures of the preceding period. The weights in the index are the quantities produced by the firm in the preceding period. Thus the larger are the realized profits of the firm in any period, the more severely will the subsequent price index be constrained. Eventually, profits are eliminated, and total surplus is maximized.[41]

It is also the case that repeated interaction with observable past performance can resolve problems of moral hazard. Radner (1984) and Linhart, Radner and Sinden (1983) show that provided the discount rate of the manager is sufficiently low and his personal costs from being dismissed are sufficiently great, he can be induced to act nearly in the regulator's interests without the imposition of undue risk.[42] The intuition commonly ascribed for their result is that with repeated play, the law of large numbers permits the regulator to distinguish more accurately between lack of diligence or effort by the firm and "bad luck" (that will be statistically offset by "good luck" over time). Consequently she is better able to motivate the desired behavior on the part of the firm. She may do so, for example, by threatening to terminate the management of the firm if performance over time is deemed sufficiently poor.

Comparisons among Agents

Repeated interaction is one source of multiple observations that allow the regulator to control better the actions of the firm. Another such source is the comparison of the performances of two or more agents. The use of comparative performance can be a powerful tool for the regulator. The work of Demski and Sappington (1984), for example, indicates that the first-best outcome can be ensured when the regulator is dealing with two risk-neutral firms whose costs are correlated (however slightly), even if the firms initially have perfect knowledge of their costs that is not shared by the regulator. In a related model, Nalebuff and Stiglitz (1983a) demonstrate how the first-best outcome can be achieved as a Nash equilibrium among privately informed regulated firms, even if they are risk-averse.

A regulatory scheme that rewards each firm according to its relative performance can mitigate the incentives that firms might otherwise have to perform poorly (e.g., exaggerate costs or shirk on effort). Essentially, the performance of one firm serves as a natural monitor of the behavior of another. Of course the value of the monitor will often depend on how similar are the characteristics (e.g., technologies and demand functions) of the firms. The greater the similarity, the more about unobservable firm behavior that can be inferred from relative performance. Because comparative performance can help alleviate the problems caused by information asymmetries, a regulator may even find it advantageous to permit entry into an industry that is known to be a natural monopoly. This possibility, which is suggested in Nalebuff and Stiglitz (1983a), is analyzed in Demski et. al. (1985). They show that the optimal regulatory policy may even entail replacing the incumbent firm with a higher-cost entrant at times in order to mitigate the incumbent's incentives to exaggerate costs.

Note too that with multiple potential producers, ex ante competition for the right to serve as a regulated monopolist can limit the ex post rents of the monopoly firm (see Demsetz 1968; McAfee and McMillan 1984).[43] Loeb and Magat (1979), for example, argue that bidding for this right can replicate the first-best outcome if the monopoly firm is subsidized according to the consumer's surplus that it generates and if there is sufficient competition for the right to operate the franchise. Riordan and Sappington (1985a) demonstrate that when potential producers receive independent estimates of the expected value of the franchise, "sufficient competition" entails an infinite number of bidders. With fewer potential producers some rents will accrue to the winning bidder. Furthermore, to limit these rents, it will generally be optimal for the regulator to induce the producer to set the price for its output strictly in excess of marginal production costs. The distortions at the production stage foster more competitive bidding and thereby limit the rents of the monopolist. (For related observations, see Laffont and Tirole 1985 and McAfee and McMillan 1986.) The magnitude of the distortions will generally be greater if the smaller is the highest private assessment of the value of the franchise (i.e., the smaller is the "winning bid").

A brief explanation of these conclusions is the following. The distortions at the production stage limit the rents that accrue to the producer when realized production costs are small. The more pronounced the distortions, the greater the rent reduction. Thus, by promising to effect more severe distortions the smaller the winning bid, potential producers are dissuaded from understating their true valuations of the franchise. Not only does a firm run a greater risk of losing the franchise to a competitor by understanding its true valuations, but, conditional on winning the franchise, it also secures a less profitable operation the smaller its bid.

Note that competitive bidding for a monopoly franchise allows the regulator to deal with two difficult problems. Bidding can both limit the rents of the eventual monopolist and help to identify the firm that is best suited for the productive task. Intuitively the firm with the lowest costs can afford to bid the most for the franchise.[44] Of course more congruent costs will promote more aggressive bidding. Again, then, greater similarity among participants will generally allow the regulator to approximate the first-best outcome more closely.

In general, specification of the optimal regulatory policy in the presence of multiple firms is a difficult and subtle exercise. Simple tournaments, for example, where a prize is awarded for the best performance, work less effectively as idiosyncratic differences among firms (e.g., abilities) become large relative to common environmental shocks (e.g., changes in key factor prices).[45] Nalebuff and Stiglitz (1983b) have shown that imposing a penalty on the "loser" can provide better incentives than rewarding the "winner." The authors also demonstrate that in more sophisticated incentive schemes, multiple equilibria can result or no equilibrium may exist at all. A key concern is to avoid excessive imitation by firms. If they are penalized too heavily for failures while being rewarded only meagerly for superior performance, incentives for efficient risk taking may be dulled, and technological progress thereby hindered. This and other related issues warrant substantially more attention.[46]

Limited Commitment

Before concluding, we briefly consider an important issue that has been avoided to this point. The issue concerns changes in regulatory policy that become necessary when the regulator cannot precommit herself for an indefinite period to carry out the terms of the announced policy. Recall that a credible commitment never to employ against the firm in the future information that can be inferred from its current performance generally allows the regulator to motivate better current performance. For example, with commitment, the firm can be induced to produce more output in every period the lower are its costs, thereby increasing consumers' surplus. However, without significant compensation for doing so, the firm will not allow itself to be identified as a low-cost producer if the regulator will subsequently eliminate all its future rents (as she will do absent a binding commitment not to). Thus the costs of tailoring the firm's performance to its capabilities (i.e., achieving "separation") increase when the regulator's ability to precommit is abrogated.

In the extreme case, where the length of the regulatory regime is infinite and the firm's discount rate is zero (as in Roberts 1984), no separation will be, or indeed can be, effected. Separation could only be achieved under these circumstances by offering the firm what amounts to an infinite bribe. With a finite planning horizon and/or positive discount rate (as in Britto et al. 1985; Baron and Besanko 1985), the payment required to induce separation will not be infinite. Therefore the optimal regulatory policy will generally entail a initial period of time in which no separation occurs, followed by a period in which separation is effected.[47] Thus with costless commitment it will generally be optimal to induce separation with continuing distortions (e.g., prices in excess of marginal cost). Absent the ability to commit, the optimal regulatory policy will generally induce more severe distortions for some period of time before all distortions are eliminated.[48]

Suggestions for Future Research

To this point, our concern has been with reviewing the insights the literature has to offer regarding the design of regulatory policy in the presence of important information asymmetries. Before concluding, we turn our attention to issues and questions in the field that warrant additional investigation.

First, note that our analysis (like the bulk of the literature) has focused on one particular principal-agent relationship. There are other such relationships of interest that characterize the regulatory environment, however. For example, owners of regulated firms must structure incentives for their managers to act on the behalf of owners. Similarly the managers must motivate employees to behave appropriately. Furthermore it may be necessary for the Congress to provide adequate incentives for the regulator to perform her job diligently. Significant research remains to be done before we can understand the delicate interplay among these many principal-agent problems.[49]

A related line of research concerns the optimal control of a regulated firm that is under the jurisdiction of more than one regulator. When the interests of these regulators are not entirely congruent, problems of conflicting regulatory mandates arise. The rationale for overlapping regulatory jurisdictions warrants additional consideration, as does the optimal structuring of incentives for the firm given such overlap.[50] Political considerations are one reason for the separation of regulatory powers. Another may be that the information required to design appropriate regulatory policy optimally resides with different regulatory bodies.[51]

It is also the case that while the literature we have reviewed contains observations regarding the general nature of efficient regulatory mechanisms, specific policy recommendations are generally absent. For instance, though we know that managers of electric utility firms should generally be forced to bear some of the social burden derived from incorrect decisions regarding nuclear power plants, the optimal extent of the burden is certainly not apparent. The optimal distribution of risk among ratepayers, shareholders, regulators, and managers of public utilities deserves much closer scrutiny. As noted earlier the issue is complicated because of a multitude of information asymmetries and interrelated principal-agent problems.

One additional information asymmetry also limits policy prescriptions on crucial regulatory matters. Because most economists lack crucial institutional knowledge of the particular industries in which policy issues arise, they are unable (or, at least, would be unwise) to offer precise policy recommendations. What seems important, then, is a sharing of private information concerning theoretical insights and institutional detail.

Notes

This chapter was written in part while J. E. Stiglitz was a visiting scholar at the Hoover Institution. Financial support from the Hoover Institution and the National Science Foundation is gratefully acknowledged. The views expressed in this chapter are not necessarily those of Bellcore. We are grateful to Elizabeth Bailey, David Besanko, Steven Salop, Jean Tirole, and an anonymous referee for helpful comments.

1. Recent literature (e.g., Baumol, Panzar and Willig 1982) has focused on the importance not only of nonconvexities but also of sunk costs. In the absence of sunk costs, efficient outcomes may be sustained, even with natural monopolies. On the other hand, even with very small sunk costs (which are pervasive in the economy), it may not be possible to sustain competitive and efficient outcomes even in the presence of small nonconvexities. See Dasgupta and Stiglitz (1985).

2. Notice, however, that private insurance firms would similarly attempt to "regulate" the behavior of the insured if they had the same powers to do so.

3. That is, when the two sides to the bargain have imperfect information concerning each other, a costly self-section process operates to enable them to differentiate themselves. For a more extended discussion of this, see Farrell (1985).

4. There are some problems that arise in the presence of nonconvexities; some allocations may not be able to be supported by linear tax-subsidy schemes. In general, however, they can be supported by nonlinear tax/subsidy schemes (see also note 5.)

5. Nonlinear tax/subsidy schemes are schemes where the payments to or from the firm are not simply proportional to the relevant variable. Thus a linear price system for pollutants would entail the polluter being charged an amount which is proportional to the amount of pollution. Simple nonlinear schedules include the pollutant being charged a fixed amount per unit of

pollution in excess of some threshold amount, or being charged a fixed amount per unit of pollution up to some threshold amount and a larger, fixed amount per unit of pollution beyond that level. Regulations often are written as if they impose a zero charge up to the threshold level and an infinite fine beyond that level. Of course the penalties imposed are seldom infinite; the polluter has the option not only to ignore the regulator but also any ensuing court order. Usually, however, the penalties for doing so are likely to be sufficiently great that compliance is achieved.

6. This ignores of course the fact that information within the utility is not shared equally by everyone. There are important control problems within the organization, as well as between the organization and the government. Our focus is on the latter class of problems, though we briefly discuss the former.

7. Thus the information literature (including the principal agent literature (Ross 1983; Stiglitz 1974) has provided a rigorous justification for the "managerial" theories of the firm, discussed earlier by Berle and Means (1932) and March and Simon (1958), among others.

8. Thus all the major alleged mechanisms for shareholder control have only limited effectiveness. While the ineffectiveness of shareholder meetings has long been recognized, the problems associated with the takeover mechanism have only recently attracted attention. See, for instance, Grossman and Hart (1980, 1981), and Stiglitz (1972, 1982, 1985).

9. There are other affected parties as well: when there are positive mobility costs (including specific human capital), workers are affected by the well-being of the firm.

10. Some discussions have emphasized the differences between "soft" budget constraints of government enterprises and their "hard" counterparts in private enterprises. There is much to the distinction, but it should not be overdrawn, particularly in the regulatory context. The firm can "persuade" the regulator to increase prices, in much the same way it attempts to persuade the government to increase subsidies. In addition, private firms often try to convince governments to provide them with subsidies when the threat of bankruptcy is imminent.

11. In traditional economic theory, all individuals are assumed never to make mistakes; any seemingly deviant behavior can be accounted for simply by inappropriate incentives. By contrast, recent work has focused on the consequences of errors (which are viewed to be inevitable) for organizational design. See, for instance, Sah and Stiglitz (1985).

12. These issues were discussed in Stiglitz (1970), parts of which were subsequently published in Stiglitz (1972). There, he noted in the context of a simple mean-variance model that shareholders would not wish the firm to maximize the market value unless they planned to sell all of their shares and that there would not be unanimity if shareholders' plans for selling shares differed. He also showed that there would be unanimity in favor of the Pareto-efficient allocation if shareholders neither planned to buy nor sell shares. A large subsequent literature (e.g., see Ekern-Wilson 1974) extended the latter result to a larger class of "spanning" conditions and showed that unanimity on the value maximizing condition could obtain under slightly weaker conditions than those associated with having a complete set of Arrow-Debreu securities. But as Grossman and Stiglitz (1980) and Radner (1974) point out, if among the actions of the firm is the choice of a debt-equity ratio, then essentially a full set of Arrow-Debreu securities is required. Moreover, as Stiglitz originally pointed out, and as Grossman and Stiglitz emphasize, in any economy with trading (either because of life cycle considerations or because different individuals obtain different information), the assumption that all individuals are planning neither to sell nor to buy securities seems inapplicable.

The importance of differences in beliefs for the behavior of the firm, in the absence of a complete set of Arrow-Debreu securities, is discussed in Stiglitz (1972).

13. In the second section we discuss how the government can enhance effective competition in the auction. That discussion also abstracts from a number of institutional drawbacks to auctions that are analyzed by Williamson (1976).

14. Boiteaux (1956) was the first to study the problem in the context of utility pricing. In the past decade an enormous literature on these issues has developed. For a survey in the context of the taxation problem, see Atkinson and Stiglitz (1980); in the context of optimal pricing, see Baumol and Bradford (1970).

15. And if one had complete confidence in the competence of the monopolist, one would trust that he would take advantage of any efficient innovation within the broadly defined confines of the franchise. But, given the informational problems within the firm that were previously discussed, we are concerned with issues of organizational slack, so we do not have complete confidence that all efficient innovations are adopted.

16. Note that we have ignored the fact that, in practice, Ramsey pricing is often misapplied, focusing on the conclusion that commodities with inelastic demands should be taxed more heavily. This ignores (1) the potentially important cross elasticity effects and (2) the important distributional concerns that often require that commodities with elastic demands be taxed more heavily (Atkinson-Stiglitz 1972, 1980).

17. Of course the government might not discriminate. Indeed, if there is an optimally chosen income tax designed to redistribute income optimally, then under certain separability conditions, if the consumers' surplus associated with consuming the output is high enough, a fixed-fee access charge along with a marginal cost price is optimal. Whatever redistribution is to be done is best done through the tax system.

18. Formally the outcome may still be within the set of Pareto-efficient outcomes, where zero weight is placed on the utility of all individuals. But this does not correspond to any "reasonable" social welfare function.

19. This is seen most clearly in the context of insurance. There, if individuals have the same risks, but differ in their risk aversion, a monopolist would price discriminate, but an egalitarian government would provide complete insurance to everyone at the actuarially fair odds.

20. Some exceptions are noted later.

21. Thus the regulator might base his review process (e.g., to ascertain, whether bad outcomes are the result of lack of effort or bad luck) on the level of certain observed outcomes such as output. Thus it might make the probability of a review an increasing function of the time since last review and a decreasing function of the integrated output since the last review. (It should be obvious that if the firm knew for certain that a review was to arrive at a certain date, its behavior at the time of review would be altered; hence, to be effective, reviews must be stochastic.)

In a complete analysis of review behavior, one must also discuss the incentives of the reviewers. Thus, if at time t a bank audit turns up a loan that should have been declared in default at the time of the previous audit, the incentives for revealing that may be different if the current auditor is different from the previous auditor than when they are the same person. On the other hand, the cost of the audit may be greatly increased by having different auditors.

22. Here we presume the regulator will choose her actions (which are assumed to be observable to all parties) and compensate the firm as she initially promised to do when she announced the regulatory policy. Before closing, we will briefly consider the possibility that the regulator cannot make such binding commitments.

23. In practice, regulators might well act to maximize their own expected benefits (e.g., income, tenure, and fame) subject to some restrictions imposed by their legal mandate. This possibility has been noted, for example, by Stigler (1971).

24. This insight is offered by Stiglitz (1974) in his analysis of the sharecropping problem. It is also recorded in a general theoretical setting by Harris and Raviv (1979), Holmstrom (1979), and Shavell (1979). Riordan's (1984) interesting solution to the peak-load pricing problem

with demand uncertainty also relies on the risk-neutrality of the firm and the symmetry of initial beliefs about the regulatory environment.

25. Stiglitz and Weiss (1981) demonstrate that in the presence of bankruptcy constraints, the optimal policy for a lender may be to deny credit to a potential borrower rather than to simply increase the charge for borrowing (i.e., raise the interest rate). Their basic insight is that an increase in the interest rate (which is paid only in the absence of bankruptcy) entails a greater effective increase in the expected cost of borrowing to those whose projects are more likely to succeed than those who are likely to declare bankruptcy. Thus an increase in the interest rate may serve only to attract less desirable borrowers. Moreover a higher interest rate may induce borrowers to undertake projects that are more risky.

26. These distortions are described in some detail in Sappington (1983a) and characterized in general by Kahn and Scheinkman (1985).

27. This observation has been made in a variety of settings other than the regulatory arena. Becker (1968), for example, notes that sufficiently large penalties need be imposed only rarely to deter criminal activity. Stiglitz (1975) shows that moral hazard problems can be costlessly resolved when the agent's action can be inferred perfectly from his performance with positive (though arbitrarily small) probability. The general observation is also recorded in Townsend (1979). Riordan and Sappington (1985b) demonstrate that the basic conclusion is true even if the result of the regulator's audit is not publicly observed, so that the firm's payment can only depend on the regulator's claim about the audit's finding and not directly on the finding itself.

28. Their analysis considers both the case in which the signal is publicly observed and that in which only the principal (regulator) can observe the signal. The first-best outcome is less likely to be feasible in the latter case, as any (regulatory) contract that employs the signal must be constrained to eliminate any incentives for the regulator to misrepresent her private observation of the signal.

29. This same assumption characterizes a host of models in related literatures. See, for example, the treatment of the insurance market in Rothschild and Stiglitz (1976) and Stiglitz (1977), the sharecropping problem in Stiglitz (1974), the optimal tax problem in Mirrless (1975), and the general treatment of signaling and screening models in Stiglitz and Weiss (1985). Self-selection problems with two or more parameters are mathematically far more difficult.

30. Some studies in the literature do not formally model the initial communication between the firm and the regulator. Thus, for example, payment to the firm is based only on the final outcome of the regulatory process. There is no loss of generality here if there is only a single firm with information that is initially perfect and if the regulator never takes an action before the firm makes its production decision. Absent these conditions, however, the presence of an initial costless communication phase may increase the regulator's expected payoff. This is true, for example, in the models of Nalebuff and Stiglitz (1983a), Weitzman (1976), Holmstrom (1982a), and Demski et al. (1985) which are described in greater detail later.

31. Technically, since the regulator's objective function is maximized at the first-best outcome, a small deviation from first-best prices (or levels of output) will have no effect on the regulator's utility level (by the envelope theorem). Thus some increase above first-best (marginal cost) prices will be optimal to limit the rents of the firm should it have lower costs for all realizations of costs except the very lowest (here c_1).

32. This basic intuition is explained in greater detail and generality in the regulatory setting in, for example, Baron and Myerson (1982) and Sappington (1982, 1983a, b). It also underlies corresponding conclusions in the optimal tax literature (e.g., Mirless 1971; Atkinson and Stiglitz 1976), the insurance literature (e.g., Rothschild and Stiglitz 1976; Stiglitz 1977), and in studies on nonlinear pricing (e.g., Goldman, Leland, and Sibley 1984; Maskin and Riley

1984). A general characterization of the solution to adverse selection problems of this nature is described in Cooper (1984).

33. Besanko (1984) also reports the gains from technological distortions.

Note that these distortions generally persist whether or not the firm's private information is initially perfect. Induced distortions in observable decision variables generally remain optimal whenever the firm's information is initially better than the regulator's. For details, see Sappington (1982, 1984).

Note also that production technologies may be intentionally distorted for a different reason. In the case of pollution control, for example, the regulator may mandate the installation of a particular technology (e.g., scrubbers) rather than impose a tax on pollutants. Though the direct control is inefficient in the sense that it does not induce firms to use their superior technological information to effect the optimal level of pollution abatement, indirect control will not be feasible when it is prohibitively costly to monitor pollution emissions.

34. It seems likely that a nonconcavity in the value of this information will exist (see Radner and Stiglitz 1984; Singh 1985). Thus signals that are only slightly correlated with the variable in question will not be "purchased" by the regulator.

35. Besanko (1984) shows that if the critical technological asymmetry in the A-J model can be reduced to a single parameter (e.g., as in the analysis of Baron and Myerson 1982), then the optimal regulatory policy will have the allowed rate of return vary inversely with the firm's level of invested capital, thereby moderating the firm's tendency toward overcapitalization.

36. Holmstrom's (1984) analysis of the delegation problem (with a single agent) can be regarded as a special case of (RP). Specifying a range within which the agent's observable actions (e.g., his capital choice) can fall amounts to a presumption that infinite penalties will be imposed if an action outside of this range is observed.

37. This observation is recorded in Rothschild and Stiglitz (1976) and analyzed in detail by Baron and Besanko (1984a).

38. Baron and Besanko (1984a), for example, examine the multiperiod extension of Baron and Myerson's (1982) model when future costs are positively but imperfectly correlated with current costs. They find distortions (prices in excess of marginal costs) that are designed to limit the firm's rents continue to characterize the optimal regulatory policy, but the magnitude of these distortions is generally diminished in periods after the first.

39. Thus the logic that underlies the scheme is similar to the basic insight of Loeb and Magat (1979). The ability of the regulator to observe historic expenditures, though, resolves the question of the distribution of rents between consumers and the firm. It should be noted, however, that the resolution may not be complete under the scheme proposed by Sappington and Sibley (1985) if there is no separation of ownership and management in the firm, and if expenditures in excess of minimal production costs provide direct utility to the owner-manager.

40. Technically, it need only be known that the firm's cost structure is characterized by decreasing ray average cost (see Panzar and Willig 1977). (This assumption assures that the firm's profits are always nonnegative under the proposed regulatory scheme.) In particular, note that (as in the models of Loeb and Magat 1979 and Sappington and Sibley 1985) the critical information asymmetry cannot be reduced to a single technological parameter whose realization is known to the firm and whose distribution is known to the regulator. It is in this sense that the information asymmetry is more severe in these models.

41. As Sappington (1980) has shown, the scheme is not immune to strategic behavior by the firm (e.g., intentional cost inflation). However, it can be shown that the authors' basic conclusions continue to hold in the presence of such behavior. In particular, prices still converge to Ramsey levels, though the speed of convergence may be slow. Finsinger and Vogelsang (1981, 1985) have also proposed attractive mechanisms for inducing managers of

public enterprises to use their superior cost and demand information to effect optimal pricing decisions. Their schemes, which require no cost or demand information to implement, effectively reward the managers in each period an amount that approximates the increment in total measured surplus that their activities generate. An interesting overview of schemes of this type is contained in Tam (1985).

42. See the analysis of Radner (1981) for a precise statement of the result, along with additional intuition.

43. Williamson (1975) cites a variety of reasons why successful franchise bidding operations may be difficult to implement.

44. Optimal franchise auctions do not necessarily guarantee that the firm with the lowest production costs will be awarded the franchise. If firms adopt mixed bidding strategies, for example, the winning bid may be submitted by other than the least-cost firm. Furthermore, as Jean Tirole has pointed out to us, when the optimal incentive scheme involves "pooling" or "bunching," the franchise may be awarded with positive probability to other than the least cost producer (see also Myerson 1981).

45. This and related results are found in Lazear and Rosen (1981) and Green and Stokey (1983).

46. The analysis of Holmstrom (1982b) and Mookherjee (1984) provide promising insights concerning the design of incentive mechanisms for multiple agents.

47. The model of Baron and Besanko (1985) is such that absent the imposition of ex post individual rationality constraints, the duration of either the initial phase or the subsequent separation phase shrinks to zero.

Freixas et al. (1985) also examine an interesting two-period model in which the regulator lacks commitment ability. The authors' analysis makes evident the losses that arise when the regulator cannot precommit to future incentive schemes. An important related multiperiod model is that of Lewis (1986).

48. A related concern in the regulatory setting is whether some forms of commitment are more readily achieved than others. For example, Sappington (1986) suggests that when commitment to a monitoring technology (i.e., the expense of observing the firm's realized costs) is more readily achieved than commitment to the frequency of use of any existing technology, there may be gains to committing to an inefficient technology. This is one of many instances where inefficiencies at one stage of the regulatory hierarchy can help compensate for the absence of commitment abilities at another stage.

49. For some thoughts on this matter, see Demski and Sappington (1986).

50. The research of Baron (1985) represents an important contribution along these lines. He examines the optimal design of regulatory policy given conflicting objectives of a public utility commission and the Environmental Protection Agency.

51. Our review has been limited to models in which the firm has better information than the regulator. It is also possible of course that the regulator's knowledge of certain aspects of the regulatory environment is better than the firm's. Interesting theoretical work on the optimal design of incentive schemes by an "informed" principal is provided by Myerson (1983). Insights concerning the optimal design of incentive structures for a single agent by many principals are recorded in Braverman and Stiglitz (1982) and Bernheim and Whinston (1984).

References

Arnott, R., and Stiglitz, J. 1985. "The Welfare Economics of Moral Hazard." Princeton University mimeo. March.

Atkinson, A., and Stiglitz, J. 1980. *Lectures in Public Economics*. New York: McGraw-Hill.

Atkinson, A., and Stiglitz, J. 1976. "The Design of Tax Structures: Direct vs. Indirect Taxation." *Journal of Public Economics* 6:55–75.

Atkinson, A., and Stiglitz, J. 1972. "The Structure of Indirect Taxation and Economic Efficiency." *Journal of Public Economics* 1:97–119.

Averch, H., and Johnson, L. 1962. "Behavior of the Firm under Regulatory Constraint." *American Economic Review* 52:1052–1069.

Baron, D. 1985. "Noncooperative Regulation of a Nonlocalized Externality." Stanford University Discussion Paper. February.

Baron, D. 1984. "Regulatory Strategies under Asymmetric Information." In M. Boyer and R. Kihlstrom, eds., *Bayesian Models in Economic Theory*. Amsterdam: North Holland, pp. 155–180.

Baron, D., and Besanko, D. 1985. "Commitment in Multiperiod Information Models." Working Paper at Stanford University. May.

Baron, D., and Besanko, D. 1984a. "Regulation and Information in a Continuing Relationship." *Information, Economics and Policy* 1:267–302.

Baron, D., and Besanko, D. 1984b. "Regulation, Asymmetric Information and Auditing." *Rand Journal of Economics* 14:447–470.

Baron, D., and Myerson, R. 1982. "Regulating a Monopolist with Unknown Costs." *Econometrica* 50:911–930.

Baron, D., and Taggart, R. 1980. "Regulatory Pricing Procedures and Economic Incentives." In M. Crew, ed., *Issues in Public Utility Economics and Regulation*. Lexington, Mass.: Lexington Books.

Baumol, W., and Bradford, D. 1970. "Optimal Departures from Marginal Cost Pricing." *American Economic Review* 60:265–283.

Baumol, W., and Klevorick, A. 1970. "Input Choices and Rate-of-Return Regulation: An Overview of the Discussion." *Bell Journal of Economics* 1:162–190.

Baumol, W., Panzar, J., and Willig, R. 1982. *Contestable Markets and the Theory of Industry Structure*. New York: Harcourt, Brace, Jovanovich.

Becker, G. 1968. "Crime and Punishment: An Economic Approach." *Journal of Political Economy* 76:169–217.

Berle, A. and Means, G. 1932. *The Modern Corporation and Private Property*. New York: Macmillan.

Bernheim, D., and Whinston, M. 1984. "Common Agency." Harvard Institute of Economic Research Paper No. 1074.

Besanko, D. 1984. "On the Use of Revenue Requirements Regulation under Imperfect Information." in M. Crew, ed., *Analyzing the Impact of Regulatory Change*. Lexington, Mass.: Lexington Books, pp. 39–58.

Boiteaux, M. 1956. "Sur la Question des Monopoles Publics Astreints a l'Equilibre Budgetaire" *Econometrica* 24:22–40.

Braverman, A., and Stiglitz, J. 1982. "Sharecropping and the Interlinking of Agrarian Markets." *American Economic Review* 72:695–715.

Britto, R., Hamilton, J., Slutsky, S., and Stiglitz, J. 1985. "Taxation and commitment." Mimeo. June.

Cooper, R. 1984. "On Allocative Distortions in Problems of Self-Selection." *Rand Journal of Economics* 15:568–577.

Dasgupta, P., and Stiglitz, J. 1985. "Sunk Costs, Competition and Welfare." Princeton University Working Paper. July.

Demsetz, H. 1968. "Why Regulate Utilities?" *Journal of Law and Economics 7*: 55–65.

Demski, J., and Sappington, D. 1986. "Hierarchical Regulatory Control." Bell Communications Research mimeo. July.

Demski, J., and Sappington, D. 1984. "Optimal Incentive Schemes with Multiple Agents." *Journal of Economic Theory 33*: 152–171.

Demski, J., Sappington, D., and Spiller, P. 1985. "The Disciplinary Role of Switching Suppliers: A Regulatory Interpretation." Working Paper at Bell Communications Research. June.

Ebrill, L., and Slutsky, S. 1985. "Pricing Rules for Intermediate and Final Good Regulated Industries." University of Florida Working Paper. March.

Ekern, S., and Wilson, R. 1974. "On the Theory of the Firm in an Economy with Incomplete Markets." *Bell Journal of Economics and Management Science 5*: 1971–180.

Farrell, J. 1985. "Allocating and Abrogating Rights: How Should Conflicts be Resolved under Incomplete Information." GTE Laboratories mimeo.

Finsinger, J., and Vogelsang, I. 1981. "Alternative Institutional Frameworks for Price Incentive Mechanisms." *Kyklos 34*: 388–404.

Finsinger, J., and Vogelsang, I. 1985. "Strategic Management Behavior under Reward Structures in a Planned Economy." *Quarterly Journal of Economics 100*: 263–270.

Friexas, X., Guesnerie, R., and Tirole, J. 1985. "Planning under Incomplete Information and the Ratchet Effect." *Review of Economic Studies 52*: 173–191.

Goldman, M., Leland, H., and Sibley, D. 1984. "Optimal Nonuniform Prices." *Review of Economic Studies 51*: 305–319.

Greenwald, B., and Stiglitz, J. 1986. "Externalities in Economies with Imperfect Information and Incomplete Markets." Princeton University Working Paper. January.

Green, J., and Stokey, N. 1983. "A Comparison of Tournaments and Contracts." *Journal of Political Economy 91*: 349–364.

Grossman, S., and Hart, O. 1980. "Takeover Bids, the Free Rider Problem, and the Theory of the Corporation." *Bell Journal of Economics 11*: 42–65.

Grossman, S., and Hart, O. 1981. "The Allocational Role of Takeover Bids in Situations of Asymmetric Information." *Journal of Finance 36*: 253–270.

Grossman, S., and Stiglitz, J. 1980. "Stockholder Unanimity in Making Production and Financial Decisions." *Quarterly Journal of Economics 94*: 543–566.

Harris, M., and Raviv, A. 1979. "Optimal Incentive Contracts with Imperfect Information." *Journal of Economic Theory 20*: 231–259.

Holmstrom, B. 1982a. "The Design of Incentive Schemes and the New Soviet Incentive Model." *European Economic Review 17*: 127–148.

Holmstrom, B. 1979. "Moral Hazard and Observability." *Bell Journal of Economics 10*: 74–91.

Holmstrom, B. 1982b. "Moral Hazard in Teams", *Bell Journal of Economics 13*: 324–340.

Holmstrom, B. 1984. "On the Theory of Delegation." In M. Boyer and R. Kihlstrom, eds., *Bayesian Models in Economic Theory*. Amsterdam: North Holland, pp. 115–142.

Kahn, C., and Scheinkman, J. 1985. "Optimal Employment Contracts with Bankruptcy Constraints." *Journal of Economic Theory 35*: 343–365.

Laffont, J., and Tirole J. 1985. "Auctioning Incentive Contracts." MIT Working Paper. October.

Laffont, J., and Tirole, J. 1986. "Using Cost Observation to Regulate Firms." *Journal of Political Economy*, forthcoming.

Lazear, E., and Rosen, S. 1981. "Rank-Order Tournaments as Optimum Labor Contracts." *Journal of Political Economy 89*: 841–864.

Lewis, T. 1985. "Reputation and Contractual Performance in Long Term Projects." Working Paper at the University of British Columbia. June.

Linhart, P., Radner, R., and Sinden, F. 1983. "A Sequential Principal-Agent Approach to Regulation." Bell Laboratories Discussion Paper.

Loeb, M., and Magat, W. 1979. "A Decentralized Method for Utility Regulation." *Journal of Law and Economics 22*: 399–404.

Loeb, M., and Magat, W. 1978. "Success Indicators in the Soviet Union: The Problem of Incentives and Efficient Allocations." *American Economic Review 68*: 173–181.

March, J., and Simon, H. 1958. *Organizations.* New York: Wiley.

Maskin, E., and Riley, J. 1984. "Monopoly with Incomplete Information." *Rand Journal of Economics 15*: 171–196.

McAfee, R., and McMillan, J. 1986. "Competition for Agency Contracts." Working Paper at University of Western Ontario. January.

McAfee, R., and McMillan, J. 1984. "Incentive Contracts and Selection of Agent by Principal." Working Paper at University of Western Ontario. May.

McFarland, H. 1985. "Ramsey Pricing of Inputs with Downstream Monopoly Power and Regulation." EPO Discussion Paper 85-2. U.S. Department of Justice.

Mirrlees, J. 1971. "An Exploration in the Theory of Optimum Income Taxation." *Review of Economic Studies 38*: 175–208.

Mookherjee, D. 1984. "Optimal Incentive Schemes with Many Agents." *Review of Economic Studies 51*: 433–446.

Myerson, R. 1983. "Mechanism Design by an Informed Principal." *Econometrica, 51*: 1767–1798.

Nalebuff, B., and Stiglitz, J. 1983a. "Information, Competition and Markets." *American Economic Review 73*: 278–283.

Nalebuff, B., and Stiglitz, J. 1983b. "Prices and Incentives: Towards a General Theory of Compensation and Competition." *Bell Journal of Economics 14*: 21–43.

Panzar, J., and Willig, R. 1977. "Free Entry and the Sustainability of Natural Monopoly." *Bell Journal of Economics 8*: 1–22.

Radner, R. 1981. "Monitoring Cooperative Agreements in a Repeated Principal-Agent Relationship." *Econometrica 49*: 1127–1148.

Radner, R. 1974. "A Note on Unanimity of Stockholders' Preferences among Alternative Production Plans." *Bell Journal of Economics 5*: 181–186.

Radner, R. 1984. "Repeated Moral Hazard with Low Discount Rates." Bell Laboratories Discussion Paper.

Radner, R., and Stiglitz, J. 1984. "A Nonconcavity in the Value of Information." In M. Boyer and R. Kihlstrom, eds., *Bayesian Models in Economic Theory.* Amsterdam: North Holland, pp. 33–52.

Ramsey, F. 1927. "A Contribution to the Theory of Taxation." *Economic Journal 37*: 47–61.

Riordan, M. 1984. "On Delegating Price Authority to a Regulated Firm." *Rand Journal of Economics 15*: 108–115.

Riordan, M., and Sappington, D. 1985a. "Awarding Monopoly Franchises." Working Paper at Stanford University and Bell Communications Research. Revised December.

Riordan, M., and Sappington, D. 1985b. "Optimal Incentive Contracts with Public and Private Ex Post Information." Working Paper at Stanford University and Bell Communications Research. June.

Roberts, K. 1984. "The Theoretical Limits to Redistribution." *Review of Economic Studies 51*: 177–196.

Ross, S. 1973. "The Economic Theory of Agency: The Principal's Problem." *American Economic Review 63*: 134–139.

Rothschild, M., and Stiglitz, J. 1976. "Equilibrium in Competitive Insurance Markets: An Essay on the Economics of Information." *Quarterly Journal of Economics 90*: 225–243.

Sah, R., and Stiglitz, J. 1985. "Human Fallibility and Economic Organization." *American Economic Review 76*: 292–297.

Sappington, D. 1986. "Commitment to Regulatory Bureaucracy." Bell Communications Research Working Paper. January.

Sappington, D. 1984. "Incentive Contracting with Asymmetric and Imperfect Precontractual Knowledge." *Journal of Economic Theory 34*: 52–70.

Sappington, D. 1983a. "Limited Liability Contracts between Principal and Agent." *Journal of Economic Theory 29*: 1–21.

Sappington, D. 1983b. "Optimal Regulation of a Multiproduct Monopoly with Unknown Technological Capabilities." *Bell Journal of Economics 14*: 453–463.

Sappington, D. 1982. "Optimal Regulation of Research and Development under Imperfect Information." *Bell Journal of Economics 13*: 354–368.

Sappington, D. 1980. "Strategic Firm Behavior under a Dynamic Regulatory Adjustment Process." *Bell Journal of Economics 11*: 360–372.

Sappington, D., and Sibley, D. 1985. "Regulatory Incentive Schemes Using Historic Cost Data." Working Paper at Bell Communications Research. Revised August.

Shapiro, C., and Stiglitz, J. 1984. "Equilibrium Unemployment as a Worker Discipline Device." *American Economic Review 74*: 433–444.

Shavell, S. 1979. "Risk Sharing and Incentives in the Principal and Agent Relationship." *Bell Journal of Economics 10*: 55–73.

Singh, N. 1985. "Monitoring and Hierarchies: The Marginal Value of Information in a Principal-Agent Model." *Journal of Political Economy 93*: 599–609.

Stigler, G. 1972. "The Theory of Economic Regulation." *Bell Journal of Economics 2*: 3–21.

Stiglitz, J. 1985. "Credit Markets and the Control of Capital." *Journal of Money, Credit, and Banking 17*: 133–152.

Stiglitz, J. 1975. "Incentives, Risk and Information: Notes Towards a Theory of Hierarchy." *Bell Journal of Economics 6*: 552–579.

Stiglitz, J. 1977. "Monopoly, Non-Linear Pricing and Imperfect Information: The Insurance Market." *Review of Economic Studies 44*: 407–430.

Stiglitz, J. 1970. "On the Optimality of the Stock Market Allocation of Investment." Paper presented at the Far Eastern Meetings of the Econometric Society, Tokyo, Japan, June 27–29.

Stiglitz, J. 1972. "Some Aspects of the Pure theory of Corporate Finance: Bankruptcies and Takeovers." *Bell Journal of Economics and Management Science 3*:458–482.

Stiglitz, J. 1974. "Risk Sharing and Incentives in Sharecropping." *Review of Economic Studies 41*:219–256.

Stiglitz, J. 1982. "Self-Selection and Pareto Efficient Taxation." *Journal of Public Economics 17*:213–240.

Stiglitz, J., and Weiss, A. 1983. "Alternative Approaches to Analyzing Markets with Asymmetric Information." *American Economic Review 73*:246–249.

Stiglitz, J., and Weiss, A. 1981. "Credit Rationing in Markets with Asymmetric Information." *American Economic Review 71*:393–410.

Stiglitz, J., and Weiss, A. 1983. "Incentive Effects of Terminations: Applications to the Credit and Labor Markets." *American Economic Review 73*:912–927.

Stiglitz, J., and Weiss, A. 1985. "Sorting Out the Differences between Screening and Signaling Models." Bell Communications Research Discussion Paper.

Tam, M. 1985. "Reward Structures in a Planned Economy: Some Further Thoughts." *Quarterly Journal of Economics 50*:279–290.

Townsend, R. 1979. "Optimal Contracts and Competitive Markets with Costly State Verification." *Journal of Economic Theory 21*:265–293.

Vogelsang, I., and Finsinger, J. 1979. "A Regulatory Adjustment Process for Optimal Pricing by Multiproduct Monopoly Firms." *Bell Journal of Economics 10*:157–171.

Weitzman, M. 1976. "The New Soviet Incentive Model." *Bell Journal of Economics 7*:251–257.

Williamson, O. 1976. "Franchise Bidding for Natural Monopolies—In General and with Respect to CATV." *Bell Journal of Economics 7*:73–104.

Williamson, O. 1975. *Markets and Hierarchies: Analysis and Antitrust Implications.* New York: The Free Press.

2

Judicial Review of Questions of Law and Policy
Stephen G. Breyer

Since the early 1930s those studying the growth of the administrative state have sounded two conflicting themes. The first is that of the need for regulation. Complex modern social, economic, and technical problems require governmental intervention, particularly into the private marketplace. Intervention means regulation by administrators acting under generally worded congressional delegations of broad policymaking authority.

The second theme is that of the need for checks and controls. These same necessary administrators must be checked in the exercise of their broad powers lest their shortsightedness or overzealousness lead to unwise policies or unfair or oppressive behavior.

Congressional action in the late 1960s and early 1970s for the most part reflected the first of these themes. Congress created many new agencies charged with problems of health, safety, and environmental protection.[1] Perhaps in reaction to the sudden, large growth in federal regulatory activity, however, public debate during the past decade has focused on the second theme: How can government guarantee wiser or fairer regulatory policies? How can it regulate the regulators?

We can find several general answers to these latter questions. One kind of answer focuses on the substance of a particular regulatory program and advocates dramatic individual substantive changes, such as deregulation of airlines,[2] trucking,[3] or financial institutions,[4] or increased taxes to control environmental pollution.[5] Another focuses more generally on the government's institutional structure. It advocates changes in that structure, such as greater supervision and control of regulators by Congress,[6] the White House,[7] or the courts.[8]

A comprehensive analysis of current regulatory problems would require an examination of both approaches. It would require an examination of many regulatory programs and also a detailed comparative account of the abilities of Congress, the White House, and the courts to supervise effectively the actions of administrative regulators.[9] This chapter examines but a small portion of that large picture, namely court efforts to control agency action, relating to the basic principles of law that govern judicial review of agency action.[10] Two important legal doctrines will, in part, govern that review. The first doctrine concerns the appropriate attitude of a reviewing court toward an agency's interpretations of law, say, the law embodied in the statute that grants the agency its legal powers. To what extent should a court make up its own mind independently about the meaning of the words of the statute? The second doctrine concerns a reviewing court's attitude toward an agency's regulatory policy. How willing should a court be to set aside such a policy as unreasonable, arbitrary, or inadequately considered?

The conclusions that emerge from the examination of current doctrines or principles are twofold. First, current doctrine is anomalous. It urges courts both to defer to administrative interpretations of regulatory statutes and to review quite strictly agency decisions of regulatory policy. Since courts have responded, like other governmental institutions, to two basically conflicting pressures—the need for regulation and for checks on regulators—this anomaly may not be surprising. Yet law that embodies so skewed a view of institutional competence is inherently unstable and likely to change. Second, the courts as presently limited by rules requiring the presentation of information through public, adversary procedures are not particularly well suited to determine the wisdom of agency policy. Thus, if we wish seriously to use them as important instruments for controlling agency policy, we must also consider whether, or how, they can obtain better information or a more global, comprehensive view of the agency's objectives and its work.

Questions of Law

Two Opposite Judicial Attitudes

We first examine a court's attitude when reviewing a claim that an agency's action violates a particular provision in a statute or that it lacks a necessary statutory authorization. How should it treat the agency's decision about the relevant interpretation of law? Should it defer to the agency or give special weight to the agency's legal views? The single most interesting observation about this question—about judicial review of an agency determination of law—is that of Judge Henry Friendly. He points out that there is no consistent "law" or "proper judicial attitude." Rather, there "are two lines of Supreme Court decisions on this subject which are analytically in conflict."[11]

Perhaps we should expect to find attitudinal inconsistency: relevant legal questions vary widely in both nature and importance. One agency, for example, may decide that a U.S. employer has placed in a "zone of special danger" an employee whose private rowboat sinks during a Sunday pleasure outing on a Korean lake.[12] The legal question—the meaning of the quoted phrase—is highly specialized, fact specific, and unlikely to have broad legal or practical implications. Alternatively, a different agency may decide that cable television systems are not engaged in broadcasting; therefore the agency has the legal power to regulate them as "common carriers."[13] The legal question—the scope of the quoted words—is of great importance for television viewers, the communications industry, and American political, social, and cultural life. Why should one expect a legal system to provide one consistent method for deciding legal questions of such varying importance?

Nevertheless, the cases seem inconsistent. One set of cases displays an attitude toward agency decisions of law that must be described as deferential. It is illustrated by *NLRB* v. *Hearst Publications, Inc.*,[14] where the Supreme Court upheld a Labor Board decision that certain newspaper distributors were "employees," as that term is used in the National Labor Relations Act. In deciding what was, under the circumstances, a question of law, the Court emphasized the need to give special weight to the agency's decision. The agency's "everyday experience in the administration of the statute gives it familiarity" with the practical problems and necessities involved in regulating the area.[15] The Court wrote: "Where the question is one of specific application of a broad statutory term in a proceeding in which the agency administering the statute must determine it initially, the reviewing court's function is limited." The Court should look to see only whether the agency's decision has "'warrant in the record' and a reasonable basis in law."[16]

A different set of cases exemplifies a judicial attitude that must be described as "independent." It is illustrated by the superficially similar case of *Packard Motor Car Co.* v. *NLRB*,[17] where the Supreme Court reviewed a Labor Board determination that shop foremen were "employees" as that term is used in the same statute. The Court upheld the determination, but it did not simply look to see whether the Board's decision had "a reasonable basis in law." To the contrary, the majority and the dissenters each made their own legal analysis; neither suggested the agency's decision should receive any special weight or deference, and neither referred to *Hearst* or to any of the cases on which *Hearst* relied.[18]

Each of these cases has spawned spiritual descendants. Many more recent Supreme Court cases, discussing the proper judicial attitude toward agency decisions of law, echo *Hearst*. In 1979, the Court wrote that if the Labor Board's "construction of the statute is reasonably defensible, it should not be rejected merely because the courts might prefer another view of the statute."[19] In 1980 the Court said it would uphold the Federal Reserve Board's interpretation of its governing statute so long as it was not "demonstrably irrational."[20] In 1981 it said, with respect to a legal interpretation by the Federal Election Commission:

> The task for the Court of Appeals was not to interpret the statute as it thought best but rather the narrower inquiry into whether the Commission's construction was 'sufficiently reasonable' to be accepted by a reviewing court.[21]

Packard, however, also has children of its own. In 1983, for example, reviewing a legal interpretation of the Bureau of Alcohol, Tobacco and Firearms, the Supreme Court cited the deference cases, but said that courts, when reviewing agency interpretations of law, must not "slip into ... judicial inertia" or "rubber stamp" agency decisions.[22] It has stated unequivocally in many cases that the judiciary is responsible for the final determination of the meaning of statutes.[23] And in numerous cases the Supreme Court, without citing the deference cases, has simply adopted what Judge Friendly, and other students of the subject, consider to be a more independent attitude.[24]

Reconciling the Conflict

One might try to reconcile this apparently conflicting case law by asking *why* a court should *ever* defer to an agency's interpretation of the law? After all, judges are charged by statute and the Constitution with deciding legal questions. Why should they ever pay *particular* attention to the agency's legal views?

One can think of two possible jurisprudential answers to these questions. First, one might believe that judges should pay special attention to the agency because the agency knows more about the particular area of the law than does the court. This answer, in part, treats agency lawyers like expert tax lawyers or real estate lawyers to whom judges may listen with particular attention when they must decide a difficult, complex case. In the context of administrative law, this answer may rest on a particularly important, highly relevant legal fact, namely the likely intent of the Congress that enacted the statute. The agency that enforces the statute may have had a hand in drafting its provisions. It may possess an internal history in the form of documents or handed-down oral tradition that casts light on the meaning of a difficult phrase or provision. Regardless, its staff, in close contact with relevant legislators and staffs, likely understands *current* congressional views, which in turn may, through institutional history, reflect prior understandings. At a minimum, the agency staff understands what sorts of interpretations are needed to make the statute work. It is virtually always proper for a court to assume Congress wanted the statute to work and, at least, did not intend a set of interpretations that would preclude its effective administration.

This better understanding of congressional will is reflected in many court statements urging deference. The District of Columbia Circuit, for example, recently wrote:

> Courts regard with particular respect the contemporaneous construction of a statute by those initially charged with its enforcement.... [W]here the agency was involved in developing the provisions, this principle applies with even greater force.[25]

Similarly courts have said they find an agency's views more persuasive when they reflect a longstanding, consistent interpretation of the statute.[26] Congress' reenactment of the statute, in the face of an agency interpretation, is also some evidence that the agency's interpretation is correct;[27] at least it suggests that the agency's interpretation does not radically violate current congressional expectations—a fact that offers some evidence about the understandings of relevant agency client groups, providing some (often weak) evidence about the original congressional understanding. There may also be some sense in which, because of "settled expectations," a statute's words, legally speaking, *come* to mean what affected parties reasonably understand them to mean over a long period of time—irrespective of a legislature's original understandings.[28] Where all these considerations are absent—where, for example, the agency adopts a radically new statutory interpretation—courts have sometimes said that the agency is not entitled to "deference."[29]

Of course, the strength and the relevance of these considerations varies from case to case. But they all reflect one type of answer to the question "Why defer?"—namely, "because the agency has a better understanding of relevant law."

A very different sort of answer to the question "Why defer?" is "Congress *told* the courts to defer in respect to this particular legal question; Congress delegated *to the agency* the power to decide the relevant question of law." Indeed, Congress may have *explicitly* delegated rule-making authority to an agency; the resulting agency rules, in a sense, are laws; and to make legislative rules is to engage in a law-declaring function.[30] But Congress is rarely so explicit about delegating the legal power to interpret a statute.

The Supreme Court, nevertheless, suggested as early as 1946 that Congress might delegate an interpretive, as well as a rule-making, power to an administrative agency. In *Social Security Board* v. *Nierotko*,[31] the Court held that the Social Security Board did *not* have the power to exclude a worker's back pay from his "wages" for the purpose of calculating benefits. The Court wrote:

> Administration, when it interprets a statute so as to make it apply to particular circumstances, acts as a delegate to the legislative power. Congress might have declared that "back pay" awards under the Labor Act should or should not be treated as wages. Congress might have delegated to the Social Security Board to determine what compensation paid by employers to employees should be treated as wages. *Except as such interpretive power may be included in the agencies' administrative functions, Congress did neither.*[32]

The italicized statement suggests that courts may sometimes find, through implication, that they should pay special attention to agency views on particular legal questions.

For the most part courts have used "legislative intent to delegate the law-interpreting function" as a kind of legal fiction. They have looked to practical features of the particular circumstance to decide whether it "makes sense," in terms of the need for fair and efficient administration of that statute in light of its substantive purpose, to infer a congressional intent that courts defer to the agency's interpretation. It is nothing new in the law for a court to imagine what a hypothetically reasonable legislator would have wanted (given the statute's objective) as an interpretive method of understanding a statutory term surrounded by silence.[33] Nor is it new to answer this question by looking to practical facts surrounding the administration of a statutory scheme.[34] And there is no reason why one could not apply these general principles, not simply to the question of what a statute's words mean but also to the question of the extent to which Congress intended that courts should defer to the agency's view of the proper interpretation.

Thus courts will defer more when the agency has special expertise that it can bring to bear on the legal question.[35] Is the particular question one that the agency or the court is more likely to answer correctly? Does the question, for example, concern common law or constitutional law, or does it concern matters of agency administration?[36] A court may also ask whether the legal question is an important one. Congress is more likely to have focused on, and answered, major questions, while leaving interstitial matters to the agencies to answer themselves in the course of the statute's daily administration.[37] A court may also look to see whether the language is "inherently imprecise" (i.e., whether the words of the statute are phrased so broadly as to invite agency interpretation).[38] It might also consider the extent to which the answer to the legal question will clarify, illuminate, or stabilize a broad area of the law.[39] Finally, a court might ask itself whether the agency can be trusted to give a properly balanced answer. Courts sometimes fear that certain agencies suffer from tunnel vision and seek to expand their power beyond the authority that Congress likely gave them.[40] Of course, reliance on any or all of these factors as a method of determining a hypothetical congressional intent on the deference question can quickly be overborne by any tangible evidence of congressional intent—say, legislative history—suggesting that Congress did resolve, or wanted a court to resolve, the statutory question at issue.[41]

These factors help explain many cases. *Hearst* (the news distributor/employee case), for example, presented a minor, interstitial question of law, which was intimately bound up with the statute's daily administration and was likely to be better understood by a technically expert agency than by a legally expert court. *Packard* (the foreman/employee case), on the other hand, presented a legal question of great importance in the field of labor relations: Does the NLRA cover shop foremen? This question raised political, as well as policy, concerns; it seems unlikely that Congress wished to leave so important and delicate a legal question to the Board to decide.

Using these factors as a means of discerning a hypothetical congressional intent about "deference" has institutional virtues. It allows courts to allocate the law-interpreting function between court and agency in a way likely to work best within any particular statutory scheme. Insofar as Congress is viewed as delegating the power to the agency, it gives the agency flexibility to adapt or to modify past policies. By contrast, a theory of deference based on the agency knowing original congressional intent "better" than the court tends to insulate administrative policies adopted early in a statute's history from later change.[42] Of course the delegation way of looking at deference tends to blur any clear distinction between legislative and interpretive rules. It suggests that Congress' intent to make agency decisions of law binding is really a question of how much deference Congress intended courts to pay to the agency's decisions—a matter of degree, not kind, and a matter to be considered by examining a particular statute in light of the various practical factors mentioned.

In sum, one can reconcile apparent conflict in case law descriptions of a proper judicial attitude toward agency decisions of law. The reconciliation process consists of asking the question, Why should courts ever defer? The reconciliation consists of two answers to this question—answers that are not mutually exclusive and that may apply in different cases. One answer rests on an agency's better knowledge of congressional intent. The other rests upon Congress's intent that courts give agency legal interpretations special weight—an intent that (where Congress is silent) courts may impute on the basis of various "practical" circumstances.

The Problem of the Chevron Case

A recent Supreme Court case, *Chevron, U.S.A. v. Natural Resources Defense Council*,[43] suggests a somewhat different test for determining the proper judicial attitude—the degree of deference—toward an agency's legal decisions. The case concerned the Environmental Protection Agency's interpretation of the words "stationary source" in the EPA's governing statute. EPA interpreted these words to refer, in part, to an entire plant. That interpretation allowed EPA to make rules[44] that treated an entire plant as a single "source," thereby allowing its owner to emit more pollutant than ordinarily permissible from one stack, provided it emitted less pollutant from another. The Court (reversing the District of Columbia Court of Appeals) upheld the EPA's interpretation.

The Court in *Chevron* described the relation of court to agency when interpreting a statute, as follows:

> First, always, is the question whether Congress has directly spoken to the precise question at issue. If the intent of Congress is clear, that is the end of the matter; for the court, as well as the agency, must give effect to the unambiguously expressed intent of Congress. If, however, the court determines Congress has not directly addressed the precise question at issue, the court does not simply impose its own construction of the statute, as would be necessary in the absence of an administrative interpretation. Rather, if the statute is silent or ambiguous with respect to the specific issue, the question for the court is whether the agency's answer is based on a permissible construction of the statute.[45]

The Court added:

> Sometimes the legislative delegation to an agency on a particular question is implicit rather than explicit. In such a case, a court may not substitute its own construction of a statutory provision for a reasonable interpretation made by the administrator or an agency.[46]

This language *may* be read as embodying the complex approach set out earlier; it speaks of "implicit" delegation of interpretative power, and the word "permissible" is general enough to embody the range of relevant factors. Yet the language may also be read as embodying a considerably simpler approach, namely first decide whether the statute is "silent or ambiguous with respect to the specific issue" and, if so, accept the agency's interpretation if (in light of statutory purposes) it is "reasonable."

Recent cases in the District of Columbia Circuit Court of Appeals indicate that the lower courts may have accepted this second interpretation of *Chevron*.⁴⁷ As so seen, *Chevron* offers a simpler view of proper judicial attitude, but a view that conflicts and competes with that offered here. Despite its attractive simplicity, however, this interpretation seems unlikely in the long run, to replace the complex approach described here for several reasons.

First, and most important, there are too many different types of circumstances—different statutes, different kinds of application, different substantive regulatory or administrative problems, different legal postures in which cases arrive—to allow "proper" judicial attitudes about questions of law to be reduced to a single simple verbal formula. These differences can be illustrated by contrasting *Chevron* with a recent First Circuit case, *Avery v. Secretary of Health and Human Services*.⁴⁸ The relevant statute said "the Secretary shall notify . . ." plaintiffs in class actions about certain recent procedural developments. The Secretary interpreted these words to authorize her to control the style and content of the relevant notices, despite the fact that the district court hearing the cases concluded that its own notices were needed to properly inform the plaintiffs, to avoid serious confusion, and to carry out the purposes of the underlying statute. Despite the provision's linguistic ambiguity, it was neither improper nor surprising that in this basically minor, procedural and court-related matter, the court would make its own (correct) interpretation of the statute.⁴⁹ To read *Avery* and to contrast it with *Chevron* leads one to recognize that questions dealing with agencies come in an almost infinite variety of sizes, shapes, and hues. To interpret *Chevron* as laying down a blanket rule, applicable to all agency interpretations of law, such as "always defer to the agency when the statute is silent," would be seriously overbroad, counterproductive, and (in a case like *Avery*) close to senseless.

A second reason why a strict interpretation of *Chevron* is undesirable is illustrated by *Railway Labor Executives Association v. United States Railroad Retirement Board*.⁵⁰ The court believed that the statute was silent on the particular question at issue, but that under *Chevron* it should see if the agency had a reasonable interpretation of the statutory language. The court found, however, that the agency had no coherent account of what the words meant; it had not considered the question in sufficient depth. The court then remanded the case to the district court in part to give the agency a chance to develop a "reasonable" interpretation of the statute.

A simpler course of judicial action would be based on a less literal reading of *Chevron*. The congressional instruction hypothetically implied from silence (and possibly other features of the situation) might be read, not as (1) "we delegate to the agency the power to create the law," but rather as (2) "Court, 'pay particular attention to a reasonable agency interpretation of the law.'" This second instruction implies that if the agency has not offered a reasonable interpretation of the statute in this case, if it has not considered the matter thoroughly, if the agency's brief lacks the power to persuade,[51] then the court should simply decide the question on its own. This second view makes practical sense from the perspective of *judicial* administration.

A third and final reason why neither a strict view of *Chevron* nor any other strictly defined verbal review formula requiring deference to an agency's interpretation of law can prove successful in the long run is that such a formula asks judges to develop a cast of mind that often is psychologically difficult to maintain. It is difficult, after having examined a legal question in depth with the object of deciding it correctly, to believe both that the agency's interpretation is legally wrong and that its interpretation is reasonable. More often one concludes that there is a better view of, say, the statute, that the better view is correct, and the alternative view is erroneous. There is not much room in this kind of thinking for the notion of "both this view and its contrary are reasonable"—a notion with which one is more at home when, say, juries apply standards to facts or agencies promulgate rules under a general delegation of authority.[52] Thus one can find many cases in which the opinion suggests the court believed the agency's legal interpretation was correct and added citations to deference cases to bolster the argument.[53] One can also find cases in which the court believed the agency's interpretation was wrong and overturned the agency, often citing nondeference cases.[54] But, it is more difficult to find cases where the opinion suggests the court believed the agency was wrong in its interpretation of a statute and nevertheless upheld the agency on deference principles.

These factors will tend to force a less univocal, less far-reaching interpretation of *Chevron* and the other "show deference on questions of law" cases. Inevitably, one suspects, we will find the courts actually following more varied approaches, sometimes deferring to agency interpretations, sometimes not, depending on the statute, the question, the context, and what makes sense in the particular litigation, in light of the basic statute and its purposes. No single simple judicial formula can capture or take account of the varying responses called for by different circumstances and needed to promote a proper, harmonious, effective, or workable agency/court relationship.

One might reformulate the two general points embodied in this brief discussion as follows. First, the main criticism that one might make of the

Supreme Court's case law describing appropriate judicial attitudes toward traditional agency interpretations of the law is that they overstate the degree of deference due the agency. If taken literally, their language suggests a greater abdication of judicial responsibility to interpret the law than seems wise, from either a jurisprudential or an administrative perspective. Second, the problem this case law language poses is not serious, for one can work out a unified set of principles roughly consistent with existing case law that allows a court to formulate a "proper" judicial attitude in individual cases. And these principles seem reasonably satisfactory from both a jurisprudential and administrative point of view.

Review of Agency Policy Decisions

We turn now to the question of when courts will hold an agency *policy* decision unlawful, essentially because it is unreasonable. The question is difficult to answer, in part because there is no set legal doctrine called "review of policy questions"; consequently the case law does not purport to authoritatively govern judicial attitude in conducting a policy review.

Nevertheless, one can focus on two sets of legal decisions that often amount in practice to a review of the wisdom and the reasonableness of agency policy.[55] First, a court sometimes will directly substitute its judgment for the agency's on a matter of substantive policy, on the ground that the agency's decision is "arbitrary, capricious, an abuse of discretion" under section 706(2)(A) of the Administrative Procedure Act. Suppose, for example, the Labor Board decides that it will permit a union business agent to buy drinks for voters before a representation election. Can a reviewing court simply find this Board policy unreasonable in light of the need for fair elections?[56] When writing an administrative law case book in the late 1970s, the authors could find only a handful of cases that faced so directly an agency policy decision and held it "arbitrary"; by the time of the second edition in 1985, they found many, many more.[57]

Second, courts more and more frequently have applied a set of procedural principles that, in effect, require the agency to take a hard look at relevant policy considerations before reaching a substantive decision. These principles require the agency to examine all relevant evidence,[58] to explain its decisions in detail,[59] to justify departures from past practices,[60] and to consider all reasonable alternatives[61] before reaching a final policy decision. In practice, these principles have far greater substantive impact than one might at first realize. A remand of an important agency rule (several years in the making) for more thorough consideration may well mean several years of additional proceedings, with mounting costs and the threat of further judicial review leading to abandonment or modification of the initial project irrespective of the merits.[62] Courts and agencies alike are aware that these doctrines, dictating more thorough consideration and a hard look, have substantive impact. To that extent, in examining the attitude with which the courts apply the doctrines, one is, in an important sense, examining the attitude with which they review the wisdom or reasonableness of agency substantive decision making.

The important attitudinal question is how closely the court will examine the agency's policy decisions. To what extent will it defer to the agency's expertise? How "hard" will the court "look" at the agency's decisions? With what state of mind is the reviewing judge to approach the question of whether the agency has inadequately considered policy considerations, failed to take a hard look at evidence or alternatives or simply adopted an unreasonable policy?

The language in several important cases decided in the last two decades suggests perhaps an increasingly less hesitant judiciary—courts that are more ready to overturn agency policy decisions that they consider unreasonable. Thus the D.C. Circuit speaks of the need for a "thorough, probing, in-depth review,"[63] and the need for a "substantial and searching" inquiry.[64] The Supreme Court has vacillated linguistically, sometimes speaking of a "thorough, probing" review[65] and sometimes speaking more traditionally about the need for courts to hesitate before substituting their judgment for that of the agency on matters of policy.[66]

The "State Farm" Case: An Example of Strict Policy Review
The airbags case, *Motor Vehicles Manufacturers of the United States* v. *State Farm Mutual Automobile Insurance Co.*,[67] provides an example of a fairly strict judicial attitude toward review of substantive agency policy. The issue in the case was whether the National Highway Traffic Safety Administration (NHTSA) acted reasonably in rescinding Motor Vehicle Safety Standard 208—a standard requiring automakers to install "passive restraints" in new cars. The regulation had a complex and convoluted history. In 1967 the Department of Transportation (DOT) required manufacturers to install ordinary lap seat belts in all cars. In 1969 it proposed a passive restraint standard that would have allowed carmakers to install either (1) seat belts that would automatically surround the driver and passenger or (2) airbags that would inflate automatically in a crash and cushion the front seat occupants. Unlike standard seat belts which passengers had to buckle, these "passive" devices required no affirmative con-

duct by the passenger. From 1973 to 1975 DOT required automakers to install either (1) these passive restraints or (2) lap and shoulder belts with an "interlock" preventing the driver from starting the car when the belts were unbuckled. Most carmakers chose the interlock option, drivers became angry, and Congress then prohibited DOT from making the interlock option a choice. After various further proposals DOT finally required automakers to install either (1) airbags or (2) detachable or spoolable (nondetachable) lap and shoulder belts that would automatically surround the front seat occupants. Most automakers indicated they would take the detachable belt option.

In 1981 the new administration simply rescinded Standard 208 on the ground that it was ineffective. Because carmakers then planned to install permanently detachable seat belts in 99 percent of all new cars, NHTSA thought that few lives would be saved.

The Court of Appeals had found the agency's action was unreasonable, but only after it applied a specially *strict* standard of review—a standard it felt justified in applying because of the legislative history of the agency's authorizing statute. The Supreme Court held that the Court of Appeals should not have applied a special review standard. It wrote that the ordinary "arbitrary and capricious" standard should apply. The Court, however, found the agency's action unreasonable even under this standard. An examination of the Court's opinion in light of NHTSA's arguments suggests the Court is holding that ordinary reasonableness review can itself be quite strict.

The Court believed NHTSA's rescission was unreasonable in three respects. First, it thought that NHTSA had failed adequately to consider whether the safety benefits of passive detachable belts would justify their cost. It accepted NHTSA's view both that driver use of existing lap belts was low and that current usage rates would have to more than double—from 11 to 24 percent—before the benefits of the more expensive nondetachable belts outweighed their cost. The Court doubted, however, whether NHTSA was reasonable in rejecting studies showing that usage more than doubled when passive, detachable belts replaced lap belts in Volkswagen Rabbits and in Chevettes. The Court thought that NHTSA should have considered the generalizability of these studies more carefully. In particular, it thought that NHTSA should study whether the inertia factor (the fact that passive, detachable belts require driver action to be decoupled, while existing lap belts require driver action to be coupled) would lead to higher usage.

NHTSA had argued that it was not unreasonable in failing to gather this extra information before rescinding the standard. It argued that it had to act quickly: automakers needed to know soon whether or not they had to comply with the standard. NHTSA said that it had no evidence that the inertia factor would make a difference and that it could not find such evidence without conducting an elaborate experiment of the sort that a previous administration had rejected in 1977. NHTSA further argued that the Volkswagen and Chevette studies did not contradict, but rather supported, its position. Drivers of such small cars, it said, tend to use seat belts far more often than others; their passive detachable belts had interlocks that made the belts unusually difficult to detach, and the car owners in the studies had voluntarily paid more money for passive belts. NHTSA pointed out that for these reasons, the passive belts usage figures could be interpreted in its favor. The studies showed that the car owners studied used passive belts 2.1 to 2.3 times more often than other drivers used ordinary lap belts in similar models, but the studies simultaneously showed that nearly one-third of those who voluntarily had sought (and paid more for) passive belts with interlocks nevertheless disconnected them. NHTSA presumably thought that a significantly higher percentage of those who were forced to use detachable belts against their will would decouple the belts. To that extent the studies supported rescission.

Second, the Court thought that NHTSA had acted unreasonably in not considering whether to require nondetachable spool-type passive belts instead of rescinding Standard 208. NHTSA had argued, however, that nondetachable belts may make it more difficult to rescue unconscious drivers, that public fears of being trapped in an accident might lead car owners to remove nondetachable belts from their cars or lead Congress to prohibit requiring them, and that Congress' responses to NHTSA's earlier proposal for passive detachable belts with interlocks (which forebade NHTSA from requiring them even as an option) showed legislative hostility to use-compelling devices. The Court did not say why it thought these arguments unreasonable. But it remanded for a more reasoned analysis.

Third, the Court unanimously[68] felt NHTSA erred in failing to consider an airbags-only alternative to Standard 208. Here the Court was on strong ground, for NHTSA had said virtually nothing about this possible alternative when it rescinded the standard. Still, NHTSA could point to several factors militating in favor of calling its decision not to consider the airbags-only alternative a reasonable one. For one thing, the specific decision

NHTSA had to make was whether or not to rescind a rule that, in practice, was a seat-belt-only rule. Although carmakers in theory could have chosen to comply by installing airbags, few, if any, intended to do so. For another thing, NHTSA had historically considered airbags to be but one way of satisfying a passive restraint standard. When NHTSA first promulgated the standard, it stated that it in no way "'favored' or expected the introduction of airbag systems to meet the [Standard 208] requirements."[69] It added that there were other "equally acceptable" ways to meet its passive restraint standard.[70] Thus it may have seen the airbags-only alternative as a new and different idea.

Moreover an airbags-only rule is a very costly way to save lives. The Court of Appeals mentioned cost estimates of $200 to $330 per car. The yearly cost to the economy would have ranged from $2 billion to $5 billion (for the annual new fleet of 10 to 15 million cars), depending on which figures one picked. Deciding whether all car buyers should pay these costs becomes difficult (even when doing so would save 9,000 lives per year) once one realizes that a buckled seat belt achieves virtually the same result at a fraction of the price.

Further NHTSA's authorizing statute mandates performance standards, not design standards. An airbags-only rule would have come close to the latter because it would have told manufacturers how to make their cars safer, not how safe their cars must be. Finally, fully considering an airbags-only rule would have taken time, and manufacturers needed to know quickly what they had to do. Unless NHTSA rescinded Standard 208 soon, they would have had to start preparing to install passive belts in all cars.

Of course NHTSA's answers to the Court's three objections did not necessarily show that its action was reasonable. But the Supreme Court's opinion does not show them to be obviously fallacious either.[71] It seems safe to conclude that in finding NHTSA's arguments insufficient, the Supreme Court applied a fairly strict review standard. Regardless of the words it used to describe what it was doing, it had to conduct a fairly thorough, detailed, and searching review of the agency's action under the "arbitrary and capricious" standard in order to undermine the plausibility of the justification for NHTSA's action. The case therefore seems to illustrate rather strict judicial scrutiny of agency policy decisions. And it has been taken as authorization for such scrutiny in several later lower court cases.[72] In light of these cases *State Farm* should not be seen as an unusual case, but rather as one example of many cases that reveal a strict review attitude.[73]

Comparative Institutional Competence
One might ask with the airbags case in mind whether the judiciary is institutionally well suited for strict policy scrutiny. To what extent can a group of men and women, typically trained as lawyers rather than as administrators or regulators, operating with limited access to information and under the constraints of adversary legal process, be counted on to supervise the vast realm of substantive agency policymaking?

First, to what extent are judges likely to sympathetically understand the problems the agency faces in setting technical standards in complex areas? In the airbags case, for example, the Supreme Court faulted NHTSA for not having more studies or more accurate studies. But was the Court fully aware of how difficult it is for an agency seeking to set standards to obtain accurate, relevant, unbiased information? Where is the agency to look? Industry information is often suspect, insofar as industry's economic interests are at stake. Consumer groups may be as suspect or biased, though perhaps in a different direction. Independent experts may not have sufficiently detailed information or may have gotten it from industry. And it may not be practicable administratively for an agency to duplicate in-house all the expertise of others outside the federal government. Some information may in fact be unobtainable. For instance, was there any practical way for NHTSA to estimate the true cost of airbags or to find out what reactions drivers would likely have to the spool-type belt? More important, how could it objectively divine Congress' reaction to the drivers' reaction? Is it then forbidden to take this factor into account? Why?

The agency must also deal with a host of complex questions in deciding what type of standard to promulgate. Should the standard aim directly at the evil targeted (traffic deaths) or at a surrogate (buckling up)? How specific should the standards be? Should it try to force technological change by making the industry achieve goals beyond its present technological capabilities? Should it use a more flexible performance standard or a more administrable design standard? The agency must have an enforcement system that will test compliance with the eventual standard. But this too is far easier said than done. The agency must design the standard with other enforcement needs and development costs in mind. Is it unreasonable to weaken or simplify standards in order to increase the likelihood of voluntary compliance or to stretch an already tight development budget?

The agency may also have to consider various competitive concerns. How will a new standard affect industry? Will it favor some existing firms over others or will it favor all existing firms by making entry into the industry more difficult?

Industry moreover is only one group whose interests the agency must consider. Whenever it regulates, the agency finds before it different groups—the industry, suppliers, consumer groups, members of Congress, and its own staff—with somewhat different interests. At the least, each group may see different aspects of the problem as important: industry may focus on costs, suppliers on competitive fairness, and consumers on safety. Each group moreover has a different weapon with which to threaten the agency. The staff can recommend changed standards. Industry can withhold or produce critical information or threaten legal or political action. Consumer groups can threaten to appeal to Congress or to the public through the press. A wise agency may recognize the weapons that the various parties wield and may shape its standards to minimize opposition. It can thus increase the likelihood of voluntary compliance and diminish the likelihood of court delays. The agency's final decision is likely to reflect some degree of compromise among all these interests. Such compromise decisions are, in a sense, political; they may not be supportable through pure logic, but are they unreasonable?

Is it surprising then that agencies and courts often disagree about what constitutes a "reasonable" decision? The court may not appreciate the agency's need to make decisions under conditions of uncertainty. Compromises made to secure agreement among the parties may strike a court as irrational because the agency cannot logically explain them.

Second, courts work within institutional rules that deliberately disable them from seeking out information relevant to the inquiry at hand. For while a judge, expert in the law, is permitted to scan all forms of legal authority and learning in reaching conclusions of law (and is given the resources to do so in the form of libraries, computer research tools, and trained law clerks), in factual matters he is limited to review of a cold record created by those over whom he has no control and who may have strong biases.

An appellate judge cannot ask an expert to answer his technical questions or go outside the record to determine the present state of scientific or technical knowledge. But the record itself tells only part of the story—the part that the advocates have chosen to let the court see. And even if fairly complete, a cold record does not allow the judge to prove the case in great depth. A judge can spend three days reading a record of 4,000 pages and still feel somewhat unfamiliar with the facts. Docket pressures make it unusual for an appellate judge to have even three days available for record reading in an individual case. The First Circuit Court of Appeals, for example, has well over 1,000 cases per year, and each judge on the court writes fifty to sixty full published opinions each year. Even if one assumes that judges of courts that review more administrative agency cases need write only three or four, instead of five to seven, opinions per month, the judges will not have time to familiarize themselves with the enormously lengthy records. How can they analyze fully a record, for example, reflecting 10,000 comments made in response to a notice of proposed rule making?[74] Can judges, when faced with such complexity and detail, do more than ask, somewhat superficially, whether the agency's result is reasonable? Can they do more than catch the grosser errors? Can they conduct the "thorough, probing, in-depth review"[75] that they promise? These realities about court review provide little basis for any hope that such review will lead to significantly better policy.

Perhaps these arguments simply restate the traditional view that agencies are more "expert" on policy matters than courts, and courts should defer to their policy expertise. In recent years it has become fashionable to doubt agency expertise, but these considerations should lead us to ask whether these doubts offer reasons for greater reliance on judicial review or whether the substantive results of such review will properly deal with the substantive problem. In short, can we be confident, given the comparative institutional settings, that strong judicial review will lead to better administrative policy?

Those skeptical of the real-world effectiveness of judicial review of agency policy decisions can find support in the long battle waged between the Court of Appeals for the District of Columbia Circuit and the Federal Communications Commission. That court, in trying to improve the quality of network broadcasting, tried to force the Commission to use intelligible station-selection standards. When the court would reverse an FCC decision, however, the FCC would typically reach the same conclusion on remand, but simply support it with a better reasoned opinion.[76]

Similarly, a recent Brookings study argues that the effect of court review on environmental regulation—an area where case law directs strict review of policy decisions—has been random. In some instances, court-imposed requirements aimed at protecting the environment have helped, but in other instances, by distorting agency enforcement priorities, they have hurt.[77] Further there is reasonably strong evidence that court review of the Federal Power Commission's regulation of natural gas caused substantial economic harm.[78]

In the airbags case the Supreme Court wrote:

We think that it would have been permissible for the agency to temporarily suspend the passive restraint requirement or to delay its implementation date while an airbags mandate was studied.[79]

If the issue in the case was really only whether Standard 208 should have been suspended for further study rather than rescinded, one might ask whether the Court's decision was likely to achieve any different substantive outcome. In fact the agency responded to the decision with a rule that will require airbags unless states with two-thirds of the nation's population enact mandatory buckle-up laws. Whether this rule takes effect or, like NHTSA's previous proposals, is eventually set aside (given the costs of airbags) remains to be seen.[80]

Moreover strict judicial review creates one incentive that, from a substantive perspective, may be perverse. The stricter the review and the more clearly and convincingly the agency must explain the need for change, the more reluctant the agency will be to change the status quo. Consider, for example, the D.C. Circuit's recent review of the Federal Highway Administration efforts to simplify the thirty-year-old truck driver logging and reporting requirements—requirements designed to help the agency enforce a different rule that limits the number of consecutive hours a truck driver may drive.[81] The major question before the agency was whether to allow the industry to use nonstandardized forms—a change that a consultant estimated would save about $160 million per year. The agency decision came after its notice of the proposed change, its receipt of 1,300 comments, and its modifications of its initial proposal. About two years elapsed from the time of public notice until the conclusion of court review. The court allowed the agency to simplify much of its standardized form, but the court set aside two changes the agency wished to make.

FHA had decided that drivers still had to use a standardized grid showing hours driven and also to include on the form: date, total miles driven today, truck number, carrier name, signature, starting time, office address, remarks. It said, however, that they could omit the name of any codriver, total mileage today, home terminal address, total hours, shipping document number or name of shipper, origin and destination points. The agency believed many of these items were redundant or unnecessary and that deletion would "reduce driver preparations by approximately 50 percent without affecting the enforcement capability." The court held to the contrary, concluding that the added items seemed useful; it would help an enforcement agency, for example, to check with a codriver or shipper to see if a log was accurate. In any event the court said FHA had not adequately explained the omissions.[82]

The agency also had decided to expand the scope of an exemption from its log rules—an exemption that originally applied to pickup and delivery drivers, defined as those who drive within a radius of 50 miles and whose driving takes place within a 15-hour period each day. In 1980, perhaps recognizing that pickup and delivery now often extends beyond 50 miles, the FHA changed the definition to 100 miles but reduced the hour period to 12. In 1982 it increased the hour period to 15. The court concluded that the agency had not adequately explained why it made these changes; it should have further investigated an alternative, namely having two exemptions, one for 50 miles/15 hours and another for 100 miles/12 hours.

One cannot tell from the opinion whether court or agency is correct about the wisdom of the agency's new policies. Yet it is easy to imagine how the head of an agency might react to the court's strict review of the policy merits of what seem rather trivial changes in reporting and examination rules. The agency head might say, Why bother? Why should I try to simplify paperwork? A decision about what specific items to include on a log, or the exact point to draw an exemption line must, within broad limits, be arbitrary. I suppose I could do cost-benefit analyses, and hire experts to field-test every possible change, but I haven't the money. I can't respond in depth to every argument made in 1,500 comments about every minor point in this record-keeping proposal. And, if I'm not even allowed to wait to see, as to these very minor matters, what a challenger says in a court brief, and then respond in my court brief, let's forget the whole thing. I'll keep whatever rules I've inherited and not try to make any minor improvements.

The reason agencies do not explore all arguments or consider all alternatives is one of practical limits of time and resources. Yet to have to explain and to prove all this to a reviewing court risks imposing much of the very burden that not considering alternatives aims to escape. Of course the reviewing courts may respond that only important alternatives and arguments must be considered. But, what counts as important? District courts often find that parties, having barely mentioned a legal point at the trial level, suddenly make it the heart of their case on appeal, emphasizing its (sudden but) supreme importance. Appellate courts typically consider such arguments as long as they have been at least mentioned in the district court. But district courts, unlike agencies dealing with policy change, do not face, say 10,000 comments challenging different aspects of complex policies.[83] And when appellate courts "answer" an argument, they write a few words or paragraphs, perhaps citing a case or two. A satisfactory answer in the agency context may mean fact-finding, empirical research, detailed investigation. Accordingly, one result of strict judicial review of agency policy decisions is a strong conservative[84] pressure in favor of the status quo.[85]

These arguments and instances are essentially anecdotal; they do not prove that strict judicial review of policy is, from a policy perspective, unhelpful or counterproductive. But they do seem strong enough to impose a burden on those advocating such review as a means toward better or wiser substantive policy to identify, to investigate, and to catalogue its successes.

Toward Appropriate Policy Review Reconciliation
Unfortunately, unlike the review of law discussed earlier in this chapter, no ready resolution of the problem of judicial review of policy is apparent, at least within the existing institutional constraints. The social imperative for control of agency power is entirely consistent with existing institutional arrangements in the context of review of law. If one believes that the more important the legal decision, the greater the need for a check outside the agency, increased judicial scrutiny automatically seems appropriate. Courts are fully capable of rigorous review of agency determinations of law, for it is the law that they are expert in and it is in interpreting law that their legitimacy is greatest.

In the review of policy area, however, these pressures for, on the one hand, control of agency power and, on the other, proper use of existing institutions are dramatically opposed. One may believe that the more important the policy decision, the greater the need for a check outside the agency. But for reasons of comparative expertise, increased judicial scrutiny seems less appropriate. It is this dilemma that makes a stable, appropriate regime for court review of policy a near-intractable problem.

One might conclude that when reviewing the reasonableness of agency policy, courts should apply the traditional law (the "arbitrary, capricious" standard of section 706(2)(A) of the Administrative Procedure Act) with the traditional attitude of deference to agency expertise. Courts would hesitate to reverse the results of a major rule-making proceeding or to remand for what is likely to amount to several years of new proceedings. They would do so only after finding major procedural violations or very unreasonable substantive results. Judges would approach cases like *State Farm* rather like they approach jury findings in a negligence action, asking whether reasonable regulators could reasonably have come to this conclusion, given not only the evidence before them but also the constraints of time and of the administrative environment in which the agency must work.

This type of standard, however, though coherent from a jurisprudential perspective, is not totally satisfactory, for it does not respond to the regulatory needs outlined at the very beginning of this article. For one thing, in applying it, the courts effectively abdicate their role in controlling agency policymaking. Yet the fact remains that Congress has delegated to administrators in the past fifteen years vast additional regulatory powers, often under vaguely worded, open-ended statutes. Simple retreat takes little account of the growth of agency power that gave rise to the demand for control. The substantive regulatory concerns that have created pressure for outside checks on the exercise of agency power continue to exist.[86] One can still argue in favor of the courts by claiming that the president's efforts will be too much affected by the politics of the day[87] and that congressional efforts may be incoherent. Judges tend to be somewhat more neutral politically; they will try to exert the force of reason on what are basically technical rules aimed at technocratic ends, and their prestige will lead the agencies to follow their guidance.

Moreover can one be certain about the overall impact of judicial scrutiny of agency policy? Does its presence act as an incentive within the agency toward more reasonable decision making, arming those who would fight an overly politicized decision-making process with a weapon—the specter of later court reversal? Would a relaxed judicial supervisory attitude be strong enough to catch the occasional agency policy decision that is in fact highly irrational?[88]

These nagging doubts are sufficiently serious to point, vaguely and suggestively, without endorsement, to an alternative approach that may warrant more serious study than it has had to date. One might examine the practicality of removing some of the institutional constraints that now prevent a court from conducting effective policy review. Could reviewing courts be given the tools to produce coherent, better, substantive agency policy? Suggestions have been made to create a specialized administrative court. But, to make the District of Columbia Court of Appeals a genuine administrative court, capable of reviewing the wisdom of substantive policy, it would need an investigative staff. It would need the power to compel the agency to produce facts not in the record. It would have to be able to question an agency about its entire enforcement program. And it would need some understanding of how that program fits in with the work of other agencies. It would need access to appropriate substantive experts. In sum, it would need many of the powers currently given to the Office of Management and Budget, insofar as it investigates and coordinates regulatory programs.

Other nations have followed this approach. Under the French system of administrative law, for example, the power to review administrative action resides in an institutional descendant of the King's Council, now an independent nonpolitical administrative court, called the Conseil d'État.[89] Membership in the Conseil is supposed to reflect relevant expertise. Some become members after a distinguished career in the French civil service; others are recent top graduates of the highly prestigious École Nationale d'Administration (ENA), where they have studied public policy and public administration. Upon entrance into the Conseil the ENA graduate is assigned the investigation of less important cases and is privy to its deliberations; he is then rotated through various operating departments of the government on special assignments and eventually returned to the Conseil. The result is a collegial body, familiar with the practical problems of creating and maintaining public policy through administration.[90]

Moreover the Conseil is not bound by the strictures of the adversary system. It has access to information throughout the administration. Its members conduct an independent investigation of each case and present the results without being confined to a formal record. The member charged with the investigation makes full use of the Conseil's internal expertise and also is expected to consult outside agencies and experts.[91] In short, the Conseil is given a wide variety of tools that enables it to discern not only whether a given policy conforms to law (as in American courts) but also whether it is wise public policy, something that our discussion suggests may be beyond the reach of our judicial system as currently organized.

Whether one could transform an existing court of appeals into an institution more closely resembling the Conseil d'Etat is debatable. Much of the Conseil's effectiveness stems from its ability to obtain information *ex parte* from within the administration and to conduct its deliberations among investigators and judges in private, without counsel present. Yet American judicial rules against *ex parte* communications are not all constitutional in nature; the use of amici curiae, special masters, and law clerks suggests that investigatory powers are not inherently beyond the judiciary's reach. And there are certain advantages to looking at the judiciary rather than, say, OMB, as the nucleus for such an institution, namely greater political independence, prestige that may mean public acceptability and the ability to process individual complaints against agency behavior, and more widespread review of agency policy within the same institution.

Analysis of such a radical transformation of existing methods of policy review is well beyond the scope of this article. This article, moreover, does not endorse the transformation. It only points to its possibility, and it suggests that more detailed analysis of its wisdom be undertaken. Given the present institutional dilemma, it may be necessary to explore quite different approaches toward making judicial review an effective check on the wisdom of substantive policymaking by agencies.

Conclusion

The present law of judicial review of administrative decision making—the heart of administrative law—contains an important anomaly. The law requires courts to defer often and strongly to agency judgments about matters of law, but it also sometimes suggests that courts conduct independent in-depth reviews of agency judgments about matters of policy. Is this not the exact opposite of a rational system? Would one not expect courts to conduct stricter review of matters of law—where courts are more expert—but more lenient review of matters of policy—where agencies are more expert?

In light of the anomaly, existing law is unstable. Change of some sort seems likely. The direction that the law might take as to review of matters of law can be spelled out with clarity. But no such clarity of direction is possible for review of policy. On the one hand, a change might amount to a retreat, with the courts leaving it up to the other branches of government to control agency excesses. On the other hand, a change might seek to make policy review more effective. But, that change implies the need for an examination of radical transformation of existing institutions of review. An examination seems warranted to determine whether such efforts should be made.

Notes

A version of this chapter will also appear in the *Administrative Law Review* for November 1987. Several of the ideas it contains originated in a paper the author prepared for a conference on Comparative Administrative Law, held in England in 1985.

1. For example, 42 U.S.C. §4321 et seq. (National Environmental Policy Act of 1969); 29 U.S.C. §651 et seq. (Occupational Safety and Health Act of 1970).

2. Pub. L. No. 95-504 (Airline Deregulation Act of 1978) (codified at scattered sections of 18, 26 and 49 U.S.C.).

3. Pub. L. No. 96-296 (Motor Carrier Act of 1980) (codified at scattered sections of 49 U.S.C.).

4. Pub. L. No. 96-221 (Depository Institutions Deregulation Act of 1980) (codified at 12 U.S.C. §3501 et seq.)

5. 42 U.S.C. §7420 (Clean Air Act Amendments of 1977).

6. The legislative veto was one notable attempt to increase Congress' supervisory control over administrative action. It gained in popularity until it was declared unconstitutional in *INS* v. *Chadha*, 462 U.S. 919 (1983).

7. For example, Exec. Order 12,291, 46 Fed. Reg. 13,193 (1981); reprinted in 5 U.S.C. §601 app. at 301-305 greatly expanded the supervisory role of the Office of Management and Budget over the federal bureaucracy.

8. For example, S.1080, 98th Cong., 1st Sess. (1983) (the Bumpers Amendment) which proposed adding the word "independently" to the judicial review section of the Administrative Procedure Act, 5 U.S.C. §706, so that it would read: "[T]he reviewing court shall *independently* decide all relevant questions of law...." See also *Motor Vehicle Manufacturers Ass'n of the United States* v. *State Farm Mutual Automobile Insurance Co.*, 463 U.S. 29 (1983) (discussed the second section of this chapter).

9. See Breyer (1984a).

10. For examination of another portion that discusses prospects for increased congressional supervision of agency, see Breyer (1984b).

11. *Pittston Stevedoring Corp.* v. *Dellaventura*, 544 F.2d 35, 49 (2d Cir. 1976), *aff'd sub nom. Northeast Marine Terminal Co.* v. *Caputo*, 432 U.S. 249 (1977); see also 5 Davis (1984) § 29.16. Similarly Judge Edwards (1984) has declared that "the results at times seemed to be jabberwok."

12. *O'Keeffe* v. *Smith, Hinchman and Grylls Associates*, 380 U.S. 359 (1965) (per curiam).

13. *FCC* v. *Midwest Video Corp.*, 440 U.S. 689 (1979) ("*Midwest II*").

14. 322 U.S. 111 (1944).

15. *Id.* at 130 (citing *Gray* v. *Powell*, 314 U.S. 402, 411 (1941)).

16. *Id.* at 131.

17. 330 U.S. 485 (1947).

18. For example, *Gray* v. *Powell*, 314 U.S. 402 (1941).

19. *Ford Motor Co.* v. *NLRB*, 441 U.S. 488, 497 (1979).

20. *Ford Motor Credit Co.* v. *Milhollin*, 444 U.S. 555, 565 (1980).

21. *FEC* v. *Democratic Senatorial Campaign Comm.*, 454 U.S. 27, 39 (1981).

22. *Bureau of Alcohol, Tobacco & Firearms* v. *FLRA*, 464 U.S. 89, 97 (1983) (quoting *American Ship Bldg. Co.* v. *NLRB*, 380 U.S. 300, 318 (1965) and *NLRB* v. *Brown*, 380 U.S. 278, 291–92 (1965)).

23. *FTC* v. *Colgate-Palmolive Co.*, 380 U.S. 374, 385 (1965) ("while informed judicial determination is dependent upon enlightenment gained from administrative experience," words setting forth "a legal standard ... must get their final meaning from judicial construction").

24. *Northeast Marine Terminal Co.* v. *Caputo*, 432 U.S. 249 (1977); *American Ship Bldg. Co.* v. *NLRB*, 380 U.S. 300, 318 (1965); *NLRB* v. *Brown*, 380 U.S. 278, 291–92 (1965); *NLRB* v. *Insurance Agents' Int'l Union*, 361 U.S. 477, 499–500 (1960); *NLRB* v. *Highland Park Mfg. Co.*, 341 U.S. 322 (1951); *Davies Warehouse Co.* v. *Bowles*, 321 U.S. 144 (1944); see 5 K. Davis, *supra* note 11, § 29.16.

25. *Middle South Energy, Inc.* v. *FERC*, 747 F.2d 763, 769 (D.C. Cir. 1984) (citing cases); see also *Norwegian Nitrogen Prods. Co.* v. *United States*, 288 U.S. 294, 315 (1933).

26. See, for example, *Massachusetts Trustees* v. *United States*, 377 U.S. 235, 241 (1964).

27. *NLRB* v. *Bell Aerospace Co.*, 416 U.S. 267, 275 (1974).

28. See *American Methyl Corp.* v. *EPA*, 749 F.2d 826, 839 n.85 (D.C. Cir. 1984); see Sunstein (1983) which discusses expectations and reliance interests that build up around regulatory scheme.

29. *Id.*

30. 5 K. Davis, *supra* note 11, § 28.6, at 279; *Schweiker* v. *Grey Panthers*, 453 U.S. 34, 43–44 (1981).

31. 327 U.S. 358 (1946).

32. *Id.* at 369 (emphasis added).

33. See *Trailways, Inc.* v. *ICC*, 727 F.2d 1284, 1288–89 (D.C. Cir. 1984).

34. See *id.* at 1289–91.

35. *Montana* v. *Clark*, 749 F.2d 740, 746 (D.C. Cir. 1985); *Mayburg* v. *Secretary of Health & Human Servs.*, 740 F.2d 100, 105–06 (1st Cir. 1984); *Constance* v. *Secretary of Health & Human Servs.*, 672 F.2d 990, 995–96 (1st Cir. 1982).

36. *Hi-Craft Clothing Co.* v. *NLRB*, 660 F.2d 910, 914–15 (3rd Cir. 1981); *Montana*, 749 F.2d at 744–45.

37. *Montana*, 749 F.2d at 746; *Mayburg*, 740 F.2d at 106; *Constance*, 672 F.2d at 995–96; *International Bhd. of Teamsters* v. *Daniel*, 439 U.S. 551, 566, n.20 (1979).

38. *Montana*, 749 F.2d at 746.

39. *Mayburg*, 740 F.2d at 106.

40. *Hi-Craft*, 660 F.2d at 916 ("government agencies have a tendency to swell, not shrink, and are likely to have an expansive view of their mission" and "therefore, an agency ruling that broadens its own jurisdiction is examined carefully").

41. *Montana*, 749 F.2d at 746.

42. See Breyer and Stewart (1985), and Edwards, *supra* note 11, at 257–58.

43. 104 S.Ct. 2778 (1984).

44. EPA possessed legislative rulemaking power delegated to it in a different part of the statute, 42 U.S.C. § 7601(a)(1) (1982).

45. 104 S.Ct. at 2781–82.

46. *Id.* at 2782.

47. *Rettig* v. *Pension Benefit Guar. Corp.*, 744 F.2d 133, 141 (D.C. Cir. 1984); *Railway Labor Executives' Ass'n* v. *United States R.R. Retirement Bd.*, 749 F.2d 856, 860 (D.C. Cir. 1984).

48. 762 F.2d 158 (1st Cir. 1985).

49. *Id.*

50. 749 F.2d 856 (D.C. Cir. 1984).

51. *Skidmore* v. *Swift & Co.*, 323 U.S. 134, 140 (1944).

52. See *Pattern Makers' League* v. *NLRB*, 53 U.S.L.W. 4928, 4934 (White, J. concurring) (U.S. June 27, 1985).

53. *See, e.g., Atlanta Gas Light Co.* v. *FERC*, 756 F.2d 191, 196–97 (D.C. Cir. 1985); *Defense Logistics Agency* v. *FLRA*, 754 F.2d 1003, 1013–14 (D.C. Cir. 1985); *South Dakota* v. *CAB*, 740 F.2d 619, 621 (8th Cir. 1984).

54. See, for example, *Bureau of Alcohol, Tobacco & Firearms* v. *FLRA*, 464 U.S. 89, 97–98 (1983).

55. Of course sometimes the wisdom of agency policy becomes relevant to the interpretation of the agency's authorizing statute. If so, review ought to be governed by the principles discussed earlier in this chapter.

56. See *NLRB* v. *Labor Services, Inc.*, 721 F.2d 13 (1st Cir. 1983).

57. Compare Breyer and Stewart (1985), *supra* note 42, at 336 n.107 (citing cases), with Breyer and Stewart (1979), at 289, n.86 (citing cases).

58. *Scenic Hudson Preservation Conf.* v. *FPC*, (*Scenic Hudson* I), 354 F.2d 608 (2d Cir. 1965).

59. See Sunstein, 1983, at 181.

60. *Id.* at 182.

61. *Id.*

62. One notable example is that of Consolidated Edison's Storm King Project, the subject of the *Scenic Hudson* litigation. "Hard look" review resulted in the demise of the project despite the Second Circuit's ultimate go ahead. See *Scenic Hudson Preservation Conf.* v. *FPC*, (*Scenic Hudson* II), 453 F.2d 463 (2d Cir. 1971), *cert. denied*, 407 U.S. 926 (1972) and Breyer and Stewart (1985), *supra* note 42, at 349–50.

63. *Pacific Legal Found.* v. *DOT*, 593 F.2d 1338, 1343 (D.C. Cir.), *cert. denied*, 444 U.S. 830 (1979).

64. *Specialty Equip. Mktg. Ass'n* v. *Ruckelshaus*, 720 F.2d 124, 132 (D.C. Cir. 1983).

65. *Citizens to Preserve Overton Park* v. *Volpe*, 401 U.S. 402, 415 (1971).

66. *Baltimore Gas & Electric Co.* v. *NRDC*, 462 U.S. 87, 103 (1983).

67. 463 U.S. 29 (1983).

68. The Court's first two decisions were by a vote of 5 to 4.

69. 35 Fed. Reg. 16,927 (1970).

70. *Id.*

71. The Court refused to accept the agency's airbags arguments in part because they were contained in the agency's brief: the agency itself had not considered them. Cf. *Burlington Truck Lines, Inc.* v. *United States*, 371 U.S. 156, 168 (1962); *SEC* v. *Chenery Corp.*, 332 U.S. 194, 196 (1947). But why is a court brief not an appropriate place for the agency to explain why it didn't consider something? Otherwise, one forces the agency explicitly to consider whether or not to consider the thing in question—thus in effect compelling the agency to consider it—which the agency shouldn't have to do if it is reasonable not to consider it.

72. *International Ladies' Garment Workers' Union* v. *Donovan*, 722 F.2d 795, 804 (D.C. Cir. 1983), *cert. denied*, 105 S. Ct. 93 (1984); *Public Citizen* v. *Steed*, 733 F.2d 93 (D.C. Cir. 1984).

73. For example, *South Terminal Corp.* v. *EPA,* 504 F.2d 646 (1st Cir. 1974); *Palisades Citizens Ass'n* v. *CAB*, 420 F.2d 188 (D.C. Cir. 1969); *Texas* v. *EPA*, 499 F.2d 289 (5th Cir. 1974); *Environmental Defense Fund* v. *Ruckelshaus*, 439 F.2d 584 (D.C. Cir. 1971).

74. *International Ladies' Garment Workers' Union* v. *Donovan*, 722 F.2d 795, 804 (D.C. Cir. 1983), *cert. denied*, 105 S. Ct. 93 (1984).

75. *See*, for example, *Ethyl Corp.* v. *EPA*, 541 F.2d 1, 35 (D.C. Cir. 1976).

76. See *Central Fla. Enters.* v. *FCC*, 683 F.2d 503 (D.C. Cir. 1982) (*Cowles II*). *See generally* Breyer and Stewart (1985), *supra* note 42, at 426–66.

77. See Melnick (1983).

78. See Breyer and MacAvoy (1973).

79. 463 U.S. at 50 n.15.

80. Some states have deliberately passed buckle-up laws that don't qualify as such under NHTSA's regulation, leaving open the possibility that drivers will face mandatory buckle-up laws and also will have to pay for airbags.

81. *International Bhd. of Teamsters* v. *United States*, 735 F.2d 1525 (D.C. Cir 1984).

82. FHA had explained its reasoning in its brief, but the court said that the brief was not a proper place for such explanation to appear for the first time. See *supra* note 71.

83. See *supra* note 74 and accompanying text.

84. Of course, the extraordinary conservative pressure exerted by strict judicial review can have worse effects. NHTSA, for example, introduced a head restraint standard in 1971. It aimed to prevent whiplash injuries by stopping the head from jerking backward when the car was hit from behind. A series of studies, however, later indicated that the standard had little safety value. NHTSA responded several times by proposing new standards, but because it could not obtain agreement from the interested parties and feared court review, it left the ineffective standard in place. There is no reason to think this kind of agency behavior is desirable.

85. Would a court have set aside airline deregulation under the former statute as unwise? Months of congressional hearings, detailed examination of the arguments, a lengthy report, and considerable study of the subject by experts and nonexperts alike, had created a broad policy consensus in favor of reform, amply supported by economic logic and empirical data. The challengers would have asked whether the agency had considered adequately, for example, the effects on fuel supply, the environment, or airport congestion; the possibility that local regulators will create local monopolies by tying up airport slots; the risk that two large airlines will control reservation systems by writing a special computer program; and other features of the case that had not been examined in depth. Opponents could have multiplied plausible-sounding alternative courses of action for the agency to investigate or explain away.

86. See *supra* text at notes 1–10.

87. This is a special concern of Judge Edwards. See Edwards, *supra* note 11, at 229–31; see also Breyer (1984a), *supra* note 9.

88. *Aqua Slide 'n' Dive Corp.* v. *Consumer Product Safety Comm'n*, 569 F.2d 831 (5th Cir. 1978) (invalidating CPSC safety regulations for pool slides).

89. See generally Brown and Garner (1983).

90. *Id.* at 30–40.

91. *Id.* at 41–57

References

Breyer, S. G. 1984a. "Reforming Regulation." *Tulane Law Review* 59:4.

Breyer, S. G. 1984b. "The Legislative Veto after Chadha." *Georgetown Law Journal* 72:785.

Breyer, S. G., and MacAvoy, P. W. 1973. "The Natural Gas Shortage and the Regulation of Natural Gas Producers." *Harvard Law Review* 86:941.

Breyer, S. G., and Stewart, R. 1985. *Administrative Law and Regulatory Policy*. 2d. ed. Boston: Little Brown.

Davis, K. 1984. *Administrative Law Treatise*. 2d. ed. K. C. Davis Publishing Co.

Brown, L. N., and Garner, J. F. 1983 *French Administrative Law*. 3d ed. Butterworths. London.

Edwards, H. 1984. "Judicial Review of Deregulation." *Kentucky Law Review* 11:229–240.

Melnick, S. 1983. *Regulation and the Courts: The Case of the Clean Air Act*. Washington, D.C.: Brookings Institution.

Sunstein, C. 1983. "Deregulation and the Hard-Look Doctrine." *1983 Supreme Court Review* 177, 204.

3

Modern Political Economy and the Study of Regulation

Thomas Romer and Howard Rosenthal

Understanding how political processes and resource allocation interact is at the core of the study of the political economy of regulation. Prior to 1970 virtually all research in the area could be neatly partitioned into two camps. Economists studied, often with substantial theoretical and econometric sophistication, the allocative effects of regulations. Political scientists engaged in largely informal and descriptive analysis of how the regulations came to be.[1]

George Stigler's "The Economic Theory of Regulation" (1971) sounded a call for an integrated, analytical attack that would view both political and economic outcomes as endogenously determined, given technology, information, and preferences. In the years preceding Stigler's seminal article, progress had been made in positive, analytical models of political processes. (This research is summarized in Riker and Ordeshook 1971.) Stigler's article does not itself make any connections to such developments. Indication that these models could be embedded in a microeconomic framework that focused on regulatory processes was provided by Klevorick and Kramer's (1973) clever study of the *Genossenschaften*, West German institutions that set Pigovian effluent taxes by majority rule. They investigated the conditions under which production decisions, water cleanup levels achieved by a *Genossenschaft*'s purification technology, voting decisions, and political power (in the form of votes that were proportional to taxes paid) could all be part of a stable equilibrium.

Unfortunately, as we argue in this essay, relatively little has been achieved on the theory side beyond the analysis of fairly simple, unidimensional majority rule situations as in the *Genossenschaften* study. Consequently there has been little progress in the development of a formal political economy that would penetrate the complex institutional structure of the central concern of participants in this conference, the regulatory structure of American federalism. Moreover what insights have been learned from formal political theory, such as the fundamentally nonmarginal nature of collective decisions, have rarely been applied in empirical work.[2]

Our review of the recent literature is carried out in two main sections. First, we review theory that has either attempted the type of integration Stigler called for or attempted an application of analytical political theory to those institutional structures, Congress in particular, that are highly relevant for regulatory policy in the United States.

Second, we survey recent empirical work dealing with the politics of regulation. Our major focus is on the U.S. federal system, with a particular emphasis on the role of Congress in setting regulatory policy, although there are passing references to state and local regulation. As in the theoretical section, our attention here is highly selective.

We stress that this essay is by no means an attempt at a broad survey of regulation, or even of the politics of regulation.[3] The emphasis throughout is on work primarily concerned with political processes in economic policy formation. So, for example, our discussion of the "economic theory" focuses primarily on what it (implicitly or explicitly) assumes about politics. Nearly all the work we discuss stresses legislative processes (where it does not ignore the details of politics altogether), with rather short shrift given to consideration of regulatory agencies or of the executive branch. To some observers of regulation, this may seem like a production of *Hamlet* without the prince. To a large extent, this apparently peculiar emphasis reflects the attention of analytical work in recent years. This in turn is due partly to the field's relatively early stage of development and the difficulties of providing tractable models that involve more than one branch of government, partly to the fact that the legislative arena is the most readily observable component of the political system, and partly to the belief of some who work in the field that the legislative branch is the dominant player in the federal regulatory game.

Theoretical Work in the Political Economy of Regulation

The work we discuss in this essay involves both economists and political scientists. Not surprisingly, in many instances, those writing from the perspective of economics tend to treat the workings of the political process as a black box, whose mechanisms conveniently—if mysteriously—adapt to economic forces to yield the outcomes predicted by whatever model is being proposed. Similarly those who model political processes often take as given the configuration of economic forces, and focus on the machinery inside the black box. What both branches of the recent work have in common, however, is the recognition that the study of regulation involves both political and economic forces, though the study of these forces may be subject to division of labor. Because it is a forceful and influential statement of some of the main themes in this line of research, we begin the survey with Stigler's 1971 paper. Together with Peltzman (1976) and Becker (1983), it has come to embody the "economic theory." We then go on to discuss recent work on formal models of politics, in which the incentives of politicians and the environment in which political decisions are made are the key features.

Figure 3.1 provides an overview of work discussed in this section. The economic models emphasize that the regulatory process is one particular channel for the economic demands for higher profits or incomes. Using this channel involves the political process, with its peculiar structure of constraints and opportunities (especially elections and majority-rule provisions), but by and large the process itself is left unmodeled. The concerns outlined in the "political process" area of figure 3.1 are a black box—the presumption being that its detailed structure is not likely to influence the broad patterns of policy.

The "political" models, by contrast, stress the importance of the structure of political decisionmaking. They are less global than the "economic" models (though they do share those models' analytical premise of constrained optimization). They look in some detail at the influence of institutional features, such as the committee system in Congress, and the procedural rules whereby legislation is made or thwarted. They emphasize the incentives and opportunities of political entrepreneurs and call attention to the way these factors influence such decisions as the creation of regulatory agencies. Perhaps most important, they point to the fundamental role of constituencies and the need to assemble critical majorities, and to the often discontinuous response of policy to economic change.

Economic Models
Stigler (1971) sought to develop a theory of the regulation of economic activity that would go beyond the traditional economic approach of looking only at the purely allocative effects of particular regulatory policies. At the same time he called for a more robust and a priori modeling strategy that would have more to say about regulation generally than the traditional public administration approach of looking at the alphabet soup of regulatory agencies noodle by noodle (one by one and period by period) and talking about regulation primarily in terms of the behavior of the agency's internal bureaucracy. The ambitious goal of the venture he proposed was to develop a theory of government intervention in economic affairs that would have approximately the same level of generality as neoclassical microeconomic theory. Since Stigler defined regulation quite broadly, to include virtually all economic acts of government, this goal was nothing less than the construction of a price theory of political economy.[4] In calling

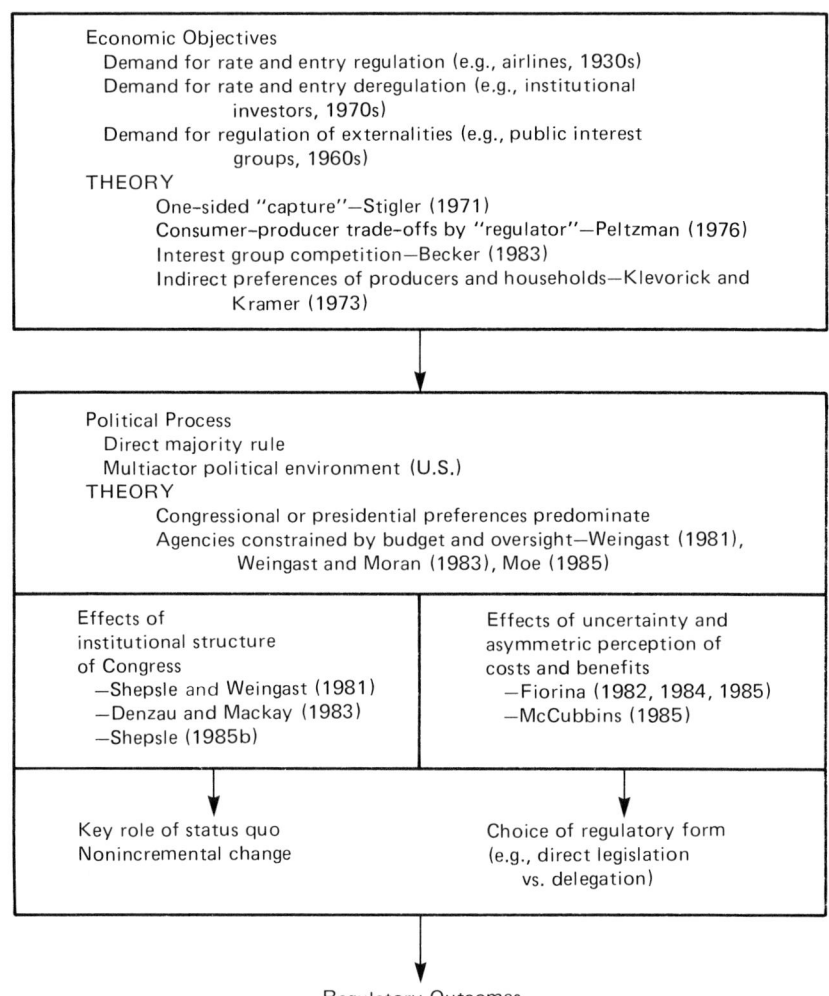

Figure 3.1 Overview of theoretical work on the political economy of regulation

for this type of analysis, Stigler was joining the already developing public choice school's approach to the study of political processes. At the heart of this approach is the assumption that agents in the political, as in the economic, arena are rational individuals, optimizing in the context of institutional environments that define constraints and opportunities. Stigler's paper focused primarily on the more general optimization aspects of the problem, rather than on the institutional elements.

Regulation confers benefits and imposes costs on various groups in the society. It creates and destroys economic opportunity. The goal of the kind of theory Stigler was attempting is to explain the patterns of costs and benefits that arise from regulation. Even more basically, it is to explain the emergence of particular forms of regulation, and the way these forms change and perhaps disappear over time. The very possibility of developing a theory of regulation of the type called for by Stigler is still the subject of debate.[5] The formal analysis required for even a basic understanding of democratic political processes is very much in its early stages. The links between such processes and economic forces are only beginning to be understood.

Though it is typically characterized as being primarily a model of the demand side of regulation, in fact much of Stigler's discussion concerns the political environment in which demand for regulation must operate. He recognizes that economic regulation, since it entails deadweight losses, would not generally pass by a direct majority vote, even if the industry that receives the benefits is in a majority. Indeed, the number of losers from most regulation of the type Stigler deals with (rate and entry regulation, e.g., of transportation, or occupational licensing) significantly exceeds the number of gainers. So even without deadweight losses, we would not expect majority rule to support regulation.

Much of the discussion in Stigler (1971) concerns the role of the political process, and why the process is likely to result in regulations that favor specific parties (especially those who are regulated). He clearly identifies perhaps the key feature of political decisions: their fundamentally non-marginal nature. This is in clear distinction to economic markets, where marginal adjustments are the norm. (Small changes in endowments or tastes induce small changes in market outcomes. More important, perhaps, small demands can generally be accommodated in already existing markets.) Because the cost of making every collective decision collectively is prohibitive, most issues are resolved by representative rather then direct democracy. As a consequence, Stigler says, only those groups that can provide enough political returns to be represented get their agendas enacted.

Political parties act as the entrepreneurs in Stigler's political world. They, in effect, aggregate political producers by forming winning coalitions. Groups that can bring to bear more political power are more likely to have policies enacted that are favorable to them than those that have little power, or are unaware of the costs imposed on them by others' preferred policies. In the context of economic regulation, Stigler argues that the political power of industries seeking to exclude entry or to control prices (i.e., maintain cartels) greatly exceeds that of individual citizens. Basically this is a concentrated-benefits–diffuse-costs story (Bernstein 1955), particularly since individual citizens are likely to be rationally ignorant of the costs of regulation: less likely to be well informed in political contexts than in issues they confront directly in markets.

Limits to the power of industries to get their way in the political arena depend on the feasibility of building viable opposing coalitions and also on the rate at which increasing group size gets traded off against returns to individual firms in the cartel. Stigler (1971, p. 11) wrote:

This does not mean that every large industry can get what it wants or all it wants: it does mean that the representative and his party must find a coalition of voter interests more durable than the anti-industry side of every industry policy proposal. A representative cannot win or keep office with the support of the sum of those who are opposed to: oil quotas, farm subsidies, airport subsidies, hospital subsidies, unnecessary navy shipyards, an inequitable housing program, and rural electrification subsidies.

An interesting aspect of Stigler's work is that there is no distinction between the political arena (legislature) and the administrative arena (regulatory agency). In this view regulatory agencies are merely neutral reflections of the political process. To the extent they have any leeway in regulating, it is due to the leeway inherent in the slack in the political arena, not due to administrative behavior. This conflation of the regulatory agency and the political entrepreneur into essentially one agent is repeated in Peltzman (1976) and Becker (1983).

Stigler has been criticized for characterizing the regulatory process as one that inevitably pays attention only to industry interests. Posner (1974) and Peltzman (1976) have argued that it is quite unlikely that political influence would be distributed in such a skewed fashion. Moreover empirical evidence suggests that even in old-line economic regulation, regulatory policy does not unambiguously follow cartel interests. In Peltzman (1976), there is again no distinction between the regulator and the political agent—his regulator looks very much like a representative in a legislature, though without any of the trappings of a political arena. In his analysis political support can be obtained from both producer and consumer groups. For a wide range of assumptions, a given politician's support is maximized when positive weight is given to both groups. Only rarely would we expect corner solutions in convex problems, so this is not really a surprising result. For Peltzman, politics is buried in a political power function. This function embodies the response of various interest groups (consumers, producers) to changes in the variables under the politician/regulator's control (output prices, industry profits). As Peltzman recognizes, to make his analysis meaningful, one ought to do one or both of the following:

• Derive the shape and properties of the appropriate political power function.
• Treat the political power function as given, and focus on how the regulatory equilibrium changes as a results of changes in the economic relationships (demand and supply shifts due to exogenous shocks).

Peltzman chooses to do the latter. From the point of view of his analysis, the relationships embedded in the political power function play the role of tastes in the neoclassical economics of consumer theory. They are unobserved (unobservable?) but can be posited to have nice properties. Having specified these properties, the analysis proceeds by looking at shifts in the economic constraints. Just as the more detailed study of tastes is outside the scope of economic analysis, so too for Peltzman is the study of the determinants of political power.

On one level this dichotomy, and Peltzman's approach to it, is a reasonable modeling strategy. But there is a pitfall in adopting this approach. The function that Peltzman takes as exogenously representing the regulator's tastes should properly be viewed as a reduced form, derived from the way the political sector aggregates preferences of, say, producer and consumer groups. All of politics is summed up in this function, and at the analytical level all would be fine if it were reasonable to suppose that the function remained fixed relative to the exogenous shifts Peltzman does analyze. The discussion of models of political processes that follows suggests, however, that it is not unreasonable to suppose that Peltzman's political power function would be susceptible to being shifted by precisely the same events that affect the economic constraints—for example, an increase in cost may well make producers more politically active, resulting in a shift in the function.

The active agent in Peltzman (1976) is the regulator. In Becker (1983) the active agents are the interest groups. In Becker's world, interest groups compete for favors from the political system. They recognize, however, that obtaining a benefit almost always imposes a cost on some other group(s), both in direct transfers and in deadweight losses. The central point of Becker's argument is that competition for political influence will lead to a policy bundle that accomplishes a given level of redistribution in such a way that deadweight losses are minimized. Politically active groups are assumed to be fully informed about the true costs and benefits of all policies. Since deadweight losses increase opposition to any particular group's subsidy, without increasing that group's gains, it is in the interest of interest groups to lobby for subsidies that have, *ceteris paribus*, low deadweight losses. (This is not to say that deadweight losses are eliminated in equilibrium, only that political competition eliminates the most wasteful policies.)

Another important facet of Becker's analysis is the emphasis on the connections among interest groups. Gains by one group at the expense of others tend to set off a chain of pressure activities as adversely affected groups respond to the change. In the new equilibrium, policy readjustments may involve many groups. Because of the need to compensate competing groups for losses due to policy changes, there may well be an inherent bias in favor of the status quo in the system. This bias may tend toward policies that protect the status quo against shocks in the private sector (Becker 1983, p. 383). This can persist only as long as the accumulated deadweight losses of policies are not too great. Over time, as these costs accumulate, those wishing policy change are on the side of reducing deadweight costs. This makes their political activity more effective, *ceteris paribus*, than that of groups attached to the status quo. Becker argues that such an explanation is valid for recent deregulatory developments.[6]

The political sector is essentially unmodeled in Becker (1983). The demands of interest groups are communicated via a pressure function whose shape is presumably determined by the responsiveness of the political process to resources devoted to political pressure. The mass electorate is seen as malleable by interest group claims, and so resources spent on swaying votes will typically have some positive effect. In turn "politicians and bureaucrats are assumed to carry out the political allocations resulting from competition among pressure groups" (p. 398). In other words, he assumes that there is nothing about the nature of political institutions or the behavior of politicians or administrators that would deflect the pressure-group equilibrium allocation from the properties that Becker claims for it.

Political Models

Recent work by political scientists has attempted to uncover and describe the black box in these models. The work we will focus on adopts, for the most part, the neoclassical view of self-interested behavior and maximization subject to constraints. In these papers the economic markets are left to operate as a black box. Emphasis is, instead, on the functioning of legislative processes and their connections to administrative (regulatory) agencies.

In a sense, the fundamental distinction between the economic and the political models of regulation is the different emphasis they place on the role of institutional structure. At one extreme, the economic model, especially that of Becker, treats institutional concerns as purely epiphenomenal. They do not serve to alter the allocations that result from the push and tug of the competition of economic interests. In some of the political models, as we shall see, institutions are of paramount importance. They define the feasible set of alternatives within which interests joust for representation. Consequently attention in these models is on the motivation and actions of a quite different set of agents than in the economic models. Here the political agents are of key importance. Although they may be representing economic interests as well as other types of constituencies, their actions are conditioned by the nature of the political environment and the arena in which this representation takes place (usually, in these models, the Congress).

In many respects formal analysis of regulation is an application of the theory of policy formation in a representative democracy. We will sketch briefly a descriptive model that captures the important elements of work in this area.

We begin with the structure of a unicameral legislature. This is the heart of most analyses of legislative processes. In these models the agent of central concern is the individual representative or member of the legislature. (This focus no doubt reflects the empirical observation that, for the federal government at least, the political entrepreneurs are individual legislators rather than political parties.) Let the legislature consist of N members.

The matters dealt with by the legislature form a policy space, Y, which may be quite broadly defined. For purposes of regulatory concern, subsets of Y may include distinct, but related, types of policy issues (Noll 1983): (1) decisions about whether to intervene in a market (to regulate or not to regulate), (2) decisions about the type of regulatory instruments to use (taxes, subsidies, command and control), and (3) decisions about the degree to which regulatory authority is to be delegated (enact regulation by detailed legislation or carry out regulation via independent agencies). The almost universal assumption is that legislators are motivated primarily by the desire to be reelected. Thus a legislator's preferences over choices in Y are induced through the interaction of (1) the relationship between policy choice and the perceived well-being of the legislator's constituents and (2) the relationship between constituent preferences and the probability of reelection.

The premise that legislators seek reelection is hardly debatable, but describing the strategies that best serve this objective remains an entirely open problem. In particular, each legislator must trade off responding to the interests of some average or median constituent against cuing on those active interests that are more likely to contribute funds, ring doorbells, or vote in primary or general elections. Despite the intuition provided by Downs' (1957) insight that a politician could be successful by forming a coalition through voting for minority (i.e., special) interests on a set of issues, work in this area has begun to develop only recently. The models of Austen-Smith (1984) and Ingberman (1985a) address only how campaign contributions affect equilibrium platforms of candidates. There has, to our knowledge, been no formal development of how the trade-off between general constituency interests and active minority interests affects the legislator's roll call voting strategy. The linkages subsumed in Becker's (1983) influence functions are so far still inside the black box.[7]

Formal models of legislatures generally combine both effects and write a legislator's preferences over policies as some function (usually single peaked) $V_i(y)$, $y \in Y$, $i = 1, \ldots, N$. The study of legislation is further bifurcated into (1) exploring the implications of individual legislators making policy choices that maximize V_i and (2) modeling the legislature's choice of policies.

Legislators' Preferences and Choice of Regulatory Form

Characterizing the properties of V_i is usually done in a highly restricted and specific context (assuming a one-or two-dimensional policy space or focusing on specific policy issues). Even so, these induced preferences will depend on the identity of the constituencies represented by a particular legislator and the particular electoral context the legislator faces (time until next election, strength of challengers, etc.).

In studying a legislator's preferences over regulatory issues, Fiorina (1982, 1985) makes the assumption that constituencies do not necessarily perceive correctly the net benefits flowing from a particular act of legislation.[8] Moreover he assumes that not all constituencies respond symmetrically to the effects of a given policy choice. In particular, there may be systematic biases associated with choices in Y and constituents' perceptions.

Legislators wish to maximize the flow of net benefits for which they are held accountable by their constituents. Regulating through commissions places the costs imposed on and benefits received by constituents at a greater remove from a legislator than does direct legislation. In this sense delegation shifts responsibility away from the legislator. With delegation, constituents will not accord the legislator as much credit for perceived regulatory benefits as they would with direct legislation. On the other hand, neither will they place on him as much of the blame for perceived regulatory costs.

Assume furthermore that the actual flows of costs and benefits are independent of the choice of regulatory form. Then a particular legislator's decision over regulatory form depends on the distribution, among his constituents, of perceived benefits and costs. For policies such that benefits are relatively clearly perceived, while costs are not (the classic concentrated-benefits–diffuse-costs example falls in this category), a legislator would usually have more to gain by claiming credit rather than shifting responsibility. In such cases Fiorina (1985) argues that we should see support for direct rather than delegated regulatory action. If, on the other hand, costs are fairly clearly perceived, while benefits are not (e.g., with diffuse benefits, concentrated costs), the legislator's incentive is to delegate, since credit claiming in this case is not as valuable as blame shifting. As an implication of this approach, we would expect that legislators whose constituencies are most likely to gain from a regulatory policy would be most in favor of direct legislation. Those whose constituencies are likely to be losers or to benefit only slightly are likely to oppose the policy. Fiorina (1985) suggests that in such cases delegation may be a compromise outcome, in which those who expect to gain from regulation give up some of the visibility they would otherwise get in return for the support of other legislators, for whom delegation provides some shield against constituents' wrath.

As an alternate approach to the question of delegation of regulatory authority, Fiorina proposes a second model, in which legislators' preferences over the mode of regulatory structure depend on the nature of the uncertainty posed by delegation as opposed to direct legislation. (This model is outlined in Fiorina 1982 and more fully developed in Fiorina

1984.) There is uncertainty with delegating authority to a regulatory agency, since congressional monitoring of the agency's actions is likely to be at best imperfect. Procedural safeguards may constrain the range of possible outcomes (cf. McCubbins 1985), but there is uncertainty about where within this constrained set agency decisions will fall. There is also uncertainty about direct legislation because legislative acts are subject to subsequent litigation and interpretation by the courts.

But the two regulatory forms differ in the shape of the distribution of future outcomes. Suppose that voting occurs over one policy dimension, y, and with direct legislation, the legislative outcome is y^*. Fiorina argues that the distribution of outcomes that would be implemented through court decisions is symmetric with mean y^*, presumably because judicial review is committed to the principle of following legislative intent. Although courts may depart from interpreting a statute exactly as it was originally intended by the legislature that passed it, the assumption is that there is no *a priori* reason for legislators to believe that such departures are likely to be systematically biased.

In creating a regulatory agency, however, the legislature may have reason to believe that the distribution is unlikely to be symmetric. Once created, an agency is relatively independent. To the extent that it is subject to congressional control, it is more likely to be responsive to the preferences of the congressional committees that are relevant to its budget and oversight. These preferences are not generally going to be a mere mirror of the preferences of the entire chamber. They are, instead, likely to reflect preferences that are away from the overall median in the legislature, as a result of self-selection onto relevant committees of members with particular constituent interests. The distribution of outcomes under delegation is therefore likely to be skewed away from y^* toward one end of the range of feasible outcomes.

The choice between delegation and direct legislation will thus depend on the distribution of legislators' preferences relative to their expectations about the direction of bias of the regulatory agency. Even in Fiorina's highly simplified model there is no unambiguous preference for delegation over direct legislation. Those with ideal points far from y^* will either be strong proponents of delegation (if they are on the same side as the bias in expected agency outcomes) or strong opponents of it (if they are on the opposite side). Those near y^* will have less clear-cut preferences: "relatively more extreme substantive preferences go along with consensus on the preferred enforcement procedure, whereas relatively more moderate substantive preferences go along with mixed feelings about the preferred enforcement procedure." (Fiorina 1984, p. 15)

McCubbins (1985) takes a related approach to studying the structural arrangements whereby regulation occurs. He too focuses on the types of uncertainty legislators face under different types of delegation. He finds that increasing uncertainty over future outcomes creates incentives for legislators to increase the amount of delegation to regulatory agencies, although at the same time there will be a tendency to adopt more stringent procedural requirements for the agency to abide by. Hence we would expect widespread support for vague, general, enabling legislation while there may be considerable division over implementation and many constraints on agency procedures. So, for example, environmental regulation was delegated to the Environmental Protection Agency (EPA) by nearly unanimous votes. Nevertheless, Congress has been quite insistent in making sure that EPA engages in quite elaborate testing procedures before acting against potentially hazardous chemicals.

Policy Choice in a Legislature

The models of Fiorina and McCubbins attempt to derive policy implications by considering primarily the incentives of individual legislators. A related strand of work looks at the behavior of legislatures as a body. Turning to these models, rather than those that discuss the preferences of individual legislators, the question becomes: What are equilibrium outcomes y^*, where by equilibrium, we mean policy choice that commands a legislative majority against any other policy choices. In general, theory tells us that the set of equilibrium outcomes Y^* is empty—there will typically be no majority winner, except under rather unusual configurations of preferences. In other words, starting only with the majority relationship and legislator preference profiles $\{V_1(y), \ldots, V_N(y)\}$ does not yield equilibrium outcomes.

Students of legislatures have long pointed to these chambers' intricate arrangement of institutional rules and internal organization. There has been recent interest in attempting to formalize these legislative institutions, both for their role in making equilibrium of a sort possible and for the way they may shape policy outcomes. Now the primitive elements of the model include not only $\{V_1(y), \ldots, V_N(y)\}$, but also S, the structure whereby the legislature makes decisions. This would include the committee system, amendment rules, and other procedural norms. Then we can ask whether a legislative voting equilibrium exists, relative to the structure S. Call this a structure-induced equilibrium, or S-equilibrium. Shepsle (1986) provides a good summary of progress to date in establishing conditions under which an S-equilibrium exists. Important elements of S-equilibrium are the following:

1. Legislative committees have jurisdiction over particular aspects of policy. This gives them some agenda control over issues falling within particular subsets of Y. Of particular importance are gatekeeping powers (Denzau and Mackay 1983) that may give committees power to forestall action on particular pieces of legislation.

2. Privileged position of the status quo. The status quo is itself some element y° of Y. Under most rules any proposed legislation must beat y° in order to be adopted. This generally means that for some policy y' to beat y°, y' must be preferred to y° by the relevant committee(s)—otherwise, the committee gate stays closed, and the bill does not come to a floor vote.[9] In addition y' must be preferred to y° by a majority of legislators, in order to gain floor passage. This potential bias toward the status quo mirrors the effect noted by Becker (1983). Here it is the nature of political decision making that tends to favor the status quo. In Becker (1983) this is reinforced by external pressures.

3. Committees are typically not random samples of representatives. There is considerable evidence of a self-selection process that results in a sorting of interests by committee, according to each committee's jurisdiction (Fenno 1973; Shepsle 1978). So the pivotal voter on a committee will not generally be the pivotal member in a floor vote. In a multidimensional context, this can easily be true for each dimension or a group of dimensions of Y.[10]

4. Policy change will not generally respond smoothly to exogenous changes that shift some or even most V_i. For example, the chamber pivot can shift on a particular issue, so that y' is preferred to y°. But if the committee pivot does not shift, so that y° is preferred by the committee to any other points that would command a floor majority, then a move away from y° may be forestalled. The success of some special interests in maintaining favorable regulation may be interpreted in this way. This is implicit in the studies of Weingast and Moran (1983) on the Federal Trade Commission (FTC), and Weingast (1984) on the Securities and Exchange Commission (SEC) (though, as we discuss in the section on empirical research, this potential for discontinuous response is not adequately captured in econometric studies).

Congressional Dominance

Because the focus of most recent theoretical work on policy formation has been in the context of legislative institutions, applications to regulation have tended to emphasize the legislative connections. This emphasis has been justified on substantive grounds by stressing the fundamental role of Congress in federal regulation. Thus it is pointed out that regulatory agencies are the creations of Congress. In each case, an act of Congress gave birth to the agency and gave it its specific charter, defining—often in the most general terms, though sometimes with considerable specificity—the agency's scope and powers. In addition Congress has the right to continue monitoring the agency's performance, through routine oversight. Congress also controls the agency's purse strings through the appropriation and authorization process. At any time Congress has the potential to change or even revoke an agency's mandate to operate in a specific arena (e.g., barring the FTC from regulating agricultural cooperatives or insurance companies) or to terminate an agency altogether (e.g., the Civil Aeronautics Board).

In such models Congress becomes the key player on the regulatory scene (Weingast 1981; Calvert and Weingast 1984). This view has come to be known as the "congressional dominance" model. Changes in regulatory behavior are in this view traceable to shifts in preferences on relevant committees or changes in committee jurisdiction rather than an independent and congressionally unsanctioned act of a regulatory agency. The congressional dominance approach is similar to the economic models in that neither approach provides an active role for the regulatory agency as a distinct component of the regulatory scene. This is in sharp contrast to the myriad descriptive analyses that focus on the internal workings of agencies, their bureaucratic structure, the politics or personalities of key staff members or commissioners. Similarly the role of the president and, to a large extent, of the courts is left outside current theoretical models.[11]

The congressional dominance model has considerable appeal, promising to wield Occam's razor to cut a swath through the jungle of regulatory analysis. To provide more theoretical underpinning to the effort, the connections between the legislature and a regulatory agency have recently been described in the language of the principal-agent models of economics (Mitnick 1980; McCubbins and Schwartz 1984; Weingast 1984; McCubbins 1985; Shepsle 1985). So far these descriptions are not themselves formal models but verbal analogies to formal models in economics. In these analogies Congress serves as the principal, while the regulatory bureaucracies are agents who respond to a system of incentives designed by Congress, keeping in mind monitoring costs and shirking opportunities.

As an illustration, consider Weingast's (1984) discussion of the link between Congress and regulatory agencies. Drawing on work by McCubbins and Schwartz (1984), Weingast argues that Congress is able to dominate bureaus in large part by relying on feedback from constituents. When agency performance gets sufficiently out of line with constituent interests—and hence congressional interests—Congress is moved to act (or, more precisely, congressmen representing those interests are moved to do so). Agencies understand this, and continual, intensive monitoring by Congress is not typically necessary. (In the terminology of McCubbins and Schwartz 1984, a "fire alarm" type of monitoring may be more efficient than "police patrols.")

The principal-agent analogy has considerable intuitive appeal, though its formal application (as opposed to invocation) in the context of regulation faces serious challenges. Probably the greatest difficulty with making the argument more formal, and structuring it in such a way that it yields robust a priori hypotheses, is that it requires a careful specification of the principal's preferences. But if individual legislators face multiple constituencies, even characterizing individual V_i may be difficult. Characterizing the preferences of Congress is subject to even more severe problems. Thus the problem is really one where there are multiple principals.[12] For congressional dominance to be a fruitful and parsimonious framework for the study of regulation, it needs to be able to predict whose protests or entreaties will be relevant for agency monitoring. Without a model of when and how legislatures listen to various voices, the analysis can do little more than identify—usually ex post—specific occasions when Congress has responded to specific interest groups. In this sense modern political economy is still some distance from providing a firm theoretical basis that links legislative and regulatory processes.

Empirical Analysis of the Political Economy of Regulation

The bulk of the empirical studies of the regulatory process has been concerned with the economic effects of regulation. Fortunately, for the literature is vast, the calculation of consumer surplus and other such topics are beyond the scope of this essay. In recent years, however, empirical analysis has been stimulated by several studies of the politics of regulation.

Regulatory Structure and Economic Behavior

These studies fall into two broad classes. The first, which emerged from the classic economic studies, is concerned with how regulatory structure directly affects regulators' economic decisions. The transition is well represented by the work of Joskow (1974) on regulatory lag. Joskow focused as much on the bureaucratic as on the directly political aspect of regulation. He argued that preferring a quiet life, public utility regulators were more attentive to changes in nominal prices than to real rates of return in periods of falling costs and were prone to lag changes in market and technological conditions in periods of rising costs.[13] A more direct concern with the outcomes of political processes is represented by Eckert's study of taxicab markets. Eckert (1973) observed that some local markets were regulated by independent commissions (e.g., a state Public Utility Commission), whereas others were regulated by agencies of a municipal bureaucracy. Like Joskow, he adopted the quiet life hypothesis with regard to independent commissions and argued that such commissions would grant service to monopoly providers with simplified rate structures. In contrast, the Niskanenesque agencies of local municipalities would seek to enhance their budgets by introducing multiple providers and complicated rate structures. Data for a sample of municipalities tended to support the hypothesis.

Further studies of how differences in regulatory structure affect market performance would be welcome, especially since, despite federal deregulatory trends, substantial regulation persists at the state and local level where the comparative approach undertaken by Eckert should readily find further application.[14]

Economic Interests and the Demand for Regulation

Our attention, however, will focus on the other side of the coin—the study of how regulatory structure responds to economic and/or political interests. In the theoretical section of this chapter, we had noted, for example, Fiorina's (1982) interest in whether regulation was legislated or delegated in terms of the interaction between constituent interests and the political process. Similar concerns have been the main emphasis of empirical research subsequent to Stigler's (1971) initial explorations into how economic interests affected occupational licensing and motor vehicle weight limits. Unfortunately these empirical studies rarely, if ever, attempt to estimate a structural model of the political process that translates the economic interests into policy. Largely omitting standard technical criticisms, we focus our discussion on two problems that arise from failure to model the political process. These problems may be termed *the pivot problem* and *the constituency interest problem.*

Pivots

Unlike markets, political processes are constantly exposed to abrupt changes because single individuals can be pivotal decision makers. Because small changes in who is the pivotal decison maker can produce large swings in policy, additive regression or limited dependent variable models, which imply that small changes in underlying variables always make small changes in (expected) policy, may well be inappropriate to the analysis of regulatory politics.

We stress that policy swings can be produced in contexts other than the "institution-free" models of multidimensional voting (as in McKelvey 1976), where cycles are endemic, or agenda setters dominate. Indeed legislatures, like Congress, that are partitioned into committees with jurisdictional power may be especially prone to policy swings. Denzau and Mackay (1983) and Shepsle (1986) have drawn our attention to the fact that such legislatures may amplify the effects of pivots. We recall the following from our discussion of theoretical developments:

1. The gatekeeping and ex post veto power of committees (Shepsle and Weingast 1985) imply that the status quo may persist long after underlying variables have changed.[15]

2. A small shift in the preferences of the pivot may result in a new policy that is a dramatic departure from the status quo.

3. Conversely, as argued by Weingast and Moran (1983), policy may change even when there is little change in the underlying preferences of the legislature simply because the committee chairmanship shifts.

Weingast and Moran (1983) provide evidence for the 1970s, when the preferences of the Senate oversight committee for the FTC shifted in a much more abrupt fashion than did preferences in the Senate as a whole. Similarly, Weingast (1984) cites data suggesting that New York Stock exchange commission rates changed abruptly after deregulatory legislation was passed by Congress in 1975. He uses these data to criticize the market analogy made by Phillips and Zecher (1981) that a new regulatory equilibrium was arrived at by a *tâtonnement* adjustment process.

Attempts at detailed modeling of the pivoting process are absent in the empirical literature. This is perhaps not surprising in various studies of Congress where very elaborate game-theoretic structures will be required for even quite stylized analyses. But such attempts might be made in simpler arenas. For example, Moe (1985) has carried out a monumental study of some 12,000 National Labor Relations Board (NLRB) decisions between 1948 and 1979. Like much of the work discussed later in the constituency interest section, Moe assumes an essentially unidimensional policy preference model, his continuum running from probusiness to prolabor. He acknowledges that NLRB decisions will be attentive to Congressional committee preferences. But he argues that there will be a stronger response to presidential preferences. Moe finds that the NLRB tilts in a probusiness fashion during Republican presidencies and reverses during Democratic administrations.

Moe's paper, however, steers clear of the internal political process in the Board, which—joyfully for modeling purposes—is a relatively simple five-person group. A first-cut look at the internal political process would argue that the tilt toward presidential preferences would not occur until the president had had the opportunity to create a 3 to 2 working majority of his appointees. Presumably the legislation that set up the independent agencies was designed to make them, at least in the short run, relatively free of presidential preferences. In contrast, Moe's specification calls for an instantaneous shift in policy by the Board once a new President takes office. By testing the 3 to 2 majority model against the instant switch model, one could begin to assess whether independence is in fact achieved. This type of test would begin to assess the value of modeling the role of pivots in regulatory decision making.[16]

Moe's approach also fails to reflect, except in the roughest way, his recognition that the NLRB has multiple *principals*. These include the president, actors in Congress, and the Courts. Because only one of the principals in this set may be decisive for a board member at a given time, it is perhaps inappropriate to estimate models in which decisions are assumed to be a simple additive function of the preferences of all the principals.

Such a problem is even more apparent in the analysis of the FTC by Weingast and Moran (1983).[17] Here FTC policy is modeled as a linear function of the average Americans for Democratic Action (ADA) rating of Congress, of subcommittees, and of subcommittee chairmen. This is clearly at odds with Weingast's own theoretical work (Shepsle and Weingast 1981, 1985), which emphasizes the nonmarginal nature of policymaking by Congress. To illustrate, suppose the activist chairman of a regulatory agency would like to make a fundamental change in public policy (e.g., severely regulate used car dealers). Suppose the chairman of the oversight committee in the House wanted the same policy as the activist agency head, while the chairman of the Senate committee preferred the status quo. Now, if the House chairman were replaced with someone with even more extreme views, it would probably make very little difference, either in the policy in question or in the agency's general dealings with Congress. But if the Senate chairman were replaced with someone willing to move away from the status quo and toward the activist's position, there probably would be a considerable policy impact. Yet both of these changes will be treated identically in the type of statistical model used by Weingast and Moran and by others.

In our hypothetical example, change was likely to lag the preferences of the activist until both committees in Congress were in phase. With reference to the Moe work, agency policies may lag because of fixed terms of appointment. Cogressional policies may also lag because of seniority powers of chairmen. Such observations illustrate how political processes possess considerable inertia, in contrast to the continual adaptations of financial markets. An additional, important source of inertia is the free-riding aspect to intitiating political change (Olson 1965). The potential benefits of change must be great before organizational costs (drafting a bill, securing its place on the agenda, etc.) are paid.

Yet this very inertia in creating change in itself provides an opportunity for great if sporadic changes. Perhaps nowhere is this more apparent than in voting on regulatory policy by initiative in statewide elections. Because the costs of changing the policy status quo are great, the status quo may be considerably distant from the policy desired by some pivotal voter before an initiative is organized. This provides the organizer with an opportunity to pass a relatively extreme proposal that, rather than giving the pivotal voter his ideal point, may just leave this voter indifferent between the status quo and the new policy (Romer and Rosenthal 1979). Indeed, econometric studies of voting returns on regulatory issues must presume that the proposal differs substantially from the status quo (e.g., see the Deacon and Shapiro (1975) study of the "coastal initiative" on policies regulating land use). If the alternatives had converged, one would not expect variation in economic variables to explain voting behavior. Nonconvergence provides opportunities to exploit the agenda. Recognition of such opportunities is implicit in the California legislature's having passed nuclear safety legislation that was stronger than the status quo prior to an antinuclear initiative vote (see also Lave and Romer 1983 on nuclear referenda).[18] Recognition that the stakes can be high is evident in the observation that expenditures by various state and national dental associations in opposing a 1978 Oregon initiative on deregulating the provision of dentures substantially exceeded the campaign expenditures of the incumbent Democratic governor and total expenditures by all sides on tax-limitation initiatives of the "Son of 13" variety.[19]

The upshot of these examples for static analysis is that we should not attempt to understand regulatory policy from a median voter or aggregate characteristic type regression. The specification will need to refer to status quo points, agenda control powers, and other aspects of political institutions.[20] To emphasize this important point, we return to it shortly in the section on defining constituency interests. At present, we also note a dynamic implication. Cross-sectional analyses usually regress current policies against current or slightly lagged values of "economic" variables. But the relevant measurements for explaining, say, California land use policies today may well be values of socioeconomic variables at the time the policy change occurred. A full model would seek to estimate when change occurs as a function of changes in underlying economic variables since a previous policy change.[21] These considerations do not apply only to initiatives and referenda. It is a sobering thought that in the absence of popular initiative in Pennsylvania, a post-Prohibition regulation of the alcoholic beverage market persists despite widespread popular opposition and campaign promises of the last two governors, one Democrat, the other Republican.

To summarize, majority rule combined with problems of organizing change implies that some policy changes will occur rarely but will be major when they occur. Although Stigler drew attention to these considerations, the consequences are not fully incorporated in his own empirical work or, almost universally, in any of the sequels.

Constituent Interests

Many recent empirical studies have analyzed roll call voting, the most readily observable aspect of Congressional behavior. The work attempts to combine the theoretical premise of the economic theory that individual interests drive regulatory outcomes with the political theorists' emphasis that Congress (rather than agencies) plays the key role in regulatory politics and that members of Congress are driven by the electoral imperative. These studies have ranged from analyses of specific regulatory issues, most notably the work of Kalt and Zupan (1984) on strip-mining, to a more global analysis of roll call voting by Peltzman (1984). The basic strategy of these models is to estimate limited dependent variable models (typically logit), where the explanatory variables have been assorted measures of constituency interest.

We preface our discussion of the constituency interest models by reviewing an alternative model, that of unidimensional spatial ("ideological") voting. After indicating that this model provides a good overall fit to a long time series of roll call data, we discuss why unidimensionality may be consistent with both economic and political theories of the regulatory process. We also present some extended examples of unidimensionality in the regulatory arena. Subsequently we discuss research based on aggregate constituency characteristics or the interests of support groups within a constituency. We find that at present these studies do not provide more insight into regulatory outcomes than does the unidimensional, "ideological" model. The latter does, however, perform poorly on questions of geographic distribution. We are not sanguine about the prospects of building parsimonious models for analyzing such issues.

Constituency Interest Models versus Ideological Voting Models
Constituency interest models have to be developed in light of a striking empirical regularity of congressional voting. Roll call voting in Congress exhibits a highly structured, basically unidimensional pattern. Moreover, given the ordering of legislators' ideal points along this dimension, it is apparent that the dimension can be thought of as liberal-conservative ideology. Liberal-conservative unidimensionality results are presented in Poole and Rosenthal (1985b). In analyzing virtually all roll calls in both Houses of Congress from 1919 through 1984, they found that, estimated on an annual or biannual basis, a single dimension can correctly classify 80 to 90 percent of the individual votes by senators and representatives.

Poole and Rosenthal go on to demonstrate that the liberal-conservative dimension is highly stable intertemporally.[22] In fact, as the "ideological" variable could readily be constructed from votes prior to a given roll call, "ideology" can readily be thought of as a lagged dependent variable that generally has strong explanatory power, regardless of the specific content of a given regulatory issue.[23]

The unidimensional pattern of roll call voting is paralleled by a largely unidimensional pattern to campaign contributions. In analyzing contributions of Political Action Committees (PACs), Poole and Romer (1985) found that most PACs give to incumbents ranging from the center of the dimension to one end or the other in a unimodal pattern, while giving to challengers (when they give to challengers at all) of incumbents located toward the opposite end, again in a largely unimodal pattern. These findings persist even when controlling for the candidate's party affiliation. Some, usually richer PACs, such as those associated with the National Rifle

Association, the dairy farmers, and the realtors simply contribute to most incumbents. In other words, giving is generally consistent with preferences that are ordered with respect to the ideological dimension, except for a small number of cases where contributions appear ideologically neutral.

The finding of an essentially unidimensional space underlying the political system is not necessarily at odds with the economic theories of regulation. Nor is it at odds with the reelection maximand advanced by political theorists. In a world of costly information, having a fairly rigid ideological lineup may (1) facilitate logrolling between adjacent legislators (who can agree to trades in such a way that the vote appears spilt along liberal-conservative lines, thus permitting legislators both to logroll and preserve their reputations with the voters), (2) facilitate cuetaking of less informed legislators from more informed legislators on the hundreds of roll calls they face each year (see Kingdon 1973); (3) facilitate cues for interest groups—an incumbent with a reputation for keeping the government off the backs of polluting industries is also likely to help ease the regulatory burdens of ones with hazardous workplaces—and (4) reduce noise in the reputational assessments made by voters. (We thus suspect there is much less "ideological" behavior in the private drafting of legislation and loopholes in legislation than in public roll call behavior.) Although authors such as Poole (1981) and Kalt and Zupan (1984) argue that empirically there is movement toward constituent preferences as reelection approaches, such movements appear slight in terms of the overall variation of legislators along the liberal-conservative dimension. These relatively constrained movements are largely consistent with the formal theory of Bernhardt and Ingberman (1985) and Ingberman (1985b) where incumbents trade off reputational losses against the benefits of conforming to changes in constituent preferences.

To illustrate the stable alignment of legislators along an ideological dimension, we have chosen some examples from specific regulatory issues that range from broad to narrow concerns and span a considerable time period. We offer these examples not as a representative sample but as an indication of how the dimension can serve as a baseline for future research. In the examples, we show how successive votes on amendments on a specific regulatory issue often fit the dimension in a consistent pattern.[24]

In order to place our analysis in a context where the status quo is invariant, we chose only sequences of amendents where all amendments, except possibly the last, failed. We preface our discussion by noting that in the Poole-Rosenthal research, the liberal-conservative dimension is parameterized to be two units in length, running from -1 to $+1$. The "yea" and

Table 3.1 Voting on wage-price controls

ICPSR number	Amend S. 2891 by exempting from wage and price controls business firms with annual revenue and employment both less than	Yes votes	No votes	Midpoint on liberal-conservative dimension
400	$50 million and 1,000 employees	11	79	−0.59
401	$5 million and 100 employees	26	62	−0.37
402	$1 million and 20 employees	36	54	−0.09

Table 3.2 Voting on OSHA

ICPSR number	Amend H.R. 16554 by barring funds when firms inspected employ	Yes votes	No votes	Midpoint on liberal-conservative dimension
906	7 employees or fewer	38	43	−0.11
908	4 employees or fewer	39	39	−0.15
910	3 employees or fewer	50	28	−0.49

"nay" alternatives in a roll call vote are modeled as being represented by two points on the dimension. The point further to the left is termed the liberal outcome, the other the conservative outcome. The roll call midpoint is the average of the two outcome locations. Legislator preferences (the V_i of the theory section) are assumed to be symmetric about ideal points. A legislator therefore is more likely to vote liberal than to vote conservative on a roll call if and only if his ideal point is to the left of the midpoint.

Our first example concerns a series of amendments introduced by Senator Proxmire (D-Wis.) on December 1, 1971, aimed at exempting small business from the wage-price controls imposed during the Nixon administration. As shown in table 3.1, the estimated midpoints were located along the dimension in a fashion that preserved the quantitative order found in the amendments.

Voting on a detailed mandate of a specific bureau, OSHA, rather than the more broadly based economic regulation inherent in wage-price controls, provides our second example. On October 3, 1972, Senator Curtis (R-Neb.) attempted to remove small firms from inspection and enforcement by the Occupational Safety and Health Administration (OSHA). After failing on seven- and four-employee limits, a three-employee limit succeeded. As the limit was lowered, the midpoint moved toward the liberal end of the dimension, as shown in table 3.2.

Our next examples concern the development of strip-mining regulation.

Table 3.3 House strip-mine voting, 1975

ICPSR number	Content	Yes votes	No votes	Midpoint on liberal-conservative dimension
43	Ottinger amendment	67	174	−0.36
44	McDade amendment	140	250	+0.14
45	Spellman amendment	136	262	−0.26
47	Blouin amendment	169	247	−0.21
48	Steiger amendment	170	248	+0.08
210	Veto override	278	143	+0.14

This issue was repeatedly before Congress over the period 1971 to 1977. Despite the sharp economic costs that such regulation would impose on certain constituencies, voting on strip-mining obeyed the usual liberal-conservative lines.

In 1974 the Hosmer (R-Cal.) amendment (ICPSR #824, 156 Yes, 255 No) sought to weaken significantly H.R. 11500, a bill with strong and broad regulatory provisions. At the same time the Heckler (D-Mass.) amendment (ICPSR #825, 69 Yes, 336 No) would have entirely eliminated surface mining. As expected, the Heckler midpoint (−0.43) was to the left of the Hosmer midpoint (+0.11).

After President Ford pocket vetoed a 1974 bill, the strip mine issue was again before the House in 1975 (H.R. 25). Representative Ottinger sought to toughen regulatory enforcement by shifting administration of strip mine regulation from the Interior Department to the EPA (see table 3.3). Representative Spellman (D-Md.) sought to toughen the bill by banning mining on slopes of 20 degrees or more. Representative Blouin (D-Iowa) sought to prohibit mining on national grasslands. The midpoints of these defeated amendments were all, as expected, to the left of the midpoint of both the vote to override President Ford's veto of the bill itself and the McDade (R-Pa.) amendment to weaken the bill by abolishing the reclamation fee and financing cleanup from outer shelf lease revenues. Interestingly a strategic amendment by Steiger of Arizona—the sixth (by the Poole-Rosenthal scaling) most conservative member of the House—ostensibly to strengthen the bill by removing anthracite exemptions, failed to generate a coalition of the extremes. The ploy was perceived, and this bill also had a midpoint to the right of center.

These contrasts were echoed in later years in the Senate. In 1975, the midpoints of the Mansfield amendment to prohibit mining of federal

Table 3.4 Senate amendment voting on strip-mining, 1975

ICPSR number	Amendment of	Yes votes	No votes	Midpoint on liberal-conservative dimension
66	Mansfield	39	56	−0.45
67	McClure	27	68	+0.24
69	Mathias	28	64	−0.68
70	Tower	18	78	+0.51
71	Fannin	19	77	+0.44

deposits where surface rights belong to others and the Mathias amendment to prohibit mining on slopes over 20 degrees were both to the left of the midpoints of the McClure amendment to permit mining of forest lands, the Fannin amendment not to pay benefits for jobs lost as a result of the bill, and the Tower amendment to allow states to opt out of the provisions of the bill (see table 3.4). Last, in 1977, the Hart amendment (ICPSR #162, defeated 37 to 45) to prohibit mining on alluvial valley floors was to the left (midpoint −0.01) of the Johnston amendment (midpoint +0.13, ICPSR #161, defeated 39 to 51) to permit states to regulate surface mining and reclamation operations.

Our final example is based on a recent paper by Krehbiel and Rivers (1985). In an attempt to combine an economic interests type of analysis with one that looks at the effects of political institutions, they studied three Senate roll calls on the minimum wage bill in 1977 (ICPSR nos. 544, 545, and 547). Rather than looking only at situations where the votes involved a sequence of proposals against a common status quo, they considered amendments to amendments as well. In addition they developed an econometric model that permits a test for the presence of sophisticated (rather than sincere) voting over the sequence.

For the three minimum wage roll calls Krehbiel and Rivers worked out an agenda tree, which maps the sequence of pairwise choices facing legislators. The agenda tree includes potential as well as actual votes, in that it shows possible pairings that are ruled out if some proposals fail. According to the Krehbiel-Rivers agenda tree, the actual votes implied the following alternatives (dollar amounts refer to minimum wage per hour):

1. $3.15 versus $2.90.
2. $3.15 versus $3.05.
3. $3.15 versus $2.30.

Krehbiel and Rivers were unable to reject the null hypothesis of sincere voting on each roll call. This finding is in accord with the Poole-Rosenthal model. The Poole-Rosenthal midpoints for the three roll calls, respectively, are 0.62, 0.35, and 0.78. If the most preferred minimum wage rates map monotonically onto the liberal-conservative dimension, this is the ordering of midpoints we should expect.[25]

These examples are all intended to suggest that on a diverse set (but not all!) of economic issues, constituency economic interests either do not play a fundamental role or are largely correlated with a simple but basic general measure of ideology. Moreover, as the preliminary results from minimum wage voting suggest, the potential for sophisticated voting does not appear to upset this correlation.

The pervasiveness of ideology is well recognized by economists and political scientists. In studies such as that of Moe (1985) on the NLRB or Beck (1982) on the Federal Reserve, the investigation centers on whether there is a "ping-ponging" in regulatory policy as a function of the party that controls the White House. Students of congressional behavior use more gradated measures of ideological preference made possible by the ratings issued by liberal or conservative interest groups. The rating most commonly used is that of the Americans for Democratic Action (ADA). This appears in the studies of Kau et al. (1982), Kalt and Zupan (1984), and Peltzman (1984), all of which are concerned with whether constituency interest measures can improve on the explanatory power of the ADA rating. In their study of how the Federal Trade Commision responded to changes in congressional preferences, Weingast and Moran (1983) use ADA ratings as their sole measure of preference, eschewing any attempt to link preferences to direct measures of economic activity in the constituencies. Similarly Moe (1985) uses ADA ratings as his sole measure of congressional preferences concerning the activities of the NLRB. The ADA ratings correlate highly with more general measures of ideology developed from scaling the ratings of a set of interest groups (Poole 1981) or from scaling roll call votes directly (Poole and Rosenthal 1985c).[26]

Aggregate Characteristics Models

Use of ADA ratings or a unidimensional spatial model is a sharp contrast to the use of socioeconomic measures of constituency interest. Introducing average or median constituency variables is the oldest and by far the most prevalent approach to investigating whether measures of constituency interest contribute to explanatory power beyond that afforded by ideology. These variables are generally derived from the distributions of income, education, age, race, labor force participation, and other relatively global socioeconomic characteristics. Following the critique of Fiorina (1974), political scientists have largely abandoned this type of research, which has been pursued by economists in recent years. The research has revealed three deficiencies that would arise in the use of these measures to explain changes in regulatory policy:

1. Explanatory power is generally low. Poole and Rosenthal (1985a), in an analysis of 568 Senate roll calls for 1977, find virtually no more explanatory power when $10 \times 568 = 5{,}680$ parameters are estimated in a linear logit model using nine average characteristics plus a constant than when 1,237 parameters are estimated in a logit representation of a one-dimensional "ideological" model. Of the average characteristics included, the political party dummy variable (included by most other investigators as well), makes by far the highest contribution to explanatory power. Of course, political party is a bogus economic characteristic. (The same might also be said of the other ad hoc choices, like education, age, and race, that social scientists routinely use simply because they are cheap goods provided by government statistical agencies.) Political party is mainly a fair to middling proxy for ideology. It explains little about roll call voting when ideology is controlled for, whereas ideology remains important even after controlling for party.

2. More generally, ideology is not explained away by these average characteristics. Kau et al., Kalt and Zupan, and Poole and Rosenthal all conclude that ideology continues to be a major determinant of roll call voting behavior, even when the average characteristics are controlled for. Essentially similar statistical results are obtained by Peltzman (1984), although Peltzman argues (mistakenly in our view) that his results support the hypothesis that ideology is determined by constituency economic interests.[27]

3. Although the average characteristics do add to the explanatory power of ideology when both types of variable appear, as shown by all the authors cited earlier, there is no theoretical structure that indicates how a given linear combination of constituency characteristics will relate to behavior. Unlike the case for ideology, where one can typically make statements of the form,"the more liberal the legislator, the more likely he or she is to vote for bill X," only in quite specific cases will one be able to claim ex ante that, for instance, "the more aged the constituents, the more likely the legislator is to vote for bill Y."

4. Most important, the average characteristics model is simply inconsistent with another significant phenomenon. Fiorina (1974) observed that when a

House seat changed party, the ADA rating of the constituency's representative flipped enormously. (Changes of 25 to 50 points on a 100 point scale are not exceptional.) The same phenomenon is true in the Senate. The general result is a "square wave" (the term is Keith Poole's) pattern to the time plot of the ideological coordinate of a given seat (see Romer and Rosenthal 1984, fig. 7, p. 470). Similarly, when the two Senate seats of a given state are split between a Democrat and a Republican, ratings and ideological coordinates vary greatly (see Bullock and Brady 1982; Peltzman 1984; Poole and Rosenthal 1984). This ideological dispersion is the echo of strong differences in roll call voting behavior across a wide set of issues, including regulatory ones. Since the average constituency characteristics vary very slowly in time, the voting flip-flops cannot readily be attributed to incremental changes in these variables. As we have already pointed out, because of the nonincremental nature of majority rule, the impacts of changes in aggregate variables are likely to be manifest in a discontinuous fashion. For example, one might argue that when constituency unemployment passed a certain threshold, the incumbent would be unseated, *ceteris paribus*. As a result the roll call voting pattern of the constituency's representative would change significantly. Nonincremental models of this type cannot be captured with the linear specifications used in past and current work.

Support Group Models
In response to the observation that average characteristics cannot explain the polarization of party voting, Peltzman (1984) took the important step of initiating research into support group characteristics. As Fenno (1977) notes, a representative responds to multiple definitions of constituency. In particular, a representative might be more attuned to the interests of those who voted for him than to those who voted against (see also McCubbins and Sullivan 1984). Peltzman attempted to capture these support groups with the following procedure. First, using county data, he regressed Senate election returns on average characteristics of the counties. Second, on a totally ad hoc basis, he used the estimated coefficients to create trichotomous variables to correspond to "pro" and "anti" groups. Variables having coefficients with t-statistics above $+1.5$ were coded $+1$ ("supporters"), those with $t < -1.5$ were coded -1 ("opponents"), and those with $|t| < 1.5$ were coded 0. The resulting variables were added to the state average characteristics in the roll call voting estimations.

Although Peltzman obtained positive results in terms of additional explanatory power, this procedure is a mild econometric nightmare.

Whether a coefficient passes the magic number of 1.5 will depend directly on the number of counties in a state and indirectly on the degree of heterogeneity across counties. Even more important, in measuring a support group effect by means of a trichotomous variable, Peltzman comes close to simply providing an alternative measure of party, one of the variables he seeks to explain as "determined" by economic interests. To see this, suppose Democratic senators tend to do relatively well in urban counties throughout the country. Then many of them will be given a $+1$ score on an urban support variable and Republicans will tend to get a -1 score. There may be few states whose senators have zero scores. In such a case the $\{+1, -1\}$ scores will closely parallel the $\{1, 0\}$ coding of the political party dummy. Finally, these support group characteristics, like the average characteristics are beset by the problem of the absence of theory that says how the characteristics will influence behavior on particular roll calls.

Despite our criticisms of Peltzman's implementation of his approach, we believe that if the constituency interest approach is to succeed at all, it will be necessary to identify support group characteristics. A more promising approach, in our view, and one partially addressed by Peltzman in his use of labor share in campaign contributions, would be to define support in terms of campaign contributions.

Since campaign contribution data can be obtained in highly disaggregated form, such an approach would permit pursuing some of the more issue-specific analyses in the spirit of Kalt and Zupan (1984). They considered roll call voting on coal strip-mining legislation. Rather than rely on highly aggregated measures of constituency interest that are applied indiscriminately to a broad sample of roll calls (à la Peltzman, Kau et al., and Poole and Rosenthal), Kalt and Zupan applied considerable diligence to measuring, for each state, the costs and benefits that relate to coal strip-mining. Variables included the regulation-induced increase in long-run average cost of surface mining in each coal-producing state, the difference between underground and surface reserves, the value to noncoal interests of strip-mined but unrestored acreage, the fraction of electricity consumption generated from coal, and other measures. In the end, however, only weak effects were found for the economic variables. Ideological primacy appeared present for their set of roll calls.

From the viewpoint of economic theories of regulation, factors that appear relevant to the negative findings obtained by Kalt and Zupan would include the following:

1. Although not general socioeconomic variables like income and education, the Kalt-Zupan variables remain average characteristics rather than support group characteristics. Thus, even though strip-mine operators and employees in a state might lose considerably from restrictive legislation, the amount of this loss may affect only senators for whom strip-mining interests form an important part of their support coalitions.

2. In terms of a standard unidimensional spatial model with probabilistic voting (e.g., see Hinich 1977), Poole and Rosenthal (1985a) have shown that a linear logit model of the Peltzman type can be reinterpreted in terms of a spatial model in which utility is quadratic in distance. The dimensions of the space are represented by the regressors of the model. Both ideal points and roll call alternatives can then be represented as points in this space. (However, the linear logit model has an important identification problem. The estimated coefficients confound the effect of the economic variable on the ideal points with the extent to which the "yea" and "nay" outcomes are spatially separate.) By computing an average percentage of anti-strip-mine votes across a set of roll calls and then regressing, Kalt and Zupan not only correctly constrained the ideal points to be constant across roll calls but also incorrectly constrained the spatial locations of roll call alternatives to be constant. However, correcting for this specification error does not alter the result that the ideological variable is far more important than the measured economic variables (Poole and Rosenthal 1985a).

3. Because strip-mining is geographically concentrated, many of the variables measured by Kalt and Zupan are likely to be important in only a minority of constituencies. For example, consider the variable measuring the regulatory impact on the average cost of surface mining. Only twenty-four states had a nonzero value on this variable. Of these twenty-four, moreover, mining would have represented an important part of the state economy in only some of the states.[28] Although senators from such states may act in terms of the state's economic self-interest, senators from other states may have a free vote that can be exercised in terms of their overall views of the desirability of governmental regulation of private enterprise.[29]

4. In reviewing the roll call votes that took place over strip-mining, one finds that many of the amendments had differential consequences on a selective geographic basis. The topics would include mining on national grasslands, mining of federally owned land, and anthracite coal. To the extent that these considerations are important, the variables measured by Kalt and Zupan, which refer to general costs and benefits of strip-mining, are unlikely to get at important aspects of specific roll calls. Geographic

redistribution is also, as we now illustrate, probably a major source of the errors of the liberal-conservative spatial voting model.

Regulation and Geographic Redistribution

The strip-mining results suggest a useful typology for understanding where the constituency interests hypothesis is most likely to find support. Some regulatory legislation is a matter of relatively uniform national policy with minimal consequences for geographic redistribution. Examples would include regulating workplace hazards, the sale of used cars, and drug trafficking. Bills on these issues should and generally do result in good fits in a pure liberal-conservative "ideology" model of voting. Other bills, like strip-mining, mix general ideological views (pro/antienvironment, pro/antiregulation) with significant economic impact on a relatively small minority of constituencies. These impacts may lead to a few votes that are out of character on liberal-conservative lines, but most legislators will continue to vote from general ideological preferences. Finally, other bills will have a minimum of ideological content and strong doses of geographic redistribution that affect nearly every constituency.

Bills of this last type fit the liberal-conservative dimension poorly. An example is furnished by the Pettingell Bill, a regulatory issue actively before Congress in the 1930s. Representative Pettingell introduced legislation to repeal Section 4 of the Interstate Commerce Act. Section 4 prohibited a railroad from charging a higher rate on short hauls than on long hauls over the same route. The Pettingell Bill passed the House easily, by a 215 to 41 vote in March of 1935 and by a 269 to 119 vote in January of 1937.[30] [The Senate refused to act on both occasions. The bill is probably an excellent illustration of committee gatekeeping (Denzau and Mackay 1983)—we found no record of Senate roll call voting on anything close to the Section 4 clause, despite overwhelming sentiment for repeal in the House.]

In voting on the bill, the liberal-conservative dimension was largely irrelevant. Although the Poole-Rosenthal procedure correctly classifies 81.5 percent of the individual votes in the 75th House (1937–38) and achieves an overall geometric mean probability[31] (gmp) of 0.664, the gmp for the Pettingell Bill in 1937 is only 0.537. (Random prediction of a fifty-fifty coin toss would have a gmp of 0.5.)

At first blush, one might think that finding the right economic variables for this bill would be easy. One would simply have to find those Congressional districts that were primarily long-haul beneficiaries on the one hand and those that were short-haul users subject to a monopoly carrier on the other. Not surprisingly, no opposition to the bill could be found in the Pacific littoral, whereas the Central Valley of California, Oregon, and Washington east of the Cascades, the Rocky Mountain area of Montana, and all the districts of Idaho, Nevada, and Arizona opposed the bill. Similarly there were no votes against the bill in Illinois, Indiana, Michigan, and Wisconsin, the four states surrounding the major long-haul terminal of Chicago. In the rest of the country the analysis gets more complicated. Opposition to the bill was found on the east coast, which proved more responsive to water carriers than to rail interests. Similar considerations prevailed in the lower Missisippi Valley. One would, then, at the least, need a model that took into account the interests of not only rails but also water carriers (and undoubtedly trucking as well). Moreover, according to Daggett (1941), in some areas specific producer interests (e.g. beet sugar in Colorado) were critical to roll call behavior. Consequently, while an economic constituency interest model looks to be preferable to an ideological model on bills involving geographic redistribution, the type of economic analysis required would appear to be so microscopic that analytical scholars are unlikely to produce findings that are more general than traditional case studies.

The problems in analyzing geographic redistribution are likely to confront us not only in roll call analysis but also if we pursue the study of regulatory decision making by agencies beyond the simple caseload counts found in a Weingast-Moran (1983) type study. To continue with the Interstate Commerce Commission, consider what it would mean to analyze ratemaking procedures. Figure 3.2, reproduced from Bigham and Roberts (1950), shows a portion of the rate structure for a single commodity, California citrus in 1948. The map indicates a price barrier to keep California citrus out of Florida, a gradient in the Rocky Mountain states designed to allow rails to meet competition from trucks on shorter hauls, and two large zones where price does not vary with distance, designed to crosssubsidize California citrus in eastern markets where it had a transportation disadvantage relative to Florida and Texas production. Policy in this area is clearly a multiplayer game involving a variety of transporation modes, producing areas, and perhaps consumers.[32] Interpretation of the figure perhaps suggests that the economic theory of regulation is alive and well, ex post. But ex ante models may be more difficult. In a corresponding map for California wine (Daggett and Carter 1947, p. 74), we do not find the New York grape afforded the same barrier as the Florida orange. In these situations of geographically distributive policies that do not fall neatly along an ideological dimension, we are not sanguine about the prospects

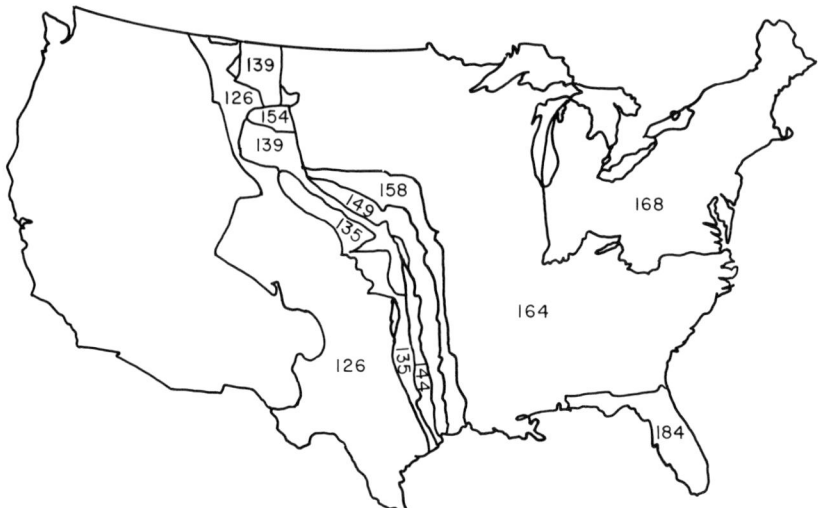

Figure 3.2 Rates on citrus fruit from Los Angeles as of August 21, 1948, in cents per 100 pounds. Source: Originally published in Daggett and Carter, (1947, p. 64); rates supplied by Bigham and Roberts (1950).

for theoretical and empirical progress that would go beyond the case study approach.

The Ideological Model Reconsidered: From Description to Prediction

A different type of problem, but one that may be more amenable to investigation, confronts pursuing the ideological model of regulatory policy formation. We have seen that many issues can be viewed as largely part of a unidimensional conflict that is repeated across a wide range of substantive policies. This insight, however, does not lead us to a predictive model of regulatory policy. Knowing that policy conflict will divide into liberal and conservative camps does not tell us where along the dimension the conflict will fall—where we will find the midpoint.

We can illustrate this problem by returning to our OSHA example where we considered three amendments introduced by Senator Curtis in October 1972 (table 3.2). Back on June 27 of that year Curtis had sought to amend OSHA legislation with a 25 employee limit. He failed, but then succeeded in passing a 15 employee limit. In the intervening four-month period, a change in how this issue projected onto the liberal-conservative dimension had occurred. As a result Senator Case was able to insert an amendment striking the 15 employee limit passed by Curtis in June. Curtis was now able to restore only a 3 employee limit. Although both in June and October voting lined up on the dimension, the mapping from quantitative limits on employees to the dimension had shifted.

When individual mappings are stable, shifts in the composition of Congress may permit prediction of policy change along the lines of Weingast and Moran (1983). The NLRB and other regulatory agencies emerged directly upon the shift to Democratic dominance in Congress occassioned by the Depression. The role of the NLRB was then profoundly modified at a later date by the Taft-Hartley Act passed by a Republican Congress (Moe 1985). But many other regulatory outcomes, in addition to our OSHA example, reflect circumstances that change the incentives or the information flows that face congressional actors and thereby influence how issues project onto the dimension. For example, General Motors' unseemly private investigation of Ralph Nader is said (Jacoby and Steinbrunner 1973, p. 10) to have been critical, in our terms, in shifting the midpoint sufficiently to permit passage of the Clean Air Act. Modeling how the ideological midpoint on a regulatory issue shifts from either information flows or structuring of the congressional agenda is the critical next step to be taken in understanding the ideological facets of regulatory policymaking.

Conclusions

On both theoretical and empirical fronts, the study of regulation continues to pose intriguing challenges for political economy. Theoretical work in the political economy of regulation has moved from the conveniently simple capture models to a recognition that the regulatory arena involves multiple competing interests. Formal models are only beginning to come to grips with how these interests are translated into constituencies that influence political and, hence, regulatory decisions. The economic and political models that we have characterized as modern political economy do provide the beginnings of an analytical framework. As yet the models are not rich enough to shed much light on the full structure of regulatory environments as complex as that of, say, the U.S. federal government. There are arguments—such as those made in support of the congressional dominance model—that suggest that it may not be necessary to tackle the full structure. But as of now, these arguments rest largely on intuition and quite casual theorizing.

The lack of a firm theoretical base has made it difficult to carry out well-specified empirical work. Empirical researchers have, for the most part, been using ad hoc formulations that seek to measure constituency characteristics in overly broad terms. In particular, empirical work has barely begun to incorporate those insights that *have* emerged from theory: the need to address the identity of political support groups in some detail; the possible impact of political institutions on policy outcomes; and because of these institutions the likelihood that the response of policy to changes in exogenous variables will be discontinuous.

At the same time theoretical development has been hampered by the lack of a substantial body of well-documented empirical regularities. Instead, much theoretical work has been done with only casual reference to observation. Often the analysis is motivated by reference to one or two examples that seem to support the model. A closer link between theory and observation would greatly enhance progress on both fronts.

Notes

We thank members of the Doctoral Seminar in Political Economy at Carnegie Mellon University (Spring 1985), especially Randall Calvert, for many stimulating discussions on the subject of this essay. We also thank Susan Rose-Ackerman and Friedrich Schneider for comments on an early draft, and Keith Poole for suggestions concerning the roll call analysis.

1. A survey of the economic studies of normative and allocative effects of regulation is provided by Joskow and Noll (1981). Mitnick (1980) is a good source for the earlier political science studies.

2. In some areas formal analysis has increased our knowledge of the linkages between economics and politics. Interestingly we seem further along in understanding outcomes at the macro level than at the micro level needed to deal with regulatory policy. For example, largely as a result of seminal papers by Kramer (1971) and Hibbs (1977), there is a substantial body of work dealing with the way macroeconomic outcomes affect elections and how electoral outcomes affect policy. (Though it should be noted that even here, the connection between theory and empirical work is often quite loose.) In another context, following Barr and Davis (1966), a large literature has developed on the relationship between spending by local governments and variations in institutional setting and economic conditions (residents' income, tax price, family size, etc.).

3. In addition to the works cited in note 1, see Noll (1983) for a broad outline of the political considerations relevant to regulation. For a collection of essays by social scientists other than economists, see Noll (1985). Breyer (1982) and Rose-Ackerman (1985) provide recent overviews of judicial aspects of regulation.

4. Regulation has been variously interpreted to include the broad sweep of government in economic life, as well as a more narrow conception restricted to those policies that work through administrative processes. Most inclusive is the definition given by Posner (1974, p. 335): Economic regulation involves "taxes and subsidies of all sorts as well as ... explicit legislative and administrative controls over rates, entry, and other facets of economic activity." Stigler (1971), Becker (1983), and to a lesser extent Noll (1983) incline to this interpretation. For arguments supporting a narrower definition of regulation, see Noll (1980), Joskow and Noll (1981), and Wilson (1975, 1980). Much of the work we discuss in this chapter deals broadly with the politics of policy formation, though some of it relates explicitly to the narrower questions of regulation by administrative agencies.

5. Rejecting the economic theory as too narrow, Wilson (1980), for example, presents a set of studies, each focusing on a different regulatory agency. In a summary chapter Wilson argues for an eclectic theory that draws not only on political and economic considerations but also those of administrative organization and bureaucratic behavior. (This theme had already been sounded in Wilson 1975.) Stigler (1980) and Shepsle (1982) have argued that such an approach is not a theory at all, since it provides little or no systematic *a priori* understanding of regulatory phenomena.

6. Although starting from quite different premises, Levine (1981) proposes a similar explanation for regulatory change. He argues that, on average, political processes move in the direction of greater efficiency, given the best current knowledge. Policymakers may make mistakes, but these mistakes tend to be corrected over time, as their welfare costs become more and more evident. Levine offers the creation (in 1938) and the dismantling (starting in 1975) of the Civil Aeronautics Board as an illustration of his paradigm. A central feature of this paradigm is the role of ideas, rather than of interests. Derthick and Quirk (1985) present a similar framework, in much greater detail. At their current level of elaboration, the approaches of Levine (1981) and Derthick and Quirk (1985) are subject to the criticisms voiced by Stigler (1980) and Shepsle (1982) (see note 5). These approaches may be useful as descriptions of specific regulatory events, rather than as a priori models.

7. Barke and Riker (1982) provide a brief outline but not a model. McCubbins and Sullivan (1984) address constituency representation but do not consider electoral competition explicitly.

8. Weingast, Shepsle, and Johnsen (1981) elaborate on this view in the context of pork-barrel legislation. Indeed, much of the analysis of government policy in general, and regulation in particular, begins with the premise that many policies are inefficient. The question then arises as to how the inefficient policies got enacted. Nearly all the analysis reposes on combining a story involving asymmetric perception of costs and benefits, combined with a rationale based on fiscal illusion. For example, in Weingast et al. (1981), there is an overcounting of the benefits generated by expenditures in a legislative district: a sewage treatment plant is valued for the direct benefits it confers in terms of the clean water it produces and also for the returns it generates to the in-district factors employed in building or running the plant. In McCubbins and Sullivan (1984) it is assumed that environmental regulation by standards more effectively hides costs and benefits than does regulation by Pigovian incentives.

The difficulty in relying on models with built-in illusion is that they are highly sensitive to the illusion assumption. In other words, the illusion can be chosen to suit particular, perhaps telling, examples. But the extent to which the examples may be generalized is open to question. Counterexamples that do not display the assumed illusion abound. (For example, while it is true that water pollution has been approached largely via treatment facilities financed out of general revenues, thus hiding their costs, it is also true that strip-mine cleanup and the Superfund have been financed by taxes on roughly the relevant producer groups.)

9. An added complication is the possibility that the bill may be forced out of the committee for a direct floor vote. Shepsle and Weingast (1985) note that though this may occur, it is procedurally difficult. An additional factor enhancing committee preferences is the ex post veto that key members may have in their role as members of conference committees that consider final versions of bills passed by both houses.

10. But what if many substantive issues (environmental safety, transportation regulation, occupational health) can be represented in terms of a single underlying dimension? In other words, what if Y is the real line, or the $V_i(y)$ can be represented as preferences over a one-dimensional issue space? Then, if all legislators have equal or nearly equal numbers of committee assignments, the median of every committee cannot differ systematically from the median of all legislators. Thus in a one-dimensional context, the key role of committees may

not stem from the features dealt with in current theoretical developments. We return to this point later when we discuss empirical developments.

11. Interestingly, a recent study of the role of courts in regulatory policy provides oblique evidence in support of the congressional dominance view. Melnick (1983), in his study of court rulings on environmental policy, suggests that courts' deference to legislative history in trying to interpret often vague regulatory statutes strengthens the power of key congressional committees and their staff, relative to the White House. This observation also has intriguing connections to Fiorina's (1984) discussion of congressional choice of legislative versus administrative form. It suggests that Congress can simultaneously delegate authority to an agency and retain considerable legislative influence via interpretation through the courts.

12. Theoretical work on principal-agent models has focused on cases where there is a single principal. For surveys, see Arrow (1985) and chapter 1 by Sappington and Stiglitz in this volume. Bernheim and Whinston (1985) develop a model in which several independent, risk-neutral principals attempt to influence a common agent. For an entertaining account that evokes some of the difficulties that face congressional principals dealing with a wily agent (the Federal Reserve), see Timberlake (1985).

13. The work of Joskow on PUCs has an interesting parallel to the papers cited in note 7, in assuming that, perhaps from pursuing rational strategies of information processing, constituents act as if they had some form of illusion. In Joskow's case, the illusion concerns nominal versus real prices. As with all models relying on illusion, more work is needed to pin down how such illusions can persist through time.

14. There have been quite a few studies comparing performance of regulated markets with unregulated ones. (Studies of the U.S. passenger airline industry are prominent among these.) But differences in regulatory structure have not been pursued with nearly the intensity of research that has examined—also using cross sections of states or municipalities—the economic performance of public versus private enterprises. See, for example, the survey by DeAlessi (1974) of a host of such studies for the electric power industry. Of the studies cited, only Mikesell (1971) looks at variation in regulatory structure across states. Borcherding et al. (1982) present a more recent survey of the public versus private studies.

Some studies attempt to explain variations in regulatory patterns across states. For example, Oster and Quigley (1977) and Noam (1982) find that the extent to which local building codes restrict cost-saving innovations is correlated with the relative power of construction unions and firms. Oster (1980) looks at the role of industry structure and the cohesiveness of consumer groups in explaining interstate differences in consumer protection regulations. Gormley (1983) emphasizes the activities of consumer advocates in influencing the behavior of state public utility commissions.

15. The most famous stylized example has great economic relevance. Control of key committees by southern conservatives permitted the maintenance of state laws that mandated economic markets segregated by race.

16. Despite our critical discussion of Moe's work, we feel it is by far the most imaginative of any of the empirical studies of the politics of regulation that we have examined. Moe is unique in exploring the complex interactions involving the expectations of underlying economic interest groups, Congress, the presidency, a regulatory board, and the board's agency bureaucracy. Much remains to be done, however, including testing Moe's hierarchical model, where economic agents take the bureaucrats' policies as given and the bureaucrats respond similarly to the Board, against alternatives where agents anticipate changes in policy induced, say, by the outcome of a presidential election. Similarly the working majority model we suggested might be refined to take into account that actual decisions are made by panels composed of three of the five members of the NLRB.

17. Calvert and Weingast (1984) present the analysis of Weingast and Moran (1983) with some data refinements and with more of a political science emphasis.

18. Mashaw and Rose-Ackerman (1984) indicate a trend for interested parties to seek their regulatory goals in a variety of political forums. Thus automobile companies sought federal legislation as an alternative to California's stringent pollution laws.

19. *Portland Oregonian*, October 18, 1978. However, spending does not guarantee victory. Proponents of deregulation spent far less and won. The spending patterns should, however, be pleasing to believers in free-rider and concentrated-cost–diffuse-benefits-type theories. (The dental associations did spend somewhat less than the successful Republican candidate for governor.)

20. In attempting to explain why the insurance industry is regulated entirely by state agencies when much might be gained by uniform national statutes, Mashaw and Rose-Ackerman (1984) are forced to conclude, "State predomination in the [area] of ... insurance may simply be [a] historical curiosit[y].... That this situation continues into the 1980s seems to reflect merely advantages to the industry from continued state regulation and the absence of a consensus in favor of any federal regulatory scheme" (p. 119). This passage nicely illustrates the force of inertia and the status quo in regulation.

21. Stigler (1971) partially addresses this problem by using values of socioeconomic variables measured close to the year in which occupational licensing took effect in a given state. Such a specification still fails to analyze the timing of regulatory change.

22. Intertemporal stability is demonstrated by a method (Poole 1983) that takes advantage of the fact that the annual or biannual scalings can be tied together as a result of the continuing presence of overlapping generations in Congress. The method is identical to principal components analysis except that allowance is made for missing data. A single factor explains 87 percent of the variation in the annual or biannual scalings for the Senate and 92 percent for the House.

23. Our use of the term "ideology" does not coincide with the way this word is applied in the Kalt-Zupan and related studies. We do not restrict it to mean simply the legislator's personal ideolgy as opposed to the interests of his constituents. Rather, in our view, ideology is a dimension on which are projected the myriad issue dimensions of politics. It is a remarkable fact that a single dimension, with considerable stability, characterizes voting in the U.S. Congress. So, in our view, voting consistently along the ideology dimension does not imply shirking by the legislator. As we explain in the text later, voting in a manner consistent with ideological location may well be consistent with close attention to constituent interest.

24. The wage-price, OSHA, and strip-mine examples were suggested by the dissertation research of Krishna Ladha at Carnegie-Mellon University. The quantitative results came from the scalings reported in Poole and Rosenthal (1985b).

25. With reference to our later analysis of aggregate characteristics models, Krehbiel and Rivers modeled each legislator's ideal point as a linear function of unemployment, wages, unionization, and party. Only unionization and the noneconomic variable of party were significant. It is difficult to compare these results to Poole-Rosenthal because of nesting problems and differences in sample. However, the exponentiated log-likelihoods per case are 0.735, 0.680, and 0.750 for Krehbiel-Rivers and 0.845, 0.743, and 0.740 for Poole-Rosenthal. The comparison suggests that aggregate characteristics models hardly explain much more than the unidimensional model.

26. There are two reasons for preferring scaled measures to the ratings of the ADA or any other single-interest group. First, as the ADA ratings are based on a small number of roll calls selected by a specific interest group, they will be relatively noisy measures. Second, as a few members of Congress may be more liberal than the ADA, the ADA ratings may be folded

(Coombs 1964) at the liberal end. The ADA rating is likely to be a poor measure of ideology for a portion of the left end of the political spectrum. For more details, see Poole and Romer (1985).

27. Peltzman performed two types of analyses. In one, he attempted to explain ADA and COPE ratings on the basis of the economic variables. Although he is correct in arguing that the marginal explanatory power of the party dummy declines as economic variables are added, he fails to note that the t-statistic on party remains greater than that on several of the economic variables. Moreover he fails to run the opposite experiment and ask what happens to the marginal explanatory power of economic variables as party is added. In a second analysis he compared the ratings and the economic variables in his logit analyses of roll call votes. A similar critique applies here.

28. We thank Kalt and Zupan for making their data available.

29. In their detailed analysis of the development of trade legislation, Bauer, Pool, and Dexter (1964) argue that legislators are frequently not harnessed to the economic interests of their constituencies. They point out that some large and potentially powerful organizations, such as DuPont, may themselves find it difficult to define their self-interest since they are multidivisional operations, each of which may be gainers or losers from a specific piece of legislation. In general, there will be a diversity of positions on an issue in a constituency that make it possible for a legislator to vote either way. As a contemporary example, consider the Senate votes on oil company mergers following the Chevron takeover of Gulf. Senators Heinz and Specter could presumably curry favor either with the numerous Pennsylvania shareholders of Gulf, about to be amply rewarded, or with Gulf's employees in the Pittsburgh area. Even though they were from the same party, the two senators split on this issue.

30. See Daggett (1941, pp. 440–446) for extensive discussion of the Pettingell Bill vote.

31. The geometric mean probability is the exponential of the quantity formed by dividing the log-likelihood by the number of observations.

32. Regulatory conflict between national and local producers of the same product is discussed by Mashaw and Rose-Ackerman (1984).

References

Arrow, K. J. 1985. "The Economics of Agency." In J. W. Pratt and R. Zeckhauser, eds., *Principals and Agents: The Structure of Business*. Boston: Harvard Business School Press, 37–51.

Austen-Smith, D. 1984. "Interest Groups, Campaign Contributions, and the Spatial Model of Voting." Mimeo. University of York.

Barke, R. P., and Riker, W. 1982. "A Political Theory of Regulation with Some Observations on Railway Abandonments." *Public Choice* 39:73–106.

Barr, J. L., and Davis, O. A. 1966. "An Elementary Political and Economic Theory of the Expenditures of Local Governments." *Southern Economic Journal* 33:149–165.

Bauer, R., Pool, I., and Dexter, L. A. 1963. *American Business and Public Policy: The Politics of Foreign Trade*. New York: Atherton Press.

Beck, N. 1982. "Presidential Influence on the Federal Reserve in the 1970's." *American Journal of Political Science* 26:415–445.

Becker, G. S. 1983. "A Theory of Competition among Pressure Groups for Political Influence." *Quarterly Journal of Economics* 98:371–400.

Bernhardt, M. D., and Ingberman, D. 1985. "Candidate Reputations and the Incumbency Effect." *Journal of Public Economic 27*: 47–67.

Bernheim, D., and Whinston, M. 1985. "Common Agency." Working Paper. Harvard University.

Bernstein, M. H. 1955. *Regulating Business by Independent Commission*. Princeton: Princeton University Press.

Bigham, T. C., and Roberts, M. J. 1950. *Citrus Fruit Rates: Development and Economic Appraisal*. Gainesville: University of Florida Press.

Borcherding, T. E., Pommerehne, W. W., and Schneider, F. 1982. "Comparing the Efficiency of Private and Public Production: The Evidence from Five Countries." In Dieter Bös, Richard A. Musgrave, and Jack Wiseman, eds., *Public Production, Zeitschrift für Nationalökonomie/ Journal of Economics, Supplement, 2*, Vienna: Springer-Verlag, 127–156.

Breyer, S. G. 1982. *Regulation and its Reform*. Cambridge: Harvard University Press.

Bullock, C. S., III, and Brady, D. 1982. "Party, Constituency, and Roll Call Voting in the U.S. Senate." *Legislative Studies Quarterly 8*: 29–43.

Calvert, R., and Weingast, B. 1984. "The Nature and Measurement of Congressional Influence over Policy Making: The Case of the FTC." Mimeo. Washington University, St. Louis.

Coombs, C. 1964. *A Theory of Data*. New York: Wiley.

Daggett, S. 1941. *Principles of Inland Transportation*, 3d ed. New York: Harper and Brothers.

Daggett, S., and Carter, J. P. 1947. *The Structure of Transcontinental Railroad Rates*. Berkeley: University of California Press.

Deacon, R., and Shapiro, P. 1975. "Private Preference for Collective Goods Revealed through Voting on Referenda." *American Economic Review 65*: 943–955.

DeAlessi, L. 1974. "An Economic Analysis of Government Ownership and Regulation: Theory and the Evidence from the Electric Power Industry." *Public Choice 19*: 1–42.

Denzau, A., and Mackay, R. 1983. "Gate Keeping and Monopoly Power of Committees." *American Journal of Political Science 27*: 740–761.

Derthick, M., and Quirk, P. 1985. *The Politics of Deregulation*. Washington, D. C.: Brookings Institution.

Downs, A. 1957. *An Economic Theory of Democracy*. New York: Harper and Row.

Eckert, R. 1973. "On the Incentives of Legislators: The Case of Taxicabs." *Public Choice 14*: 83–100.

Fenno, R. 1973. *Congressmen in Committees*. Boston: Little, Brown.

Fenno, R. 1977. *Home Style*. Boston: Little, Brown.

Fiorina, M. 1974. *Representatives, Roll Calls, and Constituencies*. Lexington, Mass.: D. C. Heath.

Fiorina, M. 1982. "Legislative Choice of Regulatory Forms: Legal Process or Administrative Process?" *Public Choice 39*: 33–66

Fiorina, M. 1984. "Legislator Uncertainty, Legislative Control and the Delegation of Legislative Power." Paper presented at the Conference on Institutional Adaptation, Stanford University.

Fiorina, M. 1985. "Group Concentration and the Delegation of Legislative Authority." In R. Noll, ed. *Regulatory Policy and the Social Sciences*. Berkeley: University of California Press.

Gormley, W. T., Jr. 1983. *The Politics of Public Utility Regulation.* Pittsburgh: University of Pittsburgh Press.

Hibbs, D. R., Jr. 1977. "Political Parties and Macroeconomic Policy." *American Political Science Review 71*: 1467–1487.

Hinich, M. J. 1977. "Equilibrium in Spatial Voting: The Median Voter Result is an Artifact." *Journal of Economic Theory 16*: 208–219.

Ingberman, D. 1985a. "Campaign Contributions and Candidate Reputations." GSIA Working Paper No. 6-84-85. Carnegie Mellon University.

Ingberman, D. 1985b. "Reputational Dynamics in Spatial Competition." GSIA Working Paper No. 21-84-85. Carnegie Mellon University.

Jacoby, H. D., and Steinbrunner, J. D. 1973. *Clearing the Air: Federal Policy on Automotive Emissions Control.* Cambridge Mass.: Ballinger.

Joskow, P. L. 1974. "Inflation and Environmental Concern: Structural Change in the Process of Public Utility Price Regulation." *Journal of Law and Economics 17*: 291–327.

Joskow, P., and Noll, R. 1981. "Regulation in Theory and Practice: An Overview." In Gary Fromm, ed., *Studies in Public Regulation.* Cambridge: MIT Press.

Kalt, J. P., and Zupan, A. M. 1984. "Capture and Ideology in the Economic Theory of Politics." *American Economic Review 74*: 301–322.

Kau, J. B., Keenan, D., and Rubin, P. H. 1982. "A General Equilibrium Model of Congressional Voting." *Quarterly Journal of Economics 96*: 271–293.

Kingdon, J. W. 1973. *Congressmen's Voting Decisions.* New York: Harper and Row.

Klevorick, A., and Kramer, G. H. 1973. "Social Choice on Pollution Management: The Genossenschaften." *Journal of Public Economics 2*: 101–146.

Kramer, G. H. 1971. "Short Term Fluctuations in U.S. Voting Behavior, 1896–1964." *American Political Science Review 65*: 131–143.

Krehbiel, K., and Rivers, D. 1985. "Congressional Roll Call Voting Strategies: Application of a New Test to Minimum Wage Legislation." Paper presented at annual meeting of American Political Science Association, New Orleans.

Lave, L. B., and Romer, T. 1983. "Specifying Risk Goals: Inherent Problems with Democratic Institutions." *Risk Analysis 3*: 217–227.

Levine, M. E. 1981. "Revisionism Revised? Airline Deregulation and the Public Interest." *Law and Contemporary Problems 44*: 179–195.

McCubbins, M. 1985 "The Legislative Design of Regulatory Structure." *American Journal of Political Science 29*: 721–748.

McCubbins, M., and Schwartz, T. 1984. "Congressional Oversight Overlooked: Police Patrols versus Fire Alarms." *American Journal of Political Science 28*: 165–179.

McCubbins, M., and Sullivan, T. 1984. "Constituency Influences on Legislative Policy Choices." *Quality and Quantity 18*: 299–319.

McKelvey, R. D. 1976. "Intransitivities in Multidimensional Voting Models and Some Implications for Agenda Control." *Journal of Economic Theory 12*: 472–482.

Mashaw, J. L., and Rose-Ackerman, S. 1984. "Federalism and Regulation." In G. Eads and M. Fix, eds., *The Reagan Regulatory Program: An Assessment.* Washington, D.C. The Urban Institute, 111–145.

Melnick, R. S. 1983. *Regulation and the Courts: The Case of the Clean Air Act.* Washington, D.C.: Brookings Institution.

Mikesell, J. L. 1971. "Regulation and Electric Utility Rate Structure." *Mississippi Valley Journal of Economics and Business* 7:82–89.

Mitnick, B. 1980. *The Political Economy of Regulation: Creating, Designing, and Removing Regulatory Forms.* New York: Columbia University Press.

Moe, T. M. 1985. "Control and Feedback in Economic Regulation: The Case of the NLRB." *American Political Science Review*, 79:1094–1116.

Noam, E. M. 1982. "Choice of Governmental Level in Regulation." *Kyklos 35*:278–291.

Noll, R. 1980. "What is Regulation?" Social Science Working Paper No. 324. California Institute of Technology, Pasadena.

Noll, R. 1983. "The Political Foundations of Regulatory Policy." *Zeitschrift für die gesamte Staatswissenchaft 139*:377–404.

Noll, R., ed. 1985. *Regulatory Policy and the Social Sciences.* Berkeley: University of California Press.

Olson, M. 1965. *The Logic of Collection Action.* New York: Shocken.

Oster, S. M. 1980. "An Analysis of Some Causes of Interstate Differences in Consumer Regulations." *Economic Inquiry 18*:39–54.

Oster, S. M., and Quigley, J. M. 1977. "Regulatory Barriers to the Diffusion of Innovation: Some Evidence from Building Codes." *Bell Journal of Economics 8*:361–377.

Peltzman, S. 1976. "Toward a More General Theory of Regulation." *Journal of Law and Economics 19*:211–240.

Peltzman, S. 1984. "Constituency Interest and Congressional Voting." *Journal of Law and Economics 27*:181–210

Phillips, S., and Zecher, R. 1981. *The SEC and the Public Interest.* Cambridge, Mass.: MIT Press.

Poole, K. T. 1981. "Dimensions of Interest Group Evaluation of the U.S. Senate 1969–1978." *American Journal of Political Science 25*:41–57.

Poole, K. T. 1983 "Recovering a Basic Space From a Set of Issue Scales." GSIA Working Paper No. 44-82-83. Carnegie-Mellon University.

Poole, K. T., and Romer, T. 1985. "Patterns of Political Action Committee Contributions to the 1980 Campaigns for the U.S. House of Representatives." *Public Choice 47*:63–111.

Poole, K. T., and Rosenthal, H. 1984. "The Polarization of American Politics." *Journal of Politics 46*:1061–1079.

Poole, K. T., and Rosenthal, H. 1985a. "The Political Economy of Roll Call Voting in the 'Multi-Party' Congress of the United States." *European Journal of Political Economy 1*:45–58.

Poole, K. T., and Rosenthal, H. 1985b. "The Unidimensional Congress, 1919–84." GSIA Working Paper No. 44-84-85. Carnegie Mellon University. Paper presented at the 1985 annual meeting of the American Political Science Association.

Poole, K. T., and Rosenthal, H. 1985c. "A Spatial Model for Legislative Roll Call Analysis." *American Journal of Political Science 29*:357–384.

Posner, R. A. 1974. "Theories of Economic Regulation." *Bell Journal of Economics and Management Science 5*:335–358.

Riker, W., and Ordeshook, P. C. 1973. *Introduction to Positive Political Theory.* Englewood Cliffs, N. J.: Prentice-Hall.

Romer, T., and Rosenthal, H. 1979. "Bureaucrats versus Voters: On the Political Economy of Resource Allocation by Direct Democracy." *Quarterly Journal of Economics* 93:563–387.

Romer, T., and Rosenthal, H. 1984. "Voting Models and Empirical Evidence." *American Scientist* 71:465–474.

Rose-Ackerman, S. 1985. "Administrative Law and Social Science: Knowledge, Politics, and Social Norms." Paper presented at the Conference on the Public Sector and the Economy, Charlottenlund, Denmark.

Shepsle, K. 1978. *The Giant Jigsaw Puzzle: Democratic Committee Assignments in the Modern House*. Chicago: University of Chicago Press.

Shepsle, K. 1982. "Review of *The Politics of Regulation*." *Journal of Political Economy* 90:216–221.

Shepsle, K. A. 1985. "Prospects for Formal Models of Legislatures." *Legislative Studies Quarterly* 10:5–19.

Shepsle, K. A. 1986. "The Positive Theory of Legislative Institutions: An Enrichment of Social Choice and Spatial Models." *Public Choice* 50:135–178.

Shepsle, K. A., and Weingast, B. R. 1981. "Structure-Induced Equilibrium and Legislative Choice." *Public Choice* 37:503–519.

Shepsle, K. A., and Weingast, B. R. 1985. "The Institutional Foundations of Committee Power." Paper presented at Caltech Weingart Conference on Formal Models of Voting, Pasadena.

Stigler, G. J. 1971 "The Economic Theory of Regulation." *Bell Journal of Economics and Management Science* 2:3–21.

Stigler, G. J. 1981. "Trying to Understand the Regulatory Leviathan." *Wall Street Journal*, August 1.

Timberlake, R. H., Jr. 1985. "Legislative Construction of the Monetary Control Act of 1980." *American Economic Review Papers and Proceedings* 75:97–102.

Weingast, B. R. 1981. "Regulation, Reregulation, and Deregulation: The Political Foundations of Agency-Clientele Relationships." *Law and Contemporary Problems* 44:147–177.

Weingast, B. R. 1984. "The Congressional-Bureaucratic System: A Principal-Agent Perspective (with Applications to the SEC)." *Public Choice* 44:147–192.

Weingast, B. R., and Moran, M. 1983. "Bureaucratic Discretion or Legislative Control? Regulatory Policymaking by the Federal Trade Commission." *Journal of Political Economy* 91:765–800.

Weingast, B. R., Shepsle, K. A., and Johnsen, C. 1981. "The Political Economy of Benefits and Costs: A Neoclassical Approach to Distributive Politics." *Journal of Political Economy* 89:642–664.

Wilson, J. Q. 1975. "The Politics of Regulation." In James W. McKie ed., *Social Responsibility and the Business Predicament*. Washington, D.C.: Brookings Institution.

Wilson, J. Q., ed. 1980. *The Politics of Regulation*. New York: Basic Books.

4

The Regulatory Surge of the 1970s in Historical Perspective

Elizabeth Sanders

> Market economy was a threat to the human and natural components of the social fabric ... what else could one expect than an urge on the part of a great variety of people to press for some sort of protection?
> Karl Polanyi, *The Great Transformation*, p. 150

Economic regulation, as Polanyi reminds us, is inevitable in human society. Far from being a natural development, free markets require consistent exertion by government to establish and maintain, and social groups of great diversity fight to harness the power of the state in order to protect themselves from the slings and arrows of outrageous markets. To understand the mode of development of the market-shaping institutions of the democratic state requires analysis of group alignments over time, and attention to the fundamental economic processes that generate those group interests.

The international flow of technology and trade, and the similarity of social groupings and electoral systems produce broad similarities in the regulatory functions of modern industrial democracies: all have welfare programs, agricultural price supports, labor laws, environmental protection units, and so on. But differences among nations are far more interesting than similarities, and the idiosyncrasies of American economic regulation cry out for explanation. Among the more remarkable features of American regulation are the climate of antagonism that prevails between business and regulators, the dual (federal/state) regulatory structure of banking and labor law, the subjection of fuel commodities to price controls, the contemporary deregulation of airlines and (to a lesser extent) trucking and railroads, the use of "independent" commissions, and an antitrust policy grounded in a unique hostility to large economic enterprise. In addition, there is the intriguing feature of periodicity: national regulatory authority in the twentieth century is largely the result of three legislative surges during the progressive era (1909–1916), the New Deal (1933–1940), and the 1970s (especially 1973–1980).

Efforts by political scientists and economists to account for the success of particular regulatory initiatives have relied on interest group,[1] ideological,[2] and "climate of the times"[3] explanations. Such analyses rely on the demonstration of discrete relationships (e.g., between "liberalism" and support for stronger environmental regulation) at a particular time. Not rooted in earlier sequences of events or connected to other economic policy initiatives, these studies offer isolated pieces of a jigsaw puzzle with little indication of a larger picture. This chapter represents an attempt to sketch that larger design, to plumb the deep structure of the American regulatory state, and to account for its uneven growth and comparative eccentricity. It is a fragment of a larger study of the development of the American regulatory state from the late nineteenth century through 1980.

The crux of my argument is that the fundamental basis of American politics has been the conflicting political imperatives of the earliest and latest (or least) industrialized regions of the country—regions that, adapting the terminology of Immanuel Wallerstein to intranational use, may be dubbed "core" and "periphery."[4] Both the periodicity and the peculiar contours of the American regulatory state are results of this conflict, whose critical role rests on (1) the original establishment, in a nation of vast geographic range, of two fundamentally different economies—the one mercantile, and then industrial; the other, slave, plantation, and agrarian—and (2) the extreme localism of American political representation, which in turn is a result of the divergence of economic interests and the early establishment of manhood suffrage in the United States. In this context local economic interests take precedence over national party doctrine. However, local interests must necessarily aggregate into national coalitions in order to contest effectively for national power. In this aggregation the two major political parties have tended to represent, at their centers (or in their "heads") the two polar regions of the country. But they are also compelled to court other regional or class-based interests in order to build national majorities. Thus the principal political agenda at any given time reflects the imperatives of one of the regional poles—imperatives determined by what is being produced in the regional economy, its level of technological advancement, and its competitive position in the national and international economy; a secondary agenda represents payoffs to extra-regional groups that are necessary to build a majority. The periodic surges of legislative activity are the consequence of the occupation of the institutions of the state by a regionally centered coalition formerly excluded from power, or a drastic change in the competitive position of the existing dominant regional interest.

For the nineteenth century and the first four or five decades of the twentieth, value added in manufacturing is the single most useful measure for differentiating between core and periphery regions at the micro (county) level. The best specification of economically interrelated regions is the "trading area" (urban center plus associated hinterland) concept that has been employed by the government in various statistical studies (including the design of the Federal Reserve System) and, in recent times, the basic unit of the Rand Commercial Atlas. The trading area boundaries used in this study coincide with those used by Bensel (1984).[5] Value-added data have been assembled by trade area from county lists in the Census of Manufacturing. (This was done by the author for the progressive era and New Deal, and by a computer run of data obtained from the Rand McNally Company for the 1970s.) The result for the progressive era can be seen in figure 4.1.

The mapping of per capita manufacturing data delineates the early industrial regions of the Northeast and Great Lakes, and their mirror images in the nonindustrial South–Plains–West. The hierarchy of industrial cities and the contours of the manufacturing belt were well defined as early as 1840.[6] There was little movement of the boundary between 1910 and 1930, except for further industrialization in Chicago and San Francisco, which elevated these two trade areas to "core" status. From the Civil War (if not earlier) until World War II the U.S. economy was marked by a stark geographic specialization between industrial metropole and extraction-based periphery. Until the late 1920s the two major parties spoke for the fundamental interests of these two poles: the Republican party, for northern capital; the Democratic party, for the southern farmer. Their political interests were diametrically opposed. The Democratic party favored free trade, soft money, punitive regulation of railroads and "trusts," decentralized and publicly controlled banking, legislative dominance (through specific, almost self-enforcing legislation) of public policy, and state power to pursue the party's "antimonopoly" agenda when the federal government refused; the Republican party leadership pursued protection, hard money, government tolerance for trusts and anticompetitive "self-regulation" of railroads and corporations, hefty subsidies and protected monopolies for the shipping industry, a centralized, big-banker controlled national bank, expanded executive and judicial power, and clear national dominance in the federal system.

Since neither pole enjoyed a majority of congressional seats, both were compelled to make outside alliances that modified the policy agenda. The principal Republican stratagem was to add products to the tariff list. A tariff on wool, whose production was less and less viable in the face of foreign competition, and on some minerals secured the allegiance of the West (fruits and nuts were added for the Pacific states). The agrarian Democrats forged their critical alliance with northern labor—an effort

Figure 4.1 Regional industrialization patterns in the early twentieth century. Sources: For trade area boundaries, Federal Reserve Bank, Eighth Annual Report of the Board of Governors, 1921 (Washington, D.C., 1922, pp. 693–699); for the outline map, Bensel (1984, p. 432); for value added in manufacturing, 1919 Census of Manufactures. Data from state-county tables were aggregated into trade areas and then divided by trade area population to get value added per capita figures.

begun by the Southern Farmers Alliance and later doggedly pursued by William Jennings Bryan and his periphery followers—by becoming the earliest and most loyal legislative promoters of trade union organizational rights. This strategy was relatively costless to the nonindustrial periphery, while causing serious difficulties for its principal antagonist, northern capital. As a result of these intraparty, interprogram trades, the leadership of both the core Republican and periphery Democratic parties could usually count on support from the allied block for their principal policy agendas. Regional and party breakdowns are shown in table 4.1.

Regulation in the Progressive Era: The Periphery Agenda

The southern-led coalition came to power in 1913 (though it dominated the House in 1911 and, in alliance with dissident periphery Republicans, in

Table 4.1 Region and party in the House of Representatives, 1913–1980

	Democrat	Republican	Total House seats
1913			
Core	90	54	150
Diverse	41	35	82
Periphery	160	42	203
1935			
Core	132	77	214
Diverse	38	7	45
Periphery	153	18	176
1975			
Core	127	71	198
Diverse	41	22	63
Periphery	125	49	174
1980			
Core	123	75	198
Diverse	41	22	63
Periphery	112	62	174
Periphery as percent of:			
1913	55.0	32.1	46.7
1935	47.4	17.6	40.5
1975	42.7	34.5	40.0
1980	40.6	39.0	40.0

Note: "Core" industrial regions are trading areas with per capita value added in manufacturing of $300 or more, according to the 1919 or 1929 Census of Manufacturing; "diverse" trade areas had per capita value added of $200–299; "periphery" trade areas, less than $200. 1973–80 regional designations follow the lines established in the 1930s—that is, a trade area is labeled "core" if its 1973 boundaries enclosed an area of $300 or more per capita value-added in 1935, and so on. Minor party votes are not broken down separately.

1910). The coalition's dominance was made possible by a breech in Republican ranks that was soon healed, but it resulted nevertheless in a momentous expansion of the regulatory state. The ICC was given unquestioned authority to suspend and fix maximum railroad rates and outlaw long-short haul differentials, and oil pipelines and telephone and telegraph lines were brought into its jurisdiction; a decentralized, publicly controlled Federal Reserve System was created; the Clayton and Federal Trade Commission acts were passed; shipping regulation was begun, the first income tax was passed (and made distinctly more progressive in 1916), farm credit and the volume of circulating currency were much expanded (through the Federal Reserve banks and the Federal Farm Loan and Warehouse Acts); the Underwood Tariff slashed duties to the lowest levels in more than half a century; and, as a payoff to northern labor allies, a child labor act, railroad eight-hour day and anti-injunction legislation were passed. Table 4.2 displays the regional and partisan bases of support for major progressive era regulatory initiatives. For the sake of brevity only House votes are tabled, although the similar Senate patterns are sometimes appended in the text or in footnotes. House districts have been mapped into trading areas according to where their population majorities lie.[7] Democratic party unity was almost complete on this progressive era legislation, as a result of interregional trades sustained by a strong party caucus organization. In the Republican party, however, periphery dissidents sometimes broke away to join the Democrats, as on Clayton Act passage, for example.

The legislative histories of these bills (including votes on earlier attempts to enact similar legislation) clearly demonstrate, as do the roll call patterns, the agrarian parentage of the early U.S. regulatory state.[8] The principal thrust of the periphery-sponsored expansion was to control the predations of corporations headquartered in the manufacturing belt, even to the extent of dismembering trusts or having government take over some of their functions. If American antitrust law is more punitive, specific, and decentralizing than that of other western industrial nations, and its banking system more obstinately localized, it is because of the early regional concentration of industry and banking and the periphery farmer's success in using his political clout to compensate for his marketplace vulnerability.

The New Deal Transition

Some of the agrarian momentum lasted into the New Deal (see table 4.3). The Reciprocal Trade Agreements Act, for example, was a weak, executive-centered version of progressive era Democratic tariff policy

Table 4.2 Support patterns for progressive era regulatory legislation (percent)

Seats held by:	Yea–nay	Yeas cast by:
1910 Mann-Elkins (Railroad Regulation) Act-Strike Commerce Court[a]		
157–176		
D 145– 1		
R 12–175		
33.5 Core	14.8–85.2	15.9
19.9 Diverse	32.4–67.6	14.0
46.5 Periphery	70.5–29.5	70.0
Underwood Tariff/Income Tax 1913 (pass)		
281–139		
D 274– 5		
R 4–125		
34.5 Core	60.0–40.0	31.0
18.9 Diverse	54.4–45.6	15.3
46.7 Periphery	77.0–23.0	53.7
Federal Reserve Act 1913 (pass)		
287–85		
D 248– 3		
R 30–80		
34.5 Core	66.9–33.1	27.5
18.9 Diverse	73.1–26.9	19.9
46.7 Periphery	85.8–14.2	52.6
1914 Clayton Antitrust (and Anti-Injunction) Act (pass)		
277–54		
D 218– 1		
*R 47–52		
34.5 Core	71.8–28.2	28.5
18.9 Diverse	83.3–16.7	21.7
46.7 Periphery	92.6– 7.4	49.8
Railroad Eight-Hour Act 1916 (pass)		
239–56		
D 167– 3		
*R 69–53		
34.5 Core	60.0–40.0	27.6
18.6 Diverse	84.1–15.9	15.5
46.9 Periphery	96.5– 3.5	56.9
1916 Create a shipping board to regulate, build, and operate ships		
209–161		
D 196– 3		
R 9–155		
34.5 Core	30.0–70.0	17.2
18.6 Diverse	36.8–63.2	12.0
46.9 Periphery	81.3–18.7	70.8

Note: The * indicates opposing core-periphery majorities within the party.
a. The Commerce Court was a device of Taft and Republican Conservatives to override ICC decisions—and was thus opposed by those who advocated strong railroad regulation. Because the final Mann-Elkins bill contained the new Court, most periphery representatives opposed it on passage. They succeeded in abolishing the Court in 1913.

Table 4.3 Party and regional support for major New Deal regulatory legislation (percent)

Seats held by:	Yea–nay	Yeas cast by:
1933 Agricultural Adjustment Act (pass)		
315–98		
D 272–24		
*R 39–73		
48.7 Core	61.9–38.1	39.7
10.3 Diverse	90.2– 9.8	11.7
40.9 Periphery	90.0–10.0	48.6
1933 National Industrial Recovery Act (pass)		
325–76		
D 267–25		
*R 54–50		
48.7 Core	76.2–23.8	45.2
10.3 Diverse	97.6– 2.4	12.6
40.9 Periphery	82.5–17.5	42.1
1934 Securities Exchange Act—recommit, weaken		
83–278		
D 8–254		
*R 75– 20		
48.7 Core	41.6–58.4	86.7
10.3 Diverse	11.8–88.2	4.8
40.9 Periphery	4.5–95.5	8.4
1934 Reciprocal Trade Agreements Act (pass)		
274–111		
D 269– 11		
R 2– 99		
48.7 Core	55.1–44.9	37.2
10.3 Diverse	74.4–25.6	11.7
40.9 Periphery	89.2–10.8	51.1
Public Utility Holding Company—"Death Sentence" provision		
155–209		
*D 139–123		
R 6– 86		
49.2 Core	27.6–85.7	31.0
10.3 Diverse	50.0–50.0	12.3
40.5 Periphery	57.9–42.1	56.8
1936 Merchant Marine Act (pass)		
194–186		
*D 139–136		
*R 55– 40		
49.2 Core	66.0–34.0	63.9
10.3 Diverse	51.3–48.7	10.3
40.5 Periphery	32.7–67.4	25.8

Table 4.3 (continued)

Seats held by:	Yea–nay	Yeas cast by:
1938 Fair Labor Standards (Minimum Wage) Act (pass)		
314–97		
D 256–55		
*R 46–42		
49.2 Core	86.7–13.3	56.1
10.3 Diverse	90.7– 9.3	12.4
40.5 Periphery	60.0–40.0	31.5
1940 Transportation Act—keep water carrier rates as low as possible		
112–212		
D 83– 95		
R 27–114		
49.2 Core	21.1–78.9	27.7
10.3 Diverse	50.0–50.0	17.0
40.5 Periphery	44.6–55.4	55.4

Note: The * indicates opposing core-periphery majorities within the party.

(which had not survived the Republican restoration). While the strong competitive position of U.S. industry dulled the core's protectionist sentiment, the Republican party reflected hardly any change, and Cordell Hull and the congressional southern Democrats labored long and hard to sell free trade to Roosevelt's "Brains Trust" who saw it as inimical to a planned economy.

The agrarian impulse to regulate and redistribute industrially created wealth could still be seen in utility regulation (the Holding Company Act of 1935), the Revenue Act of 1935, and in 1933–34 securities regulation. Southern and midwestern representatives had long attempted to outlaw or to constrain severely futures contracts (cotton contracts were brought under federal regulation in 1914 in a wave of hostility toward the New York Cotton Exchange); the Pujo hearings of 1912, chaired by a Louisiana representative, had generated a strong agrarian demand for regulation of stock trading. However, President Wilson opposed the plan in the recession year of 1914, and the idea did not come to fruition until 1933–34, when the Securities Act was passed and the SEC established. In both instances, the legislation drew substantially stronger backing in the periphery than in the core factions of both parties.[9] Agrarian regions backed a much harsher policy toward the scandal-ridden utility trusts than did the urban-industrial areas where their stockholders and managers were concentrated.[10] In addition attempts to make the income tax more progressive were still popular in the periphery (which paid less than a third of the total collected) and unpopular in the manufacturing belt, for both parties.[11]

On the whole, however, the periphery did not dominate the national policy agenda in the 1930s as it had in the progressive era. Particularly after the elections of 1934, periphery influence in the majority party was on the wane. The spread of manufacturing in the Midwest and Pacific regions and the surge of northern working and middle-class voters into the Democratic party vastly expanded core industrial influence and the agrarian percentage of Democratic House membership dropped to under 50 percent in 1935. Within the executive branch the northern labor-intelligentsia faction was in command, and it transformed the policy agenda of the Democratic party. In labor policy the northern faction was no longer content to establish organizational rights, but pressed for a national floor under wages and an end to child labor. Periphery Democrats, who had loyally backed the National Labor Relations Act of 1935, were far less loyal in 1938 (as can be seen in table 4.3). Manufacturing belt Republicans, on the other hand, were not adverse to setting a minimum national wage that might discourage the relocation of industry (particularly textiles) to the periphery regions. This pattern of regional interest (resisting labor advances on their own turf but supporting legislation that raised labor costs in other regions) could also be seen in Republican support for outlawing child labor in the 1930s (as well as the earlier, unsuccessful attempt of 1916) and in core Republican support for a new national labor law in the 1970s.[12]

The intraparty harmony that characterized Democratic ascendancy in the seventy-third Congress was severely strained by the close of the seventy-sixth (1940). Some tension of course had always been present. Periphery Democrats went along with the NIRA, as part of a trade (the AAA was passed first) and because the industrial recovery bill was packaged together with an unprecedented $3 billion dollar public works authorization attractive to periphery representatives of both parties. In the Senate, however, southern, plains, and western members attempted to scuttle the bill's antitrust immunity for price fixing. They also resisted the anticompetitive, cartelizing, and subsidizing legislation for transportation industries that succeeded the NIRA (see table 4.3 for two of the rare House roll call votes on New Deal transportation policy).[13] Regionally based differences on both transportation and antitrust policy stemmed from the northern Democratic wing's inheritance of several core political imperatives: to protect mature industries from cutthroat competition, to shore up the railroads that were vital to the region's economy, and to maintain and expand the region's depressed shipping industry. Although its labor constituency often put it into direct conflict with the party of northern capital, many regionally based interests were common to the two parties in the manufacturing belt.

Without any significant industrial base to protect, periphery representatives were much less fearful of cutthroat competition. They welcomed the challenges presented to the railroads by barge and newly developed truck transportation and resisted having these competitors brought under the jurisdiction of the presumably railroad-dominated ICC. Periphery representatives had always been inclined to break coastal shipping monopolies and allow shipping lines to purchase foreign-built ships, and opposition to maritime subsidies was a mainstay of Democratic policy for over a century. In the 1930s the newly dominant core wing of the party adopted the regional transportation policy of the core Republicans. Whereas the progressive era Democrats had instituted rate-limiting, open-conference, and antidiscriminatory regulation, the core Democrats engineered minimum rate setting and subsidies. The periphery exacted its price for this legislation (e.g., in agricultural exemptions and ICC mandates to move against regionally biased freight rates), but the major regulatory initiatives of the New Deal comprised a program of core, not periphery, design.[14]

Even in agricultural policy, the periphery was compelled to choose between policy alternatives offered by industrialist George Peek and social scientists in the Agriculture Department.[15] Had they enjoyed sufficient political power to implement their own preferred agriculture policy, the agrarian regions would not likely have settled for a bureaucracy-intensive, production-controlling program that made farmers completely dependent on the state. Farm state congressmen promoted, in the late 1920s and into the 1930s, a radically different "export debenture" plan that would have entailed considerably less federal intervention in the domestic farm economy, a much smaller bureaucracy, and a greater commitment to world trade.[16] In general, the periphery program for dealing with the economic crisis of the 1930s, a program indicated by the policy debates and voting patterns on New Deal legislation, would have looked very different from the welfare/regulatory state that is the New Deal legacy. It would have relied on inflation, progressive taxation, check-in-the-mail redistribution (through locally managed public works and direct federal payments of the sort embodied in the Veterans Bonus, Townsend and Huey Long proposals), export promotion, antitrust enforcement, and a labor policy that limited hours and protected organizational rights but set no national minimum wage.[17] What effect this program would have had on the Depression is impossible to say; at any rate it had little political support outside the periphery.

It was the program of a region more or less resigned to the status of a foodstuff and natural resource producer. In the 1940s, however, large sections of the periphery experienced a momentous change in the perception of their role in the domestic and international economy. The development of new modes of transportation (and the lowering of transportation costs), air conditioning, the effects of the war, the obvious advantage of lower labor, land and energy costs, the end of basing-point pricing and discriminatory railroad rates, and the boll weevil all played a part in this shift. It was felt first in the Midwest, and in border and outer-South states where economic development interests were not thwarted (as they were in most of the Deep South) by obsession with the race question and exclusion from the electorate of many of the potential beneficiaries of industrialization.

The data in table 4.4 chronicle the transformation of the American periphery and the concomitant slowing of industrial expansion in the original manufacturing belt. the periphery's percentage of U.S. manufacturing jobs grew from 22 percent in 1940 to 33 percent in 1975.[18] More impressively, the growth of new capital expenditures in manufacturing greatly exceeded the growth rate in the original manufacturing belt, and bank deposits expanded from 15 percent of the U.S. total to 34 percent (table 4.4). The old populist impulse to regulate and redistribute (by breaking up some of the large industrial and financial agglomerations, taxing higher incomes, and lowering the price of money and transportation services and thus reversing the regional flow of wealth) had flourished in an agrarian hinterland locked into an almost colonial relationship to the manufacturing belt. It would be surprising if populism continued to thrive in the new era of industrial transformation. And, indeed, it did not.

Regulation in the 1970s: The Reversal of Core and Periphery Roles

The industrialization of the periphery (using that term to describe contemporary trade areas that had less than $200 per capita value added in manufacturing in 1929) can be seen in table 4.5. The very highest value-added levels (over $3,700 per capita in 1977 dollars) are limited to Indianapolis and the Great Lakes portion of the old manufacturing belt, but the Nashville, Des Moines, and Charlotte trade areas now rank alongside Boston, Pittsburgh, and New York as industrial centers. Of course value added is a very crude indicator of economic system type in the modern period. It is not gross industrial production but white-collar service employment (particularly in finance, research, and development) and the

Table 4.4 The geographic realignment of industry and banking 1935–1976

	Expenditures on new plant and equipment (millions of $)				Growth rate of new capital expenditures (percent)		
	1947	1961	1968	1976	1947–61	1961–68	1968–76
Core[a] (14 states)	3,342 (55.7)	4,692 (50.6)	9,792 (47.5)	15,739 (38.6)	40.4	108.7	60.7
Periphery (28 states)	1,543 (25.7)[b]	2,897 (31.3)	6,935 (33.6)	18,042 (44.3)	87.8[b]	139.4	160.2
U.S. total	6,004 (100.0)	9,264 (100.0)	20,613 (100.0)	40,770 (100.0)	54.3	122.5	97.8

	Commercial bank deposits (millions of $)				Growth rate of bank deposits (percent)		
	1935	1947	1961	1968	1975	1935–47	1947–61	1961–68	1968–75
Core	37,081 (72.2)	97,103 (60.0)	166,208 (57.9)	220,708 (51.0)	360,199 (46.5)	161.9	71.2	32.8	63.2
Periphery	7,567 (14.7)	38,144 (23.6)	71,001 (24.7)	128,586 (32.5)	263,301 (34.0)	404.1	86.1	81.1	104.8
U.S. total	51,338 (100.0)	161,850 (100.0)	287,155 (100.0)	432,659 (100.0)	775,209 (100.0)	215.3	77.4	50.6	79.2

Source: U.S. Department of Commerce, Bureau of the Census, *Statistical Abstract*, various years.
Note: Percent of U.S. total appears in parentheses.
a. Core-periphery classifications are determined by level of industrialization in 1929 (core ≥$300 per capita value added in manufacturing; periphery <$200 per capita).
b. Hawaii excluded.

Table 4.5 Per capital value added in manufacturing by trading area, 1977

<$1,000	$1,000–2,000	$2,001–2,500	$2,501–3,000	$3,001–4,712
Honolulu	Charleston/Huntington	Atlanta/Chattanooga	Boston/Providence	Buffalo/Rochester
Miami	Denver	Birmingham	Charlotte/Greensborough/Columbia	Chicago
San Antonio	El Paso	Dallas/Ft. Worth	Columbus	Cincinnati/Dayton
Tampa/St. Petersburg	Jacksonville	Kansas City	Des Moines/Sioux City	Cleveland
	Minneapolis/St. Paul	Knoxville	Louisville/Evansville	Detroit/Toledo
	Mobile	Little Rock	Nashville	Houston
	Oklahoma City	Los Angeles	New Orleans	Indianapolis
	Omaha	Memphis	New York	Milwaukee
	Phoenix	Portland	Philadelphia	
	Salt Lake City	San Francisco/Oakland	Pittsburgh	
	Shreveport	Seattle	Richmond/Norfolk	
	Spokane	Tulsa	St. Louis	
	Washington/Baltimore		Wichita	

Source: Data supplied by Rand McNally.

concentration of financial and corporate headquarters that make San Francisco, Chicago, Boston, and New York "core" cities today.[19] Nevertheless, the data in tables 4.4 and 4.5 are fraught with political significance for the 1970s.

The interests in regulation perceived by the newly industrializing regions in the 1970s differed fundamentally from those perceived by the older industrial belt (and from the interests of the periphery in 1909–1940). The fuel shortages and price shocks of the early 1970s accelerated the decline of manufacturing in the old industrial cities but had a much less negative impact on the newly industrializing areas.[20] The latter found themselves in a position analogous to that of the manufacturing belt in the 1880s, and their representatives began to behave like nineteenth-century northeastern congressmen: that is, they behaved more like spokesmen for regions experiencing an accelerated capital accumulation process. They opposed antitrust initiatives, labor advances, inflation, redistribution through the tax code, increased government expenditures, and expanded regulation of business investment decisions; became more nationalistic (as could be seen in defense policy positions), and advocated central bank autonomy. If Phil Gramm was not the reincarnation of Nelson Aldrich, the two would at least have been ideologically compatible. Aldrich and Wright Patman most assuredly would not have been.

The Democratic party in the 1970s was again the party of regulation and redistribution, but its program was designed by the northern urban wing and was largely opposed by the periphery faction. The deindustrializing regions perceived in regulatory law a means of slowing economic decline by raising the costs of capitalization in the periphery, insulating the national economy from international economic forces, undoing the "artificial" decentralization of the economy promoted by the periphery, and divesting the corporate powerhouses that had emerged out of periphery industries. Because labor is much less mobile and adaptive than capital, this regulatory program was a *Democratic* policy agenda. However, core Republican congressmen (whose numbers were dwindling)[21] had their own political reasons for wishing to stem the flow of industry and population to the South and West, and their regulatory positions sometimes differed markedly from those of periphery Republicans. Tables 4.6 through 4.14 display party and regional voting patterns on major regulatory initiatives of the ninety-third through ninety-sixth Congresses.[22]

In order to conserve space (given the very large number of roll calls on regulatory issues in the 1970s), votes on key amendments have usually been substituted for final passage, and issues subject to repeated roll calls during these four congresses are only displayed once. The resulting tables are by no means a biased selection, but very representative of both the range of significant regulatory issues in the 1970s and the partisan and regional support patterns for these policies. Included are votes on the landmark energy, environmental, antitrust, transportation, and banking legislation of the period, as well as the unsuccessful consumer protection, labor, and planning initiatives that were part of the core Democratic agenda.

The energy crisis of the early 1970s was the catalyst for a multifaceted expansion of the regulatory state. Already suffering from a regulation-induced shortage of natural gas, the national and international competitive position of the old manufacturing belt was further undermined by the OPEC oil price increases. In the ensuing recession core representatives utilized—as had progressive era agrarians—their political power to redress market weakness.

The large, integrated petroleum companies were cast by the northern labor-intelligentsia wing of the Democratic party in the hated position of the railroads in the late nineteenth and early twentieth centuries. The shoe of exploitation was now, it seemed, on the other foot. While price increases benefited periphery state treasuries and relatively abundant energy supplies boosted manufacturing activity in those regions, manufacturing belt households and businesses felt dependent and abused. The petroleum industry in the 1970s was, like the railroads earlier, subjected to price controls and central state allocation, and (also like the railroads) its actions sparked a broad antitrust movement. The oil industry was also subjected to an unprecedented "windfall profits" tax, as well as loss of favored tax treatment in the depletion allowance.[23] By the end of the 1970s attitudes toward energy policy alternatives—whether to allow market prices to ration (and increase) supplies and encourage conservation, or to accomplish those goals through government planning—helped to define the realignment of political philosophies and parties that brought Ronald Reagan into the White House.

Periphery representatives provided the bulk of votes in opposition to the Democratic Control and Planning alternative (see table 4.6). Allied with a majority of core and diverse area Republicans, they fought to limit the expansion of controls and taxes and defeated core efforts to divest oil companies of their vertical and horizontal holdings and to create a federal authority to purchase and explore for oil.[24] Oil and gas production were significant in only a handful of states, and citizens of periphery states were, like core residents, affected by fuel price increases in the 1970s. However, the direct impact of natural gas and heating oil increases was less severe in

Table 4.6 Regulation in the 1970s: energy (percent)

Seats held by:	Yea–nay	Yeas cast by:
Strike presidential power to allocate oil and oil products (1974 NEEA)		
199–211		
D 62–168		
R 137– 43		
45.5 Core	35.9–64.1	32.7
14.5 Diverse	50.0–50.0	15.6
40.0 Periphery	61.7–38.3	51.8
Delete new oil price controls (from 1975 EPCA)		
215–199		
*D 93–184		
R 122– 15		
45.5 Core	34.9–65.1	31.6
14.5 Diverse	55.2–44.8	14.9
40.0 Periphery	71.4–28.6	53.5
Deregulate new natural gas (Brown amendment to NEA 1977)		
199–227		
D 72–210		
R 127– 17		
45.5 Core	32.3–67.7	31.2
14.5 Diverse	47.6–52.4	15.1
40.0 Periphery	62.6–37.4	53.8
1979 windfall profits tax on oil: lower rates and shorter duration		
236–183		
*D 90–173		
R 146– 10		
45.5 Core	37.6–62.4	30.1
14.5 Diverse	45.0–55.0	11.4
40.0 Periphery	81.2–18.8	58.5

Note: The * indicates opposing core-periphery majorities within the party.

the periphery than in the manufacturing belt, and the principle of federal control (which would probably mean urban consumer control) over the price and production of natural resources posed a long-term threat to producers of agricultural and other mineral commodities. The original Carter administration energy program, most of which passed the House in 1977 as the National Energy Act, had its origins in price control and coal conversion proposals designed by core Democratic congressmen in the two preceding Congresses and was implicitly a regional program that would effect a degree of income redistribution between periphery and core.[25]

Similar regional implications dogged environmental policy as it moved through the decade. The original Clean Air Act of 1970 evoked no noticeably regional opposition and passed almost unanimously. Subsequent court decisions, however, interpreted the law as a federal mandate to prevent any significant deterioration (PSD) of air quality in areas where there was currently little pollution. This mandate threatened to slow industrial development in the periphery and became a major source of contention in environmental policy. Another regional issue concerned whether new utility and industrial power plants could meet EPA air quality standards by simply burning low sulfur coal, or whether they should be compelled to install expensive scrubbing equipment. A scrubber requirement also had the advantage (to the core) of benefiting the northeastern-midwestern coal industry over western rivals and making plant expansion in the periphery more expensive.[26]

In the mid-1970s it became clear (1) that the distressed industries of the manufacturing belt could not meet the air quality deadlines in the 1970 act, (2) that the Republican administration might be lax in its enforcement of the court-mandated PSD policy, and (3) that new plants in the periphery might meet air quality standards without scrubbers. As a result amendments to the Clean Air Act became inevitable. Core representatives were, for the most part, successful in delaying implementation of auto emissions and other pollution standards and in specifying a PSD policy in the statute itself. Unable to secure statutory language requiring scrubbers, House Commerce Committee staff were able to insert in the legislative history an interpretation compelling the installation of the technological devices.[27] Periphery representatives failed in their attempts to scuttle PSD (see table 4.7) but were able to insert, in 1977, a limited local waiver authority for clean areas.[28] The periphery's preference for economic development over a cleaner (and safer) living and working environment can also be seen in voting patterns on strip-mining regulation and attempts to restrict nuclear powerplant licenses.[29]

Both the preference for privately controlled, relatively unrestricted development and the long-standing opposition to government planning that has marked the American hinterland can be seen in the periphery's defeat of the rule bringing a land-use planning bill to the floor and in persistent opposition to federal wage and price controls (see table 4.8). When at the end of the decade core representatives attempted to entice the states into planning energy conservation programs "to promote national energy objectives," even the lure of federal grant monies could not overcome the periphery's aversion to planning, and the bill was soundly defeated.[30]

Ironically, core advocacy of national planning did not go hand in hand with support for bureaucratic autonomy (or deference to agency expertise). Core Democrats were now distrustful of the regulatory bureaucracy

Table 4.7 Regulation in the 1970s: environment (percent)

Seats held by:	Yea–nay	Yeas cast by:
1976 clean air amendments: delete PSD section (Chappell amendment)		
156–199		
*D 82–161		
*R 74– 38		
45.5 Core	20.9–79.1	21.1
14.5 Diverse	38.5–61.5	12.8
40.0 Periphery	71.0–29.0	66.0
Strip-mining regulation: pass over veto (1975)		
278–143		
D 222– 60		
*R 56– 83		
45.5 Core	80.7–19.3	55.8
14.5 Diverse	76.2–23.8	17.3
40.0 Periphery	45.2–54.8	27.0
Nuclear Regulatory Commission: impose moratorium on new powerplant permits (Markey amendment, 1979)		
135–254		
*D 112–133		
R 23–121		
45.5 Core	50.6–49.4	65.2
14.5 Diverse	36.2–63.8	15.6
40.0 Periphery	16.6–83.4	19.3
Suspend auto emission standards for four years, except in areas of highest pollution (Wyman amendment to NEEA, 1973)		
180–210		
*D 77–139		
R 103– 71		
45.5 Core	31.4–68.6	30.0
14.5 Diverse	43.3–56.7	12.2
40.0 Periphery	62.7–37.3	57.8

Note: The * indicates opposing core-periphery majorities within the party.

crafted in the 1930s because of its malleability in the hands of conservative presidents. As a result manufacturing belt Democrats sponsored legislation designed to limit bureaucratic discretion via statutory specificity (as in the Clean Air Act amendments), to penetrate agency proceedings on behalf of public or consumer interests, and to establish a Consumer Protection Agency with intervenor functions. The failure of the CPA bill was largely due to periphery opposition, as can be seen in table 4.9.

Periphery opposition was also a major factor in the defeat of hospital cost controls and an FTC bill expanding the possibility for class action suits; the same opposition almost defeated the National Consumer Cooperative Bank sponsored by core Democrats to benefit low- and middle-

Table 4.8 Regulation in the 1970s: macro controls and planning (percent)

Seats held by:	Yea–nay	Yeas cast by:
Land-use planning (rule, 1974)		
204–211		
*D 156– 76		
R 48–135		
45.5 Core	64.9–35.1	58.8
14.5 Diverse	46.8–53.2	14.2
40.0 Periphery	32.7–67.3	26.9
Extend life of Council on Wage and Price Stability (1975)		
235–188		
*D 180–103		
*R 55– 85		
45.5 Core	75.0–25.0	62.6
14.5 Diverse	61.3–38.7	16.2
40.0 Periphery	30.3–69.7	21.3

Note: The * indicates opposing core-periphery majorities within the party.

Table 4.9 Regulation in the 1970s: consumer protection (percent)

Seats held by:	Yea–nay	Yeas cast by:
Consumer Protection Agency (1978, pass)		
189–227		
*D 171–102		
R 18–125		
45.5 Core	65.4–34.6	64.0
14.5 Diverse	47.5–52.5	15.3
40.0 Periphery	22.9–77.3	20.6
1977 FTC amendments: delete authority for class action suits based on FTC rulings (Krueger amendment)		
281–125		
*D 148–119		
R 133– 6		
45.5 Core	55.7–44.3	36.3
14.5 Diverse	63.9–36.1	13.9
40.0 Periphery	86.4–13.6	49.8
Create a national consumer cooperative bank (1977, pass)		
199–198		
*D 168– 91		
R 31–107		
45.5 Core	70.2–29.8	62.8
14.5 Diverse	56.7–43.3	17.1
40.0 Periphery	25.2–74.8	20.1

Note: The * indicates opposing core-periphery majorities within the party.

Table 4.10 Regulation in the 1970s: agriculture (percent)

Seats held by:	Yea–nay	Yeas cast by:
1973 agriculture bill: limit payments to $20,000 per person and prohibit lease or sale of cotton allotments (Findley amendment)		
246–163		
*D 123–104		
*R 123– 59		
45.5 Core	85.3–14.7	63.8
14.5 Diverse	69.5–30.5	16.7
40.0 Periphery	28.9–71.1	19.5
Milk support price: maintain present level, allowing only inflation adjustment (Richmond amendment, 1975)		
222–202		
*D 151–136		
*R 71– 66		
45.5 Core	66.7–33.3	58.6
14.5 Diverse	70.5–29.5	19.4
40.0 Periphery	29.2–70.8	22.1

Note: The * indicates opposing core-periphery majorities within the party.

income urban consumers (table 4.9). The urban consumer interest was paramount in limitations imposed by the House on agriculture price supports—limitations strongly opposed in the periphery (table 4.10).

Since the New Deal, urban and hinterland Democrats have logrolled across agriculture and labor policies. The trade involved core Democratic votes for agricultural price supports and reciprocal agrarian backing for minimum wage increases (or, more recently, an expanded food stamp program).[31] However, in the slow-growth climate of the late 1970s, regional competition threatened that reciprocity, as table 4.10 demonstrates. The limits of the farm-labor bargain were also indicated during repeated attempts by periphery representatives to deny food stamps to striking workers.[32] Once the periphery acquired a significant industrial base, legislation that would facilitate unionization there also strained the intraparty logroll (see table 4.11).[33] Even workplace safety became a regionally contested issue as periphery representatives, citing the need to reduce regulatory burdens for their smaller-scale industries, attempted to exempt a large class of businesses from OSHA jurisdiction (table 4.11). The small-business exemption was significantly more popular in the periphery and almost produced opposing regional majorities within the Republican party (45 percent of core Republicans opposed the Findley amendment) as well as in the Democratic Party.[34]

Nowhere is the regional reversal on regulatory policy more striking than in antitrust policy. Core dominance of the Democratic party had yielded

Table 4.11 Regulation in the 1970s: labor (percent)

Seats held by:	Yea–nay	Yeas cast by:
Legalize common site picketing 1975 (pass)		
230–177		
*D 204– 73		
R 26–104		
45.5 Core	74.2–25.8	58.7
14.5 Diverse	71.7–28.3	18.7
40.0 Periphery	31.5–68.5	22.6
1977 minimum wage act: delete indexing (Erlenborn amendment)		
223–193		
*D 97–178		
R 126– 15		
45.5 Core	35.6–64.4	30.0
14.5 Diverse	50.0–50.0	13.9
40.0 Periphery	75.3–24.7	56.1
1977 labor law revision (pass)		
257–163		
D 221– 59		
R 36–104		
45.5 Core	80.5–19.5	58.0
14.5 Diverse	66.7–33.3	16.3
40.0 Periphery	38.4–61.6	25.7
OSHA: prohibit fines for first offenses by small companies (1975 Findley amendment)		
186–231		
*D 85–194		
R 101– 37		
45.5 Core	23.2–76.8	23.7
14.5 Diverse	51.6–48.4	17.2
40.0 Periphery	66.7–33.3	59.1

Note: The * indicates opposing core-periphery majorities within the party.

little new antitrust legislation (beyond the Public Utility and Robinson-Patman Acts) in the 1930s. In 1950 hearings held by Senator Kefauver's Senate Judiciary Committee had produced a bill designed to close a court-opened loophole in the Clayton Act that had permitted a wave of postwar mergers. The Clayton Act amendments of 1950 were the last significant antitrust legislation for over two decades, as an industrializing periphery apparently lost its old inclination to oppose bigness and control corporate investment and pricing decisions. In the recession of the 1970s, as the Northeast and Midwest were stung by corporate flight and oil-gas price increases, the antitrust torch passed, for the first time, to the core industrial regions.

Core Democrats successfully sponsored legislation expanding the budgets and investigatory powers of the FTC and DOJ Antitrust Division,

Table 4.12 Regulation in the 1970s: antitrust (percent)

Seats held by:	Yea–nay	Yeas cast by:
1976 Antitrust Improvements Act: limit aggregation of damages in price-fixing cases (Flowers amendment)		
220–171		
*D 107–153		
R 113– 18		
45.5 Core	40.4–59.6	32.7
14.5 Diverse	53.7–46.3	13.2
40.0 Periphery	74.8–25.2	54.1
1976 Antitrust Civil Process Act (pass)		
254–127		
D 206– 48		
*R 48– 79		
45.5 Core	78.8–21.2	55.5
14.5 Diverse	70.9–29.1	15.4
40.0 Periphery	50.3–49.7	29.1
Deny federal leases to oil companies with competing fuel holdings (Ambro amendment to 1975 EPCA)		
158–254		
*D 148–126		
R 10–128		
45.5 Core	51.6–48.4	62.0
14.5 Diverse	42.6–57.4	16.5
40.0 Periphery	21.1–78.9	21.5

Note: The * indicates opposing core-periphery majorities within the party.

empowering them to monitor the new fuel allocation and energy standard-setting process and encouraging the FTC to issue broad, industrywide rules. The most significant and controversial of the new efforts was the Antitrust Improvements (parens patriae) Act of 1976, which authorized state attorneys general to bring antitrust suits on behalf of state citizens victimized by illegal business practices.[35] In the progressive era agrarian representatives had urged legitimation of such state initiative as a way to bring antitrust suits against corporations and railroads that the federal executive declined to prosecute. In 1976, however, periphery congressmen opposed the parens patriae legislation, and a filibuster led by Alabama and Nebraska senators almost defeated it. Reluctant to unleash state officials to bring antitrust prosecutions (perhaps against their own energy industries), these members attempted to weaken its key damage-estimating provisions, limit the scope of the suits, and require state legislative affirmation in order for the powers to be invoked.

In the House a critical mechanism for estimating aggregate damages (rather than requiring proof of each individual's loss) was weakened on an amendment offered by Representative Flowers of Alabama (table 4.12). A subsequent amendment allowing states to hire out-of-state lawyers on a contingency-fee basis to help in their suits was supported by core representatives but defeated by overwhelming periphery opposition. (Limited aggregation and auxiliary legal assistance provisions were included in the final version, however.)[36] Voting patterns of similar direction occurred on a companion Antitrust Civil Process Act empowering the DOJ to issue Civil Investigative Demands or information subpoenas against suspected antitrust violators, and on a 1977 bill authorizing class action suits based on FTC rulings (table 4.9). A House amendment to deny federal drilling leases to oil companies with competing fuel holdings was defeated on a regionally skewed vote in 1975; in the same year an amendment to ban oil company joint ventures on federal leases was narrowly defeated, with similar voting patterns.

The regional role reversal evident in support patterns for antitrust and other regulatory policy did not appear in trade policy in the 1970s. Instead, there was a dramatic *partisan* reversal. Born as the party of protection and abolition (and the two issues were linked in subtle ways), the Republican party remained committed to high tariffs through the 1930s and opposed the Reciprocal Trade Agreements Act and its periodic extensions with near unanimity. The strong postwar trade position of U.S. industry brought the first solid political evidence of a Republican shift when Eisenhower, throwing his influence behind the RTAA in the early 1950s, became the first Republican president to advocate (relatively) free trade.[37] The 1950s and most of the 1960s were therefore a period of unprecedented partisan consensus on tariff policy, made possible by American hegemony in world trade. That hegemony was clearly threatened by the end of the 1960s. In 1971 the United States experienced its first trade deficit since the late nineteenth century; the subsequent deterioration in the nation's trade balance, accelerated by the 1973 and subsequent oil shocks, is well known.

As the trade threat to labor and industry in the old manufacturing belt intensified,[38] protectionist tendencies among core Democrats increased; at the same time the Republican party's center of gravity was shifting to the West and South[39] where protectionism was less popular as a result of lower industrial factor costs, a much greater export market for midwestern corn, wheat, and soybeans, and—with the revaluing of oil and the end of import quotas—increased free trade advocacy in the domestic petroleum industry.

It is unfortunate that there are so few recorded votes on trade issues in this period, but the vote in table 4.13 (the 1974 Trade Reform Act) probably gives an accurate portrayal of regional and partisan sentiments in the 1970s. Northeastern Democrats at first attempted to defeat the rule bringing the administration bill to the floor in order to offer protectionist

Table 4.13 Regulation in the 1970s: trade (percent)

Seats held by:	Yea–nay	Yeas cast by:
1974 Trade Reform Act (pass)		
272–140		
*D 113–120		
R 159– 20		
45.5 Core	54.0–46.0	37.1
14.5 Diverse	66.7–33.3	14.0
40.0 Periphery	79.2–10.8	48.9

Note: The * indicates opposing core-periphery majorities within the party.

amendments backed by the AFL-CIO; on the final vote core Democrats opposed the granting of presidential trade expansion powers 24 to 75 percent, while periphery Democrats backed it 78 to 29.[40] Five years later an important trade bill backed by the Carter administration was passed overwhelmingly (395 to 7) because it coupled authority for U.S. participation in lowering nontariff trade barriers with a number of protectionist features (e.g., provisions speeding investigation and penalties against "dumping" that injured U.S. manufacturers).[41] The proliferation of protectionist bills in the 1980s will soon provide a larger data set for these comparisons. A cursory inspection of party and regional voting tendencies on automobile domestic content legislation in 1982 suggests that the broad patterns evident earlier still hold but that the size of the protectionist bloc is growing—which raises questions not only about the future American commitment to free trade, and but also the potential of this issue to become, once more, a fundamental line of cleavage between the two major parties.

The votes analyzed in table 4.14 caution us not to overgeneralize regional differences in support for free market versus regulatory solutions. In banking and transportation policy it is the core that advocates deregulation, and the periphery that is reluctant to abandon controls. As in most cases the position of the congressman's district in the national economy takes precedence over abstract principal. Core representatives recognized, in the 1970s, that the large, densely populated cities of the old manufacturing regions did enjoy certain natural advantages. As established commercial and banking centers, their financial institutions were strong enough to undertake a significant national expansion, if only state and federal law (much of which was erected precisely to forestall core banking penetration of the periphery) could be changed to unleash market forces. Interstate banking and deregulation of interest and checking could not only strengthen the larger banks in the Northeast, Chicago, and San Francisco but

Table 4.14 Regulation in the 1970s: decontrol of banking and transportation (percent)

Seats held by:	Yea–nay	Yeas cast by:
Banking deregulation: delete section permitting NOW accounts (Stephens amendment, 1975)		
218–134		
*D 128–112		
R 90– 22		
45.5 Core	41.7–58.3	29.8
14.5 Diverse	51.9–48.1	12.8
40.0 Periphery	88.0–12.0	57.3
1980 railroad deregulation: keep ICC jurisdiction over some rate levels (Eckhardt amendment)		
204–197		
D 148–107		
*R 56– 90		
45.5 Core	45.4–54.6	41.2
14.5 Diverse	27.6–72.4	7.8
40.0 Periphery	65.8–34.2	51.0

Note: The * indicates opposing core-periphery majorities within the party.

benefit their customers as well.[42] In the hinterland, however, old fears persisted that deregulation would lead to the "swallowing up" of its weaker banks and the draining away of local capital to the core. Periphery congressmen therefore resisted banking deregulation in the 1970s (and continue to do so in the 1980s).

Periphery representatives have also resisted the core-sponsored deregulation of transportation. As they did in the nineteenth century, congressmen from the South, Plains, and West argued that, in the absence of regulation and cross-subsidization of fares, the smaller cities and towns would have inadequate transportation services, and isolated agricultural and mineral producers would be at the mercy of the railroads. To these old arguments were added new ones. Southwestern representatives protested that, without regulation, their cities would be compelled to pay exorbitant rail rates to import (from other states) coal that their utilities and industries were forced, by federal law, to burn. Core representatives, on the other hand, saw deregulation as a way to strengthen their region's railroads and to reap the large, densely populated cities' natural advantage in competitive rail, air, and truck transportation services. Periphery representatives had limited success in modifying the rail and trucking deregulation proposals constructed by core congressmen (see table 4.14) but had much less influence on airline deregulation.[43] Having obtained some modest concessions, periphery representatives were compelled to support the deregulation bills on final passage because, without new legislation, the ICC and CAB might effect an even more drastic deregulation on the basis of the old, discretionary statutes.[44]

Conclusions

The intent of this chapter has been to call attention to the long-term forces that have expanded and structured the American regulatory state. It has been argued that the oldest and latest (or non-) industrialized regions have contended to shape both the national marketplace and the position of domestic producers in the international economic arena for at least the last hundred years. This intranational contest of very different economic systems has been particularly important when economic or political upheavals (e.g., depression or the rise to power of a new regionally based coalition) gave rise to surges of legislative creativity in regulatory policy. Party competition is a part of the political superstructure beneath which, or within which, long-term economic interests are played out. In the nineteenth and early twentieth centuries there was a sharp coincidence of party and regional interests as agrarian Democrats and mainly industrial Republicans struggled to control the political economy. When a temporary breech in the Republican party allowed the Democrats to control both Congress and the presidency, the agrarians were able to enact a good part of their regulatory agenda. The New Deal inaugurated a transitional phase in which an extraordinary Democratic majority spanned both core and periphery but was increasingly the vehicle of core interests. As a result a few pieces of early New Deal regulatory legislation reveal a lingering populist heritage, but the anticompetitive and prolabor legislation of the late 1930s reflected the core Democratic agenda. In the 1970s an extraordinary enlargement of the core wing of the party combined with the economic distress of the older industrial cities set off a new round of legislative creativity which both expanded and, in a few significant cases, contracted the regulatory state. Both regulation and deregulation initiatives served the interests of the older industrial areas and were perceived as relatively disadvantageous by representatives of agricultural or new industrial trade areas.

In the contest between core and periphery[45] that continues into the 1980s, the Democratic party has become the voice of the old industrial regions. When the national economy was healthier and the budget pie was still expanding, a degree of logrolling was possible that kept most of the periphery in the Democratic party. As expansion yielded to contraction, regional tensions within the party were exacerbated, and periphery representatives seemed increasingly attracted to the tax, budget and regulatory policy alternatives backed by the Republic party. The desire to promote capital accumulation and industrial growth has ended the periphery's longstanding support for income redistribution through the tax code,[46] as well as its enthusiasm for antitrust policy and many other forms of business regulation. The most distinctly opposed interests in American regulatory politics today are those represented by the political vehicle of labor in the old manufacturing cities and by the party of the middle and upper classes in the newly industrializing regions: in short, by core Democrats and periphery Republicans who opposed each other with near unanimity on most of the regulation votes presented here.

This argument has been, of necessity, a very broad and general one. Its logic hinges on the strong territorial incentives of American national politicians, the inclination of political actors with similar constituencies to form coalitions, and the tendency of dominant, major party factions to represent either core or periphery regions. A closer analysis of local interests on each particular regulatory policy would reveal a much more complicated picture than that which arises from the gross voting affinities displayed in the tables. The regions referred to are broad historical ones. Within the periphery, however, there are states like South Dakota and Montana whose agricultural economies have evolved little in the twentieth century. They have much less in common with Texas and Florida today than they had in 1916 and have maintained much of the old populism (whose banner has faltered so visibly in the industrializing South). There are also areas in the South and West whose economies thrive on visits from core tourists or an influx of retirees; though they remain nonindustrial, they are clearly not agrarian and have many interests in common (environmental protection, social welfare, and so on) with the core.

What is gained, I believe, by attention to broad regional imperatives is an historical understanding of continuity and change in public policy and a way of characterizing programmatic eras that does not lose sight of individual representational linkages. Thus such a political economy approach has the potential to connect the macroscopic evolution of national state power to the micro-level political incentives of elected officials. Other aggregative referents, like party or ideological affinity are, by themselves inadequate for this dual purpose. Because they represent the coalitional dynamics that shape and package policy agendas, they are a part of the description of elections and policy evolution but not part of the explanation of those processes.[47] Interregional economic conflict, on the other hand, has fundamentally shaped the structure and evolution of party and ideological competition and is central to an understanding of present and historical regulatory policy.

Notes

1. See, for example, Stigler (1971), and Schattsneider (1974).
2. See Bernstein and Horn (1981), Kenski (1980), and Mitchell (1979).
3. See Jones (1975).
4. The most complete statement of the significance of regional conflict in American politics is found in Bensel (1984).
5. Ibid.
6. See Pred (1980).
7. Trade area congressional delegations correspond to those in Bensel (1984); his methodology is described on pp. 415–442. Roll call votes are taken from tapes supplied by the Inter-University Consortium for Political and Social Research; descriptions of individual votes are taken from *Congressional Quarterly Almanac* (for the 1970s) and my own reading of the *Congressional Record*.
8. Although party lines (particularly for the Republicans) were weakening in the progressive era, party unity was quite high by contemporary standards. From 1911 to 1916 the Democrats compromised their disagreements in caucus and stood together on the floor. Democrats from core industrial areas loyally went along, for the most part, with periphery-backed initiatives, sometimes in return for direct *quid pro quos* (e.g., as on the Clayton Act where some refused to support antimonopoly legislation unless combined with anti-injection provisions). Although significant numbers (about twenty, on average) of Republicans from periphery and diverse farm areas broke with the northern capital wing of their party and stood with the Democrats on railroad, antitrust, and banking legislation, their numbers were not large enough to have much impact on the overall partisan patterns in the House.
9. In the Senate an attempt by Senator Walcott of Connecticut to weaken the bill by substituting a new title three drew 71, 58, and 19 percent, respectively, of core, diverse, and periphery votes.
10. The Senate pattern on the "death sentence" provision (mandatory dissolution within five years) was similar to that of the House (table 4.3). An attempt to strike the provision, offered in an amendment by Senator Dieterich of Illinois, drew large majorities of core Democrats and Republicans but was opposed by majorities of periphery Democrats and Republicans.
11. The House in this period did not record votes in Committee of the Whole. However, Senate amendments to the 1934–38 Revenue Acts usually found one or both parties divided on regional lines, with core members voting for lower and less progressive rates (e.g., see Senate votes on the La Follette-Couzens amendments, April 5–11, 1934; and final passage of the 1935 Act on August 15. *Congressional Record* 73-2, 6091-6402, and 74-1, 13254).
12. The Child Labor Act of 1916 passed the House 337 to 46; while a majority of periphery Democrats went along, 44 of 46 opponents were periphery (mainly southern) Democrats. Core Republicans voted 88 to 1 in favor. Similarly 10 of 12 Senate opponents were southern Democrats. In 1938, 59 percent of core Republicans backed the Fair Labor Standards Act on House passage (while periphery Republicans opposed it). In 1977, 44 percent of core Republicans supported passage of legislation facilitating unions organizing in the periphery; only 26 percent of diverse area Republicans and 4 percent of periphery Republicans did so (see table 4.11).
13. As can be seen in table 4.3, core Republicans were unhappy with the House version of the NIRA, principally because of two labor and licensing provisions; industrial area Democrats were the bill's strongest supporters. The regional conflicts that developed on New Deal legislation are described in more detail in Sanders (1982).

14. On New Deal transportation policy see, for example, Hawley (1966), Porter (1980), and Lively (1984). Contrasts between progressive era, New Deal, and 1970s transportation policy are discussed in "The Roots of Regulation," a paper I presented at the annual meeting of the American Political Science Association in Denver, Colorado on September 3, 1982.

15. See Kirkendall (1982).

16. The "export debenture" alternative is briefly explained in Benedict (1953).

17. The labor provisions of the National Industrial Recovery Act were rushed to completion in order to forestall Senator Hugo Black's increasingly popular Thirty-Hour Week Bill. The Black bill proposed a method for expanding employment that was apparently perceived as much less threatening to the periphery's infant (or anticipated) industry than minimum wage legislation.

18. U.S. Department of Commerce, Bureau of the Census, *Statistical Abstract* (Washington, D.C.: Government Printing Office, 1942, 1976).

19. The premier "headquarter cities" in 1983 (containing the largest number of headquarters of the nation's top 200 manufacturing concerns, and the top 50 banks, insurance, advertising and transportation firms) were located in the trade areas of New York (173 headquarters), Chicago (43), Los Angeles (30), Philadelphia (22), Cleveland (20), Detroit (19), San Francisco (17), and Minneapolis (16). Of these trade areas only Los Angeles and Minneapolis were not categorized as "core" trade areas on the basis of age of industrialization (i.e., 1929 value added). Of the "periphery" trade areas, only Minneapolis, Dallas, and Houston had six or more headquarters. The location of headquarters is taken from the *Rand Commercial Atlas* (Chicago, Ill.: Rand McNally, 1985), 65.

20. Bensel (1984), pp.259–268.

21. In the ninety-third Congress (1973–74) there were 102 Democrats and 96 Republicans representing core districts in the House. By the ninety-sixth (1979–80), there were 123 Democrats and 75 Republicans. In the diverse trade areas, the number of Republicans declined from 33 to 22. Only in the periphery did the number of Republican seats hold steady over the decade.

22. Because contemporary value-added data cannot distinguish the old manufacturing belt from the newly industrializing regions and because the conflict between old and new (or non-) industrial areas is posited to be a major source of conflict in regulatory policy, trade areas are described as "core" in the 1970s if their boundaries encompassed a core region (i.e., $\geq$ $300 per capita value added in the 1929 Census of manufactures); similarly 1970s "diverse" regions are those with mixed argicultural-industrial economies in 1929 ($200–299 value added per capita), and "periphery," those with nonindustrial ($200) economies in 1929. Trade area boundaries and House district groupings for the 1970s are those used in Bensel (1984).

23. The windfall profits tax is included in table 4.6 because it was in effect a *quid pro quo* for price decontrol at the end of the decade. Voting patterns on repeal of the depletion allowance paralleled those on the other energy votes.

24. In the ninety-fourth Congress, Illinois Representative Mikva proposed, as an amendment to the Energy Policy and Conservation Act (EPCA) of 1975, the creation of a federal oil purchasing authority. His amendment, which split the Democratic party on regional lines, was defeated 150 to 265. Core districts provided 59 percent of the yeas; periphery districts, only 24 percent. Core representatives also moved to expand national control over outer continental shelf reserves, to reduce the bidding power of the large petroleum companies and exert greater control over leases, and to authorize federal exploration (rather than leaving it in the hands of private companies). A 1978 amendment offered in the House by Louisiana Representative John Breaux proposed to limit both leasing reform and federal drilling. It was opposed 28 to 72 percent in the core and supported 70 to 30 percent in the periphery.

25. See, on this subject, Sanders (1981).
26. See Pashigian (1981), Blair, Fesmire, and Kaserman (1976), and Crandall (1983), ch. 8.
27. See Ackerman and Hassler (1981).
28. In 1977 Representative John Breaux of Louisiana sponsored an amendment to allow states to grant 5 percent variances from statutory targets in clean areas. The amendment passed, 237 to 172. Periphery representatives were sympathetic to the efforts of congressmen from automobile industry districts (led by Representative Dingell of Michigan) to relax auto emissions standards. A Dingell-sponsored amendment to that effect passed the House on May 26, backed 98 to 86 in the core (43 percent of core Democrats and 74 percent of Republicans voting "yea") and 128 to 28 in the periphery. In the Senate, where an amendment similar to the Breaux amendment failed, less periphery reciprocity was in evidence. When Senator Metzenbaum of Ohio proposed an amendment allowing the burning of locally produced coal in polluted industrial areas (to alleviate economic hardship), core senators backed, but periphery senators opposed the amendment. It passed 45 to 44.
29. The strip-mining bill was finally passed in 1977 after previously succumbing to Ford vetoes. Similar regionally differentiated voting patterns occurred on roll calls concerning the scope of Alaska land withdrawals, reform of federal leasing procedures, and proposals for an Energy Mobilization Board to speed development of energy supply projects.
30. The December 1, 1980, vote on Representative John Dingell's motion to suspend and pass the energy planning bill was 164 to 192; with core representatives voting in favor 65 to 35 percent, and periphery representatives against, 25 to 75 percent. A September 24, 1980, vote to extend and increase funding for the Council on Wage and Price Stability also demonstrated that despite the growing concern about inflation, the periphery remained antipathetic to planning. Fifty-six percent of periphery representatives voted against the bill; 71 percent of core representatives supported it (the proponents included 38 percent of voting core Republicans).
31. On the Democratic farm-labor trade, see Mayhew (1966), Barton (1974), and Bensel (1984), pp.216–222.
32. In the ninety-fifth Congress, for example, an amendment (offered by Representative Kelly of Florida) to deny food stamps to strikers was opposed 41 to 145 in the core, and supported 105 to 65 in the periphery, with 47 percent of periphery Democrats voting "aye." Ninety-nine percent of core Democrats and 39 percent of core Republicans voted "nay," defeating the amendment 170 to 249.
33. Labor law revision died in the Senate in 1978. The common site picketing bill (which would have enabled a construction union to shut down a construction site during a strike against any one subcontractor) was vetoed by President Ford in 1975 and defeated in the House when revived in 1977. Periphery representatives opposed the bill by an even larger margin (77 percent) in 1977.
34. In the Democratic Party, core-periphery majorities were opposed on a successful 1974 House amendment to create a safety consulting service within OSHA for small business, and on a 1979 amendment (also successful) to limit OSHA inspections at workplaces that had received state inspections in the last six months.
35. The new law also required companies planning large-scale mergers to notify the government in advance. A premerger notification bill, passed separately in the House, resulted in a voting pattern quite similar to the second vote in table 4.12.
36. The parens patriae provisions were notably weakened in a subsequent Supreme court ruling in the case of *Illinois Brick* v. *Illinois*, and core representatives were unable to secure legislation overturning the decision. Congressional Quarterly, Inc., 1978 *Congressional Quarterly Almanac* (Washington, D.C., 1979), pp.194–196.

37. See Watson (1956).

38. The threatened industrial economy included the principal southern textile region in the Carolinas—the earliest southern manufacturing region. Congressmen from this region did not oppose progressive era and New Deal tariff reductions because they remained low cost, internationally competitive manufacturers of the cruder grades of textiles in which they specialized. This was not the case, however, in the late 1960s, as indicated by the textile-protection bargain that was so important to Nixon's "southern strategy" in 1968.

39. This geographic shift moved rapidly in the 1970s. One has only to recall that Tennessee Senator Howard Baker was defeated as Republican minority leader in 1971 because, as a Southerner, he represented the "peculiar" southern fringe of the party (whose majority felt more comfortable with Senator Hugh Scott of Pennsylvania). By 1981 floor leader Baker was almost threatened with removal because he was felt to be too liberal for the southern–plains–western Republican majority. The 1976 convention had been split almost evenly between its core and periphery wings, backing, respectively, Ford and Reagan.

40. Opponents in the periphery clustered in mining, sugar bowl (southern Louisiana), and a few textile and Democratic metropolitan (presumably labor-influenced) districts. In the Senate, New Hampshire Senator McIntyre offered an amendment prohibiting the president from lowering tariffs or quotas on products when imports had exceeded one-third of U.S. consumption during three out of five years. Core Democrats backed and periphery Democrats opposed the amendment by almost equal majorities (54 to 58 percent); 36 percent of core Republicans, but only 15 percent of periphery Republicans voted "aye." The amendment failed, 35 to 49.

41. *Congressional Quarterly Almanac, 1979*, pp.296–299.

42. Core support for deregulation did not mean giving core banks a free hand in their own territories. Core Democrats in the ninety-fourth Congress sponsored legislation to eliminate "redlining" of low-income neighborhoods, and provisions to discourage the practice were included in the deregulation bill analyzed in table 4.14. A move to weaken the redlining sections was overwhelmingly opposed by core Democrats but just as strongly supported by periphery representatives. In the ninety-fifth Congress, Senator Morgan of North Carolina moved to delete a section of a Housing and Community Development bill aimed at encouraging core banks to invest in their "primary service areas," arguing that those provisions established a dangerous tendency to "allocate credit." Periphery senators backed Morgan's amendment 25 to 11, but core Republican and Democratic senators opposed it unanimously. The vote analyzed in table 4.9 (on creation of a publicly financed consumer cooperative bank) also illustrates the distinctions between core attitudes toward controlling banking prerogatives inside and outside the home region.

43. In the Senate a weakening amendment offered to the airline deregulation bill by Senator McGovern of South Dakota drew only twenty-one votes, all from periphery senators.

44. The regional implications of transportation regulation and deregulation are discussed in more detail in the paper cited in note 14. The legislative histories of the three transportation deregulation bills demonstrate strong core support, both in sponsoring bills and voting for them on the floor (as well as resisting periphery amendments to maintain existing cross-subsidies, and controls over rates and abandonments). Core legislative sponsors of major deregulation bills and amendments included Senators Edward Kennedy of Massachusetts (whose staff was actively involved both in expanding regulation of natural gas and deregulating transportation) and Adlai Stevenson III of Illinois, and Representatives James Florio of New Jersey (chairman of the House Commerce Transportation subcommittee), Alan Ertel of Pennsylvania, and Millicent Fenwick of New Jersey. Major pro-regulation amendments were offered by Senators George McGovern of South Dakota, Ernest Hollings of South Carolina, Russell Long of Louisiana, Thad Cochran of Mississippi, and Representative Bob Eckhardt

of Texas. Whether or not deregulation has put the southern, plains, and mountain regions at a disadvantage in the national economy (because they lack the dense rail networks and competitive truck, air, and water services of the manufacturing belt cities), that fear was often voiced during debate on this legislation.

45. Space constraints have prohibited discussion of the role of the "diverse" agricultural-industrial trade areas in regulatory policy. These regions produced, in the progressive era, politicians who, being sensitive to the concerns of both poles, played a very creative role in crafting legislation designed to compromise (but, in a sense, also to supersede) the interests of core and periphery. With the spread of industrialization, their numbers have diminished, and in a general sense their function seems merely to provide a fulcrum, or relatively narrow meeting ground between the polar contestants. However, the in-between position so evident in the tables is only held in the aggregate. Probably because Republicans tend to represent the nonindustrial parts of these trade areas and Democrats, the urban-industrial portions, parties in the "diverse" regions are much more sharply polarized than in core or periphery. Democrats there vote mostly like core Democrats on regulatory issues, and diverse-area Republicans tend to vote with periphery Republicans.

46. An example of the regional reversal on tax policy can be seen in voting on the 1976 Tax Reform Act. The act produced a significant overhaul of the U.S. tax code, ending or restricting a number of foreign and domestic investment tax incentives, limiting business deductions, raising taxes on the highest incomes, and extending tax cuts for lower income taxpayers. The overwhelming majority of core representatives supported the bill, while a large majority of periphery representatives opposed it.

47. For a detailed analysis of the connections between party, ideology, and regional economic and political imperatives, see Bensel (1984, pp.22-31, 368-402). Bensel describes ideological movements or organizations as "protocoalitions" that "bind together sets of public policy stands." They emerge as coalitional alternatives to the dominant party system, regionally structured when the party system is nationalized (as in the New Deal regime) but nonregional when the party system itself is regionally polarized. What is typically defined as "liberalism" in public policy reflects, not a well-developed political philosophy, but the current interests of the working class and intelligentsia of the older industrial cities; as a result the content of these policy stands changes significantly over time. So too does the relationship of ideological groups to major party structures. However, both party and ideological coalitions are shaped by the realities of regional economic competition.

References

Ackerman, B. A., and Hassler W. T. 1981 *Clear Coal, Dirty Air*. New Haven: Yale University Press.

Barton, W. V. 1974.[11] Coalition Building in the U.S. House of Representatives: Agriculture Legislation in 1973." Paper presented at the annual meeting of the American Political Science Association; August.

Benedict, M. R. 1953. *Farm Policies of the United States: 1979-1950*. New York: Twentieth Century Fund, pp.226-227.

Bensel, R. F. 1984. *Sectionalism and American Political Development*. Madison: University of Wisconsin Press.

Bernstein, R. A., and Horn, S. R. 1981. Explaining House Voting on Energy Policy. *Western Political Quarterly 34*:235-245.

Blair, R. D., Fesmire, J. M., and Kaserman, D. L. 1976. "Regional Considerations of the Clean Air Act." *Growth and Change 7.*

Crandall, R. W. 1983. *Controlling Industrial Pollution.* Washington, D. C., Brookings Institution.

Hawley, E. 1966. *The New Deal and the Problem of Monopoly.* Princeton: Princeton University Press.

Jones, C. 1975. *Clean Air.* Pittsburgh: University of Pittsburgh Press.

Kenski, H. C., and Kenski, M. C. 1980. "Partisanship, Ideology and Constituency Differences on Environmental Issues." *Policy Studies Journal 9*: 325–235.

Kirkendall, R. S. 1982. Social Scientists and Farm Politics in the Age of Roosevelt. Ames: Iowa State University Press.

Lively, R. A. 1948. "The South and Freight Rates." *Journal of Southern History 14*: 357–384.

Mayhew, D. R. 1966. *Party Loyalty among Congressmen.* Cambridge: Harvard University Press.

Mitchell, E. J. 1979. "The Basis of Congressional Energy Policy." *Texas Law Review 57.*

Pashigian, P. B. 1981. "Environomental Regulation: Whose Self-Interests are Being Served?" Research Paper. University of Chicago School of Business.

Porter, D. L. 1980. *Congress and the Waning of the New Deal.* Port Washington: Kennikat Press.

Pred, A. R. 1980. *Urban Growth and City Systems in the United States: 1840–60.* Cambridge: Harvard University Press.

Sanders, E. 1981. *The Regulation of Natural Gas: Policy and Politics, 1938–78.* Philadelphia: Temple University Press.

Sanders, E. 1982. "Business, Bureaucracy and the Bourgeoisie: The New Deal Legacy." In A. Stone and E. J. Harpham, eds., *The Political Economy of Public Policy.* Beverly Hills: Sage, pp. 115–141.

Schattsneider, E. 1974. *Politics, Pressures and the Tariff.* New York: Arno Press.

Stigler. G. 1971. "The Theory of Economic Regulation." *Bell Journal of Economics and Management Science 2*: 3–21.

Watson, R. A. 1956. "The Tariff Revolution: A Study of Shifting Party Attitudes." *Journal of Politics 18*: 678–701.

II

ASSESSMENT OF REGULATORY PERFORMANCE

5

General Equilibrium Analysis of Natural Gas Price Regulation

Dale W. Jorgenson and Daniel T. Slesnick

In this chapter we present a new approach to the general equilibrium analysis of economic policy. Our objective is to provide a complete ordering of alternative economic policies. The most desirable economic policy is the policy yielding the highest level of social welfare. This principle can be used to evaluate a specific policy change or to select the optimal policy from a set of alternatives.

We begin with a much less informative approach to the general equilibrium analysis of economic policy based on the Pareto principle. Under this principle a change in economic policy can be recommended if all consuming units are at least as well off under the policy change and at least one consuming unit is better off. The Pareto principle does not employ the concept of social welfare and provides only a partial ordering of economic policies rather than a complete ordering.

We extend the partial ordering of alternative economic policies implied by the Pareto principle to a complete ordering. For this purpose we employ the concept of a social welfare function originated by Bergson (1938) and discussed by Samuelson (1947, 1982). A social welfare function gives the level of social welfare as a function of the distribution of individual welfare over the population of consuming units. Our approach to economic policy evaluation requires measures of individual welfare that are cardinal and fully comparable among consuming units.

By contrast, the comparison of alternative economic policies by means of the Pareto principle requires only ordinal information about individual preferences. Also this principle does not require interpersonal comparability of preferences. To extend the partial ordering of economic policies based on the Pareto principle to the complete ordering represented by a social welfare function, we introduce additional information about individual preferences. This information provides measures of individual welfare that are cardinal and interpersonally comparable.

Our measures of individual welfare are derived from a model of aggregate consumer behavior. In this model systems of individual demand functions depend on the prices faced by all households. These systems also depend on levels of total expenditure and on attributes of households such as demographic characteristics. We obtain aggregate demand functions by exact aggregation over individual demand functions. The resulting system of aggregate demand functions depends on summary statistics of the joint distribution of total expenditures and attributes among consuming units.

The restrictions on individual preferences required for exact aggregation imply cardinal measures of utility that are fully comparable among individuals. The level of utility for each consuming unit can be expressed as a linear function of a single variable that incorporates the total expenditures and the attributes of the consuming unit. We define cardinal and interpersonally comparable measures of individual welfare in terms of this level of utility.

Our approach to the measurement of individual welfare is based on the indirect utility function and the individual expenditure function for each consuming unit. The indirect utility function gives the maximum attainable utility level as a function of the prices faced by the consuming unit and the level of total expenditure. The expenditure function gives the minimum level of total expenditure required to attain a stipulated level of utility as a function of the prices.

Aggregate Consumer Behavior

In this section we develop an econometric model of aggregate consumer behavior based on the theory of exact aggregation, following Jorgenson, Lau, and Stoker (1980, 1981, 1982). Our model incorporates time series data on prices and aggregate quantities consumed. We also include cross-sectional data on individual quantities consumed, individual total expenditure, and attributes of individual households such as demographic characteristics.

To represent preferences for all individuals in a form suitable for measuring individual welfare, we take households as consuming units. We assume that expenditures on individual commodities are allocated so as to maximize a household welfare function. As a consequence the household behaves in the same way as an individual maximizing a utility function, as demonstrated by Samuelson (1956) and Pollak (1981). By assuming that each household maximizes a household welfare function, we can focus on the distribution of welfare among households rather than the distribution among individuals within households.

To construct an econometric model based on exact aggregation, we first represent individual preferences by means of an indirect utility function for each consuming unit, using the following notation:

p_n Price of the nth commodity, assumed to be the same for all consuming units.

$\mathbf{p} = (p_1, p_2, \ldots, p_N)$ Vector of prices of all commodities.

x_{nk} Quantity of the nth commodity group consumed by the kth consuming unit ($n = 1, 2, \ldots, N; k = 1, 2, \ldots, K$).

$M_k = \sum_{n=1}^{N} p_n x_{nk}$ Total expenditure of the kth consuming unit ($k = 1, 2, \ldots, K$).

$w_{nk} = p_n x_{nk}/M_k$ Expenditure share of the nth commodity group in the budget of the kth consuming unit ($n = 1, 2, \ldots, N; k = 1, 2, \ldots, K$).

$\mathbf{w}_k = (w_{1k}, w_{2k}, \ldots, w_{Nk})$ Vector of expenditure shares for the kth consuming unit ($k = 1, 2, \ldots, K$).

$\ln(\mathbf{p}/M_k) = [\ln(p_1/M_k), \ln(p_2/M_k), \ldots, \ln(p_N/M_k)]$ Vector of logarithms of ratios of prices to expenditure by the kth consuming unit ($k = 1, 2, \ldots, K$).

$\ln p = (\ln p_1, \ln p_2, \ldots, \ln p_N)$ Vector of logarithms of prices.

$\mathbf{A}_k$ Vector of attributes of the kth consuming unit ($k = 1, 2, \ldots, K$).

We assume that the kth consuming unit allocates expenditures in accord with the transcendental logarithmic or translog indirect utility function,[1] say V_k, where

$$\ln V_k = G\left(\ln \frac{\mathbf{p}'}{M_k}\boldsymbol{\alpha}_p + \frac{1}{2}\ln \frac{\mathbf{p}'}{M_k} B_{pp} \ln \frac{\mathbf{p}}{M_k}\right.$$

$$\left. + \ln \frac{\mathbf{p}'}{M_k} B_{pA} \mathbf{A}_k, \mathbf{A}_k\right), \quad (k = 1, 2, \ldots, K). \tag{1}$$

In this representation the function G is a monotone increasing function of the variable

$$\ln \frac{\mathbf{p}'}{M_k}\boldsymbol{\alpha}_p + \frac{1}{2}\ln \frac{\mathbf{p}'}{M_k} B_{pp} \ln \frac{\mathbf{p}}{M_k} + \ln \frac{\mathbf{p}'}{M_k} B_{pA} \mathbf{A}_k.$$

In addition the function G depends directly on the attribute vector $\mathbf{A}_k$.[2] The vector $\boldsymbol{\alpha}_p$ and the matrices B_{pp} and B_{pA} are constant parameters that are the same for all consuming units.

The expenditure shares of the kth consuming unit can be derived by the logarithmic form of Roy's (1943) identity:[3]

$$w_{nk} = \frac{\partial \ln V_k/[\partial \ln(p_n/M_k)]}{\sum_{n=1}^{N} \partial \ln V_k/[\partial \ln(p_n/M_k)]}, \quad (n = 1, 2, \ldots, N; k = 1, 2, \ldots, K). \tag{2}$$

Applying this identity to the translog indirect utility function (1), we obtain the system of individual expenditure shares:

$$w_k = \frac{1}{D_k(p)}\left(\alpha_p + B_{pp}\ln\frac{p}{M_k} + B_{pA}A_k\right), \quad (k = 1, 2, \ldots, K), \tag{3}$$

where the denominators $\{D_k\}$ take the form:

$$D_k = i'\alpha_p + i'B_{pp}\ln\frac{p}{M_k} + i'B_{pA}A_k, \quad (k = 1, 2, \ldots, K). \tag{4}$$

The individual expenditure shares are homogeneous of degree zero in the unknown parameters: α_p, B_{pp}, and B_{pA}. By multiplying a given set of these parameters by a constant, we obtain another set of parameters that generates the same system of individual budget shares. Accordingly we can choose a normalization for the parameters without affecting observed patterns of individual expenditure allocation. We find it convenient to employ the normalization:

$$i'\alpha_p = -1.$$

Under this restriction any change in the set of unknown parameters will be reflected in changes in individual expenditure patterns.

The conditions for exact aggregation are that the individual expenditure shares are linear in functions of the attributes $\{A_k\}$ and total expenditures $\{M_k\}$ for all consuming units.[4] These conditions will be satisfied if and only if the terms involving the attributes and expenditures do not appear in the denominators of the expressions just given for the individual expenditure shares, so that

$$i'B_{pp}i = 0,$$

$$i'B_{pA} = 0.$$

The exact aggregation restrictions imply that the denominators $\{D_k\}$ reduce to:

$$D = -1 + i'B_{pp}\ln p,$$

where the subscript k is no longer required, since the denominator is the same for all consuming units. Under these restrictions the individual expenditure shares can be written:

$$w_k = \frac{1}{D(p)}(\alpha_p + B_{pp}\ln p - B_{pp}i\cdot\ln M_k + B_{pA}A_k), \quad (k = 1, 2, \ldots, K). \tag{5}$$

The individual expenditure shares are linear in the logarithms of expenditures $\{\ln M_k\}$ and in the attributes $\{\mathbf{A}_k\}$, as required by exact aggregation.

To construct an econometric model of aggregate consumer behavior based on exact aggregation we obtain aggregate expenditure shares, say $\mathbf{w}$, by multiplying individual expenditure shares (5) by expenditure for each consuming unit, adding over all consuming units, and dividing by aggregate expenditure, $M = \sum_{k=1}^{K} M_k$:

$$\mathbf{w} = \frac{\sum M_k \mathbf{w}_k}{M}. \tag{6}$$

The aggregate expenditure shares can be written:

$$\mathbf{w} = \frac{1}{D(\mathbf{p})}\left(\boldsymbol{\alpha}_p + B_{pp}\ln \mathbf{p} - B_{pp}\mathbf{i}\frac{\sum M_k \ln M_k}{M} + B_{pA}\frac{\sum M_k \mathbf{A}_k}{M}\right). \tag{7}$$

The aggregate expenditure patterns depend on the distribution of expenditure over all consuming units through summary statistics of the joint distribution of expenditures and attributes: $\sum M_k \ln M_k / M$ and $\{\sum M_k \mathbf{A}_k / M\}$. Systems of individual expenditure shares (5) for consuming units with identical demographic characteristics can be recovered in only one way from the system of aggregate expenditure shares (7).

Under exact aggregation the indirect utility function for each consuming unit can be represented in the form:

$$\ln V_k = F(\mathbf{A}_k) + \ln \mathbf{p}'(\boldsymbol{\alpha}_p + \tfrac{1}{2}B_{pp}\ln \mathbf{p} + B_{pA}\mathbf{A}_k)$$
$$- D(\mathbf{p})\ln M_k, \quad (k = 1, 2, \ldots, K). \tag{8}$$

In this representation the indirect utility function is linear in the logarithm of total expenditure $\ln M_k$, with a coefficient that depends on the prices $\mathbf{p}$ $(k = 1, 2, \ldots, K)$. This property is invariant with respect to positive affine transformations but is not preserved by arbitrary monotone increasing transformations. We conclude that the indirect utility function (8) provides a cardinal measure of utility for each consuming unit.

To provide a basis for evaluating the impact of transfers among households on social welfare, we find it useful to represent household preferences by means of a utility function that is the same for all consuming units. For this purpose, we assume that the kth consuming unit maximizes its utility, say U_k, where

$$U_k = U\left[\frac{x_{1k}}{m_1(\mathbf{A}_k)}, \frac{x_{2k}}{m_2(\mathbf{A}_k)}, \ldots, \frac{x_{Nk}}{m_N(\mathbf{A}_k)}\right], \quad (k = 1, 2, \ldots, K), \tag{9}$$

subject to the budget constraint:

$$M_k = \sum_{n=1}^{N} p_n x_{nk}, \quad (k = 1, 2, \ldots, K).$$

In this representation of consumer preferences the quantities $\{x_{nk}/m_n(\mathbf{A}_k)\}$ can be regarded as *effective quantities consumed*, as proposed by Barten (1964). The crucial assumption embodied in this representation is that differences in preferences among consumers enter the utility function U only through differences in the commodity specific household equivalence scales $\{m_n(\mathbf{A}_k)\}$.[5]

Consumer equilibrium implies the existence of an indirect utility function, say V, that is the same for all consuming units. The level of utility for the kth consuming unit, say V_k, depends on the prices of individual commodities, the household equivalence scales, and the level of total expenditure:

$$V_k = V\left[\frac{p_1 m_1(\mathbf{A}_k)}{M_k}, \frac{p_2 m_2(\mathbf{A}_k)}{M_k}, \ldots, \frac{p_N m_N(\mathbf{A}_k)}{M_k}\right], \quad (k = 1, 2, \ldots, K). \quad (10)$$

In this representation the prices $\{p_n m_n(\mathbf{A}_k)\}$ can be regarded as *effective prices*. Differences in preferences among consuming units enter this indirect utility function only through the household equivalence scales $\{m_n(\mathbf{A}_k)\}$ $(k = 1, 2, \ldots, K)$.

To represent the translog indirect utility function (1) in terms of household equivalence scales, we require some additional notation:

$\ln \dfrac{\mathbf{pm}(\mathbf{A}_k)}{M_k}$ Vector of logarithms of ratios of effective prices $\{p_n m_n(\mathbf{A}_k)\}$ to total expenditure M_k of the kth consuming unit ($k = 1, 2, \ldots, K$).

$\ln \mathbf{m}(\mathbf{A}_k) = (\ln m_1(A_k), \ln m_2(A_k), \ldots, \ln m_N(A_k))$ Vector of logarithms of the household equivalence scales of the kth consuming unit ($k = 1, 2, \ldots, K$).

We assume, as before, that the kth consuming unit allocates its expenditures in accord with the translog indirect utility function (1). However, we also assume that this function, expressed in terms of the effective prices $\{p_n m_n(\mathbf{A}_k)\}$ and total expenditure M_k, is the same for all consuming units. The indirect utility function takes the form

$$\ln V_k = \ln \frac{\mathbf{pm}(\mathbf{A}_k)'}{M_k}\alpha_p + \frac{1}{2}\ln \frac{\mathbf{pm}(\mathbf{A}_k)'}{M_k} B_{pp} \ln \frac{\mathbf{pm}(\mathbf{A}_k)}{M_k}, \quad (k = 1, 2, \ldots, K). \quad (11)$$

Taking logarithms of the effective prices $\{p_n m_n(A_k)\}$, we can rewrite the indirect utility function (11) in the form

$$\ln V_k = \ln \mathbf{m}(\mathbf{A}_k)'\alpha_p + \frac{1}{2}\ln \mathbf{m}(\mathbf{A}_k)' B_{pp} \ln \mathbf{m}(\mathbf{A}_k) + \ln \frac{\mathbf{p}'}{M_k}\alpha_p$$

$$+ \frac{1}{2}\ln \frac{\mathbf{p}'}{M_k} B_{pp} \ln \frac{\mathbf{p}}{M_k} + \ln \frac{\mathbf{p}'}{M_k} B_{pp} \ln \mathbf{m}(\mathbf{A}_k), \quad (k = 1, 2, \ldots, K). \quad (12)$$

Comparing the representation (12) with the representation (8), we see that the term involving only the household equivalence scales must take the form

$$F(\mathbf{A}_k) = \ln \mathbf{m}(\mathbf{A}_k)'\alpha_p + \frac{1}{2}\ln \mathbf{m}(\mathbf{A}_k)' B_{pp} \ln \mathbf{m}(\mathbf{A}_k), \quad (k = 1, 2, \ldots, K). \quad (13)$$

Second, the term involving ratios of prices to total expenditure and the household equivalence scales must satisfy

$$\ln \frac{\mathbf{p}'}{M_k} B_{pA} \mathbf{A}_k = \ln \frac{\mathbf{p}'}{M_k} B_{pp} \ln \mathbf{m}(\mathbf{A}_k) \quad (14)$$

for all prices and total expenditure.

The household equivalence scales $\{m_n(\mathbf{A}_k)\}$ defined by (14) must satisfy the equations:

$$B_{pA}\mathbf{A}_K = B_{pp} \ln \mathbf{m}(\mathbf{A}_k), \quad (k = 1, 2, \ldots, K) \quad (15)$$

Under monotonicity of the individual expenditure shares the matrix B_{pp} has an inverse, so we can express the household equivalence scales in terms of the parameters of the translog indirect utility function (B_{pp}, B_{pA}) and the attributes $\{\mathbf{A}_k\}$:

$$\ln \mathbf{m}(\mathbf{A}_k) = B_{pp}^{-1} B_{pA} \mathbf{A}_k, \quad (k = 1, 2, \ldots, K). \quad (16)$$

We can refer to these scales as the *commodity-specific translog household equivalence scales*.

Given the indirect utility function (12) for each consuming unit, we can express total expenditure as a function of prices, the commodity specific household equivalence scales, and the level of utility:

$$\ln M_k = \frac{1}{D(\mathbf{p})} \left\{ \ln \mathbf{m}(\mathbf{A}_k)' \alpha_p + \frac{1}{2} \ln \mathbf{m}(\mathbf{A}_k)' B_{pp} \ln \mathbf{m}(\mathbf{A}_k) \right.$$

$$\left. + \ln \mathbf{p}' \left[\alpha_p + \frac{1}{2} B_{pp} \ln \mathbf{p} + B_{pp} \ln \mathbf{m}(\mathbf{A}_k) \right] - \ln V_k \right\},$$

$$(k = 1, 2, \ldots, K). \tag{17}$$

We can refer to this function as the *translog expenditure function*. The translog expenditure function gives the minimum required for the kth consuming unit to achieve the utility level V_k, given the prices $\mathbf{p}$ ($k = 1, 2, \ldots, K$).

We find it useful to introduce household equivalence scales that are not specific to a given commodity.[6] Following Muellbauer (1974a), we define a general household equivalence scale, say m_0, as follows:

$$m_0 = \frac{M_k[\mathbf{pm}(\mathbf{A}_k), V_k^0]}{M_0(\mathbf{p}, V_k^0)}, \quad (k = 1, 2, \ldots, K), \tag{18}$$

where M_k is the expenditure function for the kth household, M_0 is the expenditure function for a reference household with commodity specific equivalence scales equal to unity for all commodities, and $\mathbf{pm}(\mathbf{A}_k)$ is a vector of effective prices $\{p_n m_n(\mathbf{A}_k)\}$.

The general household equivalence scale m_0 is the ratio between total expenditures required by the kth household and by the reference household required for the same level of utility V_k^0 ($k = 1, 2, \ldots, K$). This scale can be interpreted as the number of household equivalent members. The number of members depends on the attributes $\mathbf{A}_k$ of the consuming unit and on the prices p.

If each household has a translog indirect utility function, then the general household equivalence scale for the kth household takes the form:

$$\ln m_0 = \ln M_k - \ln M_0,$$

$$= \frac{1}{D(\mathbf{p})} \left[\ln \mathbf{m}(\mathbf{A}_k)' \alpha_p + \frac{1}{2} \ln \mathbf{m}(\mathbf{A}_k)' B_{pp} \ln \mathbf{m}(\mathbf{A}_k) \right.$$

$$\left. + \ln \mathbf{m}(\mathbf{A}_k)' B_{pp} \ln \mathbf{p} \right], \quad (k = 1, 2, \ldots, K). \tag{19}$$

We can refer to this scale as the *general translog household equivalence scale*. The translog equivalence scale depends on the attributes $\mathbf{A}_k$ of the kth household and the prices **p** of all commodities but is independent of the level of utility V_k^0.

Given the general translog equivalence scale, we can rewrite the indirect utility function (8) in the form:

$$\ln V_k = \ln \mathbf{p}'\boldsymbol{\alpha}_p + \frac{1}{2}\ln \mathbf{p}' B_{pp} \ln \mathbf{p}$$

$$- D(\mathbf{p}) \ln\left[\frac{M_k}{m_0(\mathbf{p}, \mathbf{A}_k)}\right], \quad (k = 1, 2, \ldots, K). \tag{20}$$

The level of utility for the kth consuming unit depends on prices p and total expenditure per household equivalent member $M_k/m_0(\mathbf{p}, \mathbf{A}_k)$ $(k = 1, 2, \ldots, K)$. Similarly we can rewrite the expenditure function (17) in the form:

$$\ln M_k = \frac{1}{D(\mathbf{p})}[\ln \mathbf{p}'(\boldsymbol{\alpha}_p + \tfrac{1}{2}B_{pp}\ln \mathbf{p}) - \ln V_k]$$

$$+ \ln m_0(\mathbf{p}, \mathbf{A}_k), \quad (k = 1, 2, \ldots, K). \tag{21}$$

Total expenditure required by the kth consuming unit to attain the level of utility V_k depends on prices p and the number of household equivalent members $m_0(\mathbf{p}, \mathbf{A}_k)$ $(k = 1, 2, \ldots, K)$.

The first step in analyzing the impact of alternative economic policies on the distribution of individual welfare is to select a representation of the individual welfare function. We assume that individual welfare for the kth consuming unit, say W_k $(k = 1, 2, \ldots, K)$, is equal to the logarithm of the translog indirect utility function (20):[7]

$$W_k = \ln V_k,$$

$$= \ln \mathbf{p}'\boldsymbol{\alpha}_p + \frac{1}{2}\ln \mathbf{p}' B_{pp} \ln \mathbf{p}$$

$$- D(\mathbf{p}) \ln\left[\frac{M_k}{m_0(\mathbf{p}, \mathbf{A}_k)}\right], \quad (k = 1, 2, \ldots, K). \tag{22}$$

In implementing the econometric model of consumer behavior, we divide consumer expenditures among five commodity groups:

1. *Energy* Expenditures on electricity, natural gas, heating oil, and gasoline.

2. *Food* Expenditures on all food products, including tobacco and alcohol.

3. *Consumer goods*   Expenditures on all other nondurable goods included in consumer expenditures.

4. *Capital services*   The service flow from consumer durables and the service flow from housing.

5. *Consumer services*   Expenditures on consumer services, such as car repairs, medical services, and entertainment.

We employ the following demographic characteristics as attributes of individual households:

1. *Family size*   1, 2, 3, 4, 5, 6, and 7 or more persons.

2. *Age of head*   16–24, 25–34, 35–44, 45–54, 55–64, 65 and over.

3. *Region of residence*   Northeast, North Central, South, and West.

4. *Race*   White, nonwhite.

5. *Type of residence*   Urban, rural.

Our cross-sectional observations on individual expenditures for each commodity group and on demographic characteristics of individual households are for the year 1973 from the 1972–73 Survey of Consumer Expenditures (CES).[8] Our time series observations are based on data on personal consumption expenditures from the U.S. National Income and Product Accounts (NIPA) for the years 1947 to 1982.[9] Prices for each commodity group are defined in terms of translog price indexes computed from detailed prices included in NIPA for each year. We employ time series data on the distribution of expenditures over all households and among demographic groups based on *Current Population Reports*.[10]

In our application we treat the expenditure shares for five commodity groups as endogenous variables, so that we estimate four equations. As unknown parameters we have four elements of the vector α_p, four expenditure coefficients of the vector $B_{pp}\mathbf{i}$, sixteen attribute coefficients for each of the four equations in the matrix B_{pA}, and ten price coefficients in the matrix B_{pp}, which is constrained to be symmetric. The expenditure coefficients are sums of price coefficients in the corresponding equation, so we have a total of eighty-two unknown parameters. We estimate the complete model, subject to inequality restrictions implied by monotonicity of the individual expenditure shares, by pooling time series and cross section data.[11]

In summary, for our econometric model a system of individual expenditure shares (5) can be recovered in only one way from the system of aggregate expenditure shares (7). Given a system of individual expenditure shares (5) that is integrable, we can recover the translog indirect utility function (20). This indirect utility function provides a cardinal measure of utility. We obtain a cardinal measure of individual welfare for each consuming unit (22) by setting this measure equal to the logarithm of the indirect utility function.

Money Metric Individual Welfare

The translog indirect utility function (20) and the translog individual expenditure function (21) can be employed in assessing the impacts of alternative economic policies on individual welfare. To analyze the impact of economic policy on the welfare of the kth household, we first evaluate the indirect utility function after the change in policy has taken place. Suppose that prices are $\mathbf{p}^1$ and expenditure for the kth household is M_k^1 ($k = 1, 2, \ldots, K$). The level of individual welfare for the kth consuming unit after the policy change W_k^1 is given by

$$W_k^1 = \ln V_k^1,$$
$$= \ln \mathbf{p}^{1\prime}(\alpha_p + \tfrac{1}{2} B_{pp} \ln \mathbf{p}^1)$$
$$- D(\mathbf{p}^1) \ln \left[\frac{M_k^1}{m_0(\mathbf{p}^1, \mathbf{A}_k)} \right], \quad (k = 1, 2, \ldots, K). \tag{23}$$

To evaluate the impact of alternative economic policies, we must compare the total expenditure required to attain the individual welfare resulting from each policy at prices prevailing before any change, say $\mathbf{p}^0$. For this purpose we can define *money metric individual welfare* for the kth household, say N_k, as the difference between the total expenditure required to attain W_k^1 and the expenditure required to attain W_k^0, the level before the policy change. Both are evaluated at prices $\mathbf{p}^0$:[12]

$$N_k = M_k(\mathbf{p}^0, W_k^1, \mathbf{A}_k) - M_k(\mathbf{p}^0, W_k^0, \mathbf{A}_k),$$
$$= M_k(\mathbf{p}^0, W_k^1, \mathbf{A}_k) - M_k^0, \quad (k = 1, 2, \ldots, K), \tag{24}$$

where M_k^0 is total expenditure before the policy change. If money metric individual welfare is positive, the welfare of the consuming unit is increased; otherwise, the welfare of the consuming unit is decreased or left unaffected.

We illustrate the concept of money metric individual welfare geometrically in figure 5.1. This figure represents the indifference map for a consuming unit with indirect utility function (20). For simplicity we consider

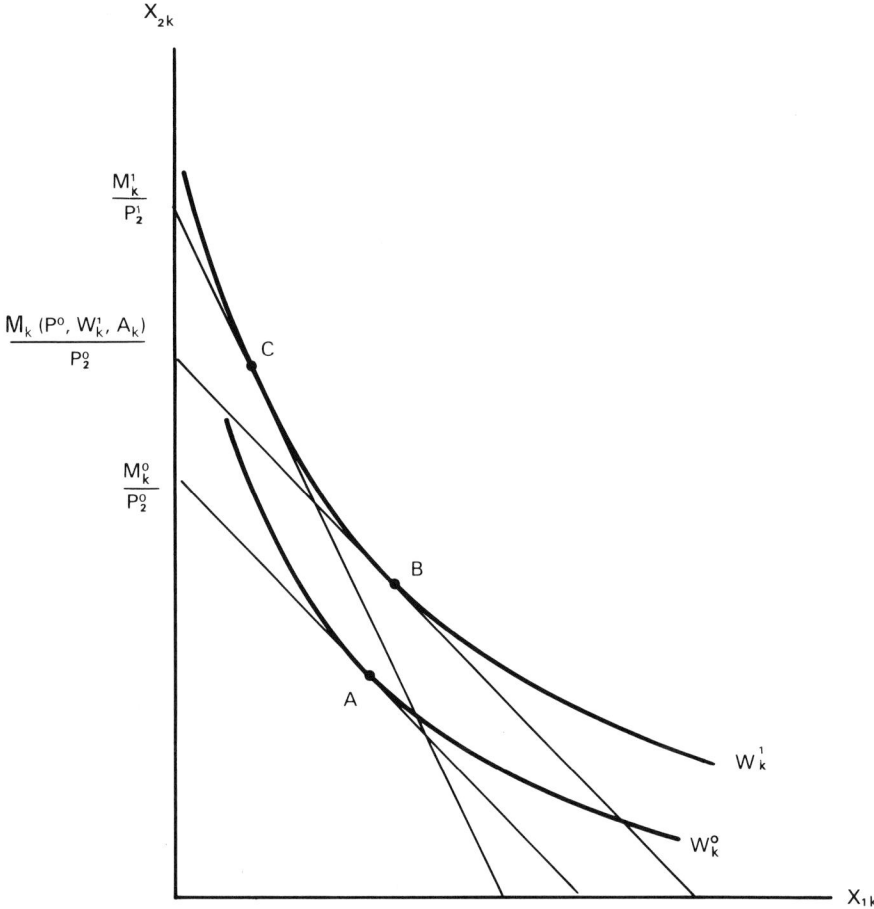

Figure 5.1 Money metric individual welfare

the case of two commodities ($N = 2$). Consumer equilibrium before the policy change is represented by the point A. The corresponding level of total expenditure $M_k^0(\mathbf{p}^0, W_k^0)$, divided by the price of the second commodity p_2^0, is given on the vertical axis. This axis gives total expenditure in units of the second commodity.

Similarly consumer equilibrium after the policy change is represented by the point C. To translate the corresponding level of welfare into total expenditure at the prices before the change, we evaluate the expenditure function (21) at this level of welfare and at the prices $\mathbf{p}^0$. The resulting level of total expenditure $M_k(\mathbf{p}^0, W_k^1, \mathbf{A}_k)$ corresponds to consumer equilibrium at the point B. Money metric individual welfare is the difference between the levels of total expenditure $M_k(\mathbf{p}^0, W_k^1, \mathbf{A}_k)$ and M_k^0.

To illustrate the measurement of individual welfare, we undertake a comparison of alternative policies for regulation of natural gas prices in the United States. These policies were analyzed by the Office of Policy, Planning, and Analysis of the U.S. Department of Energy (DOE). Our reference case for policy analysis is the policy of natural gas price decontrol called for in the Natural Gas Policy Act (NGPA) of 1978. Under this policy, price controls on natural gas remained until 1985, when prices on some types of natural gas were decontrolled. Our base case for policy analysis is the behavior of the U.S. economy under this policy.

Alternatives to current regulatory policy for natural gas prices considered by DOE were the following:

1. *Continued controls*   Under this policy, price controls on natural gas would have continued beyond 1985 and an effort would have been made to shift consumption from domestic to imported natural gas. This policy was embodied in the Gephardt bill presented to Congress in 1983.

2. *Immediate decontrol*   Under this policy, price controls would have been maintained on some types of natural gas until 1985, at which time decontrol would occur for prices on most types of natural gas. This policy was embodied in a Senate-Administration bill presented to Congress in 1983.

We have analyzed the two alternatives to current regulatory policy for natural gas prices in the United States. To evaluate these alternatives, we require projections of prices and total expenditure under each policy. We obtain these projections from the Dynamic General Equilibrium Model (DGEM) of the U.S. economy, constructed by Hudson and Jorgenson (1974, 1976, 1978a, 1978b). This model is based on a nine-sector breakdown of the U.S. economy:

1. Agriculture, nonfuel mining, construction.
2. Manufacturing, except for petroleum.
3. Transportation.
4. Communications, trade, and services.
5. Coal mining.
6. Crude petroleum and gas extraction.
7. Refined petroleum products.
8. Electric utilities.
9. Gas utilities.

The first step in analyzing alternative policies for regulation of natural gas prices is to establish projections of prices and total expenditure for all consuming units under current policy. To simulate the impact of alternatives to current regulatory policy, projections of the resulting changes in prices of natural gas to the individual industrial sectors and to final demand are incorporated into DGEM. Financial flows resulting from the alternatives to current policy are also projected and incorporated into the model.

Changes in demand for natural gas by manufacturing industries and by electric utilities are projected and incorporated into DGEM, whereas changes in demand by the other sectors of the economy are determined endogenously within the model. The response of domestic natural gas supply to changes in regulatory policy are specified exogenously. Total domestic supply is required to be equal to total domestic demand plus losses in transportation, plus the natural gas demands of natural gas producers, and less imports.

Projections of prices for each of the five commodities included in our model of aggregate consumer behavior—energy, food, consumer goods, capital services, and consumer services—are presented in table 5.1 for the reference case corresponding to current regulatory policy and for alternative policies.[13] Table 5.1 presents projections of total expenditure per household for the U.S. economy for each of the alternative regulatory policies that we consider. The projections of prices and total expenditure cover the period 1983 to 2000. It is important to note that the prices given in table 5.1 are purchasers' prices for the five commodity groups. Price projections from DGEM are given in terms of producers' prices and must be transformed by incorporating trade and transportation margins to obtain purchasers' prices.

Under continued natural gas price controls we find that the price of

Table 5.1 Projections of prices and total expenditure

a. Prices (equal to 1.000 in 1972)

Year	Energy	Food	Consumer goods	Capital services	Consumer services
Current policy					
1983	2.8452	1.8190	1.8039	2.5335	1.8067
1984	3.0394	1.8756	1.8591	2.7261	1.8620
1985	3.2794	1.9599	1.9406	2.9447	1.9394
1986	3.5175	2.0843	2.0610	3.1321	2.0553
1987	3.7893	2.1797	2.1521	3.3958	2.1332
1988	4.0712	2.2594	2.2289	3.6776	2.2051
1989	4.4023	2.3550	2.3206	3.9783	2.2877
1990	4.6296	2.5114	2.4699	4.1261	2.4232
1991	4.9263	2.6357	2.5874	4.3868	2.5240
1992	5.3241	2.7454	2.6933	4.7239	2.6297
1993	5.7350	2.8835	2.8248	5.0564	2.7503
1994	6.1258	3.1212	3.0476	5.1710	2.9395
1995	6.5515	3.3017	3.2157	5.4501	3.0855
1996	6.9604	3.3937	3.3025	5.8803	3.1774
1997	7.5162	3.5340	3.4335	6.3149	3.2962
1998	7.9925	3.7491	3.6339	6.6225	3.4783
1999	8.5172	3.9303	3.8004	7.0004	3.6230
2000	9.0189	4.1287	3.9858	7.3203	3.8061
Continued controls					
1983	2.8096	1.8182	1.8032	2.5334	1.8049
1984	3.0311	1.8753	1.8588	2.7265	1.8614
1985	3.2242	1.9575	1.9381	2.9437	1.9355
1986	3.4993	2.0826	2.0593	3.1328	2.0533
1987	3.7926	2.1794	2.1519	3.3998	2.1331
1988	4.0783	2.2598	2.2293	3.6837	2.2058
1989	4.4098	2.3556	2.3212	3.9857	2.2886
1990	4.6363	2.5122	2.4708	4.1346	2.4244
1991	4.9396	2.6371	2.5888	4.3967	2.5258
1992	5.3243	2.7463	2.6942	4.7342	2.6307
1993	5.7463	2.8851	2.8264	5.0683	2.7522
1994	6.1355	3.1229	3.0493	5.1831	2.9415
1995	6.5579	3.3034	3.2174	5.4626	3.0874
1996	6.9674	3.3955	3.3042	5.8934	3.1793
1997	7.5220	3.5358	3.4353	6.3287	3.2982
1998	7.9988	3.7510	3.6358	6.6366	3.4803
1999	8.5219	3.9322	3.8023	7.0149	3.6250
2000	9.0241	4.1308	3.9877	7.3351	3.8082

Table 5.1 (Continued)

a. Prices (equal to 1.000 in 1972)

Year	Energy	Food	Consumer goods	Capital services	Consumer services
Immediate decontrol					
1983	2.8063	1.8181	1.8031	2.5335	1.8047
1984	3.0214	1.8752	1.8587	2.7264	1.8611
1985	3.2564	1.9595	1.9401	2.9451	1.9383
1986	3.4979	2.0840	2.0607	3.1328	2.0544
1987	3.7713	2.1795	2.1520	3.3968	2.1325
1988	4.0573	2.2596	2.2291	3.6792	2.2048
1989	4.3918	2.3552	2.3208	3.9802	2.2876
1990	4.6217	2.5118	2.4703	4.1284	2.4233
1991	4.9195	2.6360	2.5877	4.3896	2.5240
1992	5.3231	2.7462	2.6941	4.7278	2.6304
1993	5.7462	2.8850	2.8263	5.0614	2.7521
1994	6.1084	3.1215	3.0480	5.1747	2.9394
1995	6.5313	3.3021	3.2162	5.4542	3.0853
1996	6.9399	3.3940	3.3027	5.8847	3.1770
1997	7.4963	3.5344	3.4339	6.3199	3.2960
1998	7.9738	3.7496	3.6344	6.6278	3.4783
1999	8.4976	3.9308	3.8009	7.0062	3.6229
2000	8.9984	4.1293	3.9864	7.3265	3.8061

b. Total expenditure per household (current prices)

Year	Current policy	Continued controls	Immediate decontrol
1983	24,576	24,572	24,573
1984	26,214	26,239	26,224
1985	28,442	28,427	28,456
1986	30,993	31,028	31,012
1987	33,141	33,188	33,165
1988	35,324	35,367	35,357
1989	37,692	37,722	37,723
1990	40,214	40,238	40,246
1991	42,765	42,795	42,786
1992	45,647	45,657	45,677
1993	48,761	48,785	48,808
1994	52,722	52,743	52,731
1995	56,927	56,945	56,933
1996	61,125	61,143	61,149
1997	65,535	65,551	65,556
1998	69,982	69,998	70,002
1999	74,618	74,634	74,636
2000	79,804	79,821	79,821

energy is lower than under the current policy for only two years. In addition the prices of all nonenergy commodities are higher under continued controls than under current policy after 1986. We also find that total expenditure per household is higher under a policy of continued controls than under current policy. It is not obvious whether individual welfare is higher or lower under continued controls than under the reference case.

To evaluate the change in individual welfare for typical households, we employ prices in the reference case as a basis for calculating money metric individual welfare (24). We make the simplifying assumption that total expenditure changes in the same proportion for all consuming units. Changes in relative levels of individual welfare are the result of differential impacts of price changes associated with changes in regulatory policy.

The dollar value of changes in individual welfare under a policy of continued controls is given for typical households in table 5.2. We present results for families of size five, with age of head 35–44, living in the Northeast region of the United States, and with average total expenditure in each year. Under continued controls all types of households gain during the period 1983 to 1989 and nonwhite households continue to gain in 1990. However, all types of families lose under continued controls beginning 1991. For example, a white urban family living in the Northeast gains $23.43 in 1983. This gain falls to $6.90 by 1989 and then becomes negative for the rest of the period. The time pattern of gains and losses for a nonwhite urban household living in the Northeast is similar to that for a white family.

With immediate decontrol of natural gas prices we find that the price of energy is lower throughout the period 1983 to 2000. Elimination of controls has very little impact on the prices of nonenergy commodities during the period of our study. We also find that total expenditure per household is slightly higher under immediate decontrol. As before, we employ prices of the reference case as a basis for calculating money metric individual welfare (24).

The dollar value of changes in welfare under a policy of immediate decontrol is given for various types of households in table 5.2. Under decontrol all households experience a gain in welfare throughout the period 1983 to 2000. As before, the time pattern of gains in welfare is similar for urban and rural households and for white and nonwhite households in the Northeast.

In summary, most of the households we have considered would be better off with immediate decontrol of natural gas prices than under current

Table 5.2 Money metric individual welfare (constant prices; Northeast region)

Year	Urban White	Urban Nonwhite	Rural White	Rural Nonwhite
Continued controls				
1983	23.43	23.61	32.07	32.26
1984	29.96	30.34	31.96	32.33
1985	37.79	38.58	49.83	50.67
1986	51.53	52.75	55.49	56.72
1987	33.30	34.92	33.42	35.04
1988	19.98	21.82	19.80	21.64
1989	6.90	8.81	6.90	8.81
1990	−1.25	0.71	−0.87	1.09
1991	−4.78	−2.77	−5.24	−3.23
1992	−9.16	−7.07	−7.52	−5.43
1993	−9.67	−7.62	−9.48	−7.43
1994	−12.53	−10.45	−11.98	−9.90
1995	−13.64	−11.56	−12.59	−10.51
1996	−13.92	−11.88	−12.91	−10.88
1997	−14.40	−12.39	−13.20	−11.18
1998	−14.87	−12.90	−13.70	−11.72
1999	−14.45	−12.49	−13.09	−11.12
2000	−14.54	−12.62	−13.22	−11.29
Immediate decontrol				
1983	27.05	27.29	36.51	36.76
1984	21.58	21.88	25.84	26.15
1985	26.72	27.09	31.92	32.31
1986	26.46	26.88	30.76	31.20
1987	26.73	27.21	30.53	31.03
1988	26.93	27.49	29.86	30.45
1989	22.09	22.69	24.31	24.93
1990	18.77	19.35	20.54	21.13
1991	11.13	11.84	12.71	13.43
1992	9.34	10.08	10.12	10.86
1993	8.98	9.64	8.13	8.78
1994	3.70	4.41	6.63	7.37
1995	1.65	2.38	4.90	5.66
1996	11.88	12.81	15.09	16.05
1997	8.50	9.46	11.56	12.56
1998	6.22	7.16	9.06	10.03
1999	4.83	5.80	7.70	8.71
2000	3.66	4.64	6.57	7.58

policy. Continued controls would eventually result in welfare losses for most households. However, these comparisons do not hold uniformly for all households and all years.

Social Welfare Function

Under the Pareto principle an economic policy can be recommended if all consuming units are as well off as under any alternative policy and at least one unit is better off. The Pareto principle provides a partial ordering of economic policies. This ordering is invariant with respect to monotone increasing transformations of individual welfare that differ among consuming units. Only welfare comparisons that are ordinal and not comparable among consuming units are required.

Money metric individual welfare (24) is a monotone increasing transformation of the measure of individual welfare (22). This transformation depends on the prices faced by all consuming units and on the attributes of the individual consuming unit. Considered as a measure of individual welfare in its own right, money metric individual welfare provides all the information about consumer preferences required for application of the Pareto principle. To obtain a complete ordering of economic policies, we next introduce a social welfare function.

We consider the set of all possible social orderings over the set of social states, say X, and the set of all possible real-valued individual welfare functions, say W_k ($k = 1, 2, \ldots, K$). A social ordering, say R, is a complete, reflexive, and transitive ordering of social states. A social state is described by the quantities consumed of N commodity groups by K individuals. The individual welfare function for the kth individual W_k ($k = 1, 2, \ldots, K$) is defined on the set of social states X and gives the level of individual welfare for that individual in each state.

To describe social orderings in greater detail, we find it useful to introduce the following notation:

x A matrix with elements $\{x_{nk}\}$ describing the social state.

$\mathbf{u} = (W_1, W_2, \ldots, W_K)$ A vector of individual welfare functions of all K individuals.

Following Sen (1970, 1977) and Hammond (1976), we define a *social welfare functional*, say f, as a mapping from the set of individual welfare functions to the set of social orderings, such that $f(\mathbf{u}') = f(\mathbf{u})$ implies $R' = R$, where

$$\mathbf{u} = [W_1(x), W_2(x), \ldots, W_K(x)],$$

$$\mathbf{u}' = [W_1'(x), W_2'(x), \ldots, W_K'(x)],$$

for all $x \in X$. Similarly we define L_k ($k = 1, 2, \ldots, K$) as the *set of admissible individual welfare functions* for the kth individual and L as the Cartesian product $\prod_{k=1}^{K} L_k$. Finally, let $\mathscr{L}$ be the partition of L such that all elements of $\mathscr{L}$ yield the same social ordering.

We can describe a social ordering in terms of the following properties of a social welfare functional:

1. *Unrestricted domain* The social welfare functional f is defined for all possible vectors of individual welfare functions $\mathbf{u}$.

2. *Independence of irrelevant alternatives* For any subset A contained in X, if $\mathbf{u}(x) = \mathbf{u}'(x)$ for all $x \in A$, then $R : A = R' : A$, where $R = f(\mathbf{u})$ and $R' = f(\mathbf{u}')$ and $R : A$ is the social ordering over the subset A.

3. *Positive association* For any vectors of individual welfare functions $\mathbf{u}$ and $\mathbf{u}'$, if for all y in $X - x$, such that

$$W_k'(y) = W_k(y),$$

$$W_k'(x) > W_k(x), \quad (k = 1, 2, \ldots, K),$$

then xPy implies $xP'y$ and $yP'x$ implies yPx, where P is a strict ordering of social states.

4. *Nonimposition* For all x, y in X there exist $\mathbf{u}, \mathbf{u}'$ such that xPy and $yP'x$.

5. *Cardinal full comparability* The set of admissible individual welfare functions that yield the same social ordering $\mathscr{L}$ is defined by:

$$\mathscr{L} = \{\mathbf{u}' : W_k'(x) = \alpha + \beta W_k(x), \quad \beta > 0, \quad k = 1, 2, \ldots, K\},$$

and $f(\mathbf{u}') = f(\mathbf{u})$ for all $\mathbf{u}' \in \mathscr{L}$.

Cardinal full comparability implies that social orderings are invariant with respect to any positive affine transformation of the individual welfare functions $\{W_k\}$ that is the same for all individuals. By contrast Arrow requires ordinal noncomparability,[14] which implies that social orderings are invariant with respect to monotone increasing transformations of the individual welfare functions that may differ among individuals:

5'. *Ordinal noncomparability* The set of individual welfare functions that yield the same social ordering $\mathscr{L}$ is defined by

$$\mathscr{L} = \{\mathbf{u}' : W_k'(x) = \phi_k[W_k(x)], \quad \phi_k \text{ increasing}, \quad k = 1, 2, \ldots, K\},$$

and $f(\mathbf{u}') = f(\mathbf{u})$ for all $\mathbf{u}'$ in $\mathscr{L}$.

The properties of a social welfare functional corresponding to unrestricted domain and independence of irrelevant alternatives are used by Arrow in proving the impossibility of a nondictatorial social ordering:

4'. *Nondictatorship* There is no individual k such that for all x, $y \in X$, $W_k(x) > W_k(y)$ implies xPy.

Under ordinal noncomparability the assumptions of positive association and nonimposition employed by Arrow imply the weak Pareto principle:

3'. *Pareto principle* For any x, $y \in X$, if $W_k(x) > W_k(y)$ for all individuals ($k = 1, 2, \ldots, K$), then xPy.

If a social welfare functional f has the properties of unrestricted domain, independence of irrelevant alternatives, the weak Pareto principle, and ordinal noncomparability, then no nondictatorial social ordering is possible. This result is Arrow's impossibility theorem. Since it is obvious that the class of dictatorial social orderings is too narrow to provide an adequate basis for expressing the implications of alternative ethical judgments, we propose to generate a class of social welfare functions suitable for the evaluation of alternative economic policies by weakening Arrow's assumptions.

If a social welfare functional f has the properties of unrestricted domain, independence of irrelevant alternatives, the weak Pareto principle, and cardinal unit comparability, there exist social orderings and a continuous real-valued social welfare function, say, W, such that if $W[\mathbf{u}(x)] > W[\mathbf{u}(y)]$, then xPy. To represent the social orderings appropriate for comparing alternative economic policies, we consider the class of social welfare functions:

$$W(\mathbf{u}, x) = \overline{W} - \gamma(x) \left[\sum_{k=1}^{K} a_k(x) | W_k - \overline{W}|^{-\rho} \right]^{-1/\rho}, \qquad (25)$$

where the function $\overline{W}(x)$ corresponds to average individual welfare:

$$\overline{W}(x) = \sum_{k=1}^{K} a_k(x) W_k(x).$$

The second part of the function $W(\mathbf{u}, x)$ is a linear homogeneous function of deviations of levels of individual welfare from the average.[15]

At this point we have generated a class of possible social welfare functions capable of expressing the implications of a variety of ethical judgments. In order to choose a specific social welfare function, we must narrow the range of possible ethical judgments by imposing further requirements on the class of social welfare functions. The parameter ρ in the representation (25) determines the curvature of the social welfare function in the individual welfare functions $\{W_k(x)\}$. We refer to this parameter as the *degree of aversion to inequality*. By selecting an appropriate value for this parameter, we can incorporate ethical judgments about inequality in the distribution of individual welfare.

If we add the assumption that the social welfare function has the property of anonymity—that is, no individual is given greater weight than any other individual in determining the level of social welfare—then the social welfare functions W in (25) must be symmetric in the individual welfare functions $\{W_k(x)\}$. To incorporate a notion of horizontal equity into the social welfare functions (25), we can impose a weak form of the property of anonymity. In particular, we require that no individual is given greater weight in the social welfare function than any other individual with an identical individual welfare function. This implies that the social welfare function is symmetric in the levels of individual welfare for identical individuals. The weights $\{a_k(x)\}$ in the social welfare functions (25) must be the same for identical individuals.

To complete the selection of a social welfare function $W(\mathbf{u}, x)$, we require that the individual welfare functions $\{W_k\}$ in (25) must be invariant with respect to any positive affine transformation that is the same for all households.[16] Under this assumption the logarithm of the translog indirect utility function is a cardinal measure of individual welfare with full comparability among households. The social welfare function takes the form:

$$W(\mathbf{u}, x) = \ln \bar{V} - \gamma(x) \left[\sum_{k=1}^{K} a_k(x) |\ln V_k - \ln \bar{V}|^{-\rho} \right]^{-1/\rho}, \tag{26}$$

where

$$\ln \bar{V} = \sum_{k=1}^{K} a_k(x) \ln V_k \left[\frac{\mathbf{pm}(\mathbf{A}_k)}{M_k} \right].$$

We can complete the specification of a social welfare function $W(u, x)$ by choosing a set of weights $\{a_k(x)\}$ for the levels of individual welfare $\{\ln V_k[\mathbf{pm}(\mathbf{A}_k)/M_k]\}$ in (26). For this purpose we must appeal to a notion of vertical equity. Following Hammond (1977), we define a distribution of total expenditure $\{M_k\}$ as more *equitable* than another distribution $\{M'_k\}$ if

i. $M_i + M_j = M_i' + M_j'$,

ii. $M_k = M_k'$ for $k \neq i, j$,

iii. $\ln V_i\left[\dfrac{\mathbf{pm}(\mathbf{A}_i)}{M_i'}\right] > \ln V_i\left[\dfrac{\mathbf{pm}(\mathbf{A}_i)}{M_i}\right] > \ln V_j\left[\dfrac{\mathbf{pm}(\mathbf{A}_j)}{M_j}\right] > \ln V_j\left[\dfrac{\mathbf{pm}(\mathbf{A}_j)}{M_j'}\right]$.

We say that a social welfare function $W(\mathbf{u}, x)$ is *equity-regarding* if it is larger for a more equitable distribution of total expenditure.

We require that the social welfare functions (26) must be equity-regarding. This amounts to imposing a version of Dalton's (1920) principle of transfers. This principle requires that a transfer of total expenditures from a rich household to a poor household that does not reverse their relative positions in the distribution of total expenditure must increase the level of social welfare.

If the social welfare functions (26) are required to be equity-regarding, then the weights $\{a_k(x)\}$ associated with the individual welfare functions $\{\ln V_k[\mathbf{pm}(\mathbf{A}_k)/M_k]\}$ must take the form:

$$a_k(x) = \frac{m_0(\mathbf{p}, \mathbf{A}_k)}{\sum_{k=1}^{K} m_0(\mathbf{p}, \mathbf{A}_k)}, \quad (k = 1, 2, \ldots, K). \tag{27}$$

We conclude that an equity-regarding social welfare function of the class (26) must take the form:

$$W(\mathbf{u}, x) = \ln \bar{V} - \gamma(x)\left[\frac{\sum_{k=1}^{K} m_0(\mathbf{p}, \mathbf{A}_k)|\ln V_k - \ln \bar{V}|^{-\rho}}{\sum_{k=1}^{K} m_0(\mathbf{p}, \mathbf{A}_k)}\right]^{-1/\rho}, \tag{28}$$

where

$$\ln \bar{V} = \frac{\sum_{k=1}^{K} m_0(\mathbf{p}, \mathbf{A}_k) \ln V_k[\mathbf{pm}(\mathbf{A}_k)/M_k]}{\sum_{k=1}^{K} m_0(\mathbf{p}, \mathbf{A}_k)},$$

$$= \ln \mathbf{p}'(\alpha_p + \tfrac{1}{2}B_{pp} \ln \mathbf{p}) - D(\mathbf{p})\frac{\sum_{k=1}^{K} m_0(\mathbf{p}, \mathbf{A}_k) \ln [M_k/m_0(\mathbf{p}, \mathbf{A}_k)]}{\sum_{k=1}^{K} m_0(\mathbf{p}, \mathbf{A}_k)}.$$

Furthermore, the condition of positive association implies that the function $\gamma(x)$ in (28) must take the form

$$\gamma(x) = \left\{\frac{\sum_{k \neq j}^{K} m_0(\mathbf{p}, \mathbf{A}_k)}{\sum_{k=1}^{K} m_0(\mathbf{p}, \mathbf{A}_k)}\left[1 + \left[\frac{\sum_{k \neq j}^{K} m_0(\mathbf{p}, \mathbf{A}_k)}{m_0(\mathbf{p}, \mathbf{A}_j)}\right]^{-(\rho+1)}\right]\right\}^{1/\rho}, \tag{29}$$

where

$$m_0(\mathbf{p}, \mathbf{A}_j) = \min_k m_0(\mathbf{p}, \mathbf{A}_k), \quad (k = 1, 2, \ldots, K).$$

In assessing the impact of changes in economic policy on levels of individual welfare for each consuming unit, we have found it useful to express the change in welfare in terms of the change in total expenditure. Similarly, to provide a basis for comparisons among social states $\{x_{nk}\}$, we propose to formulate a money measure of social welfare.[17] Following Pollak (1981), we can define the *social expenditure function* as the minimum level of total expenditure $M = \sum_{k=1}^{K} M_k$ required to attain a given level of social welfare, say, W, at a specified price system **p**. More formally, the social expenditure function $M(\mathbf{p}, W)$ is defined by

$$M(\mathbf{p}, W) = \min \left\{ M : W(\mathbf{u}, x) \geqq W; M = \sum_{k=1}^{K} M_k \right\}. \tag{30}$$

The social expenditure function (30) is precisely analogous to the individual expenditure function (21). The individual expenditure function gives the minimum level of expenditure required to attain a stipulated level of individual welfare; the social expenditure function gives the minimum level of aggregate expenditure required to attain a stipulated level of social welfare. The individual expenditure function and the indirect utility function can be employed in assessing the impact of alternative economic policies on individual welfare. Similarly the social expenditure function and the social welfare function can be employed in assessing the impacts of alternative policies on social welfare.

We can translate any level of social welfare into monetary terms by evaluating the social expenditure function at that level of welfare for a given price system p. Two different levels of social welfare can be compared with reference to a single price system by determining the minimum level of aggregate expenditure required to attain each level of social welfare for the reference prices. In addition changes in social welfare can be decomposed into changes in efficiency and changes in equity. Money measures of both components of the change in social welfare can be defined in terms of the social expenditure function and the social welfare function.

In order to determine the form of the social expenditure function $M(p, W)$ in (30), we can maximize the social welfare function (28) for a fixed level of aggregate total expenditure by equalizing total expenditure per household equivalent member $\{M_k/m_0(\mathbf{p}, \mathbf{A}_k)\}$ for all consuming units. If aggregate total expenditure is distributed so as to equalize total expenditure per household equivalent member, the level of individual welfare is the same for all consuming units. For this distribution of total expenditure the social welfare function reduces to the average level of individual welfare $\ln \bar{V}$.

For the translog indirect utility function the maximum value of social welfare for a given level of aggregate expenditure takes the form

$W(x, \mathbf{u}) = \ln \bar{V}.$

$$= \ln \mathbf{p}'(\boldsymbol{\alpha}_p + \tfrac{1}{2} B_{pp} \ln \mathbf{p}) - D(\mathbf{p}) \ln \left[\frac{M}{\sum_{k=1}^{K} m_0(\mathbf{p}, \mathbf{A}_k)} \right]. \quad (31)$$

This maximum value of social welfare reduces to average individual welfare. The average is obtained by evaluating the translog indirect utility function (20) at total expenditure per household equivalent member $M / \sum_{k=1}^{K} m_0(\mathbf{p}, \mathbf{A}_k)$ for the economy as a whole.

We can solve for aggregate expenditure as a function of the level of social welfare and prices:

$$\ln M(\mathbf{p}, W) = \frac{1}{D(\mathbf{p})} [\ln \mathbf{p}'(\boldsymbol{\alpha}_p + \tfrac{1}{2} B_{pp} \ln \mathbf{p}) - W] + \ln \left[\sum_{k=1}^{K} m_0(\mathbf{p}, \mathbf{A}_k) \right]. \quad (32)$$

We can refer to this function as the *translog social expenditure function*. The value of aggregate expenditure is obtained by evaluating the translog individual expenditure function (21) at the level of social welfare W and the number of household equivalent numbers $\sum_{k=1}^{K} m_0(\mathbf{p}, \mathbf{A}_k)$ for the economy as a whole.

To obtain a money measure of social welfare, we first evaluate the social welfare function (28) at prices $\mathbf{p}^0$ and distribution of total expenditure $\{M_k^0\}$ prevailing before any change in policy. We can express the level of social welfare before any change in policy, say, W^0, in terms of the social expenditure function:

$$\ln M(\mathbf{p}^0, W^0) = \frac{1}{D(\mathbf{p}^0)} [\ln \mathbf{p}^{0'}(\boldsymbol{\alpha}_p + \tfrac{1}{2} B_{pp} \ln \mathbf{p}^0) - W^0]$$

$$+ \ln \left[\sum_{k=1}^{K} m_0(\mathbf{p}^0, \mathbf{A}_k) \right]. \quad (33)$$

Second, we can decompose our money measure of social welfare into money measures of efficiency and equity.[18] For this purpose we evaluate the social welfare function at the maximum level, say, W^2, that can be attained through lump-sum redistributions of aggregate expenditure $M^0 = \sum_{k=1}^{K} M_k^0$. Total expenditure per household equivalent member must be equalized for all consuming units, so that the social welfare function (28) reduces to average individual welfare (31). This is the maximum level of social welfare that is potentially available and can be taken as a measure of efficiency. Evaluating the social expenditure function at the potential level of welfare, say, W^2, we obtain

$$M(\mathbf{p}^0, W^2) = M^0, \tag{34}$$

so that aggregate total expenditure M^0 is the resulting money measure of efficiency.

Given a money measure of efficiency, we can define the corresponding money measure of equity as the difference between the money measure of actual social welfare $M(\mathbf{p}^0, W^0)$ and the money measure of potential social welfare M^0. This measure of equity is nonpositive and equal to zero only for perfect equality in the distribution of individual welfare. Under perfect equality total expenditure per household equivalent member is equalized among all consuming units. Using the social expenditure function, we can express our money measure of social welfare $M(\mathbf{p}^0, W^0)$ as the sum of a money measure of efficiency M^0 and a money measure of equity $M(\mathbf{p}^0, W^0) - M^0$:

$$M(\mathbf{p}^0, W^0) = M^0 + [M(\mathbf{p}^0, W^0) - M^0]. \tag{35}$$

The critical feature of this decomposition is that all three money measures are expressed in terms of the same set of prices $\mathbf{p}^0$.

In summary, we have generated a class of social welfare function (25) that has the properties of unrestricted domain, independence of irrelevant alternatives, positive association, nonimposition, and cardinal full comparability. We can translate social welfare into a money metric by evaluating the social expenditure function (32) at the level of social welfare for a given price system. We can decompose money metric social welfare into money measures of efficiency and equity.

Money Metric Social Welfare

To analyze the impact of a change in economic policy on social welfare, we can evaluate the social welfare function (28) at prices $\mathbf{p}^1$ and distribution of total expenditure $\{M_k^1\}$ after the change in policy has taken place. In order to evaluate the impact of a change in economic policy on social welfare, we must compare the levels of aggregate total expenditure required to attain the actual levels of social welfare before and after the policy change at prices prevailing before the change. For this purpose we define *money metric social welfare*, say M_A, as the difference between the total expenditure required to attain the actual level of welfare after the policy change, say W^1, and the expenditure required to attain the actual level of welfare before the policy change W^0 at prices prevailing before the policy change $\mathbf{p}^0$:

$$M_A(\mathbf{p}^0, W^0, W^1) = M(\mathbf{p}^0, W^1) - M(\mathbf{p}^0, W^0). \tag{36}$$

If money metric social welfare is positive, the level of social welfare is increased by the policy change; otherwise, social welfare is decreased or left unaffected.

We can decompose our money measure of social welfare after the change in economic policy into money measures of efficiency and equity. For this purpose we first determine the maximum level of welfare, say W^3, that can be attained through lump-sum redistributions of aggregate total expenditure $M^1 = \sum_{k=1}^{K} M_k^1$. As before, aggregate expenditure must be distributed so as to equalize individual expenditure per household equivalent member, so that the social welfare function (28) reduces to average individual welfare (31). This is the maximum level of social welfare that is potentially available after the change in economic policy and can be taken as a measure of efficiency.

To preserve comparability between money measures of actual social welfare W^1 and potential welfare W^3 after the change in economic policy, we can evaluate the measure of potential welfare at prices prevailing before the change in policy $\mathbf{p}^0$, using the social expenditure function:

$$\ln M(\mathbf{p}^0, W^3) = \frac{1}{D(\mathbf{p}^0)} [\ln \mathbf{p}^{0'}(\boldsymbol{\alpha}_p + \tfrac{1}{2} B_{pp} \ln \mathbf{p}^0) - W^3]$$

$$+ \ln \left[\sum_{k=1}^{K} m_0(\mathbf{p}^0, \mathbf{A}_k) \right]. \tag{37}$$

The corresponding money measure of equity in terms of prices prevailing before the change in policy is given by the difference between the money measure of actual social welfare after the policy change $M(\mathbf{p}^0, W^1)$ and the money measure of potential social welfare after the policy change $M(\mathbf{p}^0, W^3)$. Our money measure of actual social welfare $M(\mathbf{p}^0, W^1)$ is the sum of money measures of efficiency and equity. All three measures are evaluated at prices prevailing before the change in policy $\mathbf{p}^0$:

$$M(\mathbf{p}^0, W^1) = M(\mathbf{p}^0, W^3) + [M(\mathbf{p}^0, W^1) - M(\mathbf{p}^0, W^3)]. \tag{38}$$

Finally, we can decompose money metric social welfare (36) into the sum of money metric efficiency and money metric equity. *Money metric efficiency*, say M_P, can be defined as the difference between the total expenditure required to attain the potential level of welfare after the policy change

W^3 and the expenditure required to attain the potential level of welfare before the policy change W^2. Both are evaluated at prices prevailing before the policy change $\mathbf{p}^0$:

$$M_p(\mathbf{p}^0, W^2, W^3) = M(\mathbf{p}^0, W^3) - M^0. \tag{39}$$

Similarly *money metric equity*, say M_E, can be defined as the difference between money measures of equity before and after the policy change, evaluated at prices before the change $\mathbf{p}^0$:

$$M_E(\mathbf{p}^0, W^0, W^1, W^2, W^3) = [M(\mathbf{p}^0, W^1) - M(\mathbf{p}^0, W^3)]$$
$$- [M(\mathbf{p}^0, W^0) - M^0]. \tag{40}$$

Money metric social welfare is the sum of money metric efficiency and money metric equity:

$$M_A(\mathbf{p}^0, W^0, W^1) = M_P(\mathbf{p}^0, W^2, W^3) + M_E(\mathbf{p}^0, W^0, W^1, W^2, W^3), \tag{41}$$

All three money measures of social welfare in this decomposition are expressed in terms of the same set of prices $\mathbf{p}^0$.

To illustrate the measurement of social welfare, we can represent the concept of money metric social welfare geometrically, as in figure 5.2. In this figure we have depicted a representative consumer with indirect utility function given by the average level of utility $\ln \bar{V}$ in (31). As before, we consider the case of two commodities ($N = 2$) for simplicity. Consumer equilibrium at the actual level of social welfare W^0 before the policy change is represented by the point A. The corresponding level of aggregate expenditure $M(\mathbf{p}^0, W^0)$, divided by the price of the second commodity $\mathbf{p}_2^0$, is given on the vertical axis. This axis provides a representation of aggregate expenditure in terms of units of the second commodity.

Aggregate expenditure M^0 is the value of the social expenditure function at the potential level of welfare W^2. This is the maximum level of welfare that can be obtained by lump-sum redistributions of aggregate expenditure. The corresponding consumer equilibrium is represented by the point B. A money measure of efficiency, expressed in terms of units of the second commodity, is given by the level of aggregate expenditure $M^0/\mathbf{p}_2^0$. The corresponding money measure of equity is provided by the distance along the x_2-axis between aggregate expenditure $M^0/\mathbf{p}_2^0$ and the value of the social expenditure function $M(p^0, W^0)/p_2^0$; each is divided by the price of the second commodity. The money measure of social welfare at A is the sum of money measures of efficiency and equity.

As before, consumer equilibrium at the level of social welfare W^1 after

General Equilibrium Analysis of Natural Gas Price Regulation

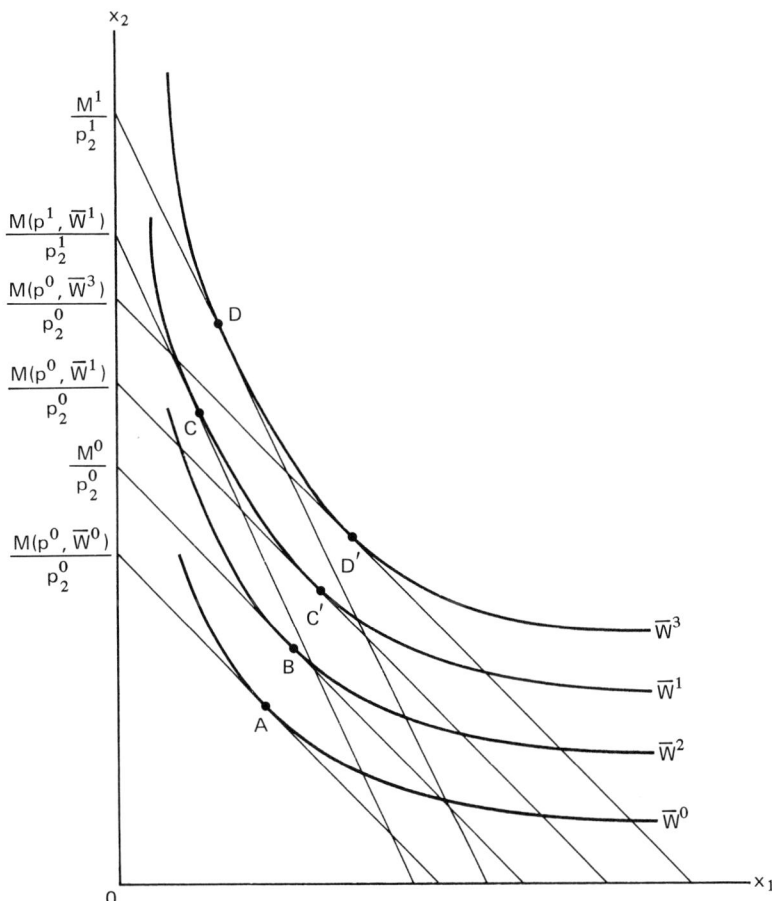

Figure 5.2 Money metric social welfare

the policy change is represented by the point C. In (36) we have determined this level of welfare by evaluating the social welfare function (28) at the prices $\mathbf{p}^1$ and the distribution of total expenditure $\{M_k^1\}$ after the change in policy has taken place. To translate the level of social welfare W^1 into aggregate expenditure at the prices prevailing before the policy change, we evaluate the social expenditure function (32) at this level of social welfare and the prices before the changes $\mathbf{p}^0$. The resulting level of aggregate expenditure $M(\mathbf{p}^0, W^1)$ corresponds to consumer equilibrium at the point C'.

The money measure of social welfare at C' is the sum of money measures of efficiency and equity that are precisely analogous to those we have defined for the measure of welfare at A. We can decompose our money measure of social welfare by first determining the maximum level of social welfare, say W^3, that can be obtained through lump-sum distributions to aggregate expenditure M^1 at prices $\mathbf{p}^1$. The corresponding consumer equilibrium is represented by the point D. We can translate this level of social welfare into aggregate expenditure at prices prevailing before the change $\mathbf{p}^0$ by evaluating the social welfare function $M(\mathbf{p}^0, W^3)$ at the point D'.

Money metric social welfare, expressed in units of the second commodity, is represented by the distance along the x_2-axis between aggregate expenditure $M(\mathbf{p}^0, W^1)/p_2^0$ and expenditure $M(\mathbf{p}^0, W^0)/p_2^0$, each divided by the price of the second commodity. Similarly money metric efficiency is represented by the distance between aggregate expenditure $M(\mathbf{p}^0, W^3)/p_2^0$ and expenditure M^0/p_2^0. Finally, money metric equity is represented by the difference between the distances $[M(\mathbf{p}^0, W^1) - M(\mathbf{p}^0, W_3)]/p_2^0$ and $[M(\mathbf{p}^0, W^0) - M^0]/p_2^0$. The distance corresponding to money metric social welfare is the sum of the distances corresponding to money metric efficiency and money metric equity.

Given methods for measuring social welfare, we are in a position to evaluate alternative policies for natural gas price regulation in the United States. As a basis for comparison of levels of social welfare associated with alternative policies, we take current policy as a reference case. Under this policy price controls are eliminated on some types of natural gas in 1985. We employ the behavior of the U.S. economy under this policy as a base case for policy analysis.

The value of social welfare depends on prices for each of the five commodities included in our model of aggregate consumer behavior—energy, food, consumer goods, capital services, and consumer services. In addition it depends on total expenditure for the U.S. economy as a whole. As before, we make the simplifying assumption that total expenditure

Table 5.3 Money metric social welfare (millions of constant dollars)

Year	Continued controls	Immediate decontrol
1983	1,492.520	1,717.652
1984	1,799.619	1,332.337
1985	2,401.407	1,650.275
1986	3,117.486	1,625.640
1987	2,004.577	1,636.300
1988	1,221.106	1,640.076
1989	452.995	1,346.813
1990	−20.729	1,144.807
1991	−239.067	695.305
1992	−467.214	579.660
1993	−519.304	532.518
1994	−681.827	276.191
1995	−740.451	160.032
1996	−759.793	768.837
1997	−786.539	569.036
1998	−816.259	429.719
1999	−789.273	349.180
2000	−796.057	280.520

changes in the same proportion for all consuming units. We employ the projection of prices and total expenditure based on the Dynamic General Equilibrium Model (DGEM) of the U.S. economy given in table 5.1.

We can translate our evaluation of alternative policies for natural gas price regulation into money measures of social welfare by employing the social expenditure function introduced in the last section. In table 5.3 we present money metric social welfare for the two alternatives to current policy described earlier in this chapter in the discussion on money metric individual welfare. Although the magnitude of money metric social welfare depends on the degree of aversion to inequality ρ, we find that the qualitative features of comparisons among alternative policies for different values of this parameter are almost identical. We present money metric social welfare for both alternatives to the base case for the degree of aversion to inequality ρ equal to minus one.

Under continued controls money metric social welfare is positive for the years 1983 to 1989 and becomes negative for the rest of the period. Money metric social welfare under immediate decontrol is positive throughout the period 1983 to 2000. Gains in social welfare under immediate decontrol exceed those under continued controls in 1983 and for all years after 1988. Our analysis of current regulatory policy for natural gas prices and the two

Table 5.4 Money metric efficiency (millions of constant dollars)

Year	Continued controls	Immediate decontrol
1983	2,162.315	2,492.543
1984	2,695.706	1,963.536
1985	3,483.171	2,434.154
1986	4,641.808	2,405.515
1987	2,978.186	2,424.443
1988	1,783.287	2,437.363
1989	611.950	1,998.672
1990	−114.416	1,697.490
1991	−438.714	1,012.105
1992	−808.774	843.876
1993	−872.335	790.947
1994	−1,125.599	361.113
1995	−1,219.799	180.499
1996	−1,246.097	1,099.865
1997	−1,287.569	797.594
1998	−1,331.449	587.833
1999	−1,291.577	464.389
2000	−1,300.480	358.882

alternative policies appears to justify immediate decontrol of natural gas prices. This policy is superior to current policy and to a policy of continued price controls.

Money metric social welfare is the sum of money metric efficiency and money metric equity. Money metric efficiency corresponds to the gain in potential social welfare associated with a change in regulatory policy and is independent of the degree of aversion to inequality ρ. We present money metric efficiency for both alternatives to the base case in table 5.4.

Under continued controls money metric efficiency is positive for 1983 to 1989 and negative for the rest of the period. Money metric efficiency under immediate decontrol is positive throughout the period. Money metric efficiency is higher for immediate decontrol than for continued controls for 1983 and 1988 to 2000. A common practice in welfare economics is to recommend the policy with the greatest efficiency. On these grounds the policy of immediate decontrol would be judged superior to current policy and to continued controls.

We next consider money measures of equity for both alternatives to current regulatory policy. Money metric equity is defined as the difference between actual and potential gains in social welfare resulting from a change in regulatory policy. Money metric equity, unlike money metric efficiency,

Table 5.5 Money metric equity (millions of constant dollars)

Year	Continued controls	Immediate decontrol
1983	−669.794	−774.890
1984	−896.087	−631.199
1985	−1,081.765	−783.880
1986	−1,524.322	−779.875
1987	−973.610	−788.143
1988	−562.181	−797.286
1989	−158.954	−651.859
1990	93.687	−552.683
1991	199.647	−316.800
1992	341.560	−264.216
1993	353.031	−258.429
1994	443.771	−84.922
1995	479.348	−20.467
1996	486.304	−331.028
1997	501.030	−228.557
1998	515.190	−158.114
1999	502.305	−115.209
2000	504.423	−78.363

depends on the degree of aversion to inequality ρ. We have found, as before, that the qualitative features of comparisons among alternative policies are almost identical for different values of this parameter, so that we present money metric equity for the two alternatives to current regulatory policy in table 5.5 for degree of aversion to inequality ρ equal to minus one.

Money metric equity for a policy of continued natural gas price controls is negative for the period 1983 to 1989 and positive for the remainder of the period 1990 to 2000, reaching a level of $515 millions in 1998. By contrast a policy of immediate decontrol reduces equity throughout the period 1983 to 2000.

Finally, by comparing the results presented in tables 5.4 and 5.5, we can see that money metric efficiency and equity move in opposite directions. For example, a policy of immediate decontrol of natural gas prices is preferred to all other policies for the period 1983 to 2000. Throughout this period money metric efficiency under immediate decontrol is positive; however, money metric equity under this policy is lower than that for current policy. Under continued controls money metric efficiency is greater than under current policy through 1989 and less than under current policy for the period 1990 to 2000. By contrast, money metric equity is lower than under current policy through 1989 and greater for 1990 to 2000.

In summary, we have translated comparisons among alternative policies for natural gas price regulation into money measures of social welfare. Money metric social welfare for a policy of immediate decontrol of natural gas prices is higher than under current policy or continued controls. Finally, we have decomposed money metric social welfare into money metric equity and money metric efficiency. We have found that money metric equity and money metric efficiency are both essential to the determination of money metric social welfare.

Notes

1. The translog indirect utility function was introduced by Christensen, Jorgenson, and Lau (1975) and extended to encompass determinants of expenditure allocation other than prices and total expenditure by Jorgenson and Lau (1975). Alternative approaches to the representation of the effects of prices and total expenditure on expenditure allocation are summarized by Barten (1977), Deaton and Muellbauer (1980, pp. 60–85), and Lau (1977a).

2. Alternative approaches to the representation of household characteristics in expenditure allocation are presented by Barten (1964), Gorman (1976), and Prais and Houthakker (1971). A review of the literature is presented by Deaton and Muellbauer (1980, pp. 191–213).

3. The specification of a system of individual demand functions by means of Roy's Identity was first employed in econometric modeling of consumer behavior by Houthakker (1960). A detailed review of econometric models based on Roy's Identity is given by Lau (1977a).

4. For further discussion, see Lau (1977b, 1982) and Jorgenson, Lau, and Stoker (1980, 1981, 1982).

5. Household equivalence scales are discussed by Barten (1964), van der Gaag and Smolensky (1982), Kakwani (1977), Lazear and Michael (1980), Muellbauer (1974a, 1977, 1980), and Prais and Houthakker (1971), among others. Alternative approaches are summarized by Deaton and Muellbauer (1980).

6. The use of household equivalence scales in evaluating transfers among individuals has been advocated by Deaton and Muellbauer (1980, esp. pp. 205–212) and Muellbauer (1974a). Pollak and Wales (1979) have presented arguments against the use of household equivalence scales for this purpose.

7. Deaton and Muellbauer (1980, pp. 227–239), King (1983a, 1983b), McKenzie (1982), and Muellbauer (1974a, 1974b) present approaches to welfare measurement based on the distribution of "real expenditure." Measures of "real expenditure" could be derived from the individual expenditure function (23) by varying the level of utility V_k for a fixed set of prices $\mathbf{p}$ ($k = 1, 2, \ldots, K$). Restrictions on preferences under which measures of social welfare defined on the distribution of real expenditure coincide with measures defined on the distribution of individual welfare are given by Roberts (1980c).

8. The 1972–73 Survey of Consumer Expenditure is discussed by Carlson (1974).

9. We employ data on the flow of services from durable goods rather than purchases of durable goods. Personal consumption expenditures in the U.S. National Income and Product Accounts are based on purchases of durable goods.

10. This series is published annually by the U.S. Bureau of the Census.

11. A detailed discussion of the stochastic specification of our model and of econometric methods for pooling time series and cross-sectional data is presented by Jorgenson, Lau, and Stoker (1982). This stochastic specification implies that time series data must be adjusted for heteroscedasticity by multiplying each observation by the statistic:

$$\rho = \frac{(\sum M_k)^2}{\sum M_k^2}.$$

12. This concept of money metric individual welfare coincides with the concept of net equivalent variation employed by Jorgenson, Lau, and Stoker (1982). Measures of equivalent variations based on the translog indirect utility function were introduced by Jorgenson, Lau, and Stoker (1981). The corresponding measures of compensating variations were introduced by Jorgenson, Lau, and Stoker (1980). The concepts of equivalent and compensating variations are due to Hicks (1942) and have been discussed by Chipman and Moore (1980), Deaton and Muellbauer (1980, pp. 184–190), Diamond and McFadden (1974), Hausman (1981), and Hurwicz and Uzawa (1971), among others. An individual ordering based on money metric individual welfare is identical to that based on Samuelson's (1974) concept of money metric utility.

13. These price projections are based on the projections of the U.S. economy under alternative regulatory policies for natural gas production by Goettle, Hudson, Jorgenson, and Slesnick (1983).

14. Arrow (1977, p. 225) has defended noncomparability in the following terms: "... the autonomy of individuals, an element of mutual incommensurability among people seems denied by the possibility of interpersonal comparisons."

15. It is important to note that the social welfare function in (25) represents a social ordering over all possible individual orderings and exemplifies the multiple profile approach to social choice of Arrow (1963) rather than the single profile approach employed by Bergson (1938) and Samuelson (1947). The literature on the existence of single profile social welfare functions is discussed by Roberts (1980b), Samuelson (1982), and Sen (1979b).

16. This assumption implies that individual welfare increases with total expenditure at a rate that is inversely proportional to total expenditure. This is also implied by the utilitarian social welfare function employed by Arrow and Kalt (1979).

17. Alternative money measures of social welfare are discussed by Arrow and Kalt (1979), Bergson (1980), Deaton and Muellbauer (1980, pp. 214–239), Roberts (1980a), and Sen (1976). A survey of the literature is presented by Sen (1979a).

18. Alternative money measures of efficiency and equity are discussed by Arrow and Kalt (1979), Bergson (1980), and Sen (1976, 1979).

References

Arrow, K. J. 1963. *Social Choice and Individual Values.* 2nd ed. New Haven: Yale University Press.

Arrow, K. J. 1977. "Extended Sympathy and the Possibility of Social Choice." *American Economic Review* 67:219–225.

Arrow, K. J., and Kalt, J. P. 1979. *Petroleum Price Regulation: Should We Decontrol?* Washington, D.C.: American Enterprise Institute.

Barten, A. P. 1964. "Family Composition, Prices, and Expenditure Patterns." In P. Hart, G. Mills, and J. K. Whitaker, eds., *Econometric Analysis for National Economic Planning: 16th Symposium of the Colston Society.* London, Butterworth, pp. 277–292.

Barten, A. P. 1977. "The Systems of Consumer Demand Functions Approach: A Review." In M. D. Intriligator, ed., *Frontiers of Quantitative Economics*. Vol. IIIA. Amsterdam: North Holland, 23–58.

Bergson, A. 1938. "A Reformulation of Certain Aspects of Welfare Economics." *Quarterly Journal of Economics 52*: 310–334.

Bergson, A. 1980. "Consumer's Surplus and Income Redistribution." *Journal of Public Economics 14*: 31–47.

Bureau of the Census (various annual issues). *Current Population Reports, Consumer Income, Series P-60*, Washington, D.C.: U.S. Department of Commerce.

Carlson, M. D. 1974. "The 1972–73 Consumer Expenditure Survey." *Monthly Labor Review 97*: 16–23.

Chipman, J. S., and Moore, J. C. 1980. "Compensating Variation, Consumer's Surplus, and Welfare." *American Economic Review 70*: 933–949.

Christensen, L. R., D. W. Jorgenson, and L. J. Lau. 1975. "Transcendental Logarithmic Utility Functions." *American Economic Review 65*: 367–383.

Dalton, H. 1920. "The Measurement of Inequality of Income." *Economic Journal 30*: 361–384.

Deaton, A., and J. Muellbauer. 1980. *Economics and Consumer Behavior*. Cambridge: Cambridge University Press.

Diamond, P. A., and McFadden, D. 1974. "Some Uses of the Expenditure Function in Public Finance." *Journal of Public Economics 3*: 3–21.

van der Gaag, J., and Smolensky, E. 1982. "True Household Equivalence Scales and Characteristics of the Poor in the United States." *Review of Income and Wealth 28*: 17–28.

Goettle, R. J., IV, Hudson, E. A., Jorgenson, D. W., and Slesnick, D. T. 1983. "The Macroeconomic Consequences of Alternative Natural Gas Policies." Cambridge: Dale W. Jorgenson Associates.

Gorman, W. M. 1976. "Tricks with Utility Functions." In M. J. Artis and A. R. Nobay, eds., *Essays in Economic Analysis: Proceedings of the 1975 AUTE Conference*. Cambridge: Cambridge University Press, pp. 211–243.

Hammond, P. J. 1976. "Equity, Arrow's Conditions and Rawl's Difference Principle." *Econometrica 44*: 793–804.

Hammond, P. J. 1977. "Dual Interpersonal Comparisons of Utility and the Welfare Economics of Income Distribution." *Journal of Public Economics 7*: 51–71.

Hausman, J. A. 1981. "Exact Consumer's Surplus and Deadweight Loss." *American Economic Review 71*: 662–676.

Hicks, J. R. 1942. "Consumers' Surplus and Index-Numbers." *Review of Economic Studies 9*: 126–137.

Houthakker, H. S. 1960. "Additive Preferences." *Econometrica 28*: 244–257.

Hudson, E. A., and, Jorgenson, D. W. 1974. "U.S. Energy Policy and Economic Growth, 1975–2000." *Bell Journal of Economics and Management Science 5*: 461–514.

Hudson, E. A., and Jorgenson, D. W. 1976. "U.S. Tax Policy and Energy Conservation." In D. Jorgenson, ed., *Econometric Studies of U.S. Energy Policy*, Amsterdam, North Holland, pp. 7–94.

Hudson, E. A., and Jorgenson, D. W. 1978a. "Energy Prices and the U.S. Economy, 1972–1976." *Natural Resources Journal 18*: 877–897.

Hudson, E. A., and Jorgenson, D. W. 1978b. "The Economic Impact of Policies to Reduce U.S. Energy Growth." *Resources and Energy 1*: 205–230.

Hurwicz, L., and Uzawa, H. 1971. "On the Integrability of Demand Functions." In J. S. Chipman et al., eds., *Preferences, Utility and Demand*. New York, Harcourt Brace, pp. 114–148.

Jorgenson, D. W., and Lau, L. J. 1975. "The Structure of Consumer Preferences." *Annals of Economic and Social Measurement 4*: 49–101.

Jorgenson, D. W., Lau, L. J., and Stoker, T. M. 1980. "Welfare Comparison under Exact Aggregation." *American Economic Review 70*: 268–272.

Jorgenson, D. W., Lau, L. J., and Stoker, T. M. 1981. "Aggregate Consumer Behavior and Individual Welfare." In D. Currie, R. Nobay, and D. Peel, eds., *Macroeconomic Analysis*. London: Croom-Helm, pp. 35–61.

Jorgenson, D. W., Lau, L. J., and Stoker, T. M. 1982. "The Transcendental Logarithmic Model of Aggregate Consumer Behavior." In R. L. Basmann and G. F. Rhodes, Jr., eds., *Advances in Econometrics*. Vol. 1. Greenwich: JAI Press, pp. 97–238.

Kakwani, N. C. 1977. "On the Estimation of Consumer Unit Scales." *Review of Economics and Statistics 59*: 507–510.

King, M. A. 1983a. "An Index of Inequality: With Applications to Horizontal Equity and Social Mobility." *Econometrica 51*: 99–115.

King, M. A. 1983b. "Welfare Analysis of Tax Reforms Using Household Data." *Journal of Public Economics 21*: 183–214.

Lau, L. J. 1977a. "Complete Systems of Consumer Demand Functions through Duality." In M. D. Intriligator, ed., *Frontiers of Quantitative Economics*. Vol. IIIA. Amsterdam: North Holland, pp. 59–86.

Lau, L. J. 1977b. "Existence Conditions for Aggregate Demand Functions." Technical Report No. 248. Institute for Mathematical Studies in the Social Sciences. Stanford University, Stanford (revised 1980 and 1982).

Lau, L. J. 1982. "A Note on the Fundamental Theorem of Exact Aggregation." *Economics Letters 9*: 119–126.

Lazear, E. P., and Michael, R. T. 1980. "Family Size and the Distribution of Real Per Capita Income." *American Economic Review 70*: 91–107.

McKenzie, G. W. 1982. *Measuring Economic Welfare: New Methods*. Cambridge: Cambridge University Press.

Muellbauer, J. 1974a. "Household Composition, Engel Curves and Welfare Comparisons between Households: A Duality Approach." *European Economic Review 5*: 103–122.

Muellbauer, J. 1974b. "Prices and Inequality: The United Kingdom Experience," *Economic Journal 84*, 32–55.

Muellbauer, J. 1977. "Testing the Barten Model of Household Composition Effects and the Cost of Children." *Economic Journal 87*: 460–487.

Muellbauer, J. 1980. "The Estimation of the Prais-Houthakker Model of Equivalence Scales." *Econometrica 48*: 153–176.

Pollak, R. A. 1981. "The Social Cost of Living Index." *Journal of Public Economics 15*: 311–336.

Pollak, R. A., and Wales, T. J. 1979. "Welfare Comparisons and Equivalent Scales." *American Economic Review 69*: 216–221.

Prais, S. J., and Houthakker, H. S. 1971. *The Analysis of Family Budgets*. 2nd ed. Cambridge: Cambridge University Press.

Roberts, K. W. S. 1980a. "Price-Independent Welfare Prescriptions." *Journal of Public Economics 13*: 277–298.

Roberts, K. W. S. 1980b. "Social Choice Theory: The Single-Profile and Multi-Profile Approaches." *Review of Economic Studies 47*: 441–450.

Roy, R. 1943. *De l'Utilite: Contributions à la Theorie des Choix*. Paris: Herman.

Samuelson, P. A. 1947. *Foundations of Economic Analysis*. Cambridge: Harvard University Press.

Samuelson, P. A. 1956. "Social Indifference Curves." *Quarterly Journal of Economics 70*: 1–22.

Samuelson, P. A. 1974. "Complementarity—An Essay on the 40th Anniversary of the Hicks-Allen Revolution in Demand Theory." *Journal of Economic Literature 12*: 1255–1289.

Samuelson, P. A. 1982. "Bergsonian Welfare Economics." In S. Rosefielde, ed., *Economic Welfare and the Economics of Soviet Socialism: Essays in Honor of Abram Bergson*. Cambridge: Cambridge University Press, pp. 223–266.

Sen, A. K. 1970. *Collective Choice and Social Welfare*. Edinburgh: Oliver and Boyd.

Sen, A. K. 1976. "Real National Income." *Review of Economic Studies 43*: 19–40.

Sen, A. K. 1977. "On Weights and Measures: Informational Constraints in Social Welfare Analysis." *Econometrica 45*: 1539–1572.

Sen, A. K. 1979a. "The Welfare Basis of Real Income Comparisons: A Survey." *Journal of Economic Literature 17*: 1–45.

Sen, A. K. 1979b. "Personal Utilities and Public Judgements: Or What's Wrong with Welfare Economics." *Economic Journal 89*: 537–558.

6

Experimental Evaluation of the Contestable Markets Hypothesis

Glenn W. Harrison

In this chapter I provide a critical evaluation of recent experimental tests of the contestable markets hypothesis by Coursey, Isaac, and Smith (1984) and Harrison and McKee (1985a). I argue that these studies do not operationalize the theory as advanced in Baumol, Panzar, and Willig (1982) in one critical respect: the "Bertrand-Nash" assumption that potential entrants are able to evaluate the profitability of entry at the incumbent firm's preentry prices. This assumption in the theory requires that hit-and-run entry-exit be allowed to occur before the incumbent is able to react. In a new series of experiments I find that the evidence in favor of the contestable markets hypothesis (CMH) is even stronger when one modifies the experimental design to correspond to the theoretical framework. Moreover this modification lies at the heart of much of the theoretical criticism of the CMH. The accumulated experimental evidence therefore demonstrates that the CMH is behaviorally robust to certain violations of one central and controversial theoretical assumption.

I argue that the experiments of Coursey, Isaac, and Smith (1984) and Harrison and McKee (1985a) should be viewed, in retrospect, as important boundary experiments on the evaluation of the CMH.[1] This is despite their support for a weak version of the CMH. Why take such a puritan methodological stance? One reason is simply to be able to determine, as I show with the Bertrand-Nash design, exactly how strong the experimental case for the CMH can be put on its own theoretical grounds.[2] I conclude that it can be put much more strongly than in previous studies.

A second reason for my methodological position questions whether the support for the CMH in previous studies is indeed so convincing. A major conclusion of the Harrison and McKee (1985a) study is precisely that market contestability, in an environment in which the Bertrand-Nash assumption is not satisfied, does not restrain monopoly effectiveness as well or as rapidly as a decentralized regulatory mechanism proposed by Loeb and Magat (1979).[3] Harrison, McKee, and Rutstrom (1987) demonstrate that this ranking of institutional performance is reversed when one considers environments in which the Bertrand-Nash assumption is satisfied. Thus whether or not one evaluates the CMH on its own theoretical ground can make a difference with respect to the comparative behavioral performance of contestability as an alternative to regulation.

A third and final reason for my methodological position is the most important: one must have a clear behavioral and theoretical foundation from which to evaluate subsequent modifications to the experimental design. At least two major directions in which the basic theoretical model should be modified have been widely discussed: the role of sunk (entry) costs and the issue of intertemporal sustainability. Each provides ample grounds for theoretical caution with respect to the general validity of the CMH, and each is amenable to experimental evaluation. It is proper to study these modifications of the basic model orthogonally from a theoretical and experimental perspective, without "contaminating" violations of the Bertrand-Nash assumption. To do this, we need to establish and agree on an experimental design that corresponds to the basic model. Without such control experiments, corresponding to theoretical models with "known" properties, it is difficult to learn much from experiments that correspond to different theoretical models (with perhaps unknown properties).

First, we provide a critical review of the recent experimental literature on contestable markets. Reviews of related experiments in monopoly behavior and monopoly regulation may be found in Plott (1982) and Harrison, McKee, and Rutström (1987). Second, we contrast the assumptions of contestability theory with existing experimental design, and propose a modification of the latter to correspond more closely to the former. Third, we present our experimental results, and fourth, we draw several conclusions.

A Review of the Experimental Literature

It is convenient to consider the recent experimental literature in two stages. First, I consider the basic and direct tests of the contestable markets hypothesis by Coursey, Isaac, and Smith (1984) and Harrison and McKee (1985a). Many of the design features of these experiments are employed in subsequent studies. Second, I examine the role of sunk costs as an entry barrier in the experiments of Coursey, Isaac, Luke, and Smith (1984).

Basic Studies

Coursey, Isaac, and Smith (1984), hereafter CIS, provided the first experimental operationalization of the contestable markets hypothesis (CMH) proposed by Baumol, Panzar, and Willig (1982). CIS adopt a design in which two potential sellers with identical decreasing-cost schedules, up to a "capacity constraint" of ten units, compete for buyers in a posted offer

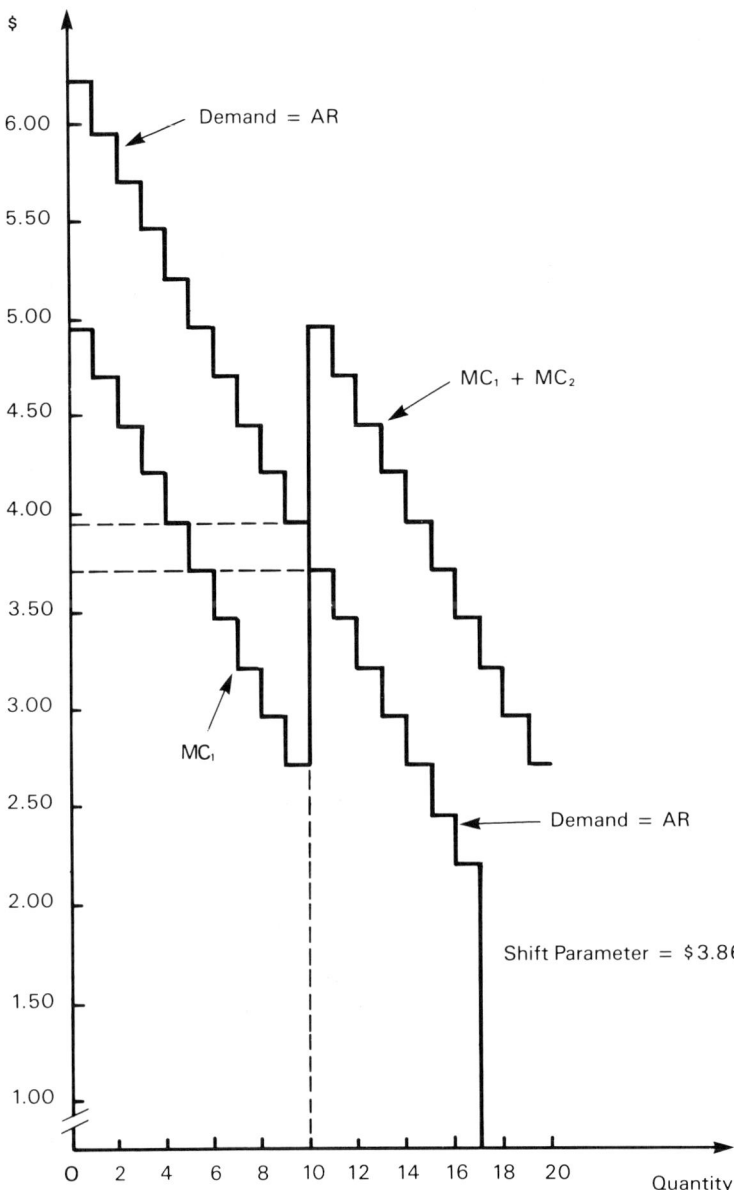

Figure 6.1 Experimental design in CIS and HM

(PO) pricing institution. Figure 6.1 illustrates the cost and demand schedules adopted. CIS present evidence that convincingly supports a "weak version" of the CMH: that observed behavior will be closer to competitive rather than monopoly predictions. Their results are somewhat less convincing with respect to a "strong version" of the CMH: that observed behavior converges to and attains competitive rather than monopoly predictions.

CIS compare their contested duopoly experiments with the outcome of four decreasing-cost monopoly experiments. Why bother conducting experiments with monopolists who know that there is no threat of entry? What can we learn from such studies that is not already entrenched in textbooks? The answer is that we must establish the extent of a behavioral monopoly "problem" as a necessary prelude to the behavioral evaluation of alternative institutions designed to mitigate that problem. If the problem does not exist behaviorally in a certain environment, then clearly there is no need to design institutions to deal with it. If the problem does exist behaviorally, we still need to establish a behavioral benchmark to measure the performance of those institutions designed to deal with it. For present purposes we may take it that the monopolists in CIS, and Harrison and McKee (1985a), hereafter HM, managed to attain the predicted monopoly outcomes. Harrison, McKee, and Rutström (1987) provide more detailed evaluations of the various monopoly experiments.

Several notable features of the CIS contested duopoly design are (1) both sellers post their price (and quantity) offers simultaneously and privately, (2) the Ramsey-optimal and "first-best" prices are identical, since $AC = MC$ at the competitive output level ($q = 10$), (3) sellers may choose to restrict their quantity offer rather than "serve the market" at the posted price, and (4) neither seller knows the (stable) demand curve. These features place the experimental operationalization of the CMH at odds with the available theoretical models. Several of these features are clearly of subsidiary interest (e.g., point 2) or theoretically uninterestingly given the focus on price-sustainable configurations of cost conditions and demand (e.g., point 3). On the other hand, points 1 and 4 are nontrivial variants of the basic theoretical model, in the sense that we do not have a consistent theoretical sense of what might happen in a market in which they do not apply. Moreover point 1 has been the center of much controversy over contestability theory. I present some evidence on the behavioral importance of these points in the next two sections.

HM provide the CMH with a "worthier institutional opponent" than unregulated monopoly, which was the only behavioral control in CIS. They consider the Loeb-Magat decentralized regulation institution, with

Table 6.1 Pooled indexes of monopoly trading effectiveness in various experiments

Period	CIS Unregulated monopoly	CIS Contested duopoly	HM Unregulated monopoly	HM Regulated monopoly	HM Contested markets
1	42	53	70	−160	22
2	57	53	57	−215	22
3	62	51	59	−142	15
4	59	36	70	−143	25
5	64	39	53	−169	20
6	71	43	73	−210	14
7	60	38	75	−340	3
8	66	37	72	−338	31
9	68	33			
10	70	9			
11	60	36			
12	57	35			
13	59	34			
14	56	−14			
15	69	10			
16	77	30			
17	59	−6			
18	56	2			
1–8	60	44	66	−217	19
All	62	29	66	−217	19
Number of replications	4	6	4	8	4

Note: The "regulated monopoly" experiments of HM refer to their R and F series.

and without franchise bidding, as a more realistic alternative to deregulation by way of contestability.[4] HM find that the regulatory institution is behaviorally more effective at restraining monopoly power, in the sense that convergence to competitive predictions was more rapid and complete than with comparable contestable markets.

Table 6.1 provides a summary of the main results of the CIS and HM experiments. A convenient and popular descriptive statistic for the observed trading behavior of each (ex post) seller is the index of monopoly effectiveness, M:

$$M = \left[\frac{\pi - \pi_c}{\pi_m - \pi_c}\right] \times 100,$$

where π denotes the observed trading profit in one or more periods, π_m denotes the theoretical monopoly trading profit, and π_c denotes the theoretical competitive trading profit. Each of the theoretical profit values can be numerically determined in each experiment, and each is reported in CIS and HM. Clearly $M = 0$ if $\pi = \pi_c$, $M = 100$ if $\pi = \pi_m$, $M > 0$ as $\pi > \pi_c$, $M < 0$ as $\pi < \pi_c$, and the maximum $M = 100$ is attained if $\pi = \pi_m$. Note that we here define π_m as the uniform-price theoretical monopoly profit, given the present focus on PO markets.

The values reported in table 6.1 demonstrate a clear tendency toward the static theoretical predictions. We would expect the unregulated and uncontested monopolies to converge to the maximum 100 percent value of M. In fact we observe that the subjects only attained 62 percent effectiveness in the CIS experiments and 66 percent effectiveness in the HM experiments. The expected value of M for the contested markets under the CMH is zero: clearly we can reject this strong form of the CMH. The CIS-contested market experiments have an average monopoly effectiveness of only 29 percent over all 18 periods, but this is significantly positive. Similarly the first eight periods of the CIS-contested duopoly experiments display significantly positive monopoly effectiveness of 19 percent. It should be noted that four of the six CIS duopoly experiments did converge to and attain the zero value of M after 10 periods; one experiment, PO52, astonishingly attained it after just one period! However, the purpose of replicating experiments is to ensure that one is not led astray by small-sample oddities. When we pool over all time periods and over all experiments, the CIS and HM results do not support the strong form of the CMH.

An important qualification to the results of CIS and HM is the length of each experiment. There is some evidence in the early duopoly experiments of Friedman (1963) of an increased tendency toward collusive outcomes with replication. Similar tendencies are noted by Friedman and Hoggatt (1980, pp. 88, 189).[5] One critical feature of these experiments is the large number of periods in each session: as many as 100 in Friedman and Hoggatt (1980). Once subjects attain a noncooperative contestable outcome, their profits are virtually zero. Hence the opportunity cost of a cooperative price signal was extremely low. Arguably, had the experiments of CIS and HM continued for more periods such collusive signals may have been observed and may have led to collusive outcomes (contrary to the CMH). It is therefore necessary to qualify out-of-sample predictions of behavioral tendencies from the observed outcomes (see CIS, pp. 108 ff.).

The results in table 6.1 show that the discipline of contestability does serve to mitigate the monopoly problem when we compare it to an unregulated monopoly over the same horizon. The monopoly effectiveness of the contested markets of both CIS and HM is significantly lower than for cases without contesting. Clearly this is one important conclusion for public policy: contestability reduces monopoly trading effectiveness over certain finite horizons. HM results are stronger than those of CIS here, since contestability showed significant beneficial effects in HM from the first period, whereas the beneficial effects in CIS are not significant until the third period.

Finally, table 6.1 demonstrates that enlightened monopoly regulation vastly outperforms contestability in terms of reducing monopoly trading effectiveness. The large negative values for the HM experiment are somewhat illusory here and reflect the fact that increases in subsidy payments offset trading losses (over the relevant range) in the regulatory scheme considered. Even if we conservatively set these values to zero, however, the comparative policy conclusion is clear: contestability does not reduce monopoly trading effectiveness as well as a decentralized regulatory institution. This conclusion is properly qualified in HM, having regard to the problems of financing subsidy payments and of the regulator knowing the demand curve. Neither problem is encountered when one considers contestability as a public policy option.

Sunk Costs and Entry Barriers

Coursey, Isaac, Luke, and Smith (1984), hereafter CILS, evaluate the CMH when sunk costs are imposed symmetrically on "incumbents" and "entrants." Their results are important by providing further evidence of the extent to which the CMH is behaviorally robust to violations of one key assumption in the basic theory: the absence of entry barriers. In these experiments one of two sellers is chosen at random to be an uncontested monopolist for five trading periods. From period six on, the other seller is allowed to post prices in direct competition with the incumbent. Each seller must purchase an "entry permit" before being allowed to post prices. Each permit is valid for five periods and costs $2. This value of the entry cost was carefully chosen by CILS (p. 72) to yield the following properties:

(1) If a firm achieves the theoretical monopoly price and quantity, it covers sunk costs in one period. (2) There exists no competitive price ... at which a seller could recoup the sunk costs in one period. (3) There are prices supporting the competitive quantity at which the sunk costs could be recouped in 2, 3, 4 or 5 periods.... (4) There are prices which cover AVC and support the competitive quantity but which do not allow the seller to cover sunk costs even if (s)he sells all 10 competitive units for 5 periods.

One interesting feature of the CILS design that CILS do not discuss is the effect of sunk costs on market efficiency when the market is openly contested.[6]

It is apparent that CILS view their symmetric sunk entry cost as an entry barrier, and yet one must proceed carefully with definitions on this point. Following Stigler (1968, p. 67), Baumol, Panzar, and Willig (1982, p. 282) define an entry barrier as "anything that requires an expenditure by a new entrant into an industry, but imposes no equivalent cost upon an incumbent." In the CILS design it is clearly not the permit payment that is the entry barrier from period 6 on, since each seller must pay the same $2 cost for every permit. Rather, it is the precommitment of the incumbent to have to purchase a permit for periods 6 through 10 that may constitute an entry barrier for those periods. Baumol, Panzar, and Willig (1982, p. 290) are quite explicit about the distinction they have in mind:

Sunk costs *to some degree* share with entry barriers the ability to impede the establishment of new firms. The need to sink money into a new enterprise ... imposes a difference between the *incremental cost and the incremental risk* that are faced by an entrant and an incumbent. The latter's funds are already committed and are already exposed to whatever perils participation in the industry entails. On the other hand, a new firm must take the corresponding amount of liquid capital and turn it into a frozen asset if he enters the business. Thus, the incremental cost, as seen by a potential entrant, includes the full amount of the sunk costs, which is a bygone to the incumbent [footnote omitted; emphasis added].

The point here is that both sellers in the CILS design are "new firms" and entrants in this sense from period 11 on. They face the same technology and virtually the same market uncertainties over these periods. However, during periods 6 through 10, and only during those periods, the sunk cost does unambiguously constitute an entry barrier as defined earlier.

Why do we care to be so "pure" in defining when the CILS sunk costs are an entry barrier and when they are not? Consider the observed effects of sunk costs on market efficiency reported in table 6.2. Market efficiency is defined here as the total surplus paid to subjects (consumer plus producer surplus) as a percentage of the maximum surplus that could have been paid out (in these experiments, at the competitive equilibrium). Table 6.2 reports the pooled efficiency values for the contested periods of the six CILS experiments with human buyers[8] and the six CIS duopoly experiments. It also shows the percentage difference in efficiency between these two series, which is attributable to the effect of sunk costs. For all eighteen periods there is a slight and statistically insignificant effect of sunk costs reducing efficiency. However, there is a significant decline in efficiency in CILS periods 6 through 10 due to sunk costs. In the remaining periods (CILS periods 11 through 23) the effect on efficiency is positive but insignificant.

These results are consistent with our classification of sunk costs in this design as an entry barrier in periods 6 through 10, and not otherwise. Thus we conclude that the CILS results are consistent with the proposition that

Table 6.2 Effects of sunk costs on market efficiency

Contested period	CILS period	Pooled efficiency of CILS human buyers experiments	Pooled efficiency of CIS contested duopoly experiments	Percentage effect of sunk costs on efficiency
1	6	55.26	76.67	−27.9
2	7	71.45	76.67	−6.8
3	8	74.15	81.67	−9.2
4	9	78.20	75.50	3.6
5	10	82.25	76.00	8.2
6	11	80.09	79.30	1.0
7	12	90.55	79.30	14.2
8	13	90.01	76.50	17.7
9	14	86.30	83.80	3.0
10	15	82.92	82.15	0.9
11	16	86.57	88.70	−2.4
12	17	82.18	90.30	−9.0
13	18	76.43	85.50	−12.7
14	19	82.66	76.90	7.5
15	20	76.25	86.50	−11.8
16	21	88.26	93.30	−5.4
17	22	84.95	81.20	4.6
18	23	86.64	85.50	1.3
1–5	6–10	72.26	77.30	−6.5
6–10	11–15	85.65	80.21	6.8
11–15	16–20	80.03	85.58	−6.5
16–18	21–23	86.61	86.67	−0.1
1–18	6–23	80.53	81.97	−1.7

entry barriers do produce a loss in efficiency. This is also consistent with one popular definition of entry barriers, expounded by Von Weizsacker (1980), that defines them directly in terms of resulting welfare losses. It is also consistent with the more operational definition proposed by Baumol, Panzar, and Willig (1982), who argue that "anything that is an entry barrier by our definition does reduce the sum of consumers' and producers' surplus ..." (p. 282).

Unfortunately there is one fundamental difficulty with the preceding (strict) interpretation of sunk costs in the CILS experiments: actual entry was never significantly diminished by the barriers to entry. The entrant always chose to enter in period 6, and there were very few periods overall in which both sellers did not own current entry permits. The importance of this observation is that we cannot categorically attribute the decline in efficiency in periods 6 through 10 to the effects of entry barriers. It is not clear what led to that decline. What this suggests is that there is a significant gap in contestability theory as to how one defines "entry barriers." As argued at length earlier, the entry permit in CILS does correspond to an entry barrier in the strict BPW sense, and yet it does not forestall actual entry. In such circumstances it is difficult to conclude that contestability theory is or is not behaviorally robust to the presence of (certain) entry barriers. More theory and experimentation are called for before any such conclusions can be drawn.

Theoretical Assumptions and Experimental Design

Baumol, Panzar, and Willig (1982, p. 5), hereafter BPW, define a perfectly contested market as a market accessible to potential entrants and having the following two properties:

First, the potential entrants can, without restriction, serve the same market demands and use the same productive techniques as those available to the incumbent firms.... Second, the potential entrants evaluate the profitability of entry at the incumbent firms' preentry prices. That is, although the potential entrants recognize that an expansion of industry outputs leads to lower prices—in accord with the market demand curves—the entrants nevertheless assume that if they undercut incumbents' prices they can sell as much of the corresponding good as the quantity demanded by the market at their own prices.

The experiments in CIS and HM operationalize the first of these properties but not the second. This is particularly unfortunate given the critical reception that the second property has received. Spence (1983, p. 982) notes:

The critical assumption in perfect competition is price-taking behavior. The reader is entitled to know what behavioral postulate replaces price-taking in the new theory and serves the same or a similar role. The answer is entry. Entry is free in the sense that there are potential competitors with the same cost functions, who can enter and leave without loss of capital *within the time frame required for incumbents to change prices.* Lest the reader close the *Journal* at this point, remember that we are talking for the moment about a theory that provides a normative standard against which market outcomes can be judged. There may also be conditions under which the theory is a reasonable descriptive approximation to reality as well.... what is set aside in the theory are elements of strategic interaction that we have come to associate with entry deterrence ... The debate will center on the empirical importance of some of these deliberately neglected aspects of industry structure [emphasis added].

In a similar vein, Brock (1983, p. 1059) argues:

Oligopolistic interactions matter. Baumol *et al.* argue that such oligopolistic indeterminacy (and hence the necessity of making unpalatable assumptions about entrants' conjectures that cannot be supported by economic "common sense") is avoided in the presence of perfectly reversible and frictionless entry. Baumol *et al.* need some argument for this conclusion because they impose the dual (equally unpalatable) assumption that entrants enter in the expectation that incumbents' *prices* remain fixed. One gets the feeling from reading the book that incumbents are forced to price competitively as the outcome of some game between incumbents and potential entrants, provided that entry is costlessly reversible.

But nowhere in the book is a game precisely defined as modern theory expects.... That is not easy, but until it is done, contestability theory must be used with caution. Unpalatable hidden assumptions may be necessary to obtain Baumol *et al.*'s conclusions.

Finally, Dixit (1982, p. 16) notes:

As a positive theory, it [contestability] needs careful handling. In most cases in practice, production requires some commitments that can only be liquidated gradually, consumers assimilate and respond to price changes with some delay, and firms need some time to calculate and implement price changes. Perfect contestability is the judgement that the third lag is the longest. There are instances where this can be argued, such as the passenger air traffic market between a given city pair. But the scope of validity of the theory is unclear. The traditional presumption in industrial organization is the opposite, that is, that prices can be changed more quickly than sunk capacity.

Similarly critical evaluations of the Bertrand-Nash behavioral assumption can be found in Knieps and Vogelsang (1982), Brock and Scheinkman (1983), and Shephard (1984).

The Bertrand-Nash assumption may be justified in several ways. We should distinguish two possible interpretations of the second property noted by BPW. One possible interpretation is of a direct structural or institutional first-mover environment, and another weaker interpretation is that it is an indirect expectational phenomenon (see BPW, p. 11, for similar interpretations). In the latter case we ask in experiments such as those of CIS and HM if the evidence is sufficient to induce such expectations or behavior consistent (on an "as if" basis) with those expectations. I argued earlier that the answer to this question is generally negative: I do not see evidence that supports the strong form of the CMH. I therefore proceed to consider the experimental effect of imposing the direct and stronger interpretation of the Bertrand-Nash assumption.

One might also justify the stronger structural interpretation in terms of the specific U.S. regulatory milieu that spawned contestability theory. Consider a system of regulation in which the incumbent is tied up by rules requiring that prices be posted, allowing entrants simply to react to those posted prices. Arguably AT&T could be thought to have been such a "tied-down" incumbent, despite the use of antitrust regulations by a potential competitor of AT&T to block the incumbent from changing it's prices (see Baumol and Ordover 1985, pp. 257 ff.). There has also been a proposal by Baumol (1979) to implement a variant of the Bertrand-Nash sequential pricing requirement as an antitrust policy to prevent predatory pricing.

BPW (pp. 11–12) provide one additional line of defence of their Bertrand-Nash assumption, alluded to by Spence in the preceding quote, but it is clear that they recognize its limitations in general. In the context of a discussion of "intertemporal unsustainability," for example, BPW (p. 428) suggest:

> There is a final and very critical reason why the implications of our unsustainability theorem may not be as drastic as they seem. A *fundamental limitation* of sustainability analysis is its implication that entrants' expectations are those of the Bertrand-Nash models. That is, each entrant is implicitly assumed to expect that after entry occurs the incumbent will keep his pre-entry prices unchanged for a period sufficiently long to make entry profitable. For only on this premise can the entrant be assumed to take advantage of any profitable entry possibilities presented by the incumbent's initial prices. However, if the potential entrant fears pricing changes after entry, then he may decide to ignore the apparently profitable entry opportunities and simply stay out of the industry. The entry threat may therefore evaporate even before it can be noticed [emphasis added].

We now turn to the treatment of this issue in the experimental literature.

For the purpose of designing experiments to test the CMH, there are two aspects of the Bertrand-Nash assumption that need to be operationalized in each trading period:

1. The incumbent firm ("incumbency" to be defined shortly) cannot change his price (and quantity) offer after seeing the offers of any potential entrants.

2. A potential entrant evaluates the profitability of various prices offers *knowing* the offer of the incumbent.

As discussed in the previous section, the experimental studies of CIS and HM adopt a posted offer marketing institution in which all potential sellers in any given trading period, whether or not we might define them as "incumbents" or "entrants," submit their price offers simultaneously and privately. These offers are publicly revealed for subsequent trading periods, but not contemporaneously—that is, in any trading period potential sellers know the prices posted in all previous periods.[9] This effectively operationalizes point 1 of the Bertrand-Nash assumption but fails to operationalize point 2 exactly.[10]

An alternative experimental design to implement both aspects of the Bertrand-Nash assumption is easily conceived. In the first period of the

CIS and HM experiments, allow all potential sellers to post their price offers simultaneously and privately (one could, alternatively, toss a coin to determine an "incumbent," but this is a somewhat arbitrary procedure). In the second period the seller who "won" the market in the first period is designated the "incumbent," and must post his/her price offer before anybody else posts theirs. Moreover the incumbent's offer can be publicly announced before the other potential sellers are required to post their offers. Subsequent periods will be handled similarly, with the incumbent being defined as the "winner" in the previous trading period.[11]

It might be argued that "hardwiring" the Bertrand-Nash assumption into a contested market experiment will automatically lead to a trivial behavioral outcome. However, such an experimental design is no more or less trivial than contestability theory itself. It is hardly consistent methodology to accept certain assumptions as interesting at a theoretical level while dismissing them as uninteresting at an empirical level. To the extent that contestability theory is at all worthy of empirical attention and scrutiny, then it is worthy of evaluation on it's theoretical domain. We also emphasize again the methodological role of our Bertrand-Nash design for the purposes of comparison with less strict designs, such as those already reported by CIS and HM.

Table 6.3 lists the experiments conducted to determine if the Bertrand-Nash assumption does matter behaviorally. We report the results of sixteen experiments with "experienced" subject[12] using computerized seller-input and *simulated buyer behavior*. All subjects were honors undergraduates in economics at the University of Western Ontario. They were told before the experiments that they would be paid a predetermined fraction of their earnings in these experiments; this fraction was set at one-tenth for all experiments, providing an expected monetary reward comfortably in excess of their likely opportunity cost for the time involved. By all casual signs subject motivation was excellent.

Following the contestable market experiments of HM, all subjects in our experiments were risk-neutral. The pretest for risk-neutrality is presented in Harrison (1986a), and the statistical basis for deciding whether a given subject was "risk-neutral" follows Harrison and Rutström (1986).[13]

All experiments were conducted on a computerized PO basis, corresponding in essentials with the institution studied by Ketcham, Smith, and Williams (1983), CIS, CILS, HM, and Harrison, McKee, and Rutström (1987). Note that the major difference between these experiments and those reported in CIS, apart from the Bertrand-Nash treatment itself, is the use of computer-simulated buyers. All subjects initially participated in an

Table 6.3 Experimental design

Experiment series ID	Individual experiment ID	Bertrand-Nash assumption satisfied?	Demand known?	Number of potential sellers	Shift parameter
C	C1	No	No	2	$3.86
	C2	No	No	2	3.86
	C3	No	No	2	3.86
	C4	No	No	3	2.66
	C5	No	No	3	2.66
	C6	No	No	3	2.66
CBN	CBN1	Yes	No	2	3.86
	CBN2	Yes	No	2	3.86
	CBN3	Yes	No	2	3.86
CBND	CBND1	Yes	Yes	2	3.86
	CBND2	Yes	Yes	2	3.86
	CBND3	Yes	Yes	2	3.86
	CBND4	Yes	Yes	3	2.66
	CBND5	Yes	Yes	3	2.66
	CBND6	Yes	Yes	3	2.66
	CBND7	Yes	Yes	3	2.66

Notes: Experiments C1 and C4 were previously reported in HM as experiments C1 and C3, respectively; experiments CBN1–CBN3 are reported in HMR as CDEBN1-3; experiment CBND7 had a "special" subject pool, as described in the text.

Uncontested Monopoly experiment with decreasing costs of at least fifteen periods duration. This preliminary experiment is qualitatively identical to the Unregulated Monopoly experiments of HM. To the extent that such "training" experiments influence subsequent behavior,[14] one would expect (on simple "hysteresis" grounds) that they bias our results against the CMH. Note that any such bias is equal to that present in HM and is the same for all of the experiments reported here.

All of the experiments reported in this study are procedural variants of the Uncontested Monopoly design. I therefore describe the procedural features of that design and then discuss the changes in procedures for the other experiments. HM present the complete set of instructions used for each of the series, with one variation to implement the Bertrand-Nash treatment.

Each subject is located at a computer terminal, and the program executed. The number of periods to be conducted is initialized in full view of the subject. In each period the seller is shown the marginal cost of each of ten units (and knows that the implicit cost of further units is infinite). The seller is rewarded by the difference between the offer price of each unit (which is uniform for all units), and the (decreasing) unit costs for the quantity sold. Inventories or carry-over of unfilled orders from buyers are not permitted (i.e., sales are "to order"); hence the given marginal cost schedule induced a theoretical flow supply schedule (see Smith 1976).

After the display of cost conditions in each period, the seller is prompted for a price and quantity offer. Given the price offer, the quantity offer is restricted in a natural way.[15] The seller is informed of the potential trading profit if all units offered are sold, and then asked to confirm or revise the prevailing price/quantity offer. Offers may be revised any number of times before the seller faces (simulated) buyers. When an offer is confirmed the seller is informed of the number of units purchased by buyers and the corresponding trading profit or loss (on a "per unit sold" and "total" basis). A trading commission of 5 cents per unit sold is also paid. All purchases were in strictly declining order of marginal valuation (i.e., inframarginal buyers were not randomized in a buying sequence as in the simulated demand procedures used in CILS).

The C series was a simple variant on the Uncontested Monopoly series. Each subject privately entered a price/quantity offer after privately being informed of the cost schedule for each period. When all offers had been initialized and "confirmed," every subject was informed of the price and quantity offers of all sellers, and the market opened to (simulated) buyers. Tied price offers were resolved by randomly choosing one of the sellers to supply first.[16] Purchases were made by the simulated buyers first from the seller posting the lowest price, and then from the seller with the next highest price, and so on, until there was no further demand or the seller's maximum quantity offer had been sold. Note that the first set of inframarginal buyers will purchase from the lowest-price seller, leaving buyers with lower marginal valuations for the next lowest-price seller, and so on. Following the previous experiments, sellers are only informed of their own sales and trading profits.

The CBN series varied from the C series only with respect to the sequential entry of price offers (the previous period incumbent makes the first offer) and the privacy of the incumbent's price offer (the experimenter making a public announcement of that price). Note that the incumbent's quantity offer was not made public. The change in experimental instructions that implements the Bertrand-Nash assumption is as follows:

In the first trading period ALL potential sellers will PRIVATELY choose their price and quantity offers. In all subsequent periods the seller who sold the largest quantity in the PREVIOUS period will enter his/her price and quantity offer before the other seller(s), and that PRICE OFFER will be announced in PUBLIC when

Table 6.4 Marginal revenue and cost schedules

Unit	Demand parameters		Marginal cost
	Average revenue	Marginal revenue	
1	$6.23	$5.98	$4.98
2	5.98	5.48	4.73
3	5.73	4.98	4.48
4	5.48	4.48	4.23
5	5.23	3.98	3.98
6	4.98	3.48	3.73
7	4.73	2.98	3.48
8	4.48	2.48	3.23
9	4.23	1.98	2.98
10	3.98	1.48	2.73
11	3.73	0.98	∞
Shift parameter assumed	3.86	3.86	3.86

it is confirmed (the QUANTITY OFFER will not be announced in public). The other seller(s) will then PRIVATELY choose their price and quantity offers for that period. In all periods, buyers will decide who they want to buy from (based on the price/quantity offers of all sellers) after ALL potential sellers have chosen their price and quantity offers.

In the CBND series we gave all subjects a listing of buyers' redemption values. It was common knowledge that all sellers received these values.

Table 6.4 presents average revenue (AR), marginal revenue (MR) and marginal costs (MC) schedules for the experiments. These are the values represented earlier in figure 6.1 for a two-seller design. A shift parameter is used as indicated in tables 6.3 and 6.4 to disguise particular cost and revenue schedules and hence the equilibrium outcomes for experienced subjects (this standard procedure follows CIS and HM).

Experimental Results

Table 6.5 presents our static theoretical predictions for all relevant variables. Our monopoly predictions adopt the familiar $MC = MR$ rule to determine quantity, and then defines price from the demand curve evaluated at that quantity. The competitive predictions are obtained from the intersection of MC and the demand curve.

The appendix at the end of this chapter lists the detailed outcomes for all experiments. Table 6.6 presents the values for the index of monopoly

Table 6.5 Theoretical predictions

Shift parameter	Variable	Monopoly predictions	Competitive predictions
$3.86	Price	$5.23	3.81
	Quantity	5	10
	Trading profit	$4.00	0.05
	Index of monopoly effectiveness, M	100	0
$2.66	Price	$4.03	2.61
	Quantity	5	10
	Trading profit	$4.00	0.05
	Index of monopoly effectiveness, M	100	0

Note: All predictions are the same across institutions; trading profit includes commissions of 5 cents per trade.

trading effectiveness.[17] Inspection of table 6.6 reveals that, with the exception of CBND3, satisfaction of the Bertrand-Nash assumption is associated with a dramatic decline in monopoly trading effectiveness. In other words, observed behavior is much closer to competitive predictions in the CBN and CBND series of experiments than in the C series. Moreover we find support in the CBND series for a strong form of the CMH that claims that observed prices will converge to and attain competitive predictions. Previous experiments by CIS and HM that did not satisfy the Bertrand-Nash assumption could only find support for a weak form of the CMH that claims that observed prices will be closer to competitive predictions than to monopoly predictions.

The results in experiment CBND3 represent a significant and important outlier. Table 6.7 shows the detailed behavior in this experiment. Price offers had fallen to the competitive level ($3.81) in period 3 and stayed there in period 4 even with a change in incumbent. However, in period 4 the incumbent successfully signalled a willingness to collude by posting a "suicidal" price offer of $5.00. The entrant appropriately chose a price of $4.99, capturing the market and selling five units for a profit of $2.80. This new incumbent then returned the favor by similarly posting a price of $5.00, allowing the other seller to capture the market with a $4.99 price offer. The two sellers repeated this collusive cycle in the final two periods. It should be noted that no explicit collusive agreement (oral or written) was allowed by the experimenter. When asked at the end of the experiment if they thought that they could have done even better (e.g., by posting prices of $4.03 and receiving the theoretical monopoly profit of $4.00), the two sellers replied that their tacit collusive agreement would probably have been too hard to maintain during the search for the maximum joint profit.

Table 6.6 Indexes of monopoly trading effectiveness

Experiments	Period								Pooled
	1	2	3	4	5	6	7	8	
C1	0.23	0	0.08	0.33	0.23	0.20	0.18	0.08	0.16
C2	0.37	0.15	0.20	0.10	0.08	0.02	0	0	0.12
C3	0.73	0.55	0.67	0.38	0.35	0.23	0.08	0.05	0.38
C1-C3	0.44	0.23	0.32	0.27	0.22	0.15	0.09	0.04	0.22
C4	0.10	0.12	0.10	0	0.08	0.13	0	0.10	0.08
C5	0.49	0.58	0.56	0.26	0.12	0.18	0.10	0.03	0.29
C6	0.31	0.28	0.49	0.82	0.91	0.58	0.20	0.10	0.46
C4-C6	0.30	0.33	0.38	0.36	0.37	0.30	0.10	0.08	0.28
C1-C6	0.37	0.28	0.35	0.31	0.30	0.23	0.09	0.06	0.25
CBN1	0.48	0.12	−0.05	−0.02	0	0	0	0	0.07
CBN2	0.61	0.60	0.12	−0.05	−0.02	0	0	0	0.16
CBN3	0.12	0.20	0.08	0.08	0	0.08	0.08	0.05	0.09
CBN1-CBN3	0.40	0.51	0.05	0	0	0.03	0.03	0.02	0.11
CBND1	0.35	0.33	0	0	0	0	0	0	0.09
CBND2	0.15	0.20	0	0	0	0	0	0	0.04
CBND3	0.60	0.08	0	0	0.70	0.70	0.70	0.70	0.44
CBND1-CBND3	0.37	0.20	0	0	0.23	0.23	0.23	0.23	0.19
CBND4	0.70	0	0	0	0	0	0	0	0.09
CBND5	0.82	0	0	0	0	0	0	0	0.10
CBND6	0.95	0	0	0	0	0	0	0	0.12
CBND4-CBND6	0.82	0	0	0	0	0	0	0	0.10
CBND1-CBND6	0.60	0.10	0	0	0.12	0.12	0.12	0.12	0.15
CBND7	0.74	0	0	−0.04	0.31	0	0	0	0.13

Table 6.7 Successful collusive behavior in experiment CBND3

Period	Seller	Price offer	Quantity offer	Quantity sold	Profit
1	1	4.20	10	9	2.43
	2	4.49	10	0	—
2	1*	3.85	10	0	—
	2	3.84	10	10	0.35
3	1	3.81	10	10	0.05
	2*	3.81	10	0	—
4	1*	3.81	10	10	0.05
	2	3.81	10	0	—
5	1*	5.00	10	0	—
	2	4.99	10	5	2.80
6	1	4.99	10	5	2.80
	2*	5.00	10	0	—
7	1*	5.00	10	0	—
	2	4.99	10	5	2.80
8	1	4.99	10	5	2.80
	2*	5.00	10	0	—

Note: Incumbent in each period is indicated by an asterisk.

Experiment CBND7 was designed to see if the collusive behavior in CBND3 would survive the introduction of a third potential seller with a history of noncollusive behavior. Sellers 1 and 2 in CBND7 were the successful colluders of CBND3, and seller 3 in CBND7 was seller 2 in CBND2. Thus all three sellers in CBND7 were experienced in the basic CBND institution with two sellers, although the experiments in which they gained their experience obviously differed as indicated above. Note also from table 6.3 that the parameters of CBND7 were different from CBND2 and CBND3.

The outcome in CBND7 was a dramatic inability to sustain any tacit collusive solution. Table 6.8 shows the detailed behavior in this experiment. Seller 3 won the market in period 1 and set a price offer 19 cents in excess of the competitive level of $2.61. Seller 2 sought control of the market in period 3 with a price offer in period 2 of $2.61. As the incumbent in period 3 he then signaled for a collusive outcome by posting a price offer of $10.00 and a quantity offer of one unit.[18] His partner in previous collusion, seller 1, responded with a price offer of $9.99, but the "newcomer," seller 3, captured the market with a price at the competitive level. Seller 3 also posted a competitive-level price as incumbent in period 4. Seller 2 then sought control of the market by posting a price 1 cent below the competitive level and incurring a loss of 5 cents. As incumbent, seller 2 again

Table 6.8 Unsuccessful collusive behavior in experiment CBND7

Period	Seller	Price offer	Quantity offer	Quantity sold	Profit
1	1	5.00	10	0	—
	2	5.00	10	0	—
	3	4.10	10	4	2.98
2	1	2.79	10	0	—
	2	2.61	10	10	0.05
	3*	2.80	10	0	—
3	1	9.99	10	0	—
	2*	10.00	1	0	—
	3	2.61	10	10	0.05
4	1	2.61	10	0	—
	2	2.60	10	10	−0.05
	3*	2.61	10	0	—
5	1	9.99	10	0	—
	2*	10.00	1	0	—
	3	5.00	10	1	1.27
6	1	2.61	10	0	—
	2	2.61	10	10	0.05
	3*	2.61	10	0	—
7	1	2.61	10	10	0.05
	2*	2.61	10	0	—
	3	2.61	10	0	—
8	1*	2.61	10	0	—
	2	2.61	10	10	0.05
	3	2.61	10	0	—

Note: Incumbent in each period is indicated by an asterisk.

signaled for a collusive outcome in period 5 by posting a price of $10.00. Again seller 1 responded with a price offer of $9.99, but this time seller 3 offered a price of $5.00 and gained a profit of $1.27. Unresponsive to the largesse of sellers 1 and 2 in period 5, seller 3 posted a price offer at the competitive level in period 6. Sellers 1 and 2 responded with identical prices, and the market collapsed to the competitive outcome in the final two periods. This pilot experiment suggests that collusive behavior in two-seller contested markets is not robust to the introduction of a third seller who does not have a history of collusive behavior.

A nonparametric statistical analysis of our results in table 6.6 strongly supports our conclusion that satisfaction of the Bertrand-Nash assumption significantly strengthens the behavioral case for the CMH. Consider the results when we pool the experiments with two and three sellers. Although some difference in outcomes is noticeable in periods 1 and 2, it is not until period 3 that this difference becomes dramatic. If we exclude experiment CBND3 as an outlier, our results are generally strengthened, especially in relation to behavior in periods 7 and 8. For reasons discussed earlier, however, we believe that the collusive result in CBND3 warrants detailed attention rather than blanket exclusion.

Concentrating only on the two-seller experiments, we cannot claim that satisfying the Bertrand-Nash assumption made any significant difference except in periods 3 and 4. This inability to identify the effect of our Bertrand-Nash treatment is largely attributable to the CBND3 outcome.

Turning now to the three-seller experiments, our statistical tests generally support the conclusion that the Bertrand-Nash assumption matters behaviorally. Note that even though the period 1 outcomes are significantly different, this is in the unusual direction of greater monopoly effectiveness in the CBND series that the C series (from table 6.6 we have $M = 0.82$ for CBND4-CBND6 and $M = 0.30$ for C4-C6). In all subsequent periods, during which the Bertrand-Nash assumption had effect, the direction of the effectiveness indexes is reversed (from table 6.6, the values pooled over all periods are $M = 0.10$ for CBND4-CBND6 and $M = 0.28$ for C4-C6). The only minor qualifications to our general conclusion for the three-seller experiments is in periods 4 and 7.

Varying the number of contestants from two to three had no significant influence on monopoly effectiveness in any period in the C series. In the CBND series the only significant effects occurred in periods 1 and 2. In all subsequent periods in the CBND1-CBND6 experiments outcomes have "degenerated" to the zero monopoly effectiveness level (again, with the exception of CBND3 in periods 5 through 8). Although the difference in behavior in period 1 is clearly significant, it is of no immediate interest given that our notion of "incumbency" and satisfaction of the Bertrand-Nash assumption does not take effect until period 2. In period 2 the increase in contestants from 2 to 3 dramatically decreases monopoly effectiveness in the CBND design, whether or not CBND7 is included.

Conclusions

Our new experimental results indicate that the Bertrand-Nash assumption indeed "matters" behaviorally. The empirical case for the CMH is significantly strengthened in an environment in which that assumption is met. Specifically, we conclude that (1) the strong version of the CMH is supported in experiments that satisfy the Bertrand-Nash assumption, whereas previous experiments were only able to find support for the weak version of the CMH, and (2) increasing the number of potential sellers from two to three does have a significant effect on behavior in environments in which the Bertrand-Nash assumption is satisfied, with significantly stronger support for the CMH during the transition to competitive outcomes.

These results nicely complement those of CIS and HM on the question of the behavioral robustness of the CMH. The present study demonstrates that an exact experimental operationalization of the theoretical model proposed by BPW yields behavior that is consistent with a strong version of their CMH. Several critics have suggested that the CMH may not be robust to "reasonable" variations from the basic model of BPW, especially with respect to alternatives to their Bertrand-Nash assumption. The results of the earlier experimental studies, in which a weak version of the CMH received empirical support in experimental operationalizations that do not match the BPW model,[19] therefore demonstrate that the CMH is behaviorally robust to certain modifications of one controversial theoretical assumption.

Appendix: Detailed Experimental Results

Experiment C1

Period	Seller	Price offer	Quantity offer	Quantity sold	Profit
1	1	4.00	10	0	—
	2	3.90	10	10	0.95
2	1	3.81	10	10	0.05
	2	3.85	10	0	—
3	1	4.00	10	0	—
	2	3.84	10	10	0.35
4	1	4.00	10	0	—
	2	3.94	10	10	1.35
5	1	3.98	10	0	—
	2	3.90	10	10	0.95
6	1	4.00	10	0	—
	2	3.89	10	10	0.85
7	1	3.88	10	10	0.75
	2	3.93	10	0	—
8	1	3.84	10	10	0.35
	2	3.99	10	0	—

Experiment C2

Period	Seller	Price offer	Quantity offer	Quantity sold	Profit
1	1	4.35	10	0	—
	2	4.10	10	9	1.53
2	1	4.08	10	0	—
	2	4.00	10	9	0.63
3	1	3.99	10	0	—
	2	3.89	10	10	0.85
4	1	3.85	10	10	0.45
	2	3.89	10	0	—
5	1	3.85	10	0	—
	2	3.84	10	10	0.35
6	1	3.83	10	0	—
	2	3.82	10	10	0.15
7	1	3.81	10	10	0.05
	2	3.83	10	0	—
8	1	3.81	10	0	—
	2	3.81	10	10	0.05

Experiment C3

Period	Seller	Price offer	Quantity offer	Quantity sold	Profit
1	1	5.95	9	0	—
	2	4.60	10	7	2.94
2	1	4.59	10	0	—
	2	4.50	10	7	2.24
3	1	4.39	10	8	2.68
	2	4.40	10	0	—
4	1	4.29	10	0	—
	2	4.10	10	9	1.53
5	1	3.95	10	10	1.45
	2	4.03	10	0	—
6	1	3.90	10	10	0.95
	2	3.92	10	0	—
7	1	3.84	10	10	0.36
	2	3.87	10	0	—
8	1	3.84	10	0	—
	2	3.83	10	10	0.25

Experiment C4

Period	Seller	Price offer	Quantity offer	Quantity sold	Profit
1	1	2.70	10	10	0.45
	2	2.80	10	0	—
	3	3.50	10	0	—
2	1	2.79	10	9	0.54
	2	2.90	10	0	—
	3	3.25	10	0	—
3	1	2.69	10	0	—
	2	2.65	10	10	0.45
	3	2.75	10	0	—
4	1	2.67	10	0	—
	2	2.61	10	10	0.05
	3	2.67	10	0	—
5	1	2.64	10	0	—
	2	2.66	10	0	—
	3	2.64	10	10	0.35
6	1	2.63	10	0	0.35
	2	2.62	10	10	0.55
	3	2.63	10	0	—
7	1	2.62	10	0	—
	2	2.61	10	10	0.05
	3	999.0	10	0	—
8	1	2.65	10	10	0.45
	2	3.00	10	0	—
	3	3.00	10	0	—

Experiment C5

Period	Seller	Price offer	Quantity offer	Quantity sold	Profit
1	1	2.95	10	9	1.98
	2	5.41	10	0	—
	3	4.04	10	0	—
2	1	3.15	10	8	2.36
	2	5.02	10	0	—
	3	3.85	10	0	—
3	1	2.99	10	0	—
	2	2.98	10	9	2.25
	3	3.20	10	0	—
4	1	2.90	10	0	—
	2	2.85	10	9	1.08
	3	2.95	10	0	—
5	1	2.79	10	9	0.54
	2	2.82	10	0	—
	3	2.80	10	0	—
6	1	2.69	10	0	—
	2	2.68	10	10	0.75
	3	2.70	10	0	—
7	1	2.65	10	10	0.45
	2	2.67	10	0	—
	3	2.68	10	0	—
8	1	2.63	10	0	—
	2	2.62	10	10	0.15
	3	2.65	10	0	—

Experiment C6

Period	Seller	Price offer	Quantity offer	Quantity sold	Profit
1	1	8.50	10	0	—
	2	4.99	10	1	1.26
	3	7.00	5	0	—
2	1	5.60	10	0	—
	2	4.90	10	1	1.17
	3	6.00	6	0	—
3	1	4.80	10	0	—
	2	4.60	10	2	1.99
	3	5.00	8	0	—
4	1	3.99	10	0	—
	2	3.89	10	5	3.30
	3	4.00	10	0	—
5	1	3.79	10	0	—
	2	3.69	10	0	—
	3	3.50	10	7	3.64
6	1	3.27	10	0	—
	2	2.99	10	9	2.34
	3	3.00	10	0	—
7	1	2.81	10	0	—
	2	2.89	10	0	—
	3	2.69	10	10	0.85
8	1	2.70	10	0	—
	2	2.65	10	10	0.45
	3	2.69	10	0	—

Experiment CBN1

Period	Seller	Price offer	Quantity offer	Quantity sold	Profit
1	1	4.15	10	9	1.95
	2	4.70	10	0	—
2	1*	3.87	9	0	—
	2	3.86	10	10	0.55
3	1	3.81	10	0	—
	2*	3.79	10	10	−0.15
4	1	3.81	10	0	—
	2*	3.80	10	10	−0.05
5	1	3.84	10	0	—
	2*	3.81	10	10	0.05
6	1	3.81	10	10	0.05
	2*	3.81	10	0	—
7	1*	3.81	10	0	—
	2	3.81	10	10	0.05
8	1	3.81	10	0	—
	2*	3.81	10	10	0.05

Note: Incumbent in each period is indicated by an asterisk

Experiment CBN2

Period	Seller	Price offer	Quantity offer	Quantity sold	Profit
1	1	5.09	10	0	—
	2	4.53	10	7	2.45
2	1	4.36	10	8	2.44
	2*	7.00	10	0	—
3	1*	3.87	10	0	—
	2	3.86	10	10	0.55
4	1	3.80	10	0	—
	2*	3.79	10	10	−0.15
5	1	3.81	10	0	—
	2*	3.80	10	10	−0.05
6	1	3.81	10	10	0.05
	2*	3.81	10	0	—
7	1*	3.81	10	10	0.05
	2	3.99	10	0	—
8	1*	3.81	10	10	0.05
	2	9.99	1	0	—

Note: Incumbent in each period is indicated by an asterisk.

Experiment CBN3

Period	Seller	Price offer	Quantity offer	Quantity sold	Profit
1	1	3.86	10	10	0.55
	2	4.29	8	0	—
2	1*	3.99	10	0	—
	2	3.89	10	10	0.85
3	1	3.85	10	0	—
	2*	3.84	10	10	0.35
4	1	3.84	10	10	0.35
	2*	3.85	10	0	—
5	1*	3.81	10	10	0.05
	2	3.82	10	0	—
6	1*	3.85	10	0	—
	2	3.84	10	10	0.35
7	1	3.84	10	10	0.35
	2*	3.84	10	0	—
8	1*	3.83	10	10	0.25
	2	3.83	10	0	—

Note: Incumbent in each period is indicated by an asterisk

Experiment CBND1

Period	Seller	Price offer	Quantity offer	Quantity sold	Profit
1	1	4.09	10	9	1.44
	2	5.48	10	0	—
2	1*	3.95	10	0	—
	2	3.94	10	10	1.35
3	1	3.81	10	0	—
	2*	3.81	10	10	0.05
4	1	3.81	10	10	0.05
	2*	3.81	10	0	—
5	1*	3.81	10	10	0.05
	2	3.81	10	0	—
6	1*	3.81	10	0	—
	2	3.81	10	10	0.05
7	1	3.81	10	10	0.05
	2*	3.81	10	0	—
8	1*	3.81	10	10	0.05
	2	3.81	10	0	—

Note: Incumbent in each period is indicated by an asterisk.

Experiment CBND2

Period	Seller	Price offer	Quantity offer	Quantity sold	Profit
1	1	5.68	8	0	—
	2	4.00	10	9	0.63
2	1	3.89	10	10	0.85
	2*	3.90	10	0	—
3	1*	3.81	10	10	0.05
	2	3.81	10	0	—
4	1*	3.81	10	10	0.05
	2	3.81	10	0	—
5	1*	3.81	10	0	—
	2	3.81	10	10	0.05
6	1	3.81	10	0	—
	2*	3.81	10	10	0.05
7	1	3.81	10	10	0.05
	2*	3.81	10	0	—
8	1*	3.81	10	10	0.05
	2	3.81	10	0	—

Note: Incumbent in each period is indicated by an asterisk.

Experiment CBND4

Period	Seller	Price offer	Quantity offer	Quantity sold	Profit
1	1	4.00	10	0	—
	2	4.85	10	0	—
	3	3.79	10	5	2.80
2	1	2.62	10	0	—
	2	2.61	10	10	0.05
	3*	2.63	10	0	—
3	1	2.61	10	10	0.05
	2*	2.61	10	0	—
	3	2.61	10	0	—
4	1*	2.61	10	0	—
	2	2.61	10	10	0.05
	3	4.50	1	0	—
5	1	2.61	10	0	—
	2*	2.61	10	10	0.05
	3	4.50	1	0	—
6	1	2.61	10	10	0.05
	2*	2.61	10	0	—
	3	5.00	1	0	—
7	1*	2.61	10	0	—
	2	2.61	10	10	0.05
	3	5.00	1	0	—
8	1	2.61	10	0	—
	2*	2.61	10	0	—
	3	2.61	10	10	0.05

Note: Incumbent in each period is indicated by an asterisk.

Experiment CBND5

Period	Seller	Price offer	Quantity offer	Quantity sold	Profit
1	1	5.80	10	0	—
	2	4.23	10	0	—
	3	3.89	10	5	3.30
2	1	2.61	10	10	0.05
	2	2.61	10	0	—
	3*	2.61	10	0	—
3	1*	2.61	10	0	—
	2	3.00	10	0	—
	3	2.61	10	10	0.05
4	1	2.61	10	10	0.05
	2	3.00	10	0	—
	3*	2.61	10	0	—
5	1*	2.61	10	10	0.05
	2	2.61	10	0	—
	3	2.61	10	0	—
6	1*	2.61	10	0	—
	2	2.61	10	10	0.05
	3	2.61	10	0	—
7	1	2.61	10	0	—
	2*	2.61	10	0	—
	3	2.61	10	10	0.05
8	1	2.61	10	0	—
	2	2.61	10	10	0.05
	3*	2.61	10	0	—

Note: Incumbent in each period is indicated by an asterisk.

Experiment CBND6

Period	Seller	Price offer	Quantity offer	Quantity sold	Profit
1	1	4.99	10	0	—
	2	3.99	10	5	3.80
	3	4.48	10	0	—
2	1	2.61	10	10	0.05
	2*	2.67	10	0	—
	3	2.61	10	0	—
3	1*	2.61	10	0	—
	2	2.61	10	10	0.05
	3	2.61	10	0	—
4	1	2.61	10	10	0.05
	2*	2.61	10	0	—
	3	2.61	10	0	—
5	1*	2.61	10	0	—
	2	2.61	10	0	—
	3	2.61	10	10	0.05
6	1	2.61	10	0	—
	2	2.61	10	10	0.05
	3*	2.61	10	0	—
7	1	2.61	10	10	0.05
	2*	2.61	10	0	—
	3	2.61	10	0	—
8	1*	2.61	10	10	0.05
	2	2.70	10	0	—
	3	2.61	10	0	—

Note: Incumbent in each period is indicated by an asterisk.

Notes

I am grateful to the Centre for Economic Analysis of Property Rights and the Social Sciences and Humanities Research Council of Canada for financial support. Helpful comments were provided by Raymond Battalio, William Brock, Curtis Eaton, Charles Holt, Mark Isaac, John Kagel, Michael McKee, John Panzar, E. E. Rutström, Edward Zajac, an anonymous referee, and seminar participants at the Australian National University, Texas A&M University, the Universities of Arizona, California at Davis, and Toronto, and the NSF-CMU Conference "Regulation at the Crossroads: Challenges of the Coming Decade" (Airlie, Virginia, September 1985).

1. Smith (1982, p. 942) motivates boundary experiments as follows: "Whenever a theory or an empirical regularity has received replicable support from several independent experiments or other empirical studies, and is thereby established as a behavioral law with some claim to generality, it is natural to ask whether one can design experiments that will test for those extreme or boundary conditions under which the law fails."

2. Some might view such experiments with disinterest on the grounds that nothing can be learned by testing a theory on its domain. I disagree. Questions of logical consistency aside, it is methodologically efficient to begin an evaluation of a theory on its domain. I therefore

agree with the methodological position of Coursey, Isaac, and Smith (1984): "... in testing [contestability] theory, we have attempted to reproduce [the] conditions specified by the theory. If the theory is falsified, we are done; that is, no further experiments are necessary. If the theory is not falsified, a wide range of questions opens about the robustness of the assumption behind the contestable markets hypothesis. This would call for further study by theoretical, empirical, and experimental economists into the limits of contesting as a discipline against monopoly behavior." I take issue, of course, on the question of whether Coursey, Isaac, and Smith (1984) (or Harrison and McKee 1985a) have indeed operationalized the theory in question. This general methodological position contrasts with the approach adopted by Cox, Smith, and Walker (1984), for example, in their rejection of certain Nash equilibrium bidding theories of discriminative auctions.

3. Restraint of monopoly effectiveness is not the only criterion for evaluating alternative institutions. This decentralized regulatory mechanism, for example, requires somewhat greater information on the part of the government about the market then does contestability. See Cox, Isaac, and Block (1985) and Harrison and McKee (1985a) for further discussion of this issue.

4. Franchising schemes are used in HM to dissipate the rent generated by the regulatory scheme. Alternative ways to reduce the subsidy payment are obvious. If we are dealing with the transition from an unregulated to a regulated monopoly, one could just pay out a subsidy equal to some fraction of the consumer surplus generated by increments in output. Cox, Isaac, and Block (1985) explore related ideas in a theoretical and experimental context.

5. Moreover Hoggatt (1967, 1969) shows that subjects will tend to respond in kind to more cooperative (albeit nonchiseling) simulated opponents in simple duopoly experiments.

6. Another interesting feature is the complete absence, to say the least, of any attempt by the incumbent to limit price in periods 1 through 5. Indeed, the CILS incumbents displayed greater monopoly effectiveness on average than the monopolists in CIS (comparing the human buyer CILS experiments with those in CIS), despite the threat of future entry hanging over the heads of the CILS incumbents.

7. The one qualification to this is the additional knowledge about market demand that the incumbent in periods 1 through 5 should have as a result of that incumbency. The entrant did not know what quantity the incumbent sold during those periods, although his price was public information.

8. The CILS experiments with computer-simulated buyer behavior are not comparable to the CIS experiments, which used human buyers.

9. Actually the offers of other potential sellers are physically revealed in the current period, but only after each seller has posted and confirmed his offer.

10. Point 2 may be viewed as applying in these experimental designs with a one-period lag, since the offers of all previous periods are public knowledge. However, point 1 does not then apply: the incumbent can set today's price offer knowing how close the offers of yesterday's entrants were to his.

11. In the HM design it was extremely rare, apart from being irrational, for any seller to restrict quantity offers. Hence the low-price seller invariably satisfied all of the market demand at that price, leaving nothing else for higher-priced sellers. The notion of a "winner" is therefore defined unambiguously.

12. Following HM, "experience" in each experiment except CBND7 consisted of having participated in a previous decreasing cost PO monopoly experiment of at least fifteen periods duration. This monopoly was uncontested and unregulated. The monopoly experiments were run immediately prior to the contestable markets experiments reported here. Two of the

subjects in experiment CBND7 were selected on the basis of previous collusive behavior in CBND3, as discussed in the text. The pilot results in Harrison, McKee, and Rutstrom (1987) on the role of subject experience do suggest an important conclusion. Although inexperienced subjects do not appear to behave in a qualitatively different way from experienced subjects in environments in which they are only learning a dominant strategy (e.g., the unregulated and regulated monopoly designs), they may exhibit highly erratic and qualitatively distinct behavior in human interaction environments (e.g., the franchise bidding and contestable markets designs). This tentative conclusion has some bearing on the relative weight we should attach to evidence about the CMH when subjects are inexperienced. It is tempting to want to evaluate recent moves toward deregulation in various sectors of the naturally occurring economy using the behavior patterns of comparably "inexperienced" firms (e.g., Bailey, Graham, and Kaplan 1985). The available experimental evidence cautions against drawing firm conclusions as to the validity of the CMH from such "transitional" evidence. On the other hand, the experimental literature does not (as yet) provide an operational criterion for identifying the end of such a transition. To address this issue experimentally would not be difficult. Rather than have unregulated or regulated monopoly experiments conducted independently of contested markets, one could run them sequentially as in CILS. The observed transitional path in such experiments may be of greater relevance for public policy than observed behavior in some terminal period (the latter has been the focus of attention in CIS and CILS).

13. The procedure is as follows. The pretest generates a utility of monetary gain (or experimental income) curve for each subject. An F-test is applied to determine if higher-order terms vanish in an OLS regression based on a Taylor series expansion of the implicit nonlinear utility function. If the hypothesis that these terms vanish cannot be rejected, at conventional levels of significance (in this case 10 percent), the subject is deemed "risk-neutral."

14. Harrison and McKee (1985b) provide a design in which the "training" role of previous experiments is of central importance. Although their results bear only on certain theories of bargaining behavior, they illustrate the potential behavioral importance of controlling for such sequence effects in general.

15. Specifically, there are four restrictions. First, the quantity offer must be an integer. Second, the quantity offer must be positive. Third, the maximum quantity offer corresponds to the last unit whose cost is less than or equal to the price offer. Fourth, the minimum quantity offer corresponds to the first unit whose cost is less than or equal to the price offer. The third and fourth restriction did not apply in the C, CBN, and CBND experiments.

16. Note that tied price offers at or near the competitive level in the CIS and CILS experiments lead to heavy losses to both traders. Such losses indeed occurred on several occasions in these experiments and could be a serious problem in variants of their designs. Kruse (1986) provides a careful discussion of these and other aspects of the CIS design, as well as proposing and implementing a number of design modifications that operationalize the key insight of contestability theory that it is the threat, rather than the actuality, of entry, that disciplines an incumbent. The major modification she considers is the provision of an alternate market: a "safe haven" providing a certain (deterministic) return. The role of alternative markets was earlier explored in Harrison (1986b), albeit with less experimental control than in Kruse (1986).

17. Several nonparametric statistical tests are used in our discussion to determine the significance of any effects on the indices in table 6.6. The Wilcoxon (or Mann-Whitney) procedure tests the null hypothesis that two random samples come from the same population against the alternative hypothesis that they come from different populations. The test adopted is two tailed, with no prediction as to whether one sample is "larger" or "smaller" than the other. We also use a two-tailed median test to determine if the two samples come from populations

with the same median. The null hypothesis of the Wilcoxon test can be rejected by any significant differences between the two populations, whereas the null hypothesis of the median test only requires that the two populations have the same median. Cover (1980, pp. 171–176, 215–223) provides a formal description of the test procedures adopted.

18. Given that only the price offers of incumbents were publicly revealed, this quantity offer restriction in fact had no signaling role.

19. It is arguable that the operationalization adopted does correspond with the spirit of the "prenatal" version of the CMH presented in Demsetz (1968). See CIS (pp. 91ff) for introductory references to this informal theoretical model.

References

Bailey, E. E., Graham, D. R., and Kaplan, D. P. 1985. *Deregulating the Airlines.* Cambridge: MIT Press.

Baumol, W. J. 1979. "Quasi Permanence of Price Reduction: A Policy for Prevention of Predatory Pricing." *Yale Law Journal 89*: 1–26.

Baumol, W. J., and Ordover, J. A. 1985. "Use of Antitrust to Subvert Competition." *Journal of Law and Economics 28*: 247–265.

Baumol, W. J., Panzar, J. C., and Willig, R. D. 1982. *Contestable Markets and the Theory of Industry Structure.* New York: Harcourt, Brace, Jovanovich.

Brock, W. A. 1983. "Contestable Markets and the Theory of Industry Structure: A Review Article." *Journal of Political Economy 91*: 1055–1066.

Brock, W. A., and Scheinkman, J. A. 1983. Free Entry and the Sustainability of Natural Monopoly: Bertrand Revisited by Cournot. In D. S. Evans, ed., *Breaking Up Bell, Essays on Industrial Organization and Regulation.* Amsterdam: North Holland, ch. 9.

Conover, W. J. 1980. *Practical Nonparametric Statistics.* 2d. ed. New York: Wiley.

Coursey, D., Isaac, R. M., Luke, M., and Smith, V. L. 1984. "Market Contestability in the Present of Sunk (Entry) Costs." *The Rand Journal of Economics 15*: 69–84.

Coursey, D., Isaac, R. M., and Smith, V. L. 1984. "Natural Monopoly and Contested Markets: Some Experimental Results." *Journal of Law and Economics 27*: 91–113.

Cox, J. C., Isaac, R. M., and Block, M. K. 1985. "Incentive Regulation: An Alternative to RORR." In M. K. Block, J. C. Cox, R. M. Isaac, D. E. Pingry, S. J. Rassenti, and V. L. Smith, eds., *Alternatives to Rate of Return Regulation.* Tucson: University of Arizona.

Cox, J. C., Smith, V. L., and Walker, J. M. 1984. "Theory and Behavior of Multiple Unit Discriminative Auctions." *Journal of Finance 39*: 983–1010.

Demsetz, H. 1968 "Why Regulate Utilities?" *Journal of Law and Economics 11*: 55–65.

Dixit, A. 1982. "Recent Developments in Oligopoly Theory." *American Economic Review (Papers and Proceedings) 72*: 12–17.

Friedman, J. W. 1963. "Individual Behavior in Oligopolistic Markets: An Experimental Study." *Yale Economic Essays 3*: 359–417.

Friedman, J. W., and Hoggatt, A. C. 1980. *An Experiment in Noncooperative Oligopoly.* Greenwich: JAI Press.

Harrison, G. W. 1986a. "An Experimental Test for Risk Aversion." *Economics Letters 21*: 7–11.

Harrison, G. W. 1986b. "Predatory Pricing in Experiments." Unpublished Manuscript. Department of Economics, University of Western Ontario.

Harrison, G. W., and McKee, M. J. 1985a. "Monopoly Behavior, Decentralized Regulation, and Contestable Markets: An Experimental Evaluation." *The Rand Journal of Economics* 16:51–69.

Harrison, G. W., and McKee, M. J. 1985b. "Experimental Evaluation of the Coase Theorem." *Journal of Law and Economics* 28:653–670.

Harrison, G. W., McKee, M. J., and Rutström, E. E. 1987. "Experimental Evaluation of Institutions of Monopoly Restraint." In L. Green and J. Kagel, eds., *Advances in Behavioral Economics*. Norwood: Ablex.

Harrison, G. W., and Rutstrom, E. E. 1986. "Measurement of Utility By A Sequential Method." Unpublished Manuscript. Department of Economics, University of Western Ontario.

Hoggatt, A. C. 1967. "Measuring Cooperativeness of Behavior in Quantity Variation Duopoly Games." *Behavioral Science* 12:109–121.

Hoggatt, A. C. 1969. "Response of Paid Students to Differential Behavior of Robots in Bifurcated Duopoly Games." *Review of Economic Studies* 36:417–432.

Ketcham, J., Smith, V. L., and William, A. W. 1984. "A Comparison of Posted-Offer and Double-Auction Pricing Institutions." *Review of Economic Studies* 51:595–614.

Knieps, G., and Vogelsang, I. 1982. "The Sustainability Concept under Alternative Behavioral Assumptions." *Bell Journal of Economics* 13:234–241.

Kruse, J. L. 1986. "Contestability in the Presence of an Alternate Market: An Experimental Examination." Unpublished Manuscript. Department of Economics, University of Arizona.

Loeb, M., and Magat, W. A. 1979. "A Decentralized Method for Utility Regulation." *Journal of Law and Economics* 22:399–404.

Plott, Charles R. 1982. "Industrial Organization Theory and Experimental Economics." *Journal of Economic Literature* 20:1485–1527.

Shepherd, W. G. 1984. "Contestability vs. Competition." *American Economic Review* 74:572–587.

Smith, V. L. 1976. "Experimental Economics: Induced Value Theory." *American Economic Review (Papers and Proceedings)* 66:274–279.

Spence, M. 1983. "Contestable Markets and the Theory of Industry Structure: A Review Article." *Journal of Economic Literature* 21:981–990.

Stigler, G. J. 1968. *The Organization of Industry*. Homewood: Irwin.

Von Weizacker, C. C. 1980. "A Welfare Analysis of Barriers to Entry." *Bell Journal of Economics* 11:399–420.

7

Risk Analysis and Relevance of Uncertainties in Nuclear Safety Decisions

M. E. Paté-Cornell

The philosophy of risk regulation in the United States has evolved considerably in the last twenty years (Okrent and Wilson 1980; Paté 1983a). The goal of absolute safety that guided, for example, the Delaney amendment to the initial Food, Drug, and Cosmetic Act, often proved economically infeasible and in many cases, was de facto abandoned. Even the convenient concepts of best available technology or best practicable technology may be so expensive that they have to be adapted to accommodate economic realities. Following more recent laws (e.g., the Fungicide, Insecticide, and Rodenticide Act), the regulator is left with the task of balancing risks, costs, and benefits without much guidance from the legislative body. Congress is extremely reluctant to face the difficult trade-offs between acceptable costs and acceptable risks. The pressure is on the regulatory agencies to make decisions that are prudent and reasonable, yet economically acceptable, and politically viable.

Agencies such as the Environmental Protection Agency, or the Nuclear Regulatory Commission, face a difficult task, and this for two reasons. First, the information regarding the risks that they are mandated to regulate is often incomplete. Understanding the facts may require considering several data bases and the opinions of several experts, some of which may provide conflicting information. To be complete, the results must reflect the corresponding uncertainties. Second, difficult value judgments have to be made to reach regulatory safety decisions. The decision process itself is a complex one involving several stages, and often several decision makers whose preferences may differ, as can their interpretation of the information. One key to the rationality and the consistency of this process is keeping risk assessment independent from risk management, while ensuring that the information provided fits the management decision framework and is properly communicated (Ruckelshaus 1983).

In the last ten years risk assessment methods have reached high levels of sophistication. In the nuclear industry, for example, tools have been developed using system analysis and probability theory to assess the reliability of nuclear power plants. The use of these technical results poses fundamental questions that are economic and political in nature. The complexity of the technical issues, on the one hand, and the difficulty of regulatory choices, on the other, call for a considerable improvement in the level of understanding among engineers, economists, and the legal profession. I attempt to address two of the key issues of nuclear safety regulation: What is the current state of the art in assessing risks and uncertainties in the nuclear industry, and how can risk analysis results be used to improve the regulatory process?

The Reactor Safety Study (USNRC 1975) was a first attempt to construct a full-scale methodology for the probabilistic risk assessment (PRA) of nuclear power plants. Since then PRA has been done for many reactors at different levels of scope and detail (Joksimovich 1984). These studies are sponsored by the Nuclear Regulatory Commission (NRC), the utility companies, or the Electric Power Research Institute. They are used along with more conventional methods for many decisions including siting, design, and operation of nuclear power plants (Daniels and Canady 1984; Bernero 1984). For the Zion Station, for example, the study was undertaken by Commonwealth Edison Company with three basic purposes (USNRC 1981):

• To provide a thorough assessment of public risk resulting from the operation of Zion Station as currently constructed and operated.
• To identify the major contributors to that risk in terms of plant design and operation. In that connection, the study postulated a variety of equipment malfunctions including those leading to the most severe reactor accident—progressive failures of multiple engineered safeguards leading to melting of the reactor core.
• To assess the benefits and risks associated with several potential plant modifications or additions designed to mitigate the effects of postulated accidents.

First, through PRA the utility company obtains insights into the interactive mechanisms of the different subsystems of the plant and the relative contribution of the different potential risk sources to the final risk. Indeed, on the basis of a PRA study, some nuclear reactors, such as the Zion power plant whose seismic safety was improved, have been modified and upgraded (USNRC 1981).

The NRC is now considering using PRA results for some of the nuclear safety regulatory decisions (Bernero 1984) and has recently proposed a set of qualitative and quantitative safety goals (USNRC 1983). PRA is an essential tool for the utility companies to show compliance with these safety goals. Finally, the PRA results are used as a basis for negotiation and discussion between the utility companies and the NRC in deciding on the extent and the scheduling of retrofit work in nuclear power plants. Altogether, probabilistic risk analysis has been in the last twenty years an informative method to approach safety evaluation and safety decisions in the nuclear power industry (Levine and Rasmussen 1984).

Major difficulties arise, however, in the risk assessment as well as the risk management part of this effort. Some of these difficulties are practical, such as doing a complete analysis of all potential accident sequences; some are more theoretical, such as the very definition of probability when used to make public sector decisions (Lewis 1980, 1984; Apostolakis et al. 1983). One particularly important question is the treatment of the uncertainties that arise in the assessment of the risk itself. In fact, as I argue in this chapter, the probability of a risky event may only be a point estimate that reflects a spectrum of experts' opinions, models, and parameters. Although such an estimate allows maximization of an expected utility, it may be insufficient in the case of a regulatory decision that does not fit directly in the classical decision analysis framework.

The problem of uncertainties is twofold: how to estimate them (and report them in the results) and how to treat them when using the results for regulatory decisions. This is not a new problem but a new formulation of an old one: how to regulate activities involving risks to the public, and in particular, risks whose nature, probabilities, and consequences are poorly known. I chose, as an illustration of this problem, the case of PRA for nuclear power plants because it is the most advanced method in practice and as such can give insights into other applications and into fundamental questions.

I examine, first, the historical reasons for doing a probabilistic assessment of nuclear power plants and the current use of the results. I describe the PRA methodology, using as an example the safety study of the Indian Point 3 reactor. I discuss some of the difficulties, practical and theoretical, in doing a PRA for a nuclear power plant.

I then focus on the problems of uncertainties in PRA and the necessity to treat them consistently for the different initiating events that contribute to the overall risk of radioactive release. The argument is illustrated by the seismic risk analysis of the Limmerick nuclear power plant. Finally, I discuss the role of uncertainties in the use of qualitative and quantitative safety goals for nuclear reactors as recently proposed by the Nuclear Regulatory Commission.

Why Probabilistic Studies for Nuclear Power Plants?

Several frameworks can be envisioned to promote the safety of nuclear power plants, for example, tort law, liability law, bankruptcy, and private negotiation. In such frameworks incentives for safety measures are provided by legal mechanisms and market mechanisms (e.g., through insurance premiums). In the United States it was decided in the 1950s to rely on a regulatory system administered initially by the Atomic Energy Commission (AEC) and currently by the Nuclear Regulatory Commission (NRC), with the primary objective of ensuring public safety. Whether regulation is an ideal way of protecting the public is debatable, but that issue will not be argued here. In this chapter the discussion is limited to safety decisions based on a regulatory process involving the agency, the industry, the experts, and the public. In this perspective the NRC, like other government agencies, such as the Environmental Protection Agency (EPA) and the Occupational Safety and Health Agency (OSHA), is facing problems of risk management involving large economic costs, large human populations, and often, conflicting interests.

Presently, the licensing and authorization procedure set by the NRC is not primarily based on probabilistic safety evaluations, but probabilistic methods have gained increasing importance and acceptance because they provide the specific information needed to replace the illusion of absolute safety. The PRA methodology was developed following a 1957 study, under the Atomic Energy Commission, of the potential consequences of accidents in nuclear power plants (AEC 1957). The unavoidable question was: What is the probability of such accidents? Subjective assessments of accident probability that were made at the time at the plant level of aggregation were vague and could clearly be improved by a detailed reliability analysis of the system. The method had to include the probabilistic study of the occurrence of internal and external accident initiators.

The Reactor Safety Study (USNRC 1975) was the first step in this development. It was reviewed by the Lewis Committee with mixed conclusions (USNRC 1978). Although the methodology was said to be "a substantial advance over previous attempts to estimate the risks of nuclear options," the report raised a certain number of objections both theoretical and practical: for example, that it was not possible to ensure the completeness of the reliability models, and that the risk uncertainties were underestimated. Following this report, the NRC seemed to move away from probabilistic methods. This move was reversed, however, after the Three Mile Island accident: a list of retrofits was then requested by the NRC for existing plants, and PRA was sometimes used to decide on the extent and the scheduling of this upgrading. The PRA results, though imperfect, gradually came to be used in NRC regulatory decisions because they provide relevant information.

Today the NRC licensing process for a new nuclear reactor is the following. First, the utility must obtain a construction permit. This requires filing a preliminary safety analysis report and an environmental report. If these reports are accepted, the utility company obtains a preliminary operating license which requires it to submit an acceptable final safety analysis and a final environmental report. Following a period of low power testing, the utility company then obtains the operating license. A PRA based on the preliminary safety study is now required in practice, if not yet in the regulation, for the preliminary operating license.

The use of PRA is particularly important for the retrofit of existing plants. For example, the NRC established a list of post-Three Mile Island requirements that operating plants must satisfy. Some of these modifications, however, could take several weeks to complete. Making the changes at a scheduled refueling time can save the utility a considerable amount of money. It is on the basis of a PRA that the NRC has sometimes accepted the delay of retrofit work until the next refueling. An argument was made, for example, that the probability of a large earthquake in New England, and therefore the risk of failure of a nuclear power plant due to earthquakes during a few months, is small enough to permit such a delay.

At this point the NRC sees PRA "as a supplement to the regulatory process, not as the sole basis of regulatory decisions" and best adapted to "the development of general licensing criteria and the evaluation of system or subsystem reliability within plants" (Bernero 1984). The use of PRA is viewed as a way to introduce more consistency and rationality into the regulatory process. For the moment, however, the process of licensing and authorization is still unstable: unpredictable changes in the rules and regulations due to new information have created heavy burdens on the nuclear industry and contributed to bringing to a complete halt the plans for new reactors in the United States.

The PRA Method

The PRA method is based on the construction of a set of scenarios in order to quantify (1) the frequency of their occurrences and (2) their consequences. Initial studies of the Atomic Energy Commission emphasized the importance of the containment structure by defining three hazard states: (1) severe core damage, (2) severe core damage and large-scale fuel melt, and (3) severe core damage, large-scale fuel melt, and significant off-site release. Only this last state can cause severe off-site losses. The construction

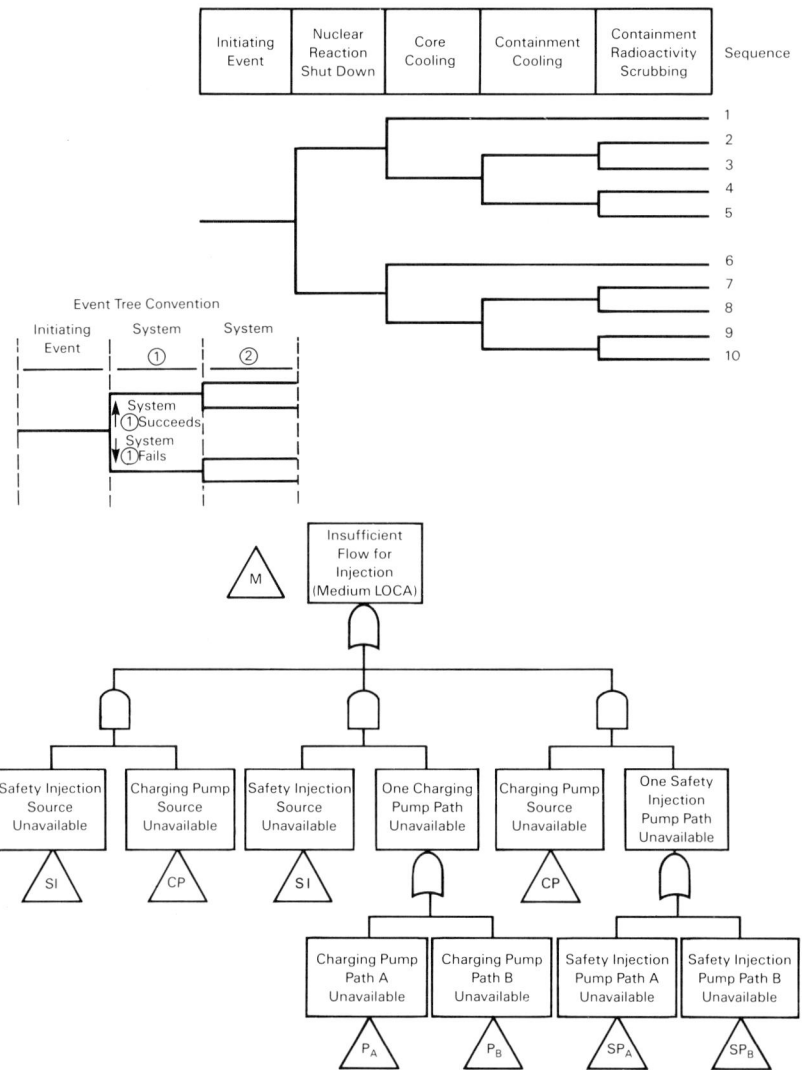

Figure 7.1 Examples of the event and fault trees used in PRA. Source: Zion Station Probabilistic Safety Study.

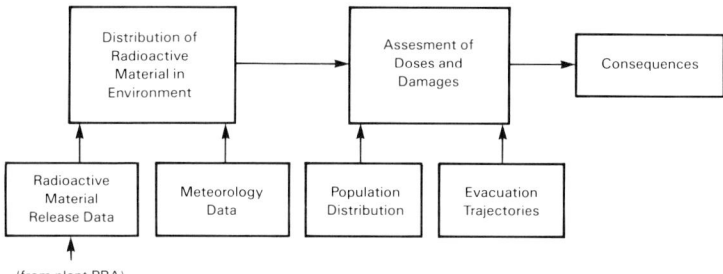

Figure 7.2 Consequence modeling: the structure of the models CRAC and CRACIT. Source: Indian Point Probabilistic Safety Study.

of the complete set of scenarios leading to different release categories is done using systems analysis (functional diagrams), fault trees, and event trees, such as those shown in figure 7.1 (Paté 1984a). The result of this part of the analysis is the annual probability or the frequency of each particular scenario. The future frequency itself can be considered as a random variable for which a probability distribution can be computed on the basis of all available information (Kaplan and Garrick 1981a). This procedure allows the evaluation of the risk uncertainties, and in particular of analytical and observational uncertainties. The former includes modeling and parametric uncertainties; the latter is the uncertainty that would remain even if all parameters and models were perfectly known. Consequence modeling is then performed using site-specific data and the general model described in figure 7.2.

Assembling these different models can be done, for example, by the method described on Figure 7.3 (USNRC 1982; Garrick 1984). This method involves the description of the plant, of the containment system, and of the site conditions and occupancy by state probabilities. The model exhibits "pinch points," that is, points in the analysis where the only information that matters is the current state of the system regardless of how this state was reached.

The results of the analysis generally include failure probabilities and consequence distributions. A first result is the probability of core melt per reactor year, usually allocated among the different release categories. In addition to the frequencies of accidents caused by the main initiating events, one may want to know the uncertainties in the estimation of these frequencies (see figure 7.4). The consequences can be described by the cumulative distribution of annual losses (e.g., early fatalities, figure 7.5). As shown in figure 7.5, one of the goals of these results is to assess the

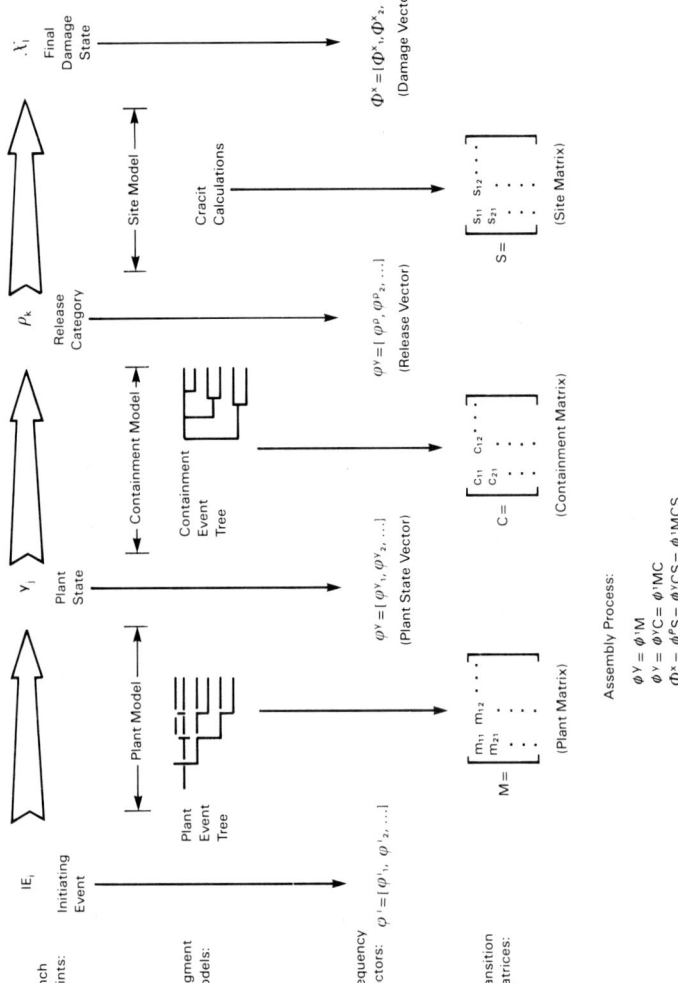

Figure 7.3 Overview of the assembly process, showing relationships of pinch points, event trees, frequency vectors, and transition matrices. Source: Garrick (1984); Indian Point Probabilistic Safety Study.

INDIAN POINT 3 ROW VECTOR ϕ^i OF INTERNAL INITIATING EVENT FREQUENCIES (MEAN VALUE)
(Frequencies in Events Per Reactor Year)

1 Large LOCA	2 Medium LOCA	3 Small LOCA	4 Steam Generator Tube Rupture	5 Steam Break Inside Containment	6 Steam Break Outside Containment	7 Loff of Main Feedwater	8 Trip of One MISV	9 Lots of RCS Flow	10 Core Power Excursion	11a Turbine Trip	11b Turbine Trip, Loss of Service Water	11c Turbine Trip, Loss of Offsite Power	12a Reactor Trip	12b Reactor Trip, Loss Of Component Cooling	V Inter- facing System LOCA
$\phi^1 = $ |2.16-3	2.16-3	2.01-2	3.37-2	2.16-3	2.16-3	3.80-0	8.98-2	1.71-1	2.57-2	2.72-0	2.66-1	2.16-3	2.86-0	2.16-3	4.64-7|

LOCA: Loss of Coolant Accident; MSIV: Main Stream Isolation Valve; RCS: Reactor Coolant System.

Note: Values are presented in abbreviated scientific notation, e.g. $1.11\text{-}5 = 1.11 \times 10^{-5}$

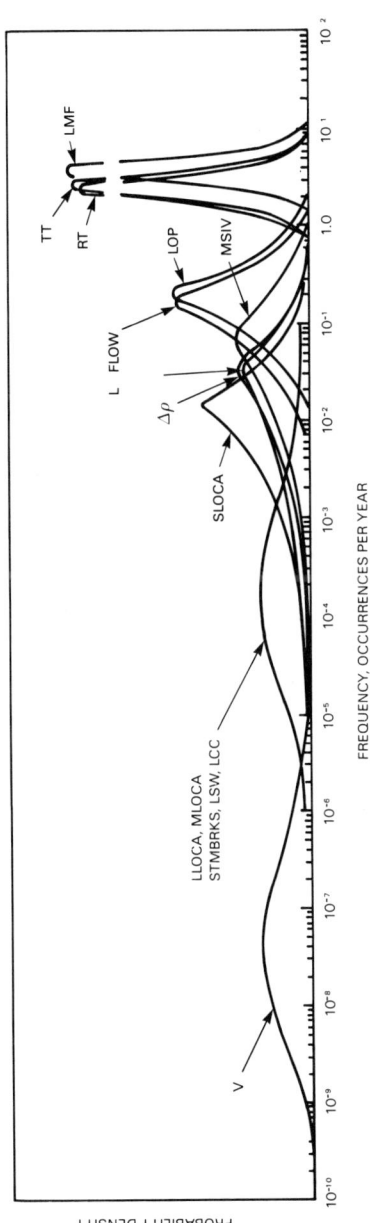

Figure 7.4 Probability of frequency of Indian Point 3 initiating events. Source: Indian Point Probabilistic Safety Study.

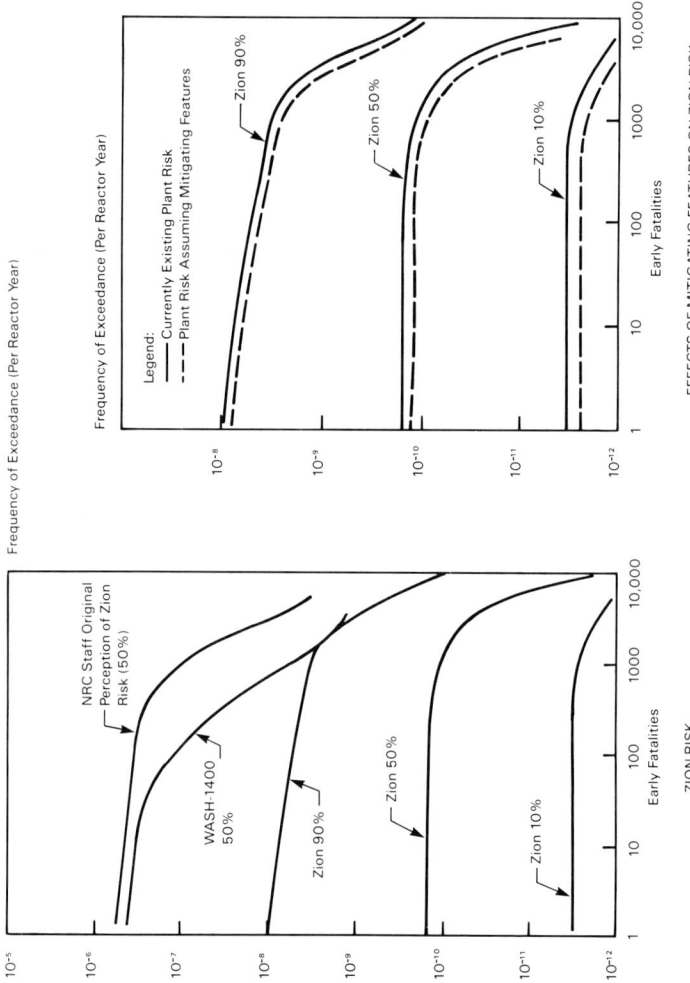

Figure 7.5 Example of PRA results for the Zion reactor. Source: Zion Station Probabilistic Safety Study.

effects of risk mitigating features for a particular reactor; these effects are measured by a shift in the risk curves.

The PRA method serves several purposes. First, it gives new insights and understanding of the performance and structure of the plant. Second, the results emphasize the main weaknesses of the plant and often lead to correction of potential defects. For example, following a PRA, Indian Point 2 was modified to reduce potential seismic effects: the space between the critical control room and another building was increased, and rubber bumpers were installed to reduce shock loads should a severe earthquake occur, that is, one of greater intensity than accounted for in the original design. The PRA method has provided guidance in many decisions of the NRC as well as the utilities to improve safety and establish priorities, thereby improving the efficiency of the decision-making process (Levine and Rasmussen 1984; Lewis 1984).

There are, however, some problems in using this technique (Lewis 1984). The main problem in risk assessment is the completeness issue. Although the construction of fault trees involves a logical, step-by-step procedure, it is impossible to be certain that no scenario has been left out. This does not apply so much to the simultaneous failure of subsystems, which can be captured in principle by an exhaustive computation, but to other physical phenomena not yet envisioned. A second problem is the weakness of the data base for component failures and human errors. These data, however, are gradually improving as more experience is gained in the field. Human error remains another difficulty. The question is the ability of the operator to diagnose and, if necessary, to correct a plant problem. Whether the opportunity for human intervention increases or decreases, the overall risk is still a debated issue in nuclear risk management.

Practical difficulties, such as the fact that fault trees and event trees cannot properly reflect accident dynamics or the treatment of common cause failures, are discussed elsewhere (Lewis 1984). These methodological points are gradually being improved with experience.

One theoretical and fundamental problem, however, remains no matter how carefully the analysis is done: the definition of probability in the regulatory framework and the significance of the results for risk management.

Probability and Judgment in Regulatory Decisions

One major problem in using probabilistic methods for regulatory decisions when the data set is weak is that expert opinion is a necessary part of the information. Bayesian probability is defined as a degree of belief, which is an intrinsically personal notion. The regulator is eventually the judge whose degree of belief matters. In making a decision for the public, however, he faces serious difficulties of calibration and aggregation of information from various sources. Furthermore, even if data were abundant and risk assessment were perfect, difficulties would remain in using this information, given the wide range of preferences and risk attitudes in the public.

Four major conceptual problems thus arise in using a probabilistic approach to regulatory decision: the definition of probability (Bayesian vs. frequentist), the aggregation of probabilistic information from different sources (statistical data and experts' judgments), the treatment of risk uncertainties, and the integration of individual preferences into collective value judgments.

Indeed, bitter quarrels about the notion of probability have divided the risk analysts between Bayesians and frequentists (e.g., Abramson 1981; Kaplan and Garrick 1981a). Bayesian methods have prevailed in the assessment of nuclear safety because they allow the use of experts' judgments in a field where statistical data are often scarce. Bayesian probability, however, is an individual notion that cannot be easily extended to collective (and in particular regulatory) decisions (Apostolakis et al. 1983). Furthermore, because Bayesian probability is based on an individual degree of belief (de Finetti 1972), one cannot be uncertain about it (which is not to say that it cannot change in time). Yet experts may disagree among themselves, which raises the question of treatment of information from different data sources.

The expert who is knowledgeable in the field of investigation can give an educated assessment of a probability. The decision maker who uses the expert's opinion then faces a calibration problem: he must make his own probability assessment using a likelihood expression that reflects his confidence in the expert. If the decision maker considers two sources of information, such as two experts or one data set and one expert, he faces the aggregation problem: he has to assess likelihood functions to reflect his confidence in each source of information and the dependencies that he sees between them (Morris 1974, 1983; Winkler 1968, 1981; Morgan et al. 1979). If two decision makers consider the same expert's opinion to assess one probability, they may attribute different likelihoods to his judgment and come up with two different figures. There is no theoretical way to resolve this problem unless one devises a procedure by which the two decision makers must first agree about the expert himself. This problem is very similar to the impossibility of constructing a collective utility function without introducing interpersonal comparison of utility (Arrow 1951).

Finally, if several decision makers, say, the five NRC commissioners, consider the opinions of several experts, they will face collectively the problems of calibrating and aggregating this information.

In theory, since the objective is to obtain "truthful" estimates of probabilities, one could approach the calibration question as a principal-agent problem. In this context the regulatory agency's strategy is to devise incentives for the experts to provide unbiased probabilities, given a reward structure. Here, however, the experts have no money at stake. What they have to lose is their overall credibility and their own self-esteem, based on their preferences in social choices. Although in theory these could be measured by willingness to pay and future gains, in practice the principal-agent model does not adapt easily, especially when the problem is to assess very low probabilities or the return periods of very rare events. For more frequent events one could design assessment procedures in which the optimal strategy of the expert is to use his best estimate. The best estimate for an expert is the value that he would use himself if he were to make bets in an actual lottery based on the probability that he assesses (Shachter 1984).

As a practical, ad hoc solution one can ask the experts to assess their confidence in their own estimates and the dependencies among them. Alternatively, one can use interactive techniques, for example, the Delphi method (Linstone and Turoff 1975). Other kinds of difficulties then arise, simply because the final consensus may or may not reflect truth or knowledge: there is no reason to believe that the most informed judgment will prevail, hence another type of uncertainty. These methods, however, are only substitutes for the calibration of information by the decision maker.

The analytical aggregation of experts' opinions by several decision makers is a complex task for two reasons: there is no "true probability," and there is no "theoretically correct" analytical solution to the aggregation problem. One can require, however, that the logic be correct and that the probabilities be "reasonable," given the evidence available. The problem is thus to minimize the effects of deliberate or unconscious biases which, in the regulatory arena, require assessment procedures that are scientifically independent and nonadversarial. An adversarial process is a good way to make a collective value judgment and a bad way to handle experts' opinions and uncertainties. Taking an extreme value on each side and picking a figure "in the middle" may defeat logic itself because one loses information about the prior probability of basic hypotheses. It is useful to provide a forum where scientific opinions from all sides can be heard and discussed, but risk management and risk assessment must be as clearly separated as practically feasible. The Environmental Protection Agency came to this conclusion some years ago and devised independent assessment procedures for product carcinogenicity (Ruckelshaus 1983). The Nuclear Regulatory Commission faces some similar problems.

The assessment of seismic activity in the eastern United States provides a good example of the challenge of aggregating divergent and sometimes biased experts' opinions. Some geoscientists, who are openly opposed to nuclear power plants, admittedly adapt their judgment about local seismicity to the decision to be made (Meehan 1984). They see it as their social responsibility to give "conservative" estimates of the probability of earthquake accelerations if it is for the nuclear industry. In effect they choose their response so that their own value judgments prevail, as opposed to the administrator's. One possible strategy is to constitute a panel of experts large enough to minimize the effects of such biases. The problem is that the choice of the panel itself determines to some extent the results. Another strategy of aggregation that tends to minimize the effects of extreme estimates is to use the median of the experts' assessments as opposed, for example, to the mean (Raiffa 1982). The median, however, is not more justified a priori than any other point of the uncertainty band. In short, there is no substitute for a complete debate on the actual foundations of the probabilistic estimates.

A multistage, Bayesian aggregation can be designed to attenuate the effects of biases (Paté 1983b). This method involves a decomposition of the random variable of interest into scenarios (e.g., fundamental hypotheses and the measure of a phenomenon given an hypothesis). One then proceeds to a sequential aggregation of experts' opinions to obtain first the aggregated probability of each hypothesis and then the aggregated conditional probability distribution for the phenomenon of interest, given each hypothesis. This procedure has several advantages. First, the overall logic of events is preserved. Second, the analyst may choose to ask the opinion of different experts for the different parts of the problem (e.g., geologists and seismologists). Third, he may find this procedure helpful to reduce the complexity of the experts' calibration problem: although calibration enters the successive aggregations, the overall result is less sensitive to extreme or unsubstantiated opinions. Finally, this method has the advantage of reducing the effects of dependencies among experts. As for the calibration question, the dependency problem remains in the aggregation of the parts, but the final result is less sensitive to this effect because it is restricted by the probability of each hypothesis.

The probability obtained by this method is a point estimate that reflects the spectrum of experts' opinions, the models that they may have used to represent physical mechanisms and the values that they may have chosen for the models' parameters. On the other hand, the administrator, depending on how he intends to use the risk analysis results, may need more complete information about the uncertainties involved.

Uncertainty in Risk Assessment

Uncertainty about a probability does not make sense in a Bayesian approach because it means uncertainty about a degree of belief. Yet, if confronted with a choice between two lotteries $(0.5, X; 0.5, Y)$, one of which is based on the tossing of a tested "fair" coin (i.e., one whose parameter is known), the other being based on an unknown coin, some people prefer the former. Even from a normative point of view, it can be argued that the uncertainties about the parameters of the problem can be relevant to the decision. In the case of nuclear safety one solution is to define the future frequency of failure of a given system, which is a random variable for which one can compute a probability distribution (USNRC 1981). This formulation allows one to define, compute, and report (1) the modeling uncertainties and (2) the parametric uncertainties. These uncertainties can possibly be reduced by further studies. By contrast, the residual observational uncertainty will always remain even if the parameters of the system are perfectly known (e.g., flipping a fair coin).

If the decision was left entirely to the judgment of an administrator using classical decision theory (Raiffa 1968; Howard 1977), uncertainties would be taken into consideration in his expected utility according to his risk attitude. The expectation is linear in the failure probability, and all parametric uncertainties would be adequately included in the expected value of the frequency with respect to parameters' distributions and models' probabilities. In the framework of quantitative safety goals, however, the questions are: What is the acceptable risk level (for example, frequency of core melt), and with what probability should this risk constraint be satisfied? This second question, if one chooses the path of numerical safety goals, has to be addressed by the regulator at the same time as setting the goal itself. The uncertainties about the future failure frequencies and about the failure consequences then have to be assessed and reported (Henrion 1982; National Research Council 1983).

Analytical uncertainties in the probabilistic risk assessment for nuclear power plants are currently the focus of many studies (USNRC 1984). They include modeling, parametric, and completeness uncertainties. Of particular interest because of their relative contribution to the uncertainty of the final result, are the uncertainties about internal and external accident frequencies (Vesely and Rasmuson 1984; Budnitz 1984). Figure 7.6, for example, represents the relative contribution of various external and internal causes to the core melt frequency for the Indian Point 3 reactor, and the uncertainties about each type of accident frequency (USNRC 1982). Much effort is currently being devoted, in particular, to the quantification of the uncertainties in the seismic part of the PRA and to the contribution of different elements of the problem to the uncertainty of the overall result.

Seismic PRA is done by combining seismic hazard analysis, components fragility curves, and plant system logic (Cornell and Newmark 1978). The goal of the seismic hazard analysis is to compute an annual frequency of exceedence of different levels of peak ground acceleration and their uncertainties: it is a probabilistic study of the ground motion at the site of the plant. The goal of the fragility studies is to compute the frequencies of failure of different components (and their uncertainties) for different levels of peak ground acceleration. The goal of a specific system analysis for seismic loads (e.g., fault tree for a seismically induced core melt) is to include in the safety study the potential effect of earthquakes on all components, including those, such as buildings, that would not fail otherwise.

The treatment of parametric and modeling uncertainties in the seismic hazard analysis is particularly important in regions such as the eastern United States, where earthquakes are rare, and where the basic seismic mechanisms are poorly known. It is then important for the completeness of the information to assess the uncertainties about the local seismic effects, given the uncertainties about the seismic mechanisms. An interesting example is the seismic PRA for the Limmerick nuclear power plant. Figure 7.7 shows the treatment in that study of different hypotheses of seismic mechanisms, and of the uncertainties about the models and their parameters. For example, a probability 0.15 has been attributed to the hypothesis that the major source area (epicenter location) is the Piedmont region and that the corresponding maximum magnitude is 5.8. More unusual still, a probability of 0.10 has been placed on a seismic mechanism called "decollement" which is a poorly known earthquake mechanism based on mass phenomena (as opposed to accumulation of energy in faults).

Figure 7.6 shows the overall result of the seismic PRA for the Indian

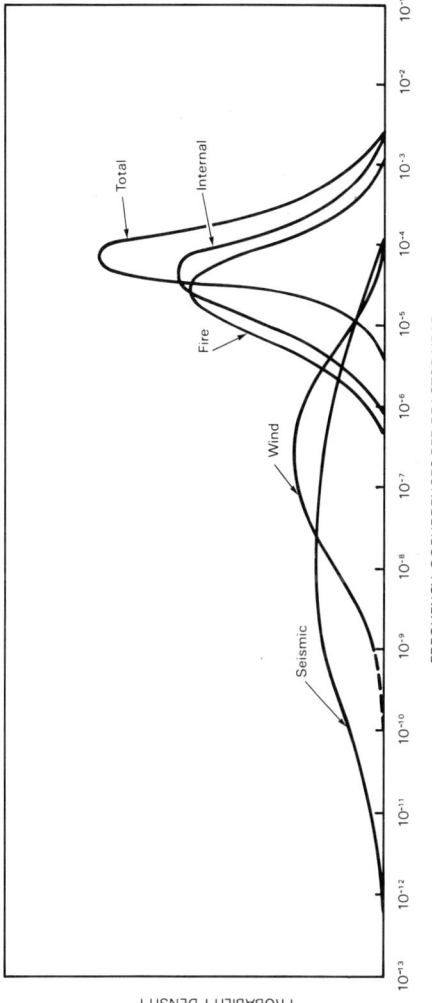

Figure 7.6 Core melt frequency from various sources for Indian Point 3. Source: Indian Point Probabilistic Safety Study.

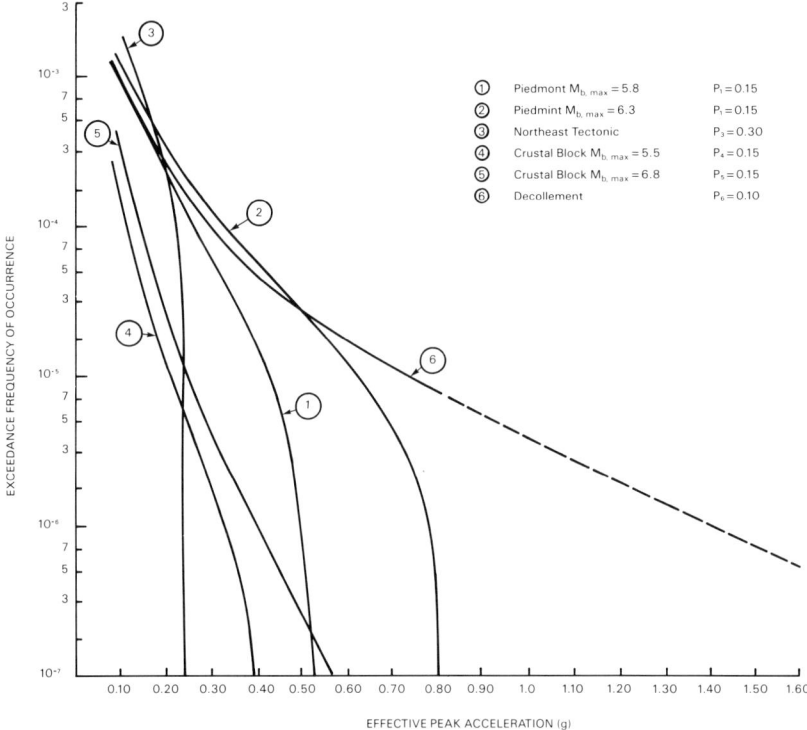

Figure 7.7 Annual frequency of exceedence versus peak acceleration for all seismogenic zones. Source: Limmerick Generating Station Probabilistic Risk Assessment.

Point reactor, including uncertainties about both the seismic hazard and components fragility. Two observations can be made about these results. First, most of the uncertainty of the seismic PRA is attributable to the uncertainty about the seismic hazard (as opposed to fragility). Second, although the uncertainty about the seismic risk seems much larger than the uncertainty about, say, the fire risk, this may be due simply to a more thorough treatment of the uncertainties in the seismic risk analysis. Uncertainty about the models (e.g., the alternate source models discussed earlier) is carefully included in the seismic study, but it is not yet included in fire risk assessments. It is therefore essential, if one is to make any conclusion about the relative contribution of different risk sources to the uncertainty of the final result, to treat consistently the uncertainties about these different sources and, in particular, to include in a coherent manner all modeling as well as parametric uncertainties in the result.

Relevance of Uncertainty in Risk Management

Assume, first, that safety decisions have to be made by a single decision maker (e.g., the industry manager) who maximizes his expected utility. In cases where the probability distribution for the outcomes depends on unknown parameters treated as random variables, there are two reasons why he may still want to know explicitly the nature and level of the uncertainties involved in the decision (Paté 1983c). First, he may want to decide whether or not to gather additional information, given that he can reduce by further investments the parametric uncertainty but not the observational uncertainty. It can be particularly crucial to gather information about seismic mechanisms, attenuation functions, or return periods of certain types of earthquakes in areas where the seismic risk may be a major contributor to the overall risk of core melt in a nuclear power plant. Second, in some cases his decision relies on a frequency that is a nonlinear function of a frequency that depends on the unknown parameters (Bier 1983). In the course of the analysis this occurs, for example, when considering the probability of simultaneous unavailability of two parts whose failure rates are dependent random variables. In this case, and more generally when studying dependent redundancies, one needs to consider the full distribution of the parameter(s). However, if the goal is to maximize an expected utility, one needs, in the end, only the expected value of the frequencies with respect to the parameters' values.

The situation is more complex in regulatory decisions where information has to be weighted by a group with different confidence levels in each information source. This problem, which was discussed earlier, constitutes, a major source of uncertainty that the administrator has to resolve finally when weighting different probabilistic assessments on the basis of fundamental assumptions. For practical reasons, however, these uncertainties and their resolutions have to be communicated to ensure the credibility of PRA. It has been shown that the public acceptance of a risk and of a decision process based on risk assessment depends, among other factors, on the novelty of the risk and how much is known about it (Slovic et al. 1979). This in turn constitutes a strong incentive to identify and reduce the major analytical uncertainties.

There are therefore at least four reasons to separate the main sources of uncertainties in risk analysis and to report them fully for public decision making: (1) The confidence of different decision makers in different sources of information may vary from person to person and for each successive variable. (2) Information can be gathered about the analytical but not the observational uncertainty. (3) Using expected values of future frequencies in the course of the analysis is insufficient when the decision is based on a probability which is nonlinear in probabilities that depend on the unknown parameters. (4) Public acceptance of risk and of risk based regulatory processes depends among other factors on the uncertainty about the future frequency of occurrence of undesirable events.

In the nuclear industry there is an additional reason for the complete treatment of uncertainties, which is the form of the proposed numerical safety goals (USNRC 1983). The goals include different types of constraints (e.g., a maximum acceptable risk), some of which are not independent. In this framework the issue of uncertainties is unavoidable. Their relevance to the decision is then more complicated than discussed earlier and varies from one constraint to another.

Safety Goals for Nuclear Power Plants and Treatment of Uncertainties

The safety goals that have recently been proposed for nuclear power plants are both qualitative and quantitative. They are meant to ensure that individuals and society are exposed to a low level of risk by the electric power industry as a whole and that the investments of the industry and society at large represent the most cost-effective allocation of safety funds (USNRC 1983). These goals should lead to a more predictable, quicker, and less costly regulatory process. For the moment, however, they are still a subject of debate, some of the question being whether these goals are based on the right concepts, whether economic considerations matter, and whether the criteria should include discounting and risk aversion (Murley 1985).

The qualitative goals are based on comparison of individual and societal risks from nuclear power plants to other risks to life and to risks of alternative electricity production methods. These goals are presented by the NRC in the following terms (USNRC 1983):

[First safety goal] Individual members of the public should be provided a level of protection from the consequences of nuclear power plant operation such that individuals bear no significant additional risk to life and health.

[Second safety goal] Societal risks to life and health from nuclear power plant operation should be comparable to or less than the risks of generating electricity by viable competing technologies and should not be a significant addition to other societal risks.

The quantitative design objectives involve numerical constraints on individual and societal mortality risks. They are the following:

The risk to an average individual in the vicinity of a nuclear power plant of prompt fatalities that might result from reactor accidents should not exceed one-tenth of one percent (0.1%) of the sum of prompt fatality risks resulting from other accidents to which members of the U.S. population are generally exposed.

The risk to the population in the area near a nuclear power plant of cancer fatalities that might result from nuclear power plant operation should not exceed one-tenth of one percent (0.1%) of the sum of cancer fatality risks resulting from all other causes.

Beyond these safety goals, a *benefit-cost guideline* has been set to evaluate additional safety measures:

The benefit of an incremental reduction of societal mortality risks should be compared with the associated costs on the basis of $1,000 per person-rem averted.

Finally, the NRC has selected a numerical design objective:

The likelihood of a nuclear reactor accident that results in a large-scale core melt should normally be less than one in 10,000 per year of reactor operation.

One can make two observations: First, the goals are not independent (plant performance, individual risk, and societal risk are directly linked). From a conceptual as well as practical point of view, it may be desirable, as we shall discuss later, to consolidate the constraints. Second, the expected values of future frequencies may be insufficient to show that the risk constraints are satisfied with "reasonable certainty." The question of uncertainties then arises. For example, under a particular stochastic model or for a particular probability distribution of a parameter, a probabilistic constraint may be satisfied but not under other reasonable assumptions. The probability distribution of the future frequency of the system's failure is generated by parameter and/or model uncertainties. There is no theoretical framework to justify the use of the mean, the median, or other characteristics of this distribution (fractiles, moments, etc.) to show compliance with any of the probabilistic constraints (risk and plant performance). Which one is to be used must be part of the goals themselves. We shall examine here which of the safety goals are essential, in what theoretical framework they can be placed, and what is the logical treatment of uncertainties in this framework.

First, some people would argue that safety levels and costs should be negotiated directly by the parties involved (Susskind 1980). This may well happen in the future when the industry and the public have gained more experience with the performance of nuclear power plants. Meanwhile regulations based on safety goals are an alternative.

There is one framework that may be useful in thinking about numerical safety goals. Starting from the perspective of individual safety, one can show that the individual willingness to pay for risk reduction depends on the level of the risk; below a certain risk level the decision becomes "delegable without compensation" and the corresponding "value of life" is constant (Howard 1980). To the extent that risk compensation to the general public is not an established process in the nuclear industry, this framework justifies a double safety goal: a maximum individual risk (above which the considered technology should simply be rejected unless private negotiations can occur that are ethically acceptable to society) and an economic constraint that is the cost of improvement below which additional safety measures should be considered.

In this framework the first safety constraint to be satisfied is on the individual risk for the most exposed person in the general public. This constraint involves health effects (immediate death and cancer) and could also include financial risk. Although risk acceptance varies in the public, the acceptability of the individual risk can be established at the minimum by comparison with like risks involved in electrical generation by alternative existing technologies. In other words, the principle of comparing risks of generating electricity by different methods, which the NRC proposes to apply to societal risk, can apply to individual risk as well. These risks of alternatives may include the potential failure of dams built for hydroelectric generation but not the professional, voluntary risks of coal mining.

Once the individual safety requirements are satisfied, additional safety measures should be considered on a cost-benefit basis to ensure that safety funds in society at large are allocated in the most cost-effective manner. This means ensuring that, beyond an already low-risk level, there is no additional measure that would imply a lower cost per life saved than measures commonly taken in other sectors for the mitigation of comparable involuntary risks. Since this constraint is economic, it involves discounting at a rate that reflects the opportunity cost of capital to society (Keeler and Cretin 1983; Paté 1984b).

Societal risk mitigation is implied by the individual risk constraint and by the cost-benefit criterion mentioned earlier. As a matter of equity, the potential isolated victims of accidents and the potential victims of large accidents should be equally protected by regulations. There is therefore no need for an additional constraint on societal risk or for risk aversion considerations. Obviously there are clear and sufficient incentives for the industry to avoid the visibility of large catastrophes.

Constraints on public safety are theoretically sufficient to guide design and operation decisions. There is, in principle, no need for the regulatory agency to introduce an additional constraint on the maximum annual frequency of severe core damage. Even if there is no off-site effect, there is great pressure on the nuclear industry to avoid severe core damage because of the disastrous effect of such accidents on the public perception of the safety of the industry as a whole, as illustrated by the Three Mile Island episode. In practice, however, a constraint on the risk of core melt can be justified by the large uncertainties associated with the containment structure performance, the dynamics of radioactive release, and the consequences of population exposure. Because there is no experience with actual release, it is particularly difficult, for example, to assess the efficiency of an emergency plan.

If one wants to relate the expected plant performance to the individual risk constraint, there are at least two site-specific elements that will influence the result: the distance from the reactor(s) of the most exposed individual, and the number of reactors on the site. Because a group of reactors increases the risks to individuals of the general public, higher safety requirements should be put on each reactor than if they were isolated. The cost-effectiveness of additional safety measures, however, is independent of that multiplicity; this means that if a safety measure costs less than $1,000 per man-rem, this is true whether there is only one reactor or a group of reactors, and this criterion does not need to be modified to account for reactor multiplicity. Similarly, for an existing nuclear reactor, the relation between the expected plant performance and the upper bound on individual risk is independent of the remaining lifetime of the plant. The cost-effectiveness of additional safety measures for existing a plant, however, is sensitive to the current time horizon of the facility.

The next question is how to ensure that the goals have been satisfied "with reasonable certainty." A common procedure is to use "conservative" estimates at every step, which means to overestimate the probabilities of initiating events, failures, accidents, and so on. The overestimation of the final result, however, is impossible to assess. It is a wrong approach that may lead to absurd figures and quite possibly to suboptimal decisions, thus defeating the purpose of conservativeness itself. This is why the analysis of uncertainties and their explicit treatment in the final decision are critical.

Once this analysis has been done, safety decisions must be made to ensure that with a high probability (e.g., 0.95) the plant is in compliance with the maximum acceptable individual risk constraints and with the maximum allowable frequency of failure. There is no compelling theoretical reason to use one fractile or a mean value rather than another criterion.

In a framework involving numerical safety goals, this certainty level must be specified by the NRC along with the safety goal.

By contrast, when making an economic decision on optimal allocation of safety funds, it is the mean value of the failure frequencies with respect to parameters and models that should be considered in order to avoid suboptimal allocation of safety funds. This is true for both internal safety funds allocation and the external cost-benefit constraint (e.g., $1,000 per man-rem) that ensures that safety funds for society at large are used efficiently.

In this framework of simplified safety goals, risk uncertainty must therefore be treated in different ways according to the constraint to be satisfied and to the intended general use of the risk analysis results. If the goal is to verify that a probabilistic threshold (e.g., individual mortality frequency) is not exceeded, it is reasonable to require that this constraint be satisfied with a probability to be specified (e.g., 0.95). One needs to consider then the probability distribution on the frequency estimates in order to reflect analytical uncertainties. If the goal is to satisfy a cost-effectiveness constraint and to ensure optimal allocation of safety funds, expected values are sufficient, and the analysis of risk uncertainties is unnecessary beyond the computation of the means. More generally, if the goal is to maximize an expected utility within cost constraints, the relevant measure of failure probability estimates is the expected value of future failure frequency, and there is no need for further reporting of the uncertainties.

In practice, PRA, and particularly uncertainty analysis in PRA, is a long and costly exercise. There is a pressing need for a standardized design that would allow for a simplified risk and uncertainty analysis. This does not mean, however, that PRA could and should be entirely standardized: plant-specific characteristics will have to be considered. In particular, the analysis of external events such as earthquakes will remain a site-specific exercise, although the procedure of analysis itself and the study of the uncertainties might be standardized. Regulatory guidance about analytical procedures is helpful for cost control and long-term planning, as long as there remains enough flexibility in the process to incorporate new knowledge and information and to adapt to unusual circumstances.

Conclusion

For controversial safety decisions, probabilistic methods and decision analysis are useful but must be adapted to the present regulatory process in the United States. This is true because of the inherently personal nature of probabilistic estimates and/or the lack of historical and statistical information. When sufficient experience has been accumulated about different types of standard nuclear power plants, negotiation and mediation will be a good way to handle the choice of a plant type and safety features and to resolve siting problems. Meanwhile, if probabilistic methods are to be used, the NRC must specify the assessment procedure, the risk and cost constraints, and the confidence level with which the risk constraints must be satisfied. Although the recent PRA guidelines have improved the assessment process, the nuclear industry is still involved in adversarial procedures in which probability can be used to express a value judgment instead of knowledge of facts. Experience, standardized plant design, and agreement about PRA procedures will help in the long run to alleviate the problem. One necessary improvement is a clear understanding of how to compute risk uncertainties in PRA and how to account for them in nuclear safety decisions.

References

Abramson, L. R. 1981. "Some Misconceptions about the Foundations of Risk Analysis." *Risk Analysis 1*: 229–230.

Apostolakis, G., Garrick, B. J., and Okrent, D. 1983. "On Quality, Peer Review, and the Achievement of Consensus in Probabilistic Risk Analysis." *Nuclear Safety 24*: 792–800.

Arrow, K. J. 1951. *Social Choice and Individual Values*. New York: Wiley.

Baecher, G. B. 1972. *Site Exploration: A Probabilistic Approach*. Dissertation. Department of Civil Engineering, Massachusetts Institute of Technology.

Baram, M. 1980. "Cost-Benefit Analysis: An Inadequate Basis for Health, Safety, and Environment Regulatory Decision-Making." *Ecology Law Quarterly 8*: 473–931.

Bier, V. M. 1983. "A Measure of Uncertainty Importance for Components of Fault Trees. Report No. LIDS-TH-1277. Massachusetts Institute of Technology.

Budnitz, R. J. 1984. "External Initiators in Probabilistic Reactor Accident Analysis—Earthquakes, Fires, Floods, Winds." *Risk Analysis 4*: 323–335.

Bernero, R. M. 1984. "Probabilistic Risk Analysis: NRC Programs and Perspectives." *Risk Analysis 4*: 287–297.

Cornell, C. A., and Newmark, N. M. 1978. "On the Seismic Reliability of Nuclear Power Plants." *Proceedings of the ANS Meeting on Probabilistic Analysis of Nuclear Reactor Safety*, Los Angeles, California, *3*: XIV.1-1–XIV.1-14.

Cramèr, H. 1946. *Mathematical Methods of Statistics*. Princeton: Princeton University Press.

Daniels, T. A., and Canady, K. S. 1984. "A Nuclear Utility's Views on the Use of Probabilistic Risk Assessment." *Risk Analysis 4*: 281–286.

De Finetti, B. 1972. *Probability, Induction, and Statistics: The Art of Guessing*. New York: Wiley.

Fischhoff, S., Lichtenstein, P., Slovic, R. K., and Derby, S. 1980. *Approaches to Acceptable Risk: A Critical Guide*. Prepared for U.S. Nuclear Commission under NRC Interagency Agreement 40-550-75, NUREG/CR-1614, ORNL/Sub-7656/1. December.

Henrion, M. 1982. *The Value of Knowing How Little You Know: The Advantages of a Probabilistic Approach to Uncertainty in Policy Analysis*. Dissertation. School of Urban and Public Affairs, Carnegie-Mellon University. March.

Howard, R. A. 1977. "Risk Preference." *Readings in Decision Analysis*. Stanford Research Institute, Menlo Park, Calif.

Howard, R. A. 1980. "On Making Life and Death Decisions." In R. C. Schwing and W. A. Albers, eds., *Societal Risk Assessment*. General Motors Symposia Series.

Joksimovich, V. 1984. "A Review of Plant Specific PRAs." *Risk Analysis 4*: 255–266.

Kaplan, S., and Garrick, B. J. 1981a. "On the Quantitative Definition of Risk." *Risk Analysis 1*: 11–27.

Kaplan, S., and Garrick, B. J. 1981b. "Some Misconceptions about Misconceptions: A Response to Abramson." *Risk Analysis 1*: 231–233.

Keeler, E. B., and S. Cretin, 1983. "Discounting of Life Saving and Other Nonmonetary Effects." *Management Science 9*: 300–306.

Levine, S., and Rasmussen, N. C. 1984. "Nuclear Plant PRA: How Far Has It Come?" *Risk Analysis 4*: 247–254.

Lewis, H. W. 1980. "The Safety of Fission Reactors." *Scientific American 242*: 53–65.

Lewis, H. W. 1984. "Probabilistic Risk Assessment: Merits and Limitations." *Proceedings of the ANS/ENS Conference*, Karlsruhe, West Germany, September.

Linstone, H., and Turoff, M. 1975. *The Delphi Method: Techniques and Applications*. North Reading, Mass. Addison-Wesley.

Meehan, R. L., 1984. *The Atom and the Fault*. Cambridge: MIT Press.

Morgan, M. G., Henrion, M., and Morris, S. C. 1979. "Expert Judgments for Policy Analysis." Report BNL-51358. Upton, N.Y.: Brookhaven National Laboratory.

Morris, P. A. 1974. "Decision Analysis Experts Use." *Management Science 20*: 1233–1241.

Morris, P. A. 1983. "An Axiomatic Approach to Expert Resolution." *Management Science 29*: 24–32.

Murley, T. E. 1985. "Implementation of Safety Goals in NRC's Regulatory Process." *Proceedings of the International ANS/ENS Topical Meeting on Probabilistic Safety Methods and Applications*, San Francisco, California, March, pp. 7-1–7-13.

National Academy of Science. 1981. *Report of the Division of Technology Assessment and Risk Analysis on their Research Program*. Washington, D.C.: Committee on Risk and Decision Making.

Okrent, D., and Wilson, R. 1980. "Safety Regulations in the United States." Energy and Environmental Policy Center. Harvard University.

Paté, M. E. 1983a. "Acceptable Decision Processes and Acceptable Risks in Public Sector Regulations." *IEEE Transactions on Systems, Man, and Cybernetics 13*: 113–124.

Paté, M. E. 1983b. "Aggregation in Risk Analysis and Decision Problems: Probabilities and Preferences." Unpublished manuscript. Department of Industrial Engineering, Stanford, Calif.

Paté, M. E. 1983c. "Relevance of Risk Uncertainties in Regulated Decisions." *Proceedings of the Conference on Seismic Risk and Heavy Industrial Facilities*, Lawrence Livermore National Laboratories, Livermore, California, pp. 129–130.

Paté, M. E. 1984a. "Fault Trees vs. Event Trees in Reliability Analysis." *Risk Analysis* 4:177–186.

Paté, M. E. 1984b. "Discounting in Risk Analysis: Capital vs. Human Safety." In *Risk, Structural Engineering and Human Error*, M. Grigoriu, ed. Waterloo, Canada: University of Waterloo Press.

Raiffa, H. 1968. *Decision Analysis*. North Reading, Mass.: Addison-Wesley.

Raiffa, H. 1982. *The Art and Science of Negotiation*. Cambridge: Harvard University Press.

Ruckelshaus, W. D. 1983. "Science, Risk, and Public Policy." *Science 221*: 1026–1028.

Shachter, R. D. 1984. "An Incentive Approach to Eliciting Probabilities." In R. A. Waller and V. T. Covells, eds., *Low Probability High Consequences Risk Analysis*. New York: Plenum, *pp. 137–152.*

Slovic, P., Fischhoff, B., and Lichtenstein, S. 1979. "Rating the Risks." *Environment 21*: 14–39.

Susskind, L., and Weinstein, A., 1980. "Towards a Theory of Environmental Disputes Resolution." *Boston College Environmental Affairs Law Review* 311–357.

U.S. Atomic Energy Commission. 1957. *Theoretical Possibilities and Consequences of Major Accidents in Large Nuclear Power Plants*, WASH-740, Washington, D.C., March.

U.S. National Research Council. 1983. Committee on the Institutional Means for the Assessment of Risk to Public Health. *Risk Assessment in the Federal Government: Managing the Process*. Washington, D.C.: National Academy Press.

U.S. Nuclear Regulatory Commission. 1984. *Probabilistic Risk Assessment Reference Document*. NUREG-1050. Washington, D.C. September.

U.S. Nuclear Regulatory Commission. 1975. *Reactor Safety Study*. WASH-1400 (NUREG-75/014). Washington, D.C. October.

U.S. Nuclear Regulatory Commission. 1978. *Risk Assessment Review, Group Report to the U.S. Nuclear Regulatory Commission*. NUREG/CR-0400. Washington, D.C. September.

U.S. Nuclear Regulatory Commission. 1983. *Safety Goals for Nuclear Power Plant Operation*. NUREG-0880, Revision 1. Washington, D.C. May.

U.S. Nuclear Regulatory Commission. 1981. *Zion Station Probabilistic Safety Study*. Docket 50-295. Washington, D.C.

U.S. Nuclear Regulatory Commission. 1982. *Indian Point Probabilistic Safety Study*. Dockets 50-247 and 50-286. Washington, D.C.

U.S. Nuclear Regulatory Commission. 1983. *Probabilistic Risk Assessment; Limmerick Generating Station*. Docket 50-352. Washington, D.C.

Vesely, W. E., and Rasmuson, D. M. 1984. "Uncertainties in Nuclear Probabilistic Risk Analysis." *Risk Analysis 4*: 313–322.

Winkler, R. L. 1968. "The Consensus of Subjective Probability Distributions." *Management Science 15*: 61–75.

Winkler, R. L. 1981. "Combining Probability Distributions from Dependent Information Sources." *Management Science 27*: 479–693.

8

Cartels That Vote:
Agricultural Marketing Boards and Induced Voting Behavior

Jonathan Cave and Stephen W. Salant

The Agricultural Marketing Act of 1937 permits the establishment of committees that, among other activities, may legally regulate industry sales for the benefit of producers. Unlike other cartels operating in the United States, these committees are exempt from antitrust penalties. Indeed, the federal government itself polices each agreement, punishing those who violate committee edicts.

Since more than half of the fruits and tree nuts and 15 percent of the vegetables produced in the United States, measured in value terms, are regulated by such committees, it seems important to understand their behavior. Figure 8.1 indicates crops currently regulated by such federal orders. Since 1937 hundreds of orders have been initiated; most have terminated for one reason or another.[1] At the moment, forty-seven different federal orders exist. Of these, twenty-four provide for some form of direct regulation of quantity. The rest purportedly regulate quality. Of the twenty-four containing quantity regulations, only a handful are commonly regarded as serious sources of resource misallocation: the orders for hops, spearmint oil, walnuts, filberts, California-Arizona navel and valencia oranges, and lemons. The rest are typically regarded as ineffective.[2] Why some quantity-restricting cartels are more effective than others is a puzzle worthy of explanation.

Our goal in this research project is to understand the behavior of administrative committees authorized to restrict volume. Understanding this behavior is interesting in its own right and in addition may clarify how other cartels operate. Like every cartel, these administrative committees must grapple with difficult collective choice problems; however, they are not burdened with the enforcement problems that beset the typical cartel. Administrative committees afford students of cartel behavior three advantages: (1) their collective choice mechanism (majority-rule voting) is explicit, (2) their meetings are open to the public, and (3) their public records reveal how each committee member voted on each proposed volume restriction (no matter whether it passed or failed).

The participants in these markets are consumers, growers, and intermediaries referred to as handlers or packinghouses. To establish an order requires a vote of the growers only (at least two-thirds of the growers

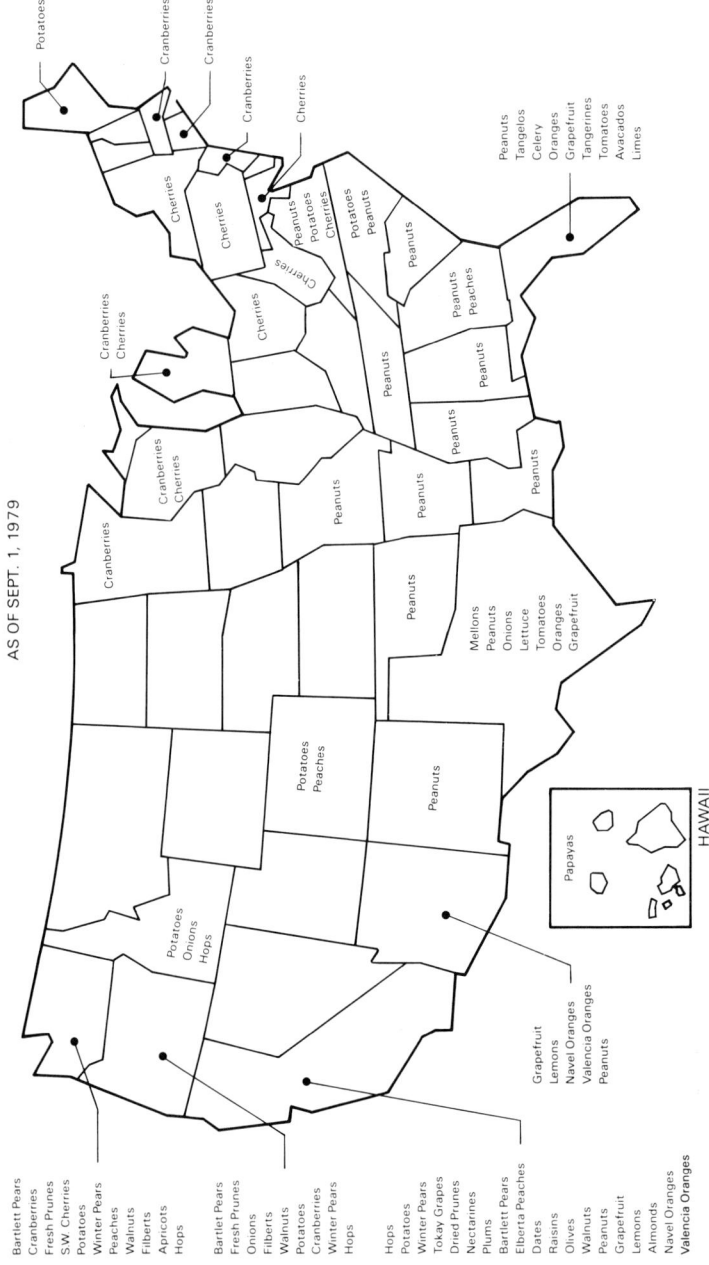

Figure 8.1 Fruit, vegetable, and nut marketing agreements and orders. Source: U.S. Department of Agriculture Marketing Service Program Aid No. 1095.

or a smaller number representing at least two-thirds of the volume). Orders generally state in detail the number of board members of each type (growers, handlers, or consumers) that growers and cooperatives can nominate. For example, the valencia committee is composed of eleven members—six growers, four handlers, and a consumer representative. Three of the growers and two of the handlers can be nominated by the cooperative that ships more than 50 percent of the crop (since time immemorial, Sunkist). The remaining cooperatives can nominate (using volume-weighted voting) one grower and one handler, whereas independent growers can nominate the two other growers and one handler. The eleventh member is selected by the other ten and must be neither a handler nor a grower. Each member serves for a term of two years.

Committees range in size from six members (Colorado potatoes) to forty-seven (raisins). Producers hold a majority on forty committees and have excluded handlers altogether on six committees.

Only the actions of the handlers are directly regulated by the committee's decisions. Under a time-honored principle known as "equitable marketing opportunity" (incorporated in sections 608 (c) (6) (C) and (D) of the Agricultural Marketing Agreement Act of 1937), all handlers are given the opportunity to ship the same percentage of the crop under their control to the regulated market, which we call the "primary" market. In practice, however, some handlers do not avail themselves of this opportunity. The divergence that typically exists between aggregate sales, on the one hand, and aggregate allotments (the amount authorized by the committee), on the other, is evidence that some handlers ship less than they are permitted. Table 8.1 reflects this stylized fact.[3] Why some handlers find it contrary to their self-interest to sell on the regulated market as much as the committee gives them the "opportunity" to sell also merits explanation. How handlers dispose of the rest of their crop depends on the specific order. Orders in which the handler can dump the rest of his crop on unregulated secondary markets are known as "market allocations" or "season-long prorates." Currently in this category are cranberries, raisins, almonds, walnuts, filberts, California dates, oranges, and lemons. Orders in which any production in excess of the allotment must be stored are known as "producer allotments." Currently in this category are hops, spearmint oil, and Florida celery.

In the next section of this chapter we review the standard model of marketing orders and discuss anecdotal evidence inconsistent with it. In subsequent sections, we develop an alternative model that, unlike the conventional model, accounts explicitly for the divergent interests of com-

Table 8.1 Illustration of divergence between aggregate allotments and sales, hops and celery from 1960 to 1980

Season beginning	Florida celery (1,000 crates)[a]		Hops (1,000 lb)	
	Allotment[b]	Sales	Allotment	Sales
1960	c	7,086	d	45,652
1961	c	7,122	d	35,454
1962	c	7,132	d	44,072
1963	c	7,372	d	51,336
1964	c	7,573	d	53,081
1965	8,055	7,770	d	56,060
1966	7,887	7,350	56,173	54,620
1967	7,887	6,867	55,753	49,498
1968	7,887	6,997	51,497	43,733
1969	7,887	6,128	46,063	41,592
1970	7,887	7,174	48,208	45,619
1971	7,887	7,069	49,601	48,057
1972	8,372	7,366	49,377	52,463
1973	8,797	6,071	55,528	55,152
1974	8,354	6,475	60,270	57,796
1975	8,326	5,686	60,270	55,593
1976	9,223	5,529	60,270	57,538
1977	8,082	5,979	60,270	54,767
1978	8,433	7,941	60,270	55,424
1979	9,644	7,900	63,234	55,254
1980	8,601	5,700[e]	76,424	75,816
1981			78,280	

Source: USDA Report No. 477, p. 40.
a. Sixty pounds per crate.
b. Quantity that may be sold in primary market outlets. Sales figures are for the primary market.
c. Order effective November 15, 1965.
d. Order effective July 22, 1966.
e. Preliminary.

mittee members and the fact that these conflicts are reconciled by voting. We clarify how the interest of each market participant depends on the restrictions adopted. Then we illustrate that these "induced preferences" need not be single-peaked even in the simplest of cases. Finally, we show that under majority rule the committee will nevertheless select the restriction most preferred by the board member with the median endowment. This chapter constitutes the theoretical underpinning of an ongoing research project.

The Standard Model of the Monolithic Marketing Board and Some Anecdotal Evidence against It

For decades agricultural marketing boards have been the subject of extensive study by economists, consumer groups, and government officials. The literature that has arisen concerning these cartels is vast.[4] In some cases it consists of comprehensive analyses of the weekly meetings of specific boards. For the most part, however, it consists of more formal, stylized models of board behavior.

These latter treatments tend to analyze the producer allotment and market allocation schemes by means of the same two models.[5] Producer allotments tend to be viewed as classic monopolies. Each committee is assumed to market whatever quantity maximizes industry profit. For example, if sale of the entire crop would cause losses at the margin, it is predicted that surplus will be discarded until the profit from an additional sale is zero. Market allocation is regarded as classic third-degree price discrimination coupled with free entry. Under this model the committee restricts sales in the inelastic primary market to the point where marginal revenues (net of any market-specific marginal handling costs) are equal in the primary and secondary markets. Since the entitlement to sell in the lucrative primary market is proportional to the size of one's crop, aggregate crop size is predicted to expand (in markets where expansion is permitted) until the losses in the secondary market offset the profits in the primary market, and total profits are dissipated.

Although this conventional view has a great deal of support among economists modeling volume-restricting marketing orders, we believe it is erroneous. The standard view fails to consider that each allotment percentage is chosen not by a benevolent dictator but by a committee operating under majority rule. If committee participants vote according to their divergent economic interests, the outcome of the voting process may differ radically from the predictions of the conventional model. In an industry of handlers of varying size, a committee dominated by small handlers, for example, can be expected to make a different collective decision than a committee composed of large handlers. The large handlers will favor tight restrictions on all fellow handlers to limit free riding. In contrast, the small handlers will prefer lax restrictions on every handler since they can depend on the larger handlers to hold up the "price umbrella" by restricting their own output even if not required by the committee to do so.

The more institution-oriented students of marketing orders have frequently emphasized that committee decisions are compromises that reconcile deep-seated divisions within a given industry. To illustrate, consider the citrus industry. The divisions within that industry were apparent even before the inception of any order. The largest cooperative (now Sunkist) had restricted sales in the inelastic market in an attempt to price discriminate, but it had failed repeatedly to get the needed cooperation of the smaller handlers and the smaller cooperative (now Pure Gold). Sunkist's problem with free riders was conveniently resolved after 1933 by federal regulations making noncompliance illegal, but, as can be imagined, the imposition of the government order was bitterly opposed by the independent handlers and Pure Gold. A half century later this conflict still smolders. Within the last year, a group of independents succeeded in pressuring the secretary of agriculture to suspend the navel order—to the great dismay of Sunkist.[6]

Size differences among market participants account for much of the conflict within the citrus industry.[7] In his comprehensive review of twenty years of weekly minutes of meetings of the orange board, Clodius (1950, p. 327) commented on a dispute that was to become chronic:

[Pure Gold] also criticized the level at which their weekly allotments were placed by the committee, holding that they always had customers who were willing to buy more of their oranges, if only the level of volume proration had not been set so low. From the viewpoint of any shipper who controls such a small part of the total supply, the amount he ships does not have any effect on the price he receives. This was the position of [Pure Gold] and the independents. Thus their criticisms of the committee in this matter were understandable. Had all the small shippers been permitted to ship what they wanted each week, these incremental supplies would probably have had a substantial price reducing effect ... The program would fail if for no other reason than that which caused the voluntary programs to fail—those whose shipments were not being restricted gained disproportionately.

These conflicts within the industry played themselves out in the decisions of the orange committee. Compromises were reached only after protracted deliberations. Clodius (1950, p. 308) reports that the independents, Pure Gold, and Sunkist would begin each meeting with widely divergent recommendations for the allotment percentage. "Rarely do the three coincide. Thereupon the groups bargain until some kind of compromise is found ..." In fact, according to Clodius (1950, p. 158), on one occasion compromise proved utterly impossible. In December 1941 the orange order had to be terminated because the board—then composed of an even number of members and lacking a tie-breaking rule—became hopelessly deadlocked.

Based on his careful examination of twenty years of such meetings, Clodius (1951, p. 1046) ultimately concluded:

Short-run maximization is also not possible because of lack of homogeneity of interests within the composition of the Committee reflecting industry attitudes. Every decision of the Committee is a result of compromise among the dominant shipper, which is a cooperative, a much smaller cooperative shipper, and the private shippers. Committee representatives tend to be prejudiced toward their own organizations. Because of the great diversity among organizations, their interests rarely tend to coincide; *thus joint maximization is impossible* [our emphasis].

What Clodius concluded about the orange committees,[8] the National Commission on Food Marketing concluded about most other administrative committees. After discussing deep conflicts in most industries—in large part related to size differences—the commission (1966, p. 348) remarked: "It is doubtful that the interests of those administering most orders coincide to the extent that an order could be operated consistently in a highly monopolistic manner."

Given the abundant evidence of widespread conflict within many administrative committees, we are skeptical of claims that they invariably act "as if" to maximize industry profits. Indeed, in our view proponents of such theories often tacitly admit that the conventional model does not apply to all orders containing volume restrictions since they never apply it to orders that they regard as somewhat competitive. Instead, at the outset they disregard such cases an uninteresting and of no "policy relevance."[9] We illustrate here an approach that we hope is applicable to the entire class of volume-restricting orders, not just to an arbitrary subset. We find that changes in the composition of the administrative committees and the rules governing them will have predictable economic consequences that policymakers may wish to consider when deciding how to reform the current system. In contrast, the conventional model suggests that such political changes will have no economic effects whatsoever.

Industry Equilibrium and Induced Preferences about the Allotment Percentage

The formal model contains n firms—the packinghouses. Firm i has at its disposal a total quantity q_i—referred to here as an "endowment" and in the trade as the "base." Handlers divide sale of their crop (regarded here as homogeneous) between a primary and a secondary market. In the primary market the demand curve is assumed to be relatively inelastic and to depend on sales in that market only.[10] Demand in the secondary market is assumed to be infinitely elastic at a price c. We have adopted these demand assumptions because they (1) simplify our problem, (2) correspond to the assumptions most often used in the literature on the alternative model of marketing orders, and (3) seem to reflect reality for certain orders.[11] Since production decisions are assumed to have taken place previously, we treat production as an endowment and therefore have no need to consider its costs. Of course c can be regarded as the opportunity cost of sales in the primary market. In the case of producer allotments, $c = 0$.[12] For concreteness, we assume that the firms are numbered in increasing order of size: $q_1 < q_2 < \cdots < q_n$. We denote by Q_i the aggregate endowment of the smallest i firms: $Q_i \equiv q_1 + \cdots + q_i$.

The marketing board sets the maximum proportion F of each firm's endowment that may be sold on the primary market. The strategy of firm i is a quantity $y_i \leq Fq_i$ to be sold on the primary market; the rest of i's endowment $(q_i - y_i)$ is sold on the secondary market. The profit of the ith firm will generally depend on its arrangement with its growers. If the packinghouse is a cooperative, it retains a percentage of the revenues and remits the remainder to the growers in proportion to the size of their crops. For simplicity, we assume this form of contractual relationship below.[13] Hence the ith handler will want to maximize revenues from the primary and secondary markets:

$$\max_{y_i \in [0, q_i F]} y_i P(y_i + Y_{-i}) + c(q_i - y_i),$$

where

$$Y_{-i} = \sum_{j \neq i} y_j.$$

Denote aggregate sales in the primary market by $Y (\equiv y_i + Y_{-i})$. If y_i is a best reply to Y_{-i}, one of the following Kuhn-Tucker conditions must hold:

$$y_i = 0 \quad \text{and} \quad P(Y) - c < 0, \tag{1}$$

$$y_i \in [0, q_i F] \quad \text{and} \quad P(Y) + y_i P'(Y) - c = 0, \quad \text{or} \tag{2}$$

$$y_i = q_i F \quad \text{and} \quad P(Y) + q_i F P'(Y) - c > 0. \tag{3}$$

A pure-strategy Nash equilibrium point is an n-tuple of strategies $(y_1, \ldots, y_n)$, each of which is a best reply to the others.

Under relatively mild assumptions it is possible to demonstrate the existence of a unique equilibrium point in pure strategies.[14] Denote the vector of equilibrium strategies by $\mathbf{y}^*(F)$ and aggregate equilibrium primary market sales by $Y^*(F)$.

We now turn to the properties of this Nash equilibrium. Since demand is strictly monotone decreasing, each handler's profit function is strictly concave in its own decision variable (y_i),[15] and only one of the Kuhn-Tucker conditions (1) through (3) can hold for each i. To ensure that the handlers will wish to sell anything at all on the primary market, we assume that $P(0) > c$, which means that (1) does not hold for any i, provided $F > 0$. Since $Y^*(F)$ is unique, we can classify handlers as constrained or unconstrained at a given F. Firm i is constrained at F iff condition (3) holds for firm i in the equilibrium associated with F; in that case we write $i \in C(F)$. If not, (2) must hold, and we say that firm i is unconstrained at F; the set of unconstrained firms is denoted $U(F)$.

If handler i is constrained, (3) holds and any smaller handler j ($j < i$) must also be constrained. If handler i is unconstrained, (2) holds, and any larger handler $j(j > i)$ must also be unconstrained. Thus $C(F)$ and $U(F)$ are intervals; there is a largest constrained handler $i(F)$ such that $C(F) = \{1, \ldots, i(F)\}$ and $U(F) = \{i(F) + 1, \ldots, n\}$.

The first-order condition characterizing the best reply of an unconstrained firm is symmetric. Hence all unconstrained firms i will sell the same quantity (denoted $y^u(F)$) on the primary market, while each constrained firm will sell the maximum feasible amount ($y_i^*(F) = q_i F$).

The profits of firm i in the unique equilibrium corresponding to a particular F are

$$\pi^1(F) = \begin{cases} \pi_u^i(F) = P(Y^*(F))y^u(F) + c(q_i - y^u(F)) & \text{if } i \in U(F), \\ \pi_c^i(F) = P(Y^*(F))q_i F + c(1 - F)q_i & \text{if } i \in C(F), \end{cases} \tag{4}$$

where

$$Y^*(F) = \sum_{i=1}^n y_i^*(F) = \sum_{i \in U(F)} y^u(F) + \sum_{i \in C(F)} q_i F.$$

These profits induce preferences of each firm over the choice of F. In turn the committee chooses F by simple majority rule, so we wish to relate the chosen F to the structure of these preferences.

The induced preferences are not single peaked even in the simplest case, where $P(\cdot)$ is linear. However, the collection of induced preferences has enough structure to ensure the existence of a unique majority-rule equilibrium to the voting game over F. We now clarify the elements of this structure on which our results will depend.

The first element of this structure we refer to as nesting. Suppose that we start with $F = 1$, in which case all firms are unconstrained. As F tightens (falls), more and more firms become constrained. In fact, associated with each firm i is a characteristic cutoff value F_i at which it just becomes constrained ($y^u(F_i) = q_i F_i$). Our previous results imply that these cutoffs are ranked in decreasing order of size: since $q_1 < \cdots < q_n$, it must be that $F_1 > \cdots > F_n$. If not, for $i > j$ there would exist F between F_i and F_j that would constrain the larger firm (i) but not the smaller (j), and $C(F)$ would not be an interval. Therefore the nesting property implies that as F falls, the smallest firms become constrained first, and firm i is constrained at F if and only if $F < F_i$. This reflects our intuition that smaller firms, having smaller inframarginal losses from additional sales in the primary market, would like to "free ride" on the voluntary (unconstrained) restraint of large firms.

The second element of this structure we refer to as scaling: by inspection of (4) it is clear that the profits of any two constrained handlers are monotonically increasing linear transformations of each other. Therefore, if F and F' are two candidate choices and if in equilibrium firms i and j are constrained at both F and F', the two firms will rank the candidates in the same way. In brief, the ordinal preferences of all constrained handlers are the same.

The third property we refer to as consistency. It requires that $\pi_c^i(F_i) = \pi_u^i(F_i)$, and it follows immediately from (4) and the definition of F_i.

Finally, the induced preferences have the property that each unconstrained handler prefers tighter restraints on its constrained rivals. We refer to this property as "unconstrained monotonicity"; it says that $\pi^i(F)$ is monotone decreasing in F throughout the range $[F_i, 1]$. Indeed, each firm's profit is continuous in F, and decreasing in F, when the firm is unconstrained.

These properties follow from the observation that the unconstrained firms are playing a symmetric Cournot quantity game. As Spence (1976), Loury (1986), and Bergstrom and Varian (1985) have remarked, Nash equilibria of symmetric games can sometimes be represented as extreme points of "potential functions." In this case, if there are k unconstrained firms, the unique Cournot equilibrium total primary market sales by the unconstrained firms can be characterized as the unique maximizer of $(k-1)CS(Q:F) + k\pi(Q:F)$, where $CS(Q:F)$ is consumer surplus and $\pi(Q:F)$ is the total revenue earned by the unconstrained firms on their primary market sales. Both of these are computed using the "residual demand curve" $P(Q:F) = P(Q + FQ_{n-k})$. This formulation shows clearly that the Cournot equilibrium associated with a smaller F's is less competitive and also that increases in the number of unconstrained firms result in more competitive outcomes for a given F.

Since the range of F is compact and the profit functions are continuous in F, it follows that each firm i has an ideal or most-preferred value of F, which we denote by I_i. It is straightforward to show that handlers in the industry with larger endowments prefer smaller allotment percentages. More precisely, if $q_1 < q_2 < \cdots < q_n$, $I_1 \geq I_2 \cdots \geq I_n$. For if $q_i < q_j$, then $F_i \geq F_j$, and (by monotonicity) either $I_i < F_j \leq F_i$ or $F_j \leq I_i < F_i$. In the former case $I_i = I_j$ (by scaling), and in the latter $I_j \leq I_i$.

The behavior of firms as F tightens is illustrated in figure 8.2 for the duopoly case. The first panel shows the two firms' unconstrained reaction functions. The unconstrained Nash equilibrium sales vector is located at their unique point of intersection, which is labeled a. In addition we have shown the endowment point, labeled q. As F tightens, the rectangle of length Fq_1 and height Fq_2, within which y must lie, shrinks. Note that since $q_2 > q_1$, the ray to the endowment point is steeper than the 45° line. As F falls, the maximum amounts that can be sold on the primary market move down this ray. From this, we can see that firm 1 (the smaller firm) is the first to become constrained, illustrating the nesting property described earlier. The allotment percentage at which firm 1 is just constrained is labeled F_1 in the figure.

The second panel shows the reaction curves for values of F where firm 1 is constrained. As F tightens, it is clear that the equilibrium sales vector moves up the unconstrained reaction curve of firm 2 until it meets the ray to the endowment point at $F_2 q$. This segment is labeled b. As F falls further, both handlers are constrained, and the vector of equilibrium sales in the primary market moves down the ray. The second panel also indicates the isoprofit curve for each packinghouse, through the equilibrium point. As figure 8.2 illustrates, locally movement along b (as F falls) benefits the unconstrained firm. This illustrates the property of "unconstrained monotonicity." The final two panels illustrate the possibilities when both firms are constrained: it is possible that both firms will benefit (or be harmed)

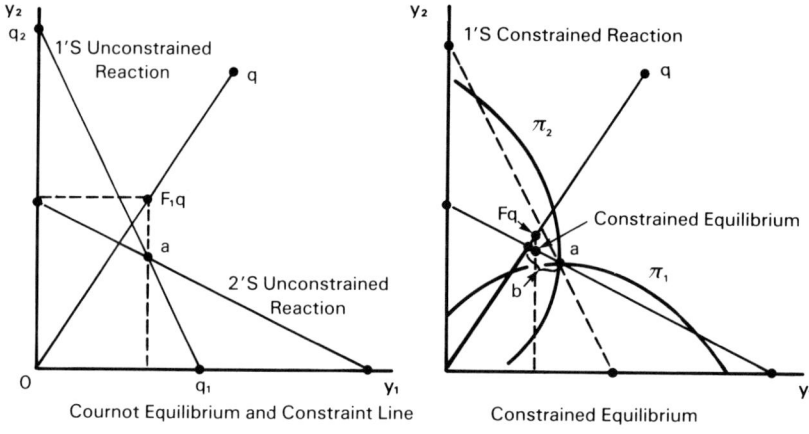
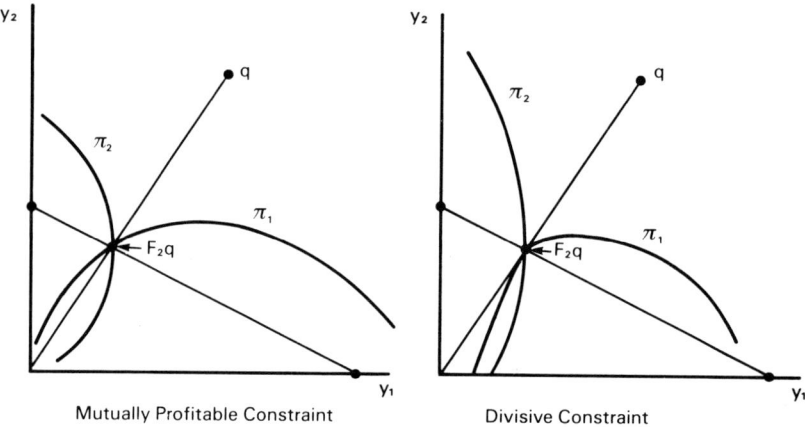

Figure 8.2 Industry equilibrium under marketing orders in the two-handler case

from tightening F, but it is also possible that only the larger firm will find this profitable.

Preferences Derived for an Example

The following example illustrates that the induced preferences derived in the previous section need not be single peaked even when inverse demand is linear:

$$P(Y) = a - bY. \tag{5}$$

Substituting this inverse demand curve into the Kuhn-Tucker conditions (1) through (3), we obtain for each i:

$$y_i = 0 \quad \text{and} \quad a - bY - c < 0, \tag{1'}$$

$$y_i \in [0, q_i F] \quad \text{and} \quad a - bY - by_i - c = 0, \quad \text{or} \tag{2'}$$

$$y_i = q_i F \quad \text{and} \quad a - bY - c > 0. \tag{3'}$$

We have already argued that (1') never holds in equilibrium. Conditions (2') and (3') characterize the unconstrained and constrained firms, respectively. From (2'), the primary sales of each unconstrained handler will be

$$y_i = y^u = \frac{(a - bY - c)}{b} \quad \text{for all } i \in U(F). \tag{6}$$

Consider the unique equilibrium associated with F. If there are k constrained firms and $n - k$ unconstrained firms, aggregate sales in the primary market will be

$$Y^*(F) = (n - k)y^u + Q_k F = \frac{(n - k)(a - c) + bFQ_k}{b(n - k + 1)}. \tag{7}$$

Hence the primary market sales of each unconstrained firm will be

$$y^u(F) = \frac{a - c - bFQ_k}{b(n - k + 1)}. \tag{8}$$

We can use this expression to find the allotment percentage F_k that is just binding on firm k. Since $y^u(F_k) = F_k q_k$,

$$F_k = \frac{a - c}{b[(n - k + 1)q_k + Q_k]}. \tag{9}$$

It is clear from this expression that the cutoffs have the nesting property derived previously:[16]

$$F_1 \geq F_2 \geq \cdots \geq F_n.$$

We now turn to the properties of the equilibrium quantities and the induced preferences. First, it will be noticed that even in the general case the preferences of the constrained and unconstrained firms can be written:

$$\pi_c^i(F) = [P(Y^*(F)) - c]q_i F + cq_i, \tag{10a}$$

$$\pi_{iu}(F) = [P(Y^*(F)) - c]y^u(F) + cq_i. \tag{10b}$$

Combining (5) and (2'), we have

$$P(F) - c = by^u(F). \tag{11}$$

From (8) it is clear that $y^u(F)$ and hence $P(F)$ are decreasing and piecewise linear in F. Moreover the limit (from either above or below) of $y^u(F)$ as $F \to F_k$ is

$$y^u(F_k) = \frac{(a-c)q_k}{[(n-k+1)q_k + Q_k]b}. \tag{12}$$

As F falls below F_k and the number of constrained firms rises from $k-1$ to k, (8) implies that the slope of $y^u(F)$, and therefore of $P(F)$, becomes more negative. To summarize, we have established that both the price and the unconstrained sales functions are continuous, piecewise linear, monotone decreasing, and convex in F. In fact they strictly decrease for $F < F_1$. These properties are illustrated in figure 8.3.

With these preliminaries established, we can consider the properties of the induced preferences. If the ith packinghouse is unconstrained ($F \geq F_i$), we can write its profits using (10b) and (11) as

$$\pi_u^i(F) = b(y^u(F))^2 + cq_i. \tag{13}$$

From the properties of $y^u(F)$, it is evident that $\pi_u^i(F)$ is continuous, decreasing and (since it is the sum of a constant and the composition of convex functions) convex in F.

On the other hand, if the ith packinghouse is constrained ($F < F_i$), we can write its profits as

$$\pi_c^i(F) = by^u(F)Fq_i + cq_i. \tag{14}$$

This is the sum of a constant and a negative definite (concave) quadratic in F. It is therefore continuous and, on each open interval (F_{k+1}, F_k),

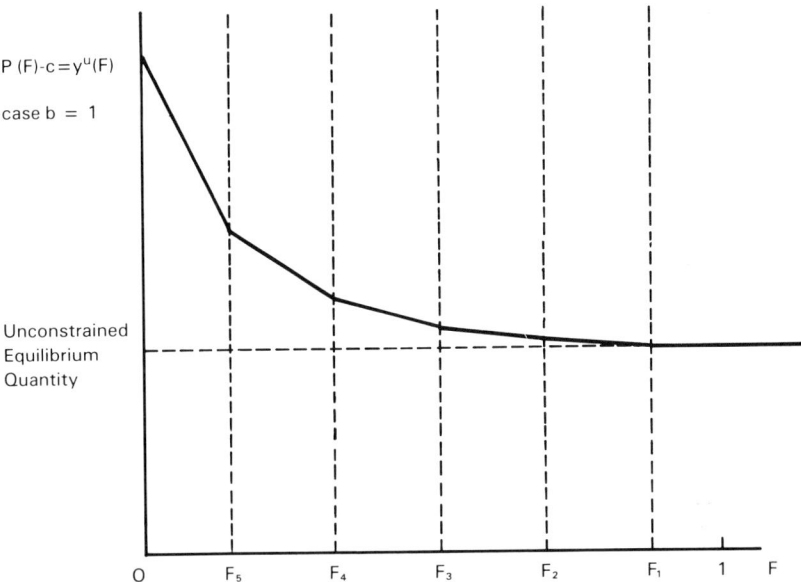

Figure 8.3 Price and unconstrained sales in the primary market as functions of F

continuously differentiable and strictly concave. On such intervals, its derivative can have either sign:

$$\frac{d\pi_c^i}{dF} = q_i b \left[F \frac{dy^u}{dF} + y^u \right]. \tag{15}$$

Since y^u is convex it follows that the slope of $\pi_c^i(F)$ increases as F increases through any boundary (F_k). As a result $\pi^i(F)$ need not be single peaked. However, since both $P(Y(F))$ and $y^u(F)$ are continuous, $\pi^i(F)$ is continuous in F.

Tables 8.2 through 8.5 numerically evaluate the induced preferences in the linear demand case for illustrative markets with three handlers. As the table headings indicate, the simulations differ with respect to individual endowments, parameters of the linear demand curve, and the price in the secondary market. To confirm that induced preferences need not be single peaked, consider the fourth and fifth columns of table 8.3. When F first binds on the smallest firm ($F = F_1$), $\pi_1 = 25.781$. As F tightens, π_1 falls. When F just binds on the largest firm ($F = F_3$), $\pi_1 = 25.669$. Still tighter F's, however, cause π_1 to reverse direction and increase. It then begins to decrease again. The reader can verify that the preferences for the handler

Table 8.2 Monopoly outcome with identical endowments

Demand parameters: $A = 10$; $B = 2$; $C = 5$
Endowments: 6.6667; 6.6667; 6.6667

	F	y^u	P	π_1	π_2	π_3
Nash	1.00	0.625	6.25	34.115	34.115	34.115
	0.2750	0.625	6.25	34.115	34.115	34.115
$F_1 = F_2 = F_3$	0.0938	0.625	6.25	34.115	34.115	34.115
	0.0750	—	7.00	34.334	34.334	34.334
$MB = JM$	0.0625	—	7.50	34.375	34.375	34.375
	0.000	—	10	33.333	33.333	33.333

F = allotment; maximum fraction permitted on primary market
y^u = fresh market sales of each unconstrained handler (if any)
P = price in primary market ($P = A - BQ$)
π_i = profit of agent i
C = price in secondary market
F_i = allotment at which firm i becomes constrained
MB = marketing board equilibrium—ideal point of firm 2
JM = joint monopoly—industry profit-maximizing allotment.

Table 8.3 Moderate diversity in endowments

Demand parameters: $A = 10$; $B = 2$; $C = 5$
Endowments: 5.0; 6.0; 9.0

	F	y^u	P	π_1	π_2	π_3
Nash	1.00	0.625	6.25	25.781	30.781	45.781
F_1	0.125	0.625	6.25	25.781	30.781	45.781
	0.1217	0.630	6.26	25.768	30.795	45.795
	0.1185	0.636	6.27	25.753	30.809	45.809
	0.1152	0.641	6.28	25.739	30.823	45.823
	0.1120	0.649	6.29	25.724	30.830	45.830
F_2	0.1087	0.652	6.30	25.709	30.851	45.851
	0.1042	0.677	6.35	25.705	30.846	45.916
	0.0997	0.702	6.40	25.699	30.839	45.985
	0.0952	0.726	6.45	25.692	30.830	46.056
	0.0907	0.751	6.50	25.681	30.818	46.128
F_3	0.0862	0.776	6.55	25.669	30.803	46.204
	0.0690	—	7.24	25.773	30.928	46.391
$MB = JM$	0.0625	—	7.5	25.781	30.937	46.406
	0.000	—	10.0	25.0	30.0	45.0

F = allotment; maximum fraction permitted on primary market
y^u = fresh market sales of each unconstrained handler (if any)
P = price in primary market ($P = A - BQ$)
π_i = profit of agent i
C = price in secondary market
F_i = allotment at which firm i becomes constrained
MB = marketing board equilibrium—ideal point of firm 2
JM = joint monopoly—industry profit-maximizing allotment.

Agricultural Marketing Boards and Induced Voting Behavior 271

Table 8.4 A committee dominated by small independents

Demand parameters: $A = 10$; $B = 2$; $C = 5$
Endowments: 1.0; 2.0; 17.0

	F	y^u	P	π_1	π_2	π_3
Nash	1.0000	0.625	6.25	5.781	10.781	85.781
F_1	0.6250	0.625	6.25	5.781	10.781	85.781
	0.5714	0.643	6.29	5.735	10.826	85.826
	0.5179	0.661	6.32	5.684	10.873	85.873
	0.4643	0.679	6.36	5.630	10.921	85.921
	0.4107	0.696	6.39	5.572	10.970	85.970
$F_2 = MB$	0.3571	0.714	6.43	5.510	11.020	86.020
	0.2992	0.801	6.60	5.479	10.959	86.284
	0.2413	0.888	6.78	5.429	10.857	86.577
	0.1834	0.975	6.95	5.358	10.715	86.901
	0.1255	1.062	7.12	5.266	10.533	87.255
F_3	0.0676	1.148	7.30	5.155	10.310	87.639
JM	0.0625	—	7.50	5.156	10.312	87.656
	0.0000	—	10.0	5.000	10.000	85.000

F = allotment; maximum fraction permitted on primary market
y^u = fresh market sales of each unconstrained handler (if any)
P = price in primary market ($P = A - BQ$)
π_i = profit of agent i
C = price in secondary market
F_i = allotment at which firm i becomes constrained
MB = marketing board equilibrium—ideal point of firm 2
JM = joint monopoly—industry profit-maximizing allotment

with the intermediate endowment (π_2) are likewise not single peaked. Nevertheless, as we prove later, the preferences have sufficient structure to avoid Condorcet cycles and ensure the existence of a majority-rule equilibrium.

Voting Equilibrium and its Properties

From the induced preferences of each packinghouse over committee decisions, we turn now to the committee's determination of the allotment percentage. Recall that committees are typically composed of a small number of growers and handlers who serve for fixed terms of several years. At the time the committee votes each grower's crop has been assigned to the packinghouse of his choice,[17] and his costs are sunk. Alternative proposals for the allotment percentage are voted on until one meets with the approval of a majority of the committee.

To proceed, we make two strategic simplifications: each voter is assumed

Table 8.5 Consequences of reduced price in secondary market

Demand parameters: $A = 10$; $B = 2$; $C = 3$
Endowments: 1.0; 2.0; 17.0

	F	y^u	P	π_1	π_2	π_3
Nash	1.0000	0.875	4.75	4.531	7.531	52.531
F_1	0.8750	0.875	4.75	4.531	7.531	52.531
	0.8000	0.900	4.80	4.440	7.620	52.620
	0.7250	0.925	4.85	4.341	7.711	52.711
	0.6500	0.950	4.90	4.235	7.805	52.805
	0.5750	0.975	4.95	4.121	7.901	52.901
$F_2 = MB$	0.5000	1.000	5.00	4.000	8.000	53.000
	0.4189	1.122	5.24	3.940	7.879	53.516
	0.3378	1.243	5.49	3.840	7.680	54.091
	0.2568	1.365	5.73	3.701	7.402	54.726
	0.1757	1.486	5.97	3.522	7.045	55.419
F_3	0.0946	1.608	6.22	3.304	6.608	56.172
JM	0.0875	—	6.50	3.306	6.613	56.206
	0.0000	—	10.0	3.000	6.000	51.000

F = allotment; maximum fraction permitted on primary market
y^u = fresh market sales of each unconstrained handler (if any)
P = price in primary market ($P = A - BQ$)
π_i = profit of agent i
C = price in secondary market
F_i = allotment at which firm i becomes constrained
MB = marketing board equilibrium—ideal point of firm 2
JM = joint monopoly—industry profit-maximizing allotment

to disregard the future interactions he will have with other members of the committee, and contracts between a grower and his packinghouse give them coincident preferences over alternative allotment percentages. These are strong assumptions, and we make them at this preliminary stage to simplify a complex problem. If the evidence suggests they are inappropriate, we will modify them in subsequent work. In the orders with which we are most familiar (e.g., the citrus orders), the board lasts for a fixed duration and then is replaced in its entirety. In such cases, as long as there is no interseasonal interaction, voting behavior in each stage of the multistage game should coincide with behavior in the one-shot game. This (and its simplicity) motivate our first assumption.[18] As for the second, in the vast majority of fruit and vegetable markets, the contracts between growers and packinghouses involve "pools."[19] As we understand such pools, the packinghouse deducts a percentage of its gross revenues to cover its costs and divides the residual among the growers according to the size of the crop each grower has assigned to the packinghouse. For such contracts our second assumption would be appropriate; other contracts of course exist for which grower and packinghouse interests diverge.[20] The practical implication of the second assumption is that the preferences and endowments of each grower can be taken to be those of his packinghouse. If we find inexplicable differences between the voting behavior of growers and handlers on the committee, we will reconsider this assumption.

In what follows, we consider the determination of the allotment percentage by the administrative committee. At the time of voting, the composition of the committee is fixed as is the size of each grower's crop and his choice of packinghouse. We treat these variables as exogenous to the problem under investigation, recognizing that they could be incorporated in a more complex model.[21] We assume there are an odd number (L) of committee members chosen from the industry of n ($\geq L$) firms. To avoid confusion, we assign a "committee index" ($i = 1, 2, \ldots, L$) to each voter in addition to his "industry index." A larger committee index of a voter indicates a larger endowment. The index we will refer to will be the committee index unless otherwise indicated. The preferences of each of the L voters have the same general characteristics as the preferences of members of the industry from which they are selected.

Assume that there are an odd number of voters and that their endowments differ. Let the committee index m denote the voter with the median endowment. Let us recall the following properties of the induced preferences:

1. The firms are numbered in (strictly) increasing order of size.

2. The cutoff levels ($F_i, i = 1, 2, \ldots, L$) below which firm i is constrained in Nash equilibrium are ranked in decreasing order of size (nesting).

3. Profits of the unconstrained firms are monotone decreasing in F on the relevant range $[F_i, 1]$ (unconstrained montonicity).

4. Profits of the constrained firms are increasing linear transformations of each other (scaling).

5. The profits of each firm i are continuous in F (continuity).

Under these conditions it is easy to demonstrate the following result.

MEDIAN PACKINGHOUSE THEOREM   There is a unique majority-rule equilibrium at I_m, the ideal point of the committee member with the median endowment.

Proof   The formal content of this theorem is that, for any F, the number of voters preferring I_m to F is at least $(L + 1)/2$. The proof is in three steps.

By continuity, each voter i ($i = 1, 2, \ldots, L$) has an ideal point I_i, and unconstrained monotonicity implies that $I_i \leq F_i$;[22] each voter's ideal point comes at a point where he is constrained. Combining this with the scaling property, we can see that if the ideal point of a small firm is smaller than the cutoff level of a larger firm, those two firms—and all firms of intermediate size—have the same ideal point. We refer to this property as "congruence given nesting."

Second, if $F < I_m$, the set of firms constrained at F includes the majority coalition $\{1, \ldots, m\}$. All the voters in this coalition are also constrained at I_m, so from the scaling property we know that they will agree as to the ranking of F and I_m. But I_m is preferred by m to F. This shows that such an F would lose to I_m in pairwise voting.

Finally, consider the only remaining possibility: that $F_{m+k} \leq I_m \leq \min\{F_{m+k-1}, F\}$ for some positive integer k. The set of firms unconstrained at F and at I_m includes the set $\{m+k, \ldots, L\}$, so every member of this set prefers I_m to F by unconstrained monotonicity. By the congruence property, I_m is also the ideal point of every voter in $\{m, \ldots, m+k-1\}$, and thus each member of this set prefers I_m to F. Therefore every voter in the majority coalition $\{m, \ldots, L\}$ prefers I_m to F. Hence for any F, I_m wins in pairwise voting. ∎

To illustrate, the preferences for a three-voter case are drawn in figure 8.4. Note that $F_1 > F_2 > F_3$, reflecting the assumption that $q_1 < q_2 < q_3$. Note also that voter i's preference is monotonically decreasing in F for $F \geq F_i$, and that the collection of preferences has the "scaling" property. The theorem therefore implies that the ideal point of the median voter (I_2) will be strictly preferred by a majority of the committee. Voter 3 would join voter 2 in defeating proposals for any larger F, while voter 1 would join voter 2 in defeating proposals for any smaller F. Hence even without single-peaked preferences, a majority-rule cycle is avoided.

The escape is a narrow one, however. If the "scaling" property did not hold a cycle could easily be produced. Suppose in figure 8.4 that π^2 and π^3 were as drawn but π^1 were modified so that $\pi^1(I_1) > \pi^1(I_3) > \pi^1(I_2)$. Then I_2 would no longer defeat I_3, and since I_1 defeats I_3 and I_2 defeats I_1, there would be no equilibrium.

Our theory does admit the possibility that the committee will vote for the restriction that maximizes industry profits. This would occur, for example, if handlers had identical endowments and hence had no conflicts of interest. But our theory also admits more competitive possibilities. These should arise when heterogeneity among the handlers creates conflicts of interest.

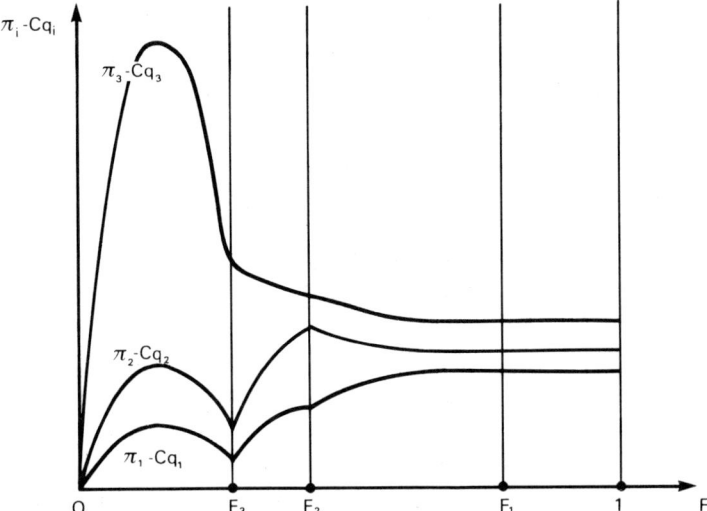

Figure 8.4 Induced preferences: not single peaked but sufficient for median voter result

The theory implies that whenever the committee does choose the monopoly restriction, each handler will sell as much as he is permitted on the primary market. Suppose in such circumstances some handler sold a smaller quantity on the primary market. Since monopoly price on the primary market would exceed the (fixed) price in the secondary market by the inframarginal loss, an additional primary sale would inflict on the profits of the entire industry, any unconstrained individual handler would have an incentive to increase his primary market sales. If the real-world conformed exactly to the assumptions of our model, then the mere evidence that some handlers sold less than they were permitted on the primary market would establish unambiguously that industry profits were not being maximized under the order and that the regulation was more competitive than is commonly supposed.[23]

Why would a committee composed of handlers and growers from the industry fail to maximize industry profits? Intuitively, the committee would select a restriction that does not maximize the profits of its members if a majority of them would lose—albeit a smaller amount than remaining members would gain—under the profit-maximizing restriction.

Given the vector of industry endowments and the demand parameters, the economic equilibrium will depend on the composition of the committee. It is instructive to regard the industry's handlers as a fixed set of preferences indexed by their endowments and the committee as some selection from this set (subject to restrictions contained in the order). Any committee whose median voter has a given endowment will vote for the same restriction no matter what is the composition of the rest of the committee.

As was previously shown, handlers in the industry with larger endowments prefer smaller allotment percentages. This suggests that industries governed by marketing orders can be made more competitive by replacing a board member whose endowment exceeds the committee's median by a member whose endowment lies below it. Such changes will lower the endowment of the median voter and will cause the committee to relax its regulation. The analysis implies moreover that there is nothing to be gained by adding a voter with an exceptionally small endowment. The greatest relaxation that can be accomplished by a single replacement is a new equilibrium at the ideal point of the current committee member with committee index $m - 1$.

By selecting committees of alternative composition, a broad range of equilibria can be generated. The largest (smallest) such F would be selected by a committee composed of the smallest (largest) L firms in the industry; they would choose the ideal point of the firm with industry index $(L + 1)/2$ (alternatively, $n - (L - 1)/2$). Notice that the induced preferences over F are entirely independent of the makeup of the committee. They reflect the distribution of endowments across all the firms affected by the marketing order regulation.

One characteristic of all such voting equilibria is that a majority of the committee must be constrained. For if a majority were unconstrained, there would exist a tighter constraint, which it would vote for, and the initial situation could not have been an equilibrium.

In any event no matter how the committee members are selected, it is not possible for the "joint-monopoly" outcome to be selected unless it happens to be the ideal point of firm $n - (L - 1)/2$. This implies that substantial asymmetry in the distribution of endowments precludes fully collusive behavior, provided the voting procedure fits our description and side payments between the firms are prohibited.

Indeed, our model suggests that marketing boards will select more competitive outcomes in highly concentrated industries. By contrast, most theories of unregulated oligopoly in which structure matters suggest that concentration leads to greater departures from competitive equilibrium. This in turn suggests that marketing boards may have more attractive welfare properties in highly concentrated industries. If marketing boards create long-term pressures for reduced concentration, they may remove both the symptom (collusion) and the cause (high concentration) of market failures.

In our analysis we have explicitly excluded side payments from consideration. In addition we have implicitly assumed sincere voting: in other words, we assume that each voter's behavior is an accurate reflection of its induced preferences. Due to the fact that preferences of constrained voters fail to be single peaked, it may not be obvious that sincere voting is a dominant strategy. What is obvious is that misrepresentation that does not displace the median voter will have no effect on the outcome. Firms that are smaller (larger) than the median firm therefore may have the power to tighten (loosen) the constraint by voting as if they were larger (smaller) than the median firm. However, from the properties of unconstrained monotonicity and scaling, it is evident that a smaller (larger) firm will only profit if it can arrange to loosen (tighten) the constraint. Thus the only changes a firm can effect are those that do not improve the outcome. It follows that sincere voting is at least a Nash equilibrium in that a firm faced with sincere voting by other committee members cannot profit by misrepresentation.

Future Research

In the next phase of this project, the predictive power of our theory will be investigated using a combination of controlled experiments and an analysis of data on committee voting and handler sales drawn from the hops, navel orange, or filbert markets. Here we outline the planned research.

Experiments

Plott (1979) studied the voting behavior of a committee of five individuals required to make a succession of twelve decisions. To pass, a proposal required the approval of a majority. On each of the twelve rounds preferences were induced for each individual by offering him a payment dependent on the committee's decision in that round. In Plott's experiment the issue space was two dimensional. Each voter's indifference curves were concentric circles around a specified ideal point. Plott found that if there existed a Condorcet winner for a particular stage, the committee almost always chose it at that stage. He reported no evidence of sophisticated voting and no evidence of interdependence between votes on successive rounds.

We plan to conduct three types of experiments to test the predictive power of our model. First, we intend to examine the voting behavior of a committee whose preferences are induced directly by the experimenter as in Plott's case. Our experiment would differ from his in two principal respects: the issue space would be one dimensional and preferences would be asymmetric. Specifically, we plan to use the nonsingle-peaked preferences derived from our linear demand case. Like Plott, we will examine the behavior of a committee that votes on a succession of issues to see if it tends to select the Condorcet winner at each stage.

The second type of experiment will concern the behavior of handlers in a regulated market. Specifically, each subject will be given an endowment to allocate between two outlets (referred to as "markets") but will be allowed to designate no more than a common exogenous percentage of that endowment for the more lucrative primary market. Participants will be paid by the experimenter as follows: a fixed reward for each unit designated for the secondary market and a per unit reward that decreases linearly in the total amount that all subjects designate for the primary market. Our goal here will be to examine the validity of the theoretical prediction that subjects will behave like Cournot competitors.

The third type of experiment will involve two stages. Participants in the market experiment will be asked first to form a committee for the purpose of deciding collectively on a common allotment percentage. Before they vote, however, they will be told that this percentage will restrict behavior in the market experiments to follow and that the experimenter will pay subjects exactly as before (i.e., according to what they designate for the two markets). Unlike the previous type of voting experiment, in this last experiment the reward to each individual from the alternative committee decisions is indirect. The experimenter does not reward him directly for alternative decisions of the committee; instead, the experimenter's reward depends on the outcome in the subsequent stage. However, that outcome will be influenced (in ways that differ across subjects) by the common constraint. The premise of the theory is that each subject will take this influence into account when voting. The experiment will be designed to permit a clear distinction between the predictions of our theory and that of the alternative in which the allocation between the two markets maximizes the total payoff of the subjects.

Experiments such as these will permit us to determine if subjects behave as the theory predicts. If they do not, the claim that marketing boards behave this way in the "naturally-occurring" world would seem questionable. If, however, the experimental evidence is consistent with the theory, questions will of course persist about the applicability of the theory to naturally-occurring marketing orders. To resolve such questions, an analysis will be undertaken of data on the voting behavior of real-world marketing boards and the sales decisions of real-world handlers.

Analysis of Real-World Data

As table 8.1 reflects, the USDA collects data for each order on the allowed and actual sales of each handler. It is clear from the aggregate data that some handlers sell less than their allotments. Our theory predicts that it is the larger packinghouses (identifiable since their allotments are larger) which will sell less than their allowed amount.[24] We hope to secure disaggregated data from USDA for various orders so that we can examine this hypothesis.

We also plan to analyze the voting behavior of members of a marketing committee. The minutes indicate how each board member voted on each proposal (whether it passed or not). It is easy to ascertain the affiliation of each board member. In most cases the packinghouse that each voter represents publishes an annual report from which information on the "endowment" of the packinghouse can be obtained. As for the distribution of endowments in the rest of the industry, this information can be obtained from the USDA data referred to earlier. We hope to use this information to test our model.

No matter which order we choose to examine, however, we anticipate that some serious questions will arise concerning the applicability of our model. Take the citrus orders as an example. In each committee, several voters represent packinghouses belonging to Sunkist growers. Each such packinghouse is regulated individually. But does each packinghouse allocate its endowment autonomously in its own interest or is it directed from above? We have been told by a packinghouse representative we interviewed that such decisions are made at the local level, and the president of Sunkist independently confirmed this. But is this information accurate? Even if sales decisions are made at the local level, a representative from a local Sunkist packinghouse may cast his vote in a way that serves the interest of Sunkist as a whole rather than that of his particular packinghouse. Despite assurances from Sunkist that such voters represent their local packinghouses as we have assumed, it may still be reasonable to question this.[25] A second questionable assumption concerns the failure of the voters to anticipate that this year's allotment percentage may affect next year's production. A third concerns the fact that committee members may come from different geographical areas with different seasonal characteristics and possibly different qualities of produce. The list could easily be expanded indefinitely.

In any of these cases the theory could be modified to handle the real-world complication. But if inability to predict can always be attributed to failures to resolve such problems, the basic theory will never be tested. The great merit of controlled experiments is that they permit a test of the basic theory. If the theory fails to predict well in the controlled environment, we would not expect it to predict better in the uncontrolled one. If, however, it predicts well in the experiments, then a failure to predict well on naturally-occurring data would lead us to examine more closely questionable assumptions such as those we have mentioned here.

Notes

The authors would like to thank (without implicating) Charles Cuff, an orange grower in District 2, and the following staff of USDA: Chuck Broder, Roland Harris, Ed Jesse, Kevin Kesecker, Chuck Martin, William Manley, Ron Miller, and Tanya Roberts. Each of these individuals patiently attempted to educate us about these complex regulations. We are also grateful for the comments and encouragement of David Levine, Roger Noll, and Hal Varian. Stephen Salant's research was supported by the National Science Foundation program on Political Science (Grant No. 8696084).

1. The reasons for such terminations have been studied by Camm (1976) and Hallagan (1985).

2. For a ranking of various orders by their social cost, see Lenard and Mazur (1985).

3. The two crops listed in table 8.1 are regulated by producer allotments. Similar divergences occur, however, under market allocation schemes and under prorates. In the 1983–84 season, for example, filbert handlers shipped substantially less in the primary "in-shell" market than their allotments permitted under the market allocations, and handlers of navel oranges from District 2 typically sold less than their allotments under the prorate. The reasons for the observed divergences may partially depend on the particular order. We hypothesize, however, that among the reasons is the concern of relatively large handlers that additional sales would depress the price in the primary market and would result in more than offsetting inframarginal losses.

4. A particularly useful, annotated bibliography for the years 1940 to 1981 is contained in USDA (1981).

5. Camm (1976), Masson, Masson, and Harris (1978), and Lenard and Mazur (1985) may be viewed as representative of such treatments.

6. For a discussion of the controversy, see Samuelson (1985) or *New York Times* (1985). The leading opponent of the navel order, Carl Pescosolido, will benefit in the long run from elimination of the order because water costs in the San Joaquin Valley, where he operates, are dramatically lower than elsewhere (see Rausser 1971, p. 118, on these costs).

7. Conflicts among districts are also serious. For example, many handlers in Central California (District 1) feel that the existing regulations are inequitable because they ignore the differential advantage of handlers in Southern California (District 2) to sell fresh fruit in the unregulated export market.

8. There is evidence that the committee tries to appear united after it has worked out a compromise allotment. Clodius (1950, pp. 307–308) noted, for example, that "in the first

twenty-one months of the federal program, determination by the Distribution committee of the weekly shipments was based on unanimous agreement in more than 90 percent of the weeks. However, the determination was nearly always a compromise, despite the unanimous vote supporting the final recommendation." This observation suggests that the final vote of a committee is less informative than prior votes and is intended to keep up appearances of solidarity for the secretary of agriculture, who must approve the final recommendations of each committee.

9. For an illustration of this common but unfortunate practice, see Lenard and Mazur (1985, p. 20).

10. Actually, since price in the secondary market is fixed, nothing would change if we allowed demand in the primary market to depend as well on price in the secondary market.

11. For example, since more than 98 percent of orange-juice concentrate comes from Florida, it is reasonable that orange growers in California and Arizona regard the price in the secondary (concentrate) market as unaffected by their sales. In general, of course the demand in each market might be regarded as a function of both prices. Smith (1961) has emphasized the importance of such demand interdependence. However, we have not yet fully explored its consequences in our model.

12. The model may have other applications as well. For example, q_i could be interpreted as the productive capacity of firm i, and the constant c interpreted as a common marginal cost of production. Indeed, this constant c could be replaced with generalized and possibly nonsymmetric opportunity cost functions $C_i(x_i)$ without necessarily vitiating the results. Certainly it is the case that if all firms share the same twice-differentiable convex cost function all the qualitative results go through.

13. An alternative contract—allegedly the "typical" arrangement between independent handlers and their growers—would instead award the packinghouse a commission that increases monotonically with the volume sold on the domestic fresh market. Such a contract would induce a handler to sell as much as possible on the domestic fresh market and—if he served on the administrative committee—to vote for the least restrictive regulation possible. Such contracts would create still another source of conflict within the committee and would constitute an additional reason to question the conventional belief that the committee chooses to maximize industry profits. Inclusion of this second form of contract would reinforce our basic point but would also complicate the analysis; it will be considered in a subsequent paper.

14. We assume that inverse demand $P(Y)$ is everywhere nonnegative, monotone decreasing and twice differentiable. Where price $P(Y)$ is positive, we require that $P'(Y)$ be negative. To ensure that positive quantities are sold on the primary market when $F > 0$, we assume that $P(0) > c$. These assumptions suffice for existence. To ensure uniqueness, we assume that for every feasible aggregate amount Y placed on the primary market and for every feasible individual amount $x < \min\{Y, q_n\}$,

$$\left[\frac{3P'(Y)}{2}\right] + xP''(Y) \leq 0.$$

15. This follows since marginal revenue in the secondary market is assumed to be constant and marginal revenue in the primary market will be strictly decreasing in own sales given the final inequality in note 14.

16. It will also be noted that it is possible for F_k to exceed 1 for some or all k. This means that the outputs of some or all firms are below the quantities they would wish to sell in the primary market even in the absence of the marketing order system.

17. We ignore the fact that a few growers use more than one packinghouse.

18. Moreover our assumption about how a committee behaves when making a finite set of decisions in sequence by majority-rule voting conforms with the experimental evidence reported in Plott (1979).

19. See the National Commission on Food Marketing (1966, p. 270) for a discussion of these "single-pool" systems.

20. See note 13.

21. How a self-interested, foresighted grower chooses a particular packinghouse for his crop deserves some comment. Assume provisionally that each packinghouse is equidistant from each grower and that each has the same convex cost of processing. In an equilibrium in which growers had foresight, no grower would assign his crop to a shipper anticipated to be unconstrained under the forthcoming allotment percentage. Such handlers would be so large that they would have lower per-unit revenues. The fact that some packinghouses are unconstrained and do have customers (see table 8.1 and note 3) suggests that the preceding assumption is inappropriate. In particular, a grower will tend to pick a packinghouse in his immediate area because of transport and transactions costs. In our analysis we do not attempt to explain why a particular packinghouse has a particular "endowment"; instead we take such data as given.

22. The property of consistency is used to ensure that each handler is actually constrained at his ideal point. If it were possible for π^i to jump up as handler i just becomes unconstrained, his ideal point could be exactly F_i, and yet he would not be constrained at that point.

23. In reality, of course, handlers sometimes sell less than their allotments for reasons not included in our model and in such cases valid inferences cannot be drawn merely from the evidence of undershipping. For example, navel handlers in District 2 have a differential advantage in the lucrative but limited export market and typically sell much of their endowment abroad. As a result their allotments often exceed what they ship to the regulated fresh market.

24. In examining this hypothesis, care should be taken to control for district and contract type, as discussed in notes 3 and 13.

25. Further assurance that Sunkist voters represent the disparate interests of their local packinghouse comes from the USDA representative who attends each navel meeting. According to Roland Harris, it is not uncommon for representatives of different Sunkist packinghouse to oppose each other in the voting. We plan to check this ourselves once we obtain the voting data.

References

Benedict, M., and Stine, O. C. 1956. *The Agricultural Commodity Programs: Two Decades of Experience* Twentieth Century Fund.

Bergstrom, T. C., and Varian, H. R. 1985. "Two Remarks on Cournot Equilibria." *Economic Letters* 19:5–8.

Camm, F. 1976. *Political Exchange and Agricultural Marketing Order*. Dissertation. University of Chicago, August.

Clodius, R. L. 1951. "An Analysis of Statutory Market Control Programs in the California-Arizona Orange Industry." *Journal of Farm Economics* 33:1043–1048.

Clodius, R. L. 1950. *An Analysis of Statutory Marketing Control Programs in the California-Arizona Orange Industry*. Dissertation. University of California, Berkeley. September.

Consumer Reports. 1982. "What's a Marketing Order?" February, 106–107.

Hallagan, W. S. 1985. "Contracting Problems and the Adoption of Regulatory Cartels." *Economic Inquiry 23*: 37–56.

Lenard, T., and Mazur, M. P. 1985. "Harvest of Waste: The Marketing Order Program." *Regulation 9*: 19–26.

Loury, G. 1986. "A Theory of Oiligopoly 'Oil'igopoly: Cournot Equilibrium in Exhaustible Resource Markets with Fixed Supplies." *International Economic Review 27*: 285–301.

Masson, A., Masson, R. T., and Harris, B. C. 1978. "Cooperatives and Marketing Orders." In B. W. Marion, ed., *Agricultural Cooperatives and the Public Interest*, N.C., Project 117, Mono. No. 4, September 1978.

National Commission on Food Marketing. 1966. *Organization and Competition in the Fruit and Vegetable Industry*. Technical Study No. 4. Washington, D.C.: Government Printing Office. June.

New York Times. 1985. "Citrus Growers Divided on a Possible End to U.S. Regulation." April 28.

Plott, C. R. 1979. "The Application of Laboratory Experimental Methods to Public Choice." In Clifford Russell, ed., *Collective Decision Making: Applications from Public Choice Theory, Resources for the Future*. Johns Hopkins University Press.

Rausser, G. 1971. *A Dynamic Econometric Model of the California-Arizona Orange Industry*, Dissertation. University of California, Davis.

Roll, R. 1984. "Orange Juice and Weather." *American Economic Review 74*: 861–880.

Samuelson, R. J., 1985. "The Economics of Nostalgia." *Newsweek*, March 25, p. 76.

Smith, R. J., 1961, "The Lemon Prorate in the Long Run." *Journal of Political Economy 69*: 573–586.

Spence, M. 1976 "Product Selection, Fixed Costs, and Monopolistic Competition." *Review of Economic Studies 43*: 217–235.

U.S. Department of Agriculture. 1981. *A Review of Federal Marketing Orders for Fruits, Vegetables and Speciality Crops: Economic Efficiency and Welfare Implications*. Agricultural Economic Report, No. 477. November.

9

An Assessment of the Efficiency Effects of U.S. Airline Deregulation via an International Comparison

Douglas W. Caves, Laurits R. Christensen, Michael W. Tretheway, and Robert J. Windle

Introduction

Airline deregulation was a major event in the U.S. transportation scene in the mid-1970s, paving the way for profound changes in the airline industry. Among the changes that ensued were the bankruptcies of two major airlines, fare wars, and the emergence of a host of upstart airlines and expanded commuter carriers. Speculation on the benefits and costs of deregulation has been plentiful, but scientific evidence is scarce. To date, consensus on the effects of deregulation and the proper direction for policy has not been achieved.

On the positive side are observations by Bailey, Graham, and Kaplan (1985, p. 202) who summarize their extensive study with the statement that "the changes that we have observed indicate that the industry is using its resources better; deregulation is leading to a substantially more efficient airline system." But there remain numerous detractors and skeptics, for example, Melvin A. Brenner, Frederick C. Thayer, and Secor D. Browne, who expressed their views in Foster et al. (1983).

The basic problem with assessing airline deregulation is common to the assessment of many national economic policies: there is no ready control group against which the observed effects of deregulation can be compared. We can observe the course of the industry since deregulation, but it is difficult to say what the course would have been had deregulation not occurred. Some studies have used the period immediately prior to deregulation to gain insight on trends and thereby project what would have happened in the absence of deregulation. Bailey, Graham, and Kaplan (1985), Caves, Christensen, and Tretheway (1984), and Meyer and Oster (1981) are examples of this approach. Though such an approach has merit, there are pitfalls. Even if trends can be established for the preregulation period, there is no guarantee that such trends would have held in the post deregulation period.

The problem of assessing deregulation could be eased if data were available for air carriers that did not face regulatory change during the period of interest. There are such carriers operating in other countries where, until 1984, relatively little airline deregulation had taken place. For the past two years we have been gathering and processing data on these carriers to create a control group against which the performance of U.S. airlines under deregulation may be assessed.[1] In this chapter we report on the outcome to date of our investigation.

The airline industry is particularly well suited for international comparison. The nature of its production process is much more similar across countries than is true for most other industries; moreover there are relatively few types of aircraft used throughout the world. Another factor favoring such a comparison is the existence of a large carrier-specific data base compiled by the International Civil Aviation Organization (ICAO). Using this source we have been able to compile a data base that includes twenty-seven non-U.S. air carriers for all or part of the 1970 to 1983 time period. These data, along with those for twenty-one U.S. carriers used in Caves, Christensen, and Tretheway (1984), form the basis for our analysis of the effects of U.S. airline deregulation.

U.S. deregulation did not occur as a single action at a specific point in time. Instead, there were a series of actions liberalizing pricing and entry rules. Meyer and Oster (1981) provide an extensive history of the transition period and conclude that the transition to a deregulated environment had begun by 1976. Thus we analyze airline deregulation by comparing performance in the 1970 to 1975 period with performance in the 1976 to 1983 period for both U.S. and non-U.S. airlines.

There are a number of aspects one would investigate in a complete cost-benefit analysis of deregulation, including changes in air carrier performance and changes in consumer utility. This study confines its attention to the question of productive efficiency. Two complementary measures of productive efficiency are analyzed: total factor productivity and unit cost. Analysis of unit cost requires statistical estimation and carries with it the usual assumptions required for such estimation. Analysis of total factor productivity avoids such assumptions at the cost of foregoing detail on the sources of changes in productive efficiency.

For U.S. airlines the results show that the rate of growth in productive efficiency was at least as good after deregulation as before. This is not true for non-U.S. airlines: comparing the same time periods the rate of growth in productive efficiency declined by nearly 40 percent. Using the non-U.S. experience as an indication of what would have occurred in the United States in the absence of deregulation, we estimate that by 1983 deregulation had lowered U.S. airline unit costs by 10 percent. This resulted in a savings in 1983 alone of over $4 billion.

There are several reasons to believe that the $4 billion estimate understates the benefits due to deregulation. First, our estimate accounts only for cost savings available in the operations of the major interstate scheduled passenger airlines. Welfare gains flowing from the operations of new entrants to the airline industry, former intrastate, charter, or freight airlines, and from expanded commuter service operations are not included. The new entrants appeared only in the last few years covered by our study, so we cannot measure the trend in productive efficiency for such carriers.[2] Second, we do not correct the productivity performance of non-U.S. carriers by the gains that might be due to increased competition in international markets. At the same time deregulation was occurring in the United States, competition was also increasing in important international markets, such as U.S.–Europe travel. This may have induced efficiency gains in non-U.S. carriers competing in such markets. Third, we do not completely control for the quality of air service produced by U.S. carriers. Numerous allegations of increases or decreases in service quality have been made. However, the most detailed study to date of this issue, Morrison and Winston (1985), shows that on net, service quality has risen dramatically since deregulation.

Regulatory Environments: U.S. and the Rest of the World

Since its infancy air transport has been the subject of considerable public interest. In almost every country regulation of air transport was implemented shortly after airlines commenced regular operations. Outside the United States air transport objectives were often achieved through government ownership of airlines or through government regulation. Government ownership or regulation generally is justified because it prevents monopoly pricing and provides uneconomic service to small communities. In Saudi Arabia, for example, the social need for transportation links between traditionally independent tribes outweighs the economic losses incurred on many domestic routes.[3]

In the United States, however, as markets changed and technology matured, economists began to question the need for continued regulation or ownership of air transport.[4] The United States was the first country to deregulate its airlines, and recently other countries, namely Chile, New Zealand, and Canada, have taken similar steps. Presently other countries, European and Mideastern, are seriously considering privatization of government airlines. Two of the arguments given in favor of abandoning regulation are that it stifles innovation of technical efficiency (e.g., see

Capron 1971) and that it induces firms to produce at nonoptimal points on the production locus (e.g., see Douglass and Miller 1974).

U.S. Deregulation
The passage of the Civil Aeronautics Act in 1938 brought the U.S. air transport industry under tight regulation enforced by the Civil Aeronautics Board (CAB).[5] Prices, entry into the industry, and entry onto routes were regulated. In the early 1960s economists began to question the benefits of airline regulation. By the mid-1970s economic evidence of the damaging effects of airline regulation began to fuel deregulatory momentum within the political arena. The 1975 Economic Report of the President criticized the regulatory policies of the CAB, and President Gerald Ford sent to Congress the Aviation Act of 1975. This was the first of several bills that would have substantially reduced the CAB's ability to regulate fares and entry, but none of these bills resulted in legislation.[6]

Although the first attempts to legislate airline deregulation were unsuccessful, the CAB responded to the political climate by voluntarily relaxing regulatory restraints. The first year in which there was substantial change in the CAB's policies was 1976, when John Robson was chairman.[7] When Alfred Kahn was appointed CAB chairman by President Jimmy Carter in 1977, the CAB accelerated the process of deregulation by further administrative actions that permitted substantial fare discounts on many routes. In addition the CAB made new route awards, often authorizing more than one new entrant at a time. Finally, in October 1978 the Airline Deregulation Act (ADA) was passed by Congress and signed by President Carter. The ADA provided for a seven-year phased deregulation, but in fact the CAB proceeded to deregulate the industry by 1979.

Domestic Airline Regulation in Other Countries
Most countries have followed the former U.S. practice of regulating fares and restricting entry into the industry and to other routes. Many of these countries, however, have extended regulatory control to include varying degrees of capacity limitation.[8] Government ownership of airlines is also common. Table 9.1 lists the non-U.S. air carriers included in this study and indicates the form of ownership.

Domestic deregulation of air transport in the United States has provided an example for regulatory reform. Two other countries have already moved to complete deregulation: Chile deregulated in 1979, and New Zealand deregulated at the end of 1983. In addition some countries, Canada, for example, have liberalized regulation while not going to com-

Assessment of Efficiency Effects of Airline Deregulation 289

Table 9.1 Non-U.S. air carriers in this study and their average annual growth rate of total factor productivity

Carrier	Percentage of government ownership		1983 percentage of international traffic[e]	1983 revenue ton-miles (billions)	TFP annual growth rate, 1970–1975	TFP annual growth rate, 1975–1983
	1983[c]	1960[d]				
AerLingus/Aerlinte	NI	95/100	98	0.20	−0.4	0.0
Air Canada	100	100	51	1.41	4.9	1.1
Air France	100	100	86	2.60	4.6	3.4
Air India	100	100	98	0.68	7.3	3.0
Air Inter	50	NI	0	0.26	1.2	5.3
Air Portugal	100	0	84	0.28	1.3	0.2
Alitalia	99	84	91	1.01	1.7	1.6
British Airways	100	100	97	2.39	−0.6	6.3
British Caledonian	0	NI	97	0.50	−2.1	6.4
Canadian Pacific	0	NI	64	0.73	4.5	2.2
Dan Air Skyways	0	NI	95	0.22	14.6	2.9
Finnair	76	0	88	0.25	1.6	3.7
Iberia	GC	100	76	1.08	5.9	−0.1
Indian Airlines	100	100	5	0.33	11.2	1.7
Japan Airlines	38	75	87	3.01	5.9	3.2
KLM	64	70	100	1.57	6.9	2.1
Korean Airlines	0	100	97	0.99	11.5	5.3
Lufthansa	74	50	94	2.38	5.7	2.0
Pacific Western	100[a]	0	20	0.13	4.0	2.4
Pakistan International	NI	65	83	0.36	2.3	3.5
Sabena	98	65	100	0.55	6.0	2.6
SAS	50[b]	50	86	0.82	4.0	−1.4
Singapore	83	NI	100	1.48	−0.7	4.9

Table 9.1 (continued)

Carrier	Percentage of government ownership		1983 percentage of international traffic[e]	1983 revenue ton-miles (billions)	TFP annual growth rate, 1970–1975	TFP annual growth rate, 1975–1983
	1983[c]	1960[d]				
Swissair	22	30	98	1.00	5.8	3.2
Thai International	100	70	100	0.57	10.5	3.8
UTA	0	0	100	0.57	2.0	4.0
Varig	1	0	73	0.63	6.6	−1.0

Note: TFP = total factor productivity; GC = government controlled; NI = no information.
a. PWA was owned (99.9 percent) by the Canadian Province of Alberta from 1974 to 1983. Following a general sale of stock in December 1983, the province retained a 4 percent ownership share. No one individual or group of individuals may vote more than 4 percent of PWA's stock.
b. SAS is owned on a 3:2:2 share ratio by companies in Sweden, Denmark, and Norway. Each of these is 50 percent government owned.
c. Source: Martin (1983).
d. Source: Straszheim (1969).
e. We use ton-miles of freight and passenger service as a measure of traffic for the purpose of this column.

Table 9.2 Recent changes in non-U.S. air transport policy

Country	Changes
Australia	Deregulation of third-level carriers (in some states) 1979
Canada	Partial deregulation of domestic transport 1984; Considering privatization of Air Canada
Chile	Deregulated domestic air transport 1979
EEC	Some deregulation of commuter airlines 1983; committee approves plan to ease airline regulation 1984 (not expected actually to take place at this time)
Gulf States[a]	Partial privatization of GulfAir 1985
Japan	Conducting review of air transport policy 1984–present
Malaysia	Announced intent to privatize Malayasian Airline System 1985
Mexico	Nationalized Mexicana 1983
New Zealand	Deregulated domestic air transport 1983 (phase 1) and 1984 (phase 2)
Peoples Republic of China	Reorganizing Civil Aviation Administration of China into a regulatory body (1984) with several provincial and national carriers, possibly competing with each other
Turkey	Announced intent to privatize and break up Turkish Airlines 1985
United Kingdom	Signed liberal bilateral with Netherlands 1984; considering privatization of British Airways in 1986; conducted review of domestic air transport 1984
West Germany	Announced intent to privatize partially Lufthansa 1985

a. Baharain, Oman, Qatar, and United Arab Emirates (Abu Dhabi, Ajman, Al Fujayrah, Dubai, Ras al Khaimah, Sharjah, Ummal Qquayn).

plete deregulation.[9] In the case of Canada some pricing freedom was granted in 1979, but little additional change occurred until 1984.

In general, most countries have resisted the notion of air transport deregulation. The United States International Air Competition Act of 1979, though confining itself to intercountry movements of U.S. air traffic, was viewed by many governments as an attempt to export deregulation forcibly.[10] Recently, there has been some softening of positions. The Reagan administration has backed away from its hardline position, and other countries are considering some aspects of regulatory reform or privatization. Table 9.2 summarizes recent changes in air transport policy around the world.

Non-U.S. Regulation of Air Transport

Table 9.1 for non-U.S. carriers and Table 9.3 for U.S. carriers indicate the relative importance of international services for each carrier in our study. The regulation of intercountry air transportation is governed by a maze of bilateral and multilateral treaties and agreements, between governments

Table 9.3 U.S. carriers and their average annual growth rate of total factor productivity

Carriers	1983 percentage of international traffic[a]	1983 revenue ton-miles (billions)	TFP annual growth rate 1970–1975[b]	TFP annual growth rate 1975–1983[b]
American	7	3.11	3.0	3.1
Braniff	—	—	1.8	2.7[c]
Continental	11	0.91	3.0	0.8[d]
Delta	7	2.50	2.4	1.5
Eastern	8	2.63	2.0	2.0
Frontier	2	0.34	3.4	3.3
Hughes Air West	—	—	7.3	4.9[c]
National	—	—	9.3	8.1[c]
North Central	—	—	0.7	3.9[c]
Northeast	—	—	−1.8[c]	—
Northwest	50	2.31	8.2	2.7
Ozark	0	0.23	0.7	5.5
Pan Am	77	3.21	1.9	7.4(1.1)[e]
Piedmont	0	0.45	1.0	5.8
Republic	3	0.86	—	11.1(8.3)[e]
Southern	—	—	5.0	5.3[c]
Texas International	—	—	1.7	5.9[c]
TWA	41	2.67	3.3	2.9
United	3	4.34	2.3	4.3
U.S. Air	3	0.64	1.9	3.0
Western	6	0.91	4.7	1.1

Note: Dash means information not available for stated time period.
a. We use ton miles of freight and passenger service as a measure of traffic for the purpose of this table.
b. If a strike occurred in either end point year, that year is not included.
c. Firm did not exist for entire time period.
d. Growth rate for Continental before merger with Texas International.
e. Growth rate for pre-merger years; post-merger growth rate in parentheses.

and between air carriers. The model for most routes has been the 1946 Bermuda I agreement between the United States and the United Kingdom. This treaty established that bilateral negotiations between countries would determine how many carriers of each nation would be allowed on a route. It was left to the individual country to determine which carriers would be authorized to provide the service. Fares were determined by the International Air Transport Association (IATA) on a multilateral basis.

This pattern of bilateral regulation of route entry and multilateral cartel pricing was generally adhered to until the United States began to sign a series of liberal bilateral agreements with countries such as Belgium, Israel, and Germany in 1978. These liberal agreements generally authorized more air carriers to serve routes and effectively broke from IATA's cartel-like pricing. Fare structures tend to be country-of-origin or double-veto, in which carrier-proposed fares prevail unless rejected by both countries. The liberal bilateral agreements, coupled with other events, such as Laker Airway's entry into the North Atlantic markets in 1977, unleashed the forces of competition into many North Atlantic markets, resulting in the virtual elimination of IATA's rate-making ability in this geographic area.[11]

It was not until 1984 that pricing competition began to appear within Europe. In June, the United Kingdom successfully negotiated a new bilateral agreement with the Netherlands (and later Belgium) that allowed unilateral authorization of routes and fares.[12]

In sum, the early years of U.S. deregulation also witnessed a change in regimes in the regulation of international air transport. These international changes, however, were largely confined to the North Atlantic. Not until 1984 was there a major change in international air transport regulation outside of U.S. markets. Although deregulation of the North Atlantic may lessen the applicability of certain non-U.S. carriers as a control group, almost all non U.S. carriers have some North Atlantic traffic. Thus we do not feel it is possible to drop them from the study or include them as deregulated carriers without specifying an arbitrary cutoff point for North Atlantic traffic.[13]

The International Air Transport Operating Environment

The task of comparing productive efficiency between U.S and non-U.S. air carriers is eased by the similarity in airline operations across countries. During the 1970 to 1983 period the firms in our sample used very few types of aircraft. Most of these aircraft were produced in the United States, the United Kingdom, or France. Although aircraft manufacturers emphasize differences among their models, the technology is in fact very similar, much more similar, for example, than the differences among countries in auto production technology.

Operation and maintenance of aircraft are governed by strict international standards. Traditionally the United States has taken the lead in setting standards and requirements. Important roles are also played in these areas by two international agencies, ICAO and IATA. The result is that the conduct of aircraft operations and maintenance is remarkably similar among the countries in our sample.

The very fact that major portions of many air carriers' services involves the movement of their customers between countries has resulted in great similarity in the nonflight operations of carriers (e.g., ticketing and promotions). International treaties or conventions generally cover items such as insurance requirements, liability for lost baggage, and exchange of tickets.

Carriers purchase two important inputs, aircraft and fuel, in world rather than domestic markets. For many carriers, ground equipment and many elements of materials are also purchased internationally. Even for labor, international standards of qualification and some important work rules often prevail for the key groups of pilots, flight attendants, and maintenance workers. Prices for labor may vary greatly among countries, but it is straightforward to control for price differences in our analysis.

Non-U.S. Airlines as a Control Group

The ideal control group for assessing the U.S. experience with deregulation would consist of a group of firms experiencing the same events as U.S. carriers, except for deregulation. In particular, they would face the same increase in fuel prices, the same recession, the same secular growth in airline markets, the same changes in engineering technology, the same air traffic controllers strike, and so on. Such an ideal control group rarely exists in economic production studies, and it does not exist here.

Nevertheless, similarities in the operating environment should permit meaningful comparisons between U.S. and non-U.S. carriers. The non-U.S. carriers faced the same increase in fuel prices as their U.S. counterparts. Although the timing and depth varied, most of the non-U.S. countries in our study experienced a major economic contraction during the 1976 to 1983 time period. If anything, secular trends (i.e., nonprice-induced traffic growth) may have been stronger outside of the United States as rising incomes promote increased air travel.

Some would point out that government ownership of many non-U.S. airlines makes comparisons difficult. Here we compare growth rates of airline performance. Since there were no dramatic changes in government ownership or social duties charged to air carriers during the time period of our study, we believe that the growth rate comparisons are legitimate. Our analysis, lacking an ideal control group, may not be definitive, but we believe it is suggestive of the impact of deregulation.

Sample and Data

Our data consist of annual observations on U.S. and non-U.S. airlines for the years 1970 through 1983. The U.S. airlines include all the trunk and local service airlines, thirteen of which are present for the full time period and eight for a portion of the period. There are 235 U.S. airline observations in the sample. The airlines that were included in the sample are listed in table 9.3, which also shows revenue ton-miles in 1983 as a measure of carrier size.[14]

The non-U.S. carriers in our sample are listed in table 9.1.[15] They were selected from all carriers reporting to ICAO in the years 1970 through 1983. Carriers were dropped from our sample if they failed to report the necessary data for eight or more of the fourteen years. This left us with fifty carriers, many of which are very small in relation to U.S. airlines. To control for size differences, we eliminated carriers with less than 300 million passenger kilometers in 1983 and less than twenty aircraft.[16] This eliminated airlines that were substantially smaller than any U.S. trunk or local airline and reduced our sample of non-U.S. carriers to the twenty-seven listed in table 9.1. These carriers provided 351 annual observations on non-U.S. airline operations. Our sample of twenty-seven non-U.S. airlines includes most of the major free world carriers, including seventeen of the twenty-two carriers that carried more than 1 billion revenue ton-kilometers in 1983, and twenty-two of the thirty-two carriers that carried more than 0.5 billion revenue ton-kilometers.

We attempted throughout data development and processing to treat both the U.S. and non-U.S. carriers identically. In appendix A we document the differences in data treatment from our earlier studies and provide additional details on our handling of the non-U.S. data.

Our productivity comparisons involve measures of real input and output as well as shares in cost or revenues. Thus our analysis is largely independent of exchange rates. Homogeneity of degree one in input prices also ensures that estimated cost function results do not depend on exchange rates.[17]

Productivity measurement requires detailed data on prices and quantities of inputs. We employ five categories of inputs: labor, fuel, flight equipment, ground property and equipment (GPE), and all other inputs, referred to as "materials". Labor is formed as a multilateral index of three categories of employees.[18] Fuel is based on the number of gallons used. Labor and fuel prices are computed as labor and fuel costs divided by their respective quantity indexes. Flight equipment is formed from a multilateral index of nine aircraft categories, using current annual aircraft lease costs as weights. GPE cost is measured by applying a capital service price reflecting interest, economic depreciation, capital gains, and taxes to the stock of GPE capital formed by using the perpetual inventory method. Total capital stock is computed as a multilateral index of GPE and flight equipment. Time series materials price indexes were collected for each country, but within each country for a particular year the price of materials is assumed constant across firms.[19] Intercountry links for materials indexes were provided by purchasing power parities found in Kravis, Heston, and Summers (1982) for seven commodity or service categories.[20] Annual changes in materials price is given by a Tornqvist index of the seven categories of materials input.

We recognize four categories of output: revenue passenger-miles of scheduled service, revenue ton-miles (RTM) of nonscheduled or charter service, RTM of mail and RTM of all other freight. Scheduled service accounts for the bulk of revenues for almost all carriers in the sample.[21] Because of the small revenue shares for the other outputs, we do not believe it would be fruitful to maintain separate outputs in cost function estimation. Thus we aggregated the four output types by using the multilateral index procedure.

The model incorporates three characteristics of airline operations: load factor, average stage length, and points served. Load factor is the ratio of seat miles sold to seat miles actually flown. Average stage length is the average distance between takeoffs and landings. An airport, rather than a city, constitutes a point served.[22]

Improvement in Productive Efficiency as Measured by Total Factor Productivity

We begin investigation of productive efficiency by comparing rates of growth in total factor productivity (TFP) indexes for U.S. and non-U.S. airlines during the time periods before and after U.S. deregulation. The TFP results are free of the assumptions required for statistical cost analysis and are known to be representative of quite general production processes.²³ The limitation of the TFP indexes is their inability to indicate whether growth in productive efficiency is due to pure technical change or to economies of scale, density, or utilization. Attribution of TFP to these sources requires statistical cost estimation, which we undertake in the next section.

Our TFP study builds upon two earlier papers, Caves, Christensen, and Tretheway (1981, 1983), in which we estimated TFP for U.S. trunk and local service air carriers. In those papers we developed the basic procedures for measuring airline inputs, outputs, and prices. We use the same basic procedures in this chapter, but we have added three years of data, 1981 to 1983, and extended the data base to include non-U.S. air carriers.

We use the method of translog multilateral comparisons of output, input, and TFP, which has been proposed by Caves, Christensen, and Diewert (1982b). The translog multilateral comparison of output of firms k and j can be written

$$\ln Y_k - \ln Y_j = \sum_i \frac{R_{ik} + \bar{R}_i}{2} \ln \frac{Y_{ik}}{\tilde{Y}_i} - \sum_i \frac{R_{ij} + \bar{R}_i}{2} \ln \frac{Y_{ij}}{\tilde{Y}_i}, \qquad (1)$$

where Y_{ik} is output of type i for airline k, R_{ik} is the revenue share of output i for airline k, $\bar{R}_i$ is the arithmetic mean of the revenue share of output i over all observations in the sample, and $\tilde{Y}_i$ is the geometric mean of output i over all observations in the sample. The translog multilateral comparison of aggregate input of firms k and j can be written

$$\ln X_k - \ln X_j = \sum_i \frac{W_{ik} + \bar{W}_i}{2} \ln \frac{X_{ik}}{\tilde{X}_i} - \sum_i \frac{W_{ij} + \bar{W}_i}{2} \ln \frac{X_{ij}}{\tilde{X}_i}, \qquad (2)$$

where the X_{ik} are the inputs, and the W_{ik} are the cost shares. The translog multilateral comparisons of TFP of firms k and j can be written

$$\ln \text{TFP}_k - \ln \text{TFP}_j = (\ln Y_k - \ln Y_j) - (\ln X_k - \ln X_j). \qquad (3)$$

Using equations (1), (2), and (3), we compute a TFP index for each carrier for each year in our sample. The growth rates of the indexes are shown in table 9.3 for U.S. carriers and in table 9.1 for non-U.S. carriers. There are seventeen U.S. carriers for which we can compare the same entity before and after deregulation. Of these seventeen, nine showed increases after deregulation, seven showed decreases, and one showed no change. Of the twenty-seven non-U.S. carriers, only eight showed increases in the

Table 9.4 Average annual growth rates for U.S. and non-U.S. airlines before and after U.S. airline deregulation

	Output		Input		TFP	
	U.S.	Non-U.S.	U.S.	Non-U.S.	U.S.	Non-U.S.
Pderegulation, 1970–1975	4.1	9.9	1.1	5.4	2.9	4.5
Postderegulation, 1975–1983	5.6	6.8	2.5	4.0	3.1	2.8

Table 9.5 Annual growth rates for U.S. and non-U.S. airlines, 1970–1983

	Output		Input		TFP	
	U.S.	Non-U.S.	U.S.	Non-U.S.	U.S.	Non-U.S.
1970–71	2.0	9.3	−0.8	9.0	2.8	0.4
1971–72	10.7	15.6	2.9	5.3	7.8	10.2
1972–73	6.7	12.8	4.9	4.5	1.8	8.2
1973–74	1.2	6.0	−1.1	4.4	2.3	1.5
1974–75	−1.0	6.8	−0.8	4.4	−0.2	2.5
1975–76	9.0	9.0	1.9	3.2	7.1	5.8
1976–77	7.5	7.1	3.0	6.3	4.5	0.7
1977–78	13.2	12.1	3.0	8.4	10.2	3.7
1978–79	10.2	10.3	6.7	4.5	3.5	5.8
1979–80	−4.6	3.5	5.3	1.9	−9.8	1.6
1980–81	−5.4	5.1	−5.1	−0.4	−0.3	5.5
1981–82	1.7	−0.1	−3.4	1.0	5.1	−1.1
1982–83	9.0	1.6	6.2	3.1	2.7	−1.4

rate of growth of TFP after 1975. The other nineteen all showed decreases in the rate of growth.

We form U.S. and non-U.S. average growth rates by taking a cost share weighted average of the individual carrier growth rates. The cost share weight assigned to each carrier is the average of its shares in total industry costs in the beginning and ending years of the period under consideration.[24] The average annual U.S. and non-U.S. growth rates for the periods before and after U.S. airline deregulation are shown in table 9.4. Table 9.5 presents the annual growth rates.

The results show that U.S. airline output growth increased substantially after deregulation. But input growth also increased substantially so that the rate of growth of TFP increased from 2.9 percent per year prior to deregulation to 3.1 percent per year after deregulation. For the non-U.S. carriers, output growth declined substantially in the period following U.S. deregulation. Input growth also declined, but not to the same extent as output. The result was a decline in the average rate of growth in TFP for non-U.S. airlines.

It should be noted that the higher TFP growth of non-U.S. carriers in the early 1970s has still left them at a lower level of TFP than the U.S. carriers. In 1970 aggregate TFP was 22 percent higher for U.S. carriers than for non-U.S. carriers. By 1975 this had been reduced to a 15 percent higher level for U.S. carriers, but by 1983 it had increased to an 18 percent advantage. Although it might be argued that the high growth rate of TFP for the non-U.S. carriers in the early 1970s represents some catching up to the U.S. level of TFP, there does not appear to be any evidence to suggest that this should have ended in 1975. The non-U.S. carriers were still at a substantially lower level than their U.S. counterparts at that time.

The non-U.S. experience provides the only backdrop we have for judging U.S. experience under deregulation. The U.S. experience by itself shows a small increase in the rate of growth of TFP in the post-deregulation period. However, the non-U.S. carriers, which did not experience deregulation, underwent a 38 percent decline in the rate of TFP growth between the earlier and later periods. Against this backdrop we conclude that deregulation had a positive influence on productive efficiency for U.S. carriers. Had U.S. airline TFP dropped by the same percentage as non-U.S. airline TFP during the deregulation period, the U.S. average would have been 1.8 percent per year rather than 3.1 percent per year during the deregulation period. Accumulation of these differences over the eight year deregulation period would have yielded 1983 costs 10 percent above actual costs under deregulation.

We can probe deeper into the pattern of U.S. and non-U.S. airline TFP by considering the annual growth rates displayed in table 9.5. Prior to deregulation, non-U.S. airline TFP growth exceeded U.S. airline TFP growth in three of the five years. After the transition to deregulation began in 1976, U.S. TFP growth exceeded non-U.S. TFP growth in five of the eight years.

It should be noted that during the first transition year, 1976, U.S. TFP growth exceeded non-U.S. TFP growth by 1.3 percent. Some observers might be hesitant to attribute this first-year growth difference to the emerging transition. Omitting this year from the post deregulation period would reduce the U.S. postderegulation average growth from 3.1 to 2.5 percent per year. This would imply that U.S. airline TFP declined from 2.9 percent per year prederegulation to 2.5 percent per year postderegulation. However, if we carry out the same exercise for non-U.S. carriers, we find that omission of 1976 would decrease non-U.S. average TFP growth after U.S. deregulation from 2.8 to 2.4 percent per year. Thus the omission of

1976 from the analysis does not alter the relationship of U.S. and non-U.S. carriers: U.S. growth falls below non-U.S. growth in the preregulation period and above it in the postderegulation period. Had the U.S. suffered the same relative decline as the non-U.S. carriers in this period, U.S. growth would have been only 1.7 percent per year in the postderegulation period.

Some observers might also identify 1977 as a transition year. The omission of both 1976 and 1977 results in average U.S. TFP growth falling from 2.9 percent per year preregulation to 2.2 percent postderegulation, while average non-U.S. TFP growth fell from 4.5 percent preregulation to 2.6 percent postderegulation. If U.S. TFP growth had fallen by the same percentage as non-U.S. TFP, its annual growth rate would have been reduced to 1.8 percent rather than 2.2 percent.

Unit Cost Analysis of Changes in Productive Efficiency

The Variable Cost Function

The TFP results of the previous section reflect all sources of change in productive efficiency. The sources include exploitation of economies of scale, traffic density, and utilization of capital, as well as changes in technical efficiency. It is of some interest to distinguish productivity changes due to changes in scale, density, and utilization. which we hereafter refer to as changes in operating characteristics, from changes in technical efficiency. The former represents movements along the cost function, and the later represents shifts in the function.

Either source may be influenced by deregulation. Shifts in the function may occur at an increased rate as air carriers strive for more efficiency in the face of competition. Movements along the function in directions that lower unit costs may occur as airlines take advantage of pricing and entry freedom to rationalize routes and traffic patterns. Table 9.6 shows the

Table 9.6 Average rate of growth per year of operating characteristics of U.S. and non-U.S. airlines

	Preregulation		Postderegulation	
	U.S.	Non-U.S.	U.S.	Non-U.S.
Output	4.1	9.9	5.6	6.8
Load factor	1.4	0.7	1.4	1.4
Stage length	0.6	2.0	2.9	1.4
Points served	1.0	0.6	3.6	1.0
Stock	2.2	8.9	4.0	6.9

growth rates for U.S. and non-U.S. carriers for the individual factors that make up operating characteristics. The growth rates are weighted averages of individual firm growth rates, the weights being shares in industry cost. The U.S. experienced a substantial increase in service as measured either by output (traffic) or by points served. The rate of growth of output increased by more than one-third, and the rate of growth of points served more than tripled. The non-U.S. rate of growth of points served also increased substantially, but the non-U.S. rate of growth of output declined by nearly one-third. Other factors also show substantial differences between the U.S. and the rest of the world.

In the remainder of this section we develop estimates of the variable cost function to determine the effect of each of these factors on cost. We then use the results to allocate efficiency changes between technical change and changes in operating characteristics. The allocation requires estimation of a neoclassical cost function using our data on U.S. and non-U.S. air carriers. The methodology is the same as that employed by Caves, Christensen, and Tretheway (1984) to obtain cost function estimates for U.S. trunk and local service airlines.

Because our data set consists of pooled time series cross-sectional data, we employ an analysis of covariance estimator (Mundlak 1961, 1978) to avoid potential bias from unobserved firm-specific effects.[25] Important among the unobserved effects are social goals, such as job creation that governments may set for airlines that they own or regulate. By including the firm effects in the model, we reduce the bias that might be induced by correlation between the observed independent variables and the unobserved effects that are constant within firms.

To allow for the possibility that capital input is not always in equilibrium, we treat it as a quasi-fixed input and estimate the variable cost function:

$$C_V = C_V(Y, W, K, Z, t, f, g), \tag{4}$$

where C_V is variable cost, Y is aggregate output, W is a vector of input prices for variable inputs, K is the real flow of services from capital input, Z is a vector of output attributes, t is a vector of technology variables; representing time periods, f is a vector of individual firm shift variables, and g is a binary variable signifying government ownership as in Tretheway (1984).[26] All variables except t, f, and g are measured in natural logarithmic units. The output attributes include: the number of points served, stage length, and load factor.[27]

We represent (4) using the translog functional form:

$$C_V = \alpha_0 + \sum_t \alpha_t + \sum_f \alpha_f + \alpha_g g + \alpha_Y Y + \sum_i \beta_i W_i + \beta_K K + \sum_i \phi_i Z_i$$

$$+ \frac{1}{2}\delta_{YY}(Y)^2 + \frac{1}{2}\sum_j\sum_j \gamma_{ij} W_i W_j + \frac{1}{2}\gamma_{KK}(K)^2$$

$$+ \frac{1}{2}\sum_i\sum_j \psi_{ij} Z_i Z_j + \sum_i \rho_{Yi} YW_i + \rho_{YK} YK$$

$$+ \sum_i \mu_{Yi} YZ_i + \sum_i \lambda_{iK} W_i K + \sum_i\sum_j \lambda_{ij} W_i Z_j + \sum_i \tau_{iK} Z_i K, \tag{5}$$

where $\gamma_{ij} = \gamma_{ji}$, $\psi_{ij} = \psi_{ji}$, the α_t are time period effects, and the α_f are firm effects. A cost function must be homogeneous of degree one in input prices, which implies the following restrictions on the parameters of the translog cost function:

$$\sum_i \beta_i = 1, \quad \sum_i \gamma_{ij} = 0, \quad \sum_i \rho_{Yi} = 0, \quad \sum_i \lambda_{iK} = 0, \quad \sum_i \lambda_{ij} = 0, \tag{6}$$

for all j.

Shephard's (1953) lemma implies that the input shares (C_i) can be equated to the logarithmic partial derivatives of the cost function with respect to the input prices:

$$C_i = \beta_i + \sum_j \gamma_{ij} W_j + \gamma_{iK} K + \rho_{Yi} Y + \sum_j \lambda_{ij} Z_j. \tag{7}$$

It has become standard practice to specify classical disturbances for (5) and (7) and to estimate the parameters of the cost function by treating (5) and (7) as a multivariate regression. This procedure is followed, using a modification of Zellner's (1962) technique for estimation.[28]

The data described earlier is used to estimate equations (5) and (7). Prior to estimation all the variables are normalized by the sample means for U.S. firms. To reduce the number of parameters, the multilateral index procedure is used to aggregate the two types of capital. This leaves 121 parameters to be estimated. Full details of the regression results are shown in appendix B.

Allocation of Productive Efficiency

Our interest is in decomposing unit costs into sources of unit cost changes. Drawing on the properties of translog aggregation functions, Caves and Christensen (1984) showed that a decomposition of the logarithmic total cost difference between observation 1 and 0 $(C^1 - C^0)$ can be obtained from the variable cost function using the following formula:

$$\begin{aligned}C^1 - C^0 = S[&\tfrac{1}{2}(\partial_y^1 C_V + \partial_y^0 C_V) \cdot (Y^1 - Y^0) \\ &+ \tfrac{1}{2}(\partial_w^1 C_V + \partial_w^0 C_V) \cdot (W^1 - W^0) \\ &+ \tfrac{1}{2}(\partial_z^1 C_V + \partial_z^0 C_V) \cdot (Z^1 - Z^0) \\ &+ \tfrac{1}{2}(\partial_k^1 C_V + \partial_k^0 C_V) \cdot (K^1 - K^0) \\ &+ \tfrac{1}{2}(\partial_t^1 C_V + \partial_t^0 C_V) \cdot (t^1 - t^0)] \\ &+ (1 - S)((W_K^1 + W_K^0) + (K^1 - K^0)),\end{aligned} \quad (8)$$

where the superscripts denote observations 1 and 0, W_K is the price of capital input, S denotes the average share of variable in total cost for observations 1 and 0 (i.e., $1/2(C_V^1/C^1 + C_V^0/C^0)$), $\partial_X^i C_V$ denotes the derivative of C_V (log variable costs) with respect to argument X evaluated at i, and the dots denote vector multiplication.

Equation (8) is reorganized and expanded to achieve the following: (1) express the decomposition in terms of total unit costs $[c^1 - c^0 = (C^1 - C^0) - (Y^1 - Y^0)]$, (2) recognize differences in firm effects and government ownership, and (3) combine the capital input price with variable input prices. This yields

$$\begin{aligned}c^1 - c^0 = &S[\tfrac{1}{2}(\partial_w^1 C_V + \partial_w^0 C_V) \cdot (W^1 - W^0)] \\ &+ (1 - S)(W_K^1 + W_K^0) \quad \text{all input prices} \\ &+ S[\tfrac{1}{2}(\partial_y^1 C_V + \partial_y^0 C_V) \cdot (Y^1 - Y^0)] - (Y^1 - Y^0) \quad \text{traffic} \\ &+ S[\tfrac{1}{2}(\partial_z^1 C_V + \partial_z^0 C_V) \cdot (Z^1 - Z^0)] \quad \text{operating characteristics} \\ &+ [\tfrac{1}{2}S(\partial_k^1 C_V + \partial_k^0 C_V) + (1 - S)](K^1 - K^0) \quad \text{capital} \\ &+ S[\tfrac{1}{2}(\partial_t^1 C_V + \partial_t^0 C_V) \cdot (t^1 - t^0)] \quad \text{time or technical efficiency} \\ &+ S[\tfrac{1}{2}(\partial_f^1 C_V + \partial_f^0 C_V) \cdot (f^1 - f^0)] \quad \text{firm effect} \\ &+ S[\tfrac{1}{2}(\partial_g^1 C_V + \partial_g^0 C_V) \cdot (g^1 - g^0)] \quad \text{government ownership.}\end{aligned} \quad (9)$$

Equation (9) provides a decomposition of changes in unit costs. Each line represents the portion of unit cost change that is attributable to the source listed to the right of the line. It is useful to consider three major groupings of the sources of changes in unit costs. The first source is the change in input prices, line 1. The second source is the change in operating

Table 9.7 Average annual percentage decline in unit costs and sources of unit cost for U.S. and non-U.S. carriers for the pre- and postderegulation period

Sources	Prederegulation (1970–1975)		Postderegulation (1975–1983)	
	U.S.	Non-U.S.	U.S.	Non-U.S.
Productive efficiency				
Operating characteristics (1)	1.8	3.1	2.2	2.0
Technical efficiency (2)	1.2	1.4	1.1	0.8
Total productive efficiency (3) = (1) + (2)	3.0	4.5	3.4	2.8

characteristics, lines 2, 3, and 4. This includes changes due to traffic, density, firm size (scale), stage length, load factor, and capital utilization. The remaining three lines represent changes in technical efficiency associated with time, firms, and government ownership. The firm effects represent differences across firms that are constant over time. Because this study is concerned with productivity changes over time, rather than across firms, the firm effects are zero for all comparisons.

We use the estimated parameters of the cost function (appendix B) along with the observed data on the cost function arguments to evaluate the decomposition terms in equation (9). The first four lines are evaluated directly, and the technical efficiency term is constructed as the difference between the observed change in unit costs and the portion of the change accounted for by the first four terms. For each individual carrier we used this procedure to decompose changes in unit cost for the 1970 to 1975 period and the 1975 to 1983 period. We then aggregated the individual carrier results using the same procedures that we used to aggregate productivity indexes in the previous section.

Table 9.7 summarizes the decomposition results. The bottom line shows the overall results, which are very comparable to the TFP results in table 9.4.[29] The rate of growth of U.S. productive efficiency increased from 3.0 percent per year in the prederegulation period to 3.4 percent per year in the postderegulation period. Comparing the same two periods the rate of growth of non-U.S. productive efficiency shows a decline from 4.5 percent per year to 2.8 percent per year.

The first and second lines of table 9.7 show the allocation of changes in productive efficiency into two sources: operating characteristics and technical efficiency. For U.S. airlines we find that changes in operating characteristics accounted for a 1.8 percent per year increase in productive efficiency prior to deregulation. Following deregulation this figure increased to 2.2 percent per year. For non-U.S. airlines, changes in operating characteristics accounted for a 3.1 percent per year increase in productive efficiency prior to U.S. deregulation. Following U.S. deregulation, this figure declined to 2.0 percent per year.

The rate of growth of technical efficiency, line 2, remained virtually constant during the pre- and postderegulation periods for U.S. airlines. But for non-U.S. airlines the rate of growth of technical efficiency declined from 1.4 percent per year in the first period to 0.8 percent per year in the second.

Had the U.S. growth in technical efficiency fallen in proportion to that of the non-U.S. carriers, the U.S. growth rate would have been 0.7 percent per year after deregulation instead of 1.1 percent. The difference of 0.4 percent per year amounts to over 3 percent in total costs by 1983, over a billion dollars.

The differences in the effects of operating characteristics are larger than the differences in technical efficiency. Non-U.S. airlines were gaining 1.3 percent per year more than U.S. airlines from this source prior to deregulation. After deregulation U.S. performance was slightly above that of the non-U.S. airlines. Had the U.S. declined in the same proportion as the rest of the world, the U.S. would have been at 1.2 percent per year in the later period rather than 2.2 percent. This would have increased U.S. costs by 8 percent in 1983 over their actual value. A more conservative estimate of the effect of deregulation would be that deregulation stimulated the U.S. increase in the face of the decline experienced by the world. This would attribute 0.4 percent per year to deregulation or a total of over 3 percent cost reduction in 1983 alone.[30]

Results from a Total Cost Function

The results in table 9.7 were obtained from a variable cost function, which treats capital as a quasi-fixed input. We now alter the treatment of capital by permitting capital to be a variable input. This requires estimation of the total cost function, which is identical in form to the variable cost function except that the left-hand variable is total cost instead of variable cost and capital on the right-hand side is replaced by its price. The productivity allocation formula is the same as equation (9) except that the variable S and the capital stock line do not appear.

The results of using the total cost function are shown in table 9.8. The results are very similar to those of the variable cost function. The postderegulation decline in growth of technical efficiency for the non-U.S. is somewhat larger than was indicated by the variable cost results in table 9.7.

Table 9.8 Average annual percentage decline in unit costs and sources of unit cost for U.S. and non-U.S. carriers for the pre- and postderegulation period

Sources	Prederegulation (1970–1975)		Postderegulation (1975–1983)	
	U.S.	Non-U.S.	U.S.	Non-U.S.
Productive efficiency				
Operating characteristics (1)	1.6	3.3	2.2	2.4
Technical efficiency (2)	1.4	1.2	1.1	0.4
Total productive efficiency (3) = (1) + (2)	3.0	4.5	3.3	2.8

Appendix A: Data

In constructing the data for non-U.S. air carriers, we have attempted to adhere as closely as possible to our procedures for development of the U.S. carrier data as outlined in Caves, Christensen, and Tretheway (1981, 1983). The ultimate data source for the non-U.S. carriers is the statistical data reported by individual air carriers to the International Civil Aviation Organization (ICAO). These data are published in a series of annual statistical publications, containing traffic, financial, and fleet and personnel statistics. Most statistics are reported on a yearly basis, but traffic is reported monthly. Since ICAO does not collect the same data as the CAB in some instances, some changes in our data procedures were necessary in order to ensure compatibility of the U.S. and non-U.S. data sets. The remainder of this appendix will discuss these changes and our treatment of non-U.S. carriers.

Missing data are a sizable problem in analyzing non-U.S. air carriers because carriers outside the United States often decline or neglect to report data in one or more categories for one or more years. However, our interest is in broad trends rather than specific observations, so we have replaced missing data by interpolation of available data whenever we felt such practice would be reliable. This practice was aided by the fact that missing data generally were limited to specific numbers rather than broad data categories. In some cases where interpolation was not possible, the observation was dropped. In particular, we omitted annual observations whenever the carrier failed to report any financial or traffic data. We also omitted an annual observation whenever the carrier failed to report annual fleet and personnel data and interpolation was not possible. This generally occurred at the beginning and end of our time series for each firm. In the course of data collection and processing every effort was made to utilize the supplements, addenda, and corrigenda to the ICAO statistical publications. These updates contained most of the data that were missing from the original publications.

We distinguish four categories of output: scheduled passenger service, charter service (freight and passenger), freight (scheduled), and mail (scheduled). This is a slight modification of our previous practice for U.S. airlines of including charter freight with scheduled freight. In addition we measure output as deflated revenues rather than as a direct output index. This modification is required because certain non-U.S. carriers provided no service in a particular category for some years. Because our index number procedure requires nonzero quantities for all observations, we were unable to construct a quantity index. However, we could construct the dual price index since prices can be estimated even for carriers that do not supply a particular service. Firms that did not supply a particular output category were assigned the mean price for that category in that year. Then the output quantity index was constructed as the ratio of total revenue to the price index.

Non-U.S. airline data are further complicated by fiscal year reporting of financial data and calendar year reporting of traffic data. To ensure appropriate output measures for countries whose fiscal years do not coincide with the calendar year, we collected monthly traffic data and formed our own annual data consistent with each airline's fiscal year.

Labor input is formed using the six ICAO labor categories: (1) pilots and copilots, (2) other cockpit personnel, (3) cabin attendants, (4) maintenance and overhaul personnel, (5) ticketing sales and promotional personnel, and (6) other personnel. These categories are further aggregated before forming the labor index. Categories 1 and 2 are combined because not all airlines have labor in both these categories and our index number procedure requires nonzero entries for all categories. Categories 4, 5, and 6 are combined into a single category because of evidence indicating that the airlines do not maintain a consistent definition of these categories. There are numerous instances for both the U.S. and non-U.S. carriers where large numbers of personnel are shifted from one of these categories to another in adjacent years. Thus we have formed our labor index using three types of labor.

Our method for treatment of ground property and equipment is based on Christensen and Jorgenson (1969). We begin by using the perpetual inventory method to estimate the real stock of ground, property, and equipment. We use historical real investment data with geometrically declining weights to estimate the stock for each carrier for each year.[31] We assume that the flow of capital services is proportional to the stock. Finally, we estimate the annual cost of using ground, property and equipment by imputing interest and depreciation expenses, adjusted for income taxes, property taxes, and capital gains.[32]

Indexes of aircraft and fuel were constructed in an identical manner to the procedure used previously for U.S. carriers. A major problem was lack of readily available data on fuel consumption: ICAO does not collect such information. We contacted each of the airlines in our sample and requested fuel data, but only nine carriers complied with the request. We estimated fuel gallons for the remaining carriers. This estimation was carried out by estimating the relationship between fuel consumption and aircraft miles, available ton-miles, load factor, aircraft hours, aircraft departures, time effects and plane types.[33] The relationship was estimated as a multiple regression using the available U.S. data. The estimated equation was used to estimate gallons consumed by non-U.S. carriers.

Materials expenditures include all operating expenses not attributable to labor, capital, or fuel. A material index is constructed by applying a price deflator to expenditures on materials. In the United States this price index is a discrete time Divisia index of seven separate national income and product account deflators. For the non-U.S. carriers a country specific price deflator is formed as a discrete time Divisia index of seven separate price indexes. These price indexes are formed by first obtaining inter-country purchasing power parities for each component from Kravis, Heston, and Summers (1983) for 1975. These intercountry comparisons are then expanded into full time series by applying each country's GNP deflator to the individual indexes. This produces a materials deflator specific to goods purchased in the home country. The appropriate price deflator for materials is a function of where the particular good is purchased. Since non-U.S. airlines purchase much of their materials (spare parts, food, etc.) in foreign countries, the domestic price deflator may be inappropriate. For all non-U.S. airlines we have averaged the U.S. and home country price deflator to arrive at a final materials deflator.

Appendix B: Cost Function Results

All variables used in the cost function were first normalized by dividing each value by the mean value of the U.S. carriers. The mean of the U.S. carriers was used rather than the over all sample mean in order to facilitate comparison with our earlier work, which included only the U.S. firms. The results (including standard errors for any given point on the cost function) are independent of this normalization, which allows one to interpret all first-order coefficients as cost elasticities evaluated at the U.S. mean.

The cost function (5) has 121 parameters to be estimated. These parameters include 13 time effects for the U.S. carriers, 13 additional time effects for non-U.S. carriers and 58 firm effects.[34] The parameter estimates are presented in table 9B.1.

All first-order coefficients have the expected sign and are highly significant, except for stage length, which is not significantly different from zero. The elasticities of cost with respect to the factor prices are equivalent to shares in variable cost. Thus at the U.S. mean, labor accounts for approximately 42 percent of airline variable costs, while fuel accounts for 20 percent and materials for 38 percent. Load factor has the expected negative sign and indicates that a 1 percent increase in load factor results in a 0.18 percent reduction in variable costs. The sign on capital stock is positive indicating that for a 1 percent increase in capital stock variable costs will rise by 0.22 percent. This is consistent with excess capacity in the airline industry.

Caves, Christensen, and Tretheway (1984) define returns to density (RTD) as

$$\text{RTD} = \frac{1 - \partial C_V/\partial K}{\partial C_V/\partial Y}, \tag{B1}$$

and returns to scale (RTS) as

$$\text{RTS} = \frac{1 - \partial C_V/\partial K}{(\partial C_V/\partial Y + \partial C_V/\partial P)}, \tag{B2}$$

where P represents points served, a measure of network size. Our cost function results produce an estimate of returns to density of 1.63 with a standard error of 0.09. This represents significant increasing returns to density. Caves, Christensen, Tretheway, and Windle (1985) show that when dealing with panel data, measurement of returns to scale should utilize the between firm estimator.[35] We have computed the between firm estimator and used it to evaluate (B2): this results in an estimate of returns to scale of 0.99—indicating constant returns to scale at the U.S. mean.

Chamberlain (1982) demonstrated that the firm effects estimator used in this chapter is consistent only if the regressors are strictly exogenous. Chamberlain (1979) also demonstrated that if the regressors are not exogenous, then leads and lags of the regressors will in general improve the fit of the estimating equation. In order to test the exogeneity of output, we

Table 9B.1 Variable cost function results

Coefficient on	Estimate and standard error
First-order terms	
Constant	13.298
	(0.039)
Output	0.481
	(0.039)
Labor price	(0.423)
	(0.003)
Fuel price	0.200
	(0.002)
Stage length	0.006
	(0.044)
Load factor	−0.175
	(0.069)
Points	0.121
	(0.032)
Stock	0.217
	(0.036)
Second-order terms	
$(\text{Labor})^2$	0.111
	(0.006)
$(\text{Fuel})^2$	0.120
	(0.003)
Labor-fuel	−0.063
	(0.003)
$(\text{Output})^2$	−0.069
	(0.078)
$(\text{Points})^2$	0.033
	(0.067)
$(\text{Stock})^2$	−0.191
	(0.069)
$(\text{Stage length})^2$	−0.215
	(0.072)
$(\text{Load factor})^2$	0.631
	(0.479)
Load factor–fuel price	−0.083
	(0.017)
Stock–labor price	0.045
	(0.011)
Stock–fuel price	0.017
	(0.008)
Stage length-ouptut	0.130
	(0.061)
Load factor–output	−0.178
	(0.164)
Points–output	−0.176
	(0.058)
Stock–output	0.164
	(0.067)

Table 9B.1 (continued)

Coefficient on	Estimate and standard error
Stage length–load factor	0.041
	(0.103)
Output–labor price	−0.067
	(0.011)
Output–fuel price	0.026
	(0.008)
Points–labor price	0.074
	(0.006)
Points–fuel price	−0.051
	(0.004)
Stage length–labor price	0.000
	(0.006)
Stage length–fuel price	−0.043
	(0.004)
Load factor–labor price	0.033
	(0.023)
Points–load factor	0.114
	(0.112)
Points–stage length	0.051
	(0.052)
Stock–stage length	−0.149
	(0.052)
Stock–load factor	−0.071
	(0.167)
Stock–points	0.100
	(0.053)
U.S. time effects	
1970	0.116
	(0.022)
1971	0.066
	(0.021)
1972	0.085
	(0.019)
1973	0.081
	(0.019)
1974	0.055
	(0.019)
1975	0.048
	(0.018)
1976	0.024
	(0.017)
1978	−0.010
	(0.019)
1979	0.009
	(0.022)
1980	0.039
	(0.022)
1981	−0.005
	(0.022)

Table 9B.1 (continued)

Coefficient on	Estimate and standard error
1982	−0.077
	(0.024)
1983	−0.058
	(0.024)
Non-U.S. time effects	
1970	0.085
	(0.021)
1971	0.092
	(0.020)
1972	0.057
	(0.018)
1973	0.020
	(0.017)
1974	−0.002
	(0.016)
1975	−0.017
	(0.015)
1976	−0.028
	(0.015)
1978	0.021
	(0.015)
1979	−0.002
	(0.015)
1980	−0.020
	(0.016)
1981	−0.070
	(0.016)
1982	−0.072
	(0.017)
1983	−0.066
	(0.018)
Government ownership effect	
	0.154
	(0.026)
U.S. firm effects—former trunks	
American	0.109
	(0.035)
Continental (before merger)	−0.288
	(0.041)
Continental (after merger)	−0.160
	(0.066)
Eastern	0.118
	(0.025)
Northwest	−0.339
	(0.035)
Pan Am (before merger)	0.049
	(0.061)

Table 9B.1 (continued)

Coefficient on	Estimate and standard error
Pan Am (after merger)	0.042
	(0.055)
TWA	0.109
	(0.039)
United	0.064
	(0.036)
Western	−0.244
	(0.042)
U.S. firm effects—former locals	
US Air	−0.131
	(0.040)
Frontier	−0.422
	(0.057)
Ozark	−0.373
	(0.056)
Piedmont	−0.284
	(0.054)
Republic (before merger)	−0.183
	(0.067)
Republic (after merger)	−0.110
	(0.051)
U.S. firm effects—airlines no longer in existence	
Braniff	−0.172
	(0.039)
National	−0.264
	(0.047)
Northeast	−0.288
	(0.072)
Air West	−0.321
	(0.054)
North Central	−0.302
	(0.058)
Southern	−0.394
	(0.059)
Texas International	−0.487
	(0.059)
U.S. firm effects—new entrants	
Air California	−0.399
	(0.097)
Midway	−0.50
	(0.093)
New York Air	0.018
	(0.063)
Pacific Southwest Airlines	0.051
	(0.059)
People Express	−0.331
	(0.068)

Table 9B.1 (continued)

Coefficient on	Estimate and standard error
Southwest	−0.101
	(0.061)
World	−0.513
	(0.123)
Muse Air	−0.898
	(0.096)
Non-U.S. firm effects	
AerLingus/Aerlinte	−0.293
	(0.070)
Air Canada	−0.296
	(0.050)
Air France	−0.054
	(0.059)
Air India	0.101
	(0.083)
Air Portugal	0.033
	(0.070)
Alitalia	−0.194
	(0.055)
British Airways	0.192
	(0.060)
British Caledonian	−0.187
	(0.064)
Canadian Pacific	−0.339
	(0.065)
Dan Air Skyways	−0.031
	(0.086)
Finnair	−0.447
	(0.065)
Iberia	−0.146
	(0.049)
Indian Airlines	−0.127
	(0.064)
Japan Airlines	0.054
	(0.060)
KLM	−0.212
	(0.064)
Korean Airlines	−0.086
	(0.076)
Air Inter	−0.068
	(0.065)
Lufthansa	−0.046
	(0.051)
Pacific Western	−0.722
	(0.067)
Pakistan Int'l	0.018
	(0.065)

Table 9B.1 (continued)

Coefficient on	Estimate and standard error
Sabena	−0.141 (0.065)
SAS	−0.278 (0.051)
Singapore	−0.214 (0.078)
Swissair	−0.173 (0.051)
Thai Int'l	−0.335 (0.082)
UTA	−0.075 (0.091)
Varig	−0.080 (0.062)

estimated the cost function and associated share equations with a single lead and lag on output added to the cost equation. Tests showed that the coefficients on the leading and lagging values of output were individually zero and that both coefficients were jointly zero at the 1 percent significant level. The F-statistic for the test that both coefficients are zero was 4.45. The 1 percent critical value of the F-statistic is 4.62. Also the coefficients on the other regressors do not change appreciably when the lead and lag on output are included.

Notes

The authors gratefully acknowledge the support of the National Science Foundation, the University of British Columbia, and the Center for International Studies at the University of British Columbia.

1. Experts on the study of regulation have recently emphasized the gains to be obtained by giving more attention to international comparisons. For example, Joskow and Noll (1981, p. 57) state: "Most of the empirical literature on regulation focuses entirely on U.S. industries. Little effort has been made to exploit available data on the costs, prices, quality, and rate of technological change in the same industries in other developed countries." See also Peltzman (1981).

2. Our ongoing airline research includes a comparison of productive efficiency of established and new entrant carriers.

3. See "Saudia Concentrating on Self Reliance," *Air Transport World*, January 1984, pp. 58–59.

4. Byrnes (1985) has a good discussion of the future ability of U.S. airlines to keep pace with maturing markets and technological change.

5. Effective economic regulation of the U.S. airlines extends back to a 1930 amendment to the Contract Air Mail Act. See Davies (1972).

6. Rakowski and Johnson (1979) provide a legislative history of the events leading up to deregulation in 1978.

7. Meyer and Oster (1981, p. 4) state: "While deregulation did not formally begin until passage of the Deregulation Act in October 1978, 1976 marked the beginning of the transition to a less regulated environment. In particular, the CAB in 1976 reversed its established policy and began allowing the airlines considerable freedom to compete on the basis of price."

8. Examples of capacity regulation include limits on numbers of flights or size of aircraft. A few countries, such as Australia, have also regulated flight schedules.

9. As this was written (November 1985), Canada was considering an introduction of complete deregulation in 1986.

10. See Taneja (1980) for a discussion of the act.

11. Pacific routes originating in the U.S. were also affected, although many markets in Asia have always had a degree of price competition. See Sampson (1984, pp. 173–178) for a discussion of competition in the Pacific.

12. See "Don't Be Vague, Ask for The Hague," *The Economist*, June 23, 1984, pp. 66–67.

13. Data on passengers carried over the North Atlantic for the first six months of 1982 and 1983 are provided in *Aviation Week and Space Technology* (November 12, 1984). These data are for fifteen of our twenty-seven non-U.S. carriers. The percentage of passengers carried over the North Atlantic ranges from a high of 15.9 percent for Sabena to a low of 2.5 percent for Iberia. Even non-European carriers such as Canadian Pacific (8.4 percent) and Air Canada (5.8 percent) had substantial North Atlantic traffic. The lack of a clear distinction among carriers serving the North Atlantic has led us to retain all non-U.S. carriers in the control group.

14. Observations that include strikes of more than twenty-five days were excluded from the analysis. These include Eastern, 1980; Continental, 1983; National, 1970, 1974, 1975; Northwest, 1970, 1972, 1978; TWA, 1973; United, 1979; Air West, 1972, 1979; Ozark, 1973, 1979, 1980; and Texas International, 1974, 1975.

15. Data problems caused some individual airline years to be excluded from the sample. See appendix A for a list of these observations.

16. For comparison of tables 9.1 and 9.3, 300 million passenger-kilometers are equivalent to 190 million passenger-miles.

17. It can be shown that the cost function is invariant to exchange rate differences.

18. See Caves, Christensen, and Diewert (1982) for a theoretical discussion of multilateral index procedures. Caves, Christensen, and Tretheway (1981) apply this theory to the measurement of airline inputs.

19. Data for U.S. airlines are more complete and show some variation in materials' prices among firms.

20. For those countries not included in Kravis, Heston, and Summers, we followed their recommendation of estimating the parities from a regression on gross domestic product per capital.

21. Dan-Air is the one exception. Nonscheduled RTM account for the bulk of its revenues.

22. Points served for the U.S. carriers were collected from the CAB publication, *Airport Activity Statistics*, (June 30 issue for each year). Points served for the world carriers were obtained directly from the carriers or were compiled from the world wide edition of the *Official Airline Guide*.

23. Caves, Christensen, and Diewert (1982a).

24. For some carriers data were not available for all years. If a carrier was missing an end point year, we used its TFP growth rate for the longest span of years available within the period under consideration. For carriers missing end point years, we multiplied the weight by the ratio of available years to total years in the period.

25. This estimator is obtained by including a binary variable for each firm in the regression.

26. There are some changes in government ownership during the 1970 to 1983 period. This has allowed us to identify an ownership shift variable separate from the firm shifts.

27. Caves, Christensen, and Tretheway (1984) discuss the choice of these variables. See also Oum and Tretheway (1985) for further discussion.

28. To overcome the problem of singularity of the contemporaneous covariance matrix, we delete one of the share equations before carrying out the second stage of Zellner's technique for estimation. The resulting estimates are asymptotically equivalent to maximum likelihood estimates. Moreover the use of all equations at the first stage ensures that the estimates are invariant to the choice of equation to be deleted at the second stage.

29. The difference in the overall results result from slight differences in the formulas and from the use of fitted cost shares in the cost function estimates as opposed to actual cost shares in the TFP indexes.

30. Caves, Christensen, Tretheway, and Windle (1985) track productivity growth for U.S. airlines for the entire 1947 to 1981 period.

31. For U.S. carriers our benchmark is 1945 net book value. For non-U.S. carriers our benchmark in 1960 net book value adjusted by the U.S. ratio of net book value to computed capital stock for 1960. Some non-U.S. carriers did not have financial data available back to 1960. For these carriers we use the most recent year available adjusted by the U.S. ratio of net book value to computed capital stock in that year.

32. Information on tax laws and rates were compiled from the Price Waterhouse "Doing Business in" series and the Organization for Economic Cooperation and Development publication, *International Comparison of Tax Depreciation Practices* (1975). Interest rates were compiled from corporate bond yields in the publication *World Financial Markets*, or, when not available there, from the interest rate series published in *International Financial Statistics*.

33. Plane type variables were computed as percents of total aircraft gross vehicle takeoff weight. The plane types used were our aircraft aggregate categories used in forming our aircraft index.

34. Twenty-seven for non-U.S. carriers, twenty-three for U.S. carriers, and eight for U.S. new entrant carriers. These new entrant carriers are included in the sample as part of ongoing research. Removing them from the sample has no appreciable effect on any of the results.

35. The between firm estimator replaces each observation with its firm mean.

References

Bailey, E., Graham, D. R., and Kaplan, D. P. 1985. *Deregulating the Airlines*. Cambridge: MIT Press.

Banks, H. 1982. *The Rise and Fall of Freddie Laker*. London: Faber.

Brenner, M. A. 1983. "The Economic Effects of Airline Deregulation." In J. R. Foster et al., eds., *Airline Deregulation: Lessons for Public Policy Formation*. Washington, D.C.: Institute for Study of Regulation.

Browne, S. D. 1983. "Salvage of the United States Air Transport System." In J. R. Foster et al., eds., *Airline Deregulation: Lessons for Public Policy Formation*. Washington, D.C.: Institute for Study of Regulation.

Byrnes, J. L. S. 1985. *Diversification Strategies for Regulated and Deregulated Industries: Lessons from the Airlines*. Lexington, Mass.: Lexington Books.

Capron, W. M. 1971. *Technological Change in Regulated Industries*. Washington D.C.: Brookings Institution.

Caves, D. W., and Christensen, L. R. 1984. "The Importance of Economies of Scale, Capacity Utilization and Density in Explaining Interindustry Differences in Productivity Growth." Paper presented at AEI Conference on Interindustry Differences in Productivity Growth, Washington, D.C.

Caves, D. W., Christensen, L. R., and Diewert, W. E. 1982a. "The Economic Theory of Index Numbers and the Measurement of Input, Output, and Productivity." *Econometrica* 50: 1393–1414.

Caves, D. W., Christensen, L. R., and Diewert, W. E. 1982b. "Multilateral Comparisons of Output, Input, and Productivity Using Superlative Index Numbers." *Economic Journal* 92: 73–86.

Caves, D. W., Christensen, L. R., and Swanson, J. A. 1981. "Productivity Growth, Scale Economies and Capacity Utilization in U.S. Railroads, 1955–1974." *American Economic Review* 71: 994–1002.

Caves, D. W., Christensen, L. R., and Tretheway, M. W. 1981. "U.S. Trunk Air Carriers, 1972–1977: A Multilateral Comparison of Total Factor Productivity." In T. Cowing and R. Stevenson, eds., *Productivity Measurement in Regulated Industries*. New York: Academic Press.

Caves, D. W., Christensen, L. R., and Tretheway, M. W. 1983. "Productivity Performance of U.S. Trunk and Local Service Airlines in the Era of Deregulation." *Economic Inquiry* 21: 312–324.

Caves, D. W., Christensen, L. R., and Tretheway, M. W. 1984, "Economies of Density versus Economies of Scale: Why Trunk and Local Service Airline Costs Differ." *Rand Journal of Economics* 15: 471–489.

Caves, D. W., Christensen, L. R., Tretheway, M. W., and Windle, R. J. 1985. "Network Effects and the Measurement of Returns of Scale and Density for U.S. Railroads." In A. F. Daughety, ed., *Analytical Studies in Transport Economics*. Cambridge: Cambridge University Press.

Caves, R. E. 1962. *Air Transport and Its Regulators*, Cambridge: Harvard University Press.

Chamberlain, G. 1982. "Multivariate Regression Models for Panel Data." *Journal of Econometrics* 18: 5–46.

Chamberlain, G. 1979. "Heterogeneity, Omitted Variable Bias, and Duration Dependence." Discussion Paper 691. Harvard Institute of Economic Research. March.

Christensen, L. R., and Jorgenson, D. W. 1969. "The Measurement of U.S. Real Capital Input, 1929–1967." *Review of Income and Wealth*, December, 292–320.

Davies, R. E. G. 1972. *Airlines of the United States Since 1914*. Washington, D.C.: Smithsonian.

Douglas, G. W., and Miller, J. C., III. 1974. *Economic Regulation of Domestic Air Transport: Theory and Policy*. Washington D.C.: Brookings Institution.

Foster, J. R., Hall, G. R., Holmberg, S. R., Phillips, C. F. Jr., and Wallace R. L. eds. 1983. *Airline Deregulation: Lessons for Public Policy Formation*. Washington, D.C.: Institute for Study of Regulation.

International Civil Aviation Organization (various years). *Fleet and Personnel*. Montreal.

International Civil Aviation Organization. *Financial Data*. Montreal.

International Civil Aviation Organization. *Traffic*. Montreal.

Jordan, W. A. 1970. *Airline Regulation in America: Effects and Imperfections*. Baltimore: Johns Hopkins University Press.

Joskow, P. L., and Noll, R. C. 1981. "Regulation in Theory and Practice: An Overview." In G. Fromm, ed., *Studies in Public Regulation*. Cambridge: MIT Press, pp. 1–65.

Kravis, I. B., Heston, A., and Summers, R. 1982. *World Product and Income: International Comparisons of Real Gross Product*. Washington, D.C.: World Bank.

Levine, M. 1965. "Is Regulation Necessary? California Air Transportation and National Regulatory Policy." *Yale Law Journal 74*: 1416–1447.

Martin, P. K. 1983. *The Airline Handbook: 1983–1984*. Cranston, R.I.: Aerotravel Research.

Meyer, J. R., and Oster, C. V., Jr., eds. 1981. *Airline Deregulation: The Early Experience*. Boston: Auburn House.

Meyer, J. R., and Oster. C. V., Jr., eds. 1984. *Deregulation and the New Airline Entrepreneurs*. Cambridge: MIT Press.

Morrison, S. A., and Winston, C. 1985. *The Economic Effects of Airline Deregulation*. Washington D.C.: Brookings Institution.

Mundlak, Y. 1961. "Empirical Production Functions Free of Management Bias." *Journal of Farm Economics 43*: 44–56.

Mundlak, Y. 1978. "On the Pooling of Time Series and Cross Section Data." *Econometrica 46*: 69–85.

Official Airline Guide, (various issues) North American Edition. Oak Brook, Ill.: Reuben H. Donnelley.

Oum, T. H., Gillen, D. W., and Noble, D. S. E. 1984. "Demands for Fareclasses and Pricing in Airline Markets." Working Paper No. 1004. Faculty of Commerce, University of British Columbia.

Oum, T. H., and Tretheway, M. W. 1985. "Hedonic versus General Specifications of the Translog Cost Function." Faculty of Commerce and Business Administration, University of British Columbia, Vancouver. Paper presented to Canadian Economics Association, May.

Peltzman, S. 1981. "Current Developments in the Economics of Regulation." In G. Fromm, ed., *Studies in Public Regulation*. Cambridge: MIT Press, pp. 371–384.

Rakowski, J. P., and Johnson, J. 1979. "Airline Deregulation: Problems and Prospects." *Quarterly Review of Economics and Business 19*: 65–78.

Sampson, A. 1984. *Empires of the Sky*. London: Hodder and Stoughton.

Strassmann, D. L. 1981. "Impacts on Air Fares and Traffic." In J. R. Meyer and C. V. Oster, eds., *Airline Deregulation: The Early Experience*. Boston: Auburn House.

Straszheim, M. R. 1969. *The International Airline Industry*. Washington, D.C.: Brookings Institution.

Taneja, N. K. 1980. *U.S. International Aviation Policy*. Lexington, Mass.: Lexington Books.

Thayer, F. C. 1983. "Excessive Competition Equals Collapse: Regulation Equals Recovery." In J.R. Foster et al., eds., *Airline Deregulation: Lessons for Public Policy Formation.* Washington, D.C.: Institute for Study of Regulation.

Tornqvist, L. 1936. "The Bank of Finland's Consumption Price Index." *Banks of Finland Monthly Bulletin*, No. 10, pp. 1–8.

Tretheway, M. W. 1984. "An International Comparison of Airlines." *Proceedings Canadian Transportation Research Forum*, May.

Zellner, A. 1962. "An Efficient Method of Estimating Seemingly Unrelated Regressions and Tests for Aggregation Bias." *Journal of the American Statistical Association* 58:977–992.

10

Occupational Disease Remedies: The Asbestos Experience

Leslie I. Boden and Carol Adaire Jones

In this chapter we assess the impact of the labor market, product liability, and workers' compensation on incentives to control asbestos hazards in the workplace. First, we develop criteria for efficient incentives to reduce occupational disease. Then we compare these norms with the observed performance of the compensation systems for asbestos insulation workers.

Introduction

Estimates of the number and severity of occupational disease cases vary widely: from 4 percent (Doll and Peto 1981) to 20 percent (Bridbord et al. 1978) of annual cancer deaths have been attributed to occupational cancer. The low figure represents about 15,000 fatalities per year; the high estimate implies approximately 75,000 fatalities per year. Noncancer occupational illnesses also account for substantial morbidity and mortality. For example, it has been estimated that 30,000 American textile workers have developed totally disabling byssinosis (Bouhuys et al. 1977) and that 59,000 have silicosis (U.S. Department of Labor 1980).

Asbestos is generally considered to be the single largest source of occupational disease. Projections for cancer deaths caused by asbestos between the years 1980 and 2000 range from 85,000 (Enterline 1981) to over 200,000 (Hogan and Hoel 1981). In addition it has been estimated that over 35,000 workers currently suffer from disabling asbestosis (Walker 1982). Given the perception that the labor market does not effectively internalize the costs of occupational disease, a variety of postdamage compensation and predamage regulatory policies have been implemented. The workers' compensation program, designed in the early twentieth century as a no-fault scheme to compensate for workplace accidents, has slowly expanded its scope to cover occupational diseases. Many have argued that workers' compensation has provided inadequate incentives to companies to reduce occupational hazards. In the last two decades Congress has designed regulatory schemes to reduce occupational hazards. The Coal Mine Health and Safety Act of 1969 established maximum permissible exposures to coal mine dust and created an extensive regulatory structure to enforce the exposure limits. The Occupational Safety and Health Act of 1970 established a regulatory system covering most American workplaces, to promulgate occupational health standards that limit exposures with engineering control and work practice requirements.

In the mid-1970s the courts expanded the role of third-party liability suits by establishing the principle of strict liability for asbestos-related damages. The number of suits outstanding against asbestos manufacturers has grown from a handful in the early 1970s to more than 30,000 today. Access to remedies under tort for other kinds of occupational diseases, however, remains highly restricted.

The asbestos litigation has provoked considerable controversy about the effectiveness of workers' compensation and product liability litigation in providing incentives to reduce occupational disease risks and in compensating those suffering from work-related diseases. Some analyses of occupational disease compensation have emphasized serious impediments to the efficient functioning of both systems, including lack of information among potential claimants and their physicians and serious difficulties with proof of causation (Barth and Hunt 1980). Recently, however, the product liability system has been attacked for having excessive legal costs and for providing too much compensation to asbestos disease victims. The latter charge has been fueled by three bankruptcies in the asbestos manufacturing sector, attributed by the manufacturers to high asbestos tort costs. This assertion runs directly counter to the hypothesis that the systems undercompensate for occupational disease.

Until recently adequate documentation of the costs imposed by the compensation systems on manufacturers and employers has not been available. Most of the relevant data exist only for individuals who have filed for compensation. Yet it is essential to examine how the systems function, not just for those who file but for all people conceptually eligible for compensation because of disability or death from occupational disease. In order to remedy this data problem, the U.S. Department of Labor supported the development of economic and health data for asbestos insulators identified to have died from asbestos-related disease. The insulators were members of the International Association of Heat and Frost Insulators and Asbestos Workers, AFL-CIO, CLC, hereafter referred to as the Asbestos Workers Union (AWU) (Selikoff 1983).

We bring together evidence from these data and other related studies of AWU members. Our purpose is to assess the level of incentives to reduce

Table 10.1 Deaths among asbestos insulation workers in the United States and Canada, January 1, 1967–December 31, 1976

Underlying cause of death	Expected[a]	Observed[b]		Ratio O/E[b]	
		(BE)	(DC)	(BE)	(DC)
Total deaths, all causes	1,658.9	2,271	2,271	1.37	1.37
Total cancer, all sites	319.7	995	922	3.11	2.88
Cancer of lung	105.6	486	429	4.60	4.06
Mesothelioma	c	175	104	—	—
Cancer of the kidney	8.1	19	18	2.36	2.23
Digestive system cancers	74.2	131	119	1.77	1.60
All other cancer	131.8	184	252	1.40	1.91
Asbestosis	c	168	78	—	—

Source: From Selikoff et al. (1983).
Note: Number of workers were 17,800; man-years of observation were 166,853.
a. Expected deaths are based on white male age-specific U.S. death rates calculated by the U.S. National Center for Health Statistics for 1967–1976.
b. (BE) = best evidence of the number of deaths categorized after review of best available information (autopsy, surgical, clinical); (DC) = number of deaths as recorded from death certificate information only.
c. Rates are not available, but these are extremely rate causes of death in the general population.

asbestos-related disease risks imposed by the labor market and by the liability and workers' compensation systems. We focus on the deterrence function of the systems; we will not discuss directly the compensation function.

The Asbestos Case

Incidence of Asbestos-Related Disease

Asbestos is widely recognized to cause three major diseases: asbestosis (a scarring disease of the lungs), mesothelioma (a cancer of the lining of the lungs or abdominal cavity), and lung cancer. In addition evidence suggests that asbestos exposure is associated with cancer of the larynx and cancers of the digestive system.

The pattern of excess incidence of disease observed by Selikoff (1983) in North American insulation workers (members of AWU) during 1967 to 1976 appears in table 10.1. The compensation data are from workers identified to have died from an asbestos-related disease. The observed mortality for all cancers is three times the expected rate for individuals not exposed to asbestos. The ratio of observed to expected mortality, the standardized mortality ratio (SMR), is over 4 for lung cancer. Ratios cannot be calculated individually for mesothelioma or asbestosis because the diseases are so rare in the general population that incidence data do not exist; generally, all cases of both diseases are attributed to asbestos exposures. Other identified cancers have SMR's ranging from 1.5 to 2.5.

During the ten-year period covered by the Selikoff data, the death rate was 37 percent higher than expected. Deaths attributable to asbestos—defined as excess deaths from cancers, asbestosis, and noninfectious pulmonary diseases—represent 44 percent of all deaths according to Selikoff's "best-evidence" determination.

Epidemiological studies confirm that asbestos exposure and smoking have a multiplicative effect on the incidence of some asbestos-related diseases. In the general population, cigarette smokers have a ten- to fifteen-fold excess risk of lung cancer. In a 1979 study Hammond et al. observed a fivefold excess of lung cancer among nonsmoking asbestos workers compared with nonsmokers in the general population, but smokers exposed to asbestos had a fifty-threefold excess when compared to the general population of nonsmokers. Smoking appears to aggravate the effects of asbestosis. Mesothelioma, on the other hand, appears not to be influenced by smoking.

Worker Exposure

Workers' exposure to asbestos occurs during any of the stages of the production cycle—during the mining and milling of asbestos fiber and the manufacture of primary asbestos products—and during the installation of asbestos products in final demand goods, and, finally, during the repair and demolition of such goods. The primary manufacturers of asbestos products not only affect the safety level in their own plants but also the safety levels down the chain of the production process. When information about those risks is provided to consumers, decisions can be made that control risks in sectors concerned with installation and repair or demolition.

Most worker exposures occur downstream from manufacturing. Seventy percent of asbestos is supplied to the construction industry for industrial, commercial, and residential use. Another 20 percent is directed to the automotive sector. The final 10 percent goes to miscellaneous industries and a small consumer sector. The approximate numbers of workers exposed to asbestos in 1972 are 21,000 in primary manufacturing, 26,000 in secondary manufacturing, 250,000 in construction and demolition, 350,000 in the automotive aftermarket, and 4,000 in shipbuilding.

Theory-Based Norms for Performance Evaluation

The Labor Market and the Role of Information

The theory of compensating differentials suggests that, under certain conditions, workers will be fully compensated with higher wages and benefits for bearing more risk on the job. The higher wages and benefits create an incentive for employers to reduce workplace hazards to the cost-minimizing level, where the cost of increased safety will just equal the value the workers place on safety.

In recent years a substantial number of studies have demonstrated that workers in hazardous occupations receive extra pay (see Smith 1979; Violette and Chestnut 1983). The existence of some wage premium, however, does not necessarily indicate that the wage payments reflect the full cost of workplace hazards. Two conditions must be met for firms to have efficient deterrence incentives. First, workers must have other comparable job opportunities, which implies that workers on the margin are not receiving firm-specific rents. If workers are receiving rents from job-specific capital or union monopoly, the incremental price of risk they demand will tend to be reduced by the value of the rents: as a result the employer will not receive the correct signal as to how much safety is valued. The lack of comparable job opportunities is a general problem, particularly prominent in unionized contexts.

Second, workers and employers must have adequate information about on-the-job hazards. Workers may find it relatively easy to assess injury risks in alternative jobs (Viscusi 1983). However, a variety of factors make it much more difficult to determine the risks of workplace exposure to toxic substances.

To evaluate accurately the risk premium associated with a given job, workers must have knowledge about both the toxicity of varying exposures to workplace hazards and the exposure levels in potential places of employment. To determine the acceptable hazard level, employers also must have knowledge about toxicity and exposures. In addition employers need to know how the labor supply schedule shifts with changes in the health risks and what the costs of control technologies are.

We consider separately the problems in developing toxicity and exposure information, turning first to the toxicity data. Many occupational diseases are difficult for physicians to distinguish from other diseases. If diseases are successfully diagnosed, another difficulty arises: diseases can frequently be attributed to both occupational and nonoccupational hazards. Often the initial manifestation of an occupational disease may not occur for fifteen to thirty years, and the people who develop the disease may no longer be working with the causal agent. In the case of worker exposure to asbestos, long-term epidemiological studies have been necessary to clarify statistically the relationships between asbestos exposure and disease.

Even if a hazard is recognized in the health literature, workers are not likely to have full information about what substances are present in the workplace, much less information about specific exposure levels. Recent federal and state "right-to-know" laws, however, are beginning to establish workers' legal rights to have at least partial access to such information (Baram 1984).

Without the threat of liability for subsequent damages, neither the manufacturer of a hazardous product nor the employer who uses the product in the workplace has an incentive to collect and disseminate risk information (Viscusi 1980). Workers do have an incentive, but the high minimum cost and the public good nature of the toxicity information may lead to substantially less than optimal investment in such activity. Though unions are in a better position to collect information than individual workers, they do not have sufficient incentives to invest in producing the optimal amount of toxicity information when many nonunion workers are exposed to the hazard. They are more able to appropriate the benefits of exposure information in specific workplaces. However, they are unlikely to be able to produce exposure information at a lower cost than employers.

Optimal Design of the Liability of Manufacturers, Employers, and Workers: The Information Transfer Case

Three parties affect the incidence of occupational disease: manufacturers, employers, and workers. Each group affects occupational health risk levels in different ways. Our compensation data are for downstream workers (insulation installers), however. Thus we will focus on the decisions by these groups that directly affect downstream workers' risk levels.

First, firms manufacturing asbestos products for industrial use affect hazard levels in downstream workplaces with decisions on whether to inform their customers of the hazards associated with their products. We assume that manufacturers cannot redesign their products to reduce their hazards in use. Then, downstream employers affect safety levels in their own plants by the choice of inputs in the production process. We treat the level of occupational risk as a function of the level of asbestos products used, the amount of labor employed, the level of controls for reducing exposures, and the degree of supervision of work practices. Finally, workers affect their own safety through the care they exercise at work in handling hazardous materials and through their personal non-work habits.

The Information Transfer Problem

We consider the simplest case in which the manufacturer of a product knows the product is hazardous but does not make the knowledge publicly available. In this simple case information is modeled as a dichotomous variable: a product is, or is not, known to be hazardous. It will be efficient for the information to be provided if the cost of dissemination is less than the value of reduced occupational disease net of extra prevention costs (incurred at the efficient level of safety, given that information was provided). The value of occupational disease risks can be measured by the amount that knowledgeable workers would require to accept these risks relative to safe, but otherwise identical, employment.

We propose the following liability rules that would, with perfect markets, provide incentives in the information transfer case for the efficient dissemination of information and for efficient levels of workplace risk:

1. Manufacturers should be liable for the harm resulting from use of their product if they were aware of its health risks but did not warn those to whom the product was sold.

2. Informed employers should be liable for the full costs of occupational disease if workers were not informed at the time of harmful exposure. To provide both efficient safety and insurance levels, this liability should be apportioned in three parts: (a) payments for disability to workers that equate the pre-injury and post-injury marginal utilities of income, (b) payments to survivors of workers who die prematurely, to take the place of the life insurance that informed workers would have purchased, and (c) fines equal to the costs of occupational disease net of the compensation received.

3. When both employers and workers are informed, the sum of the employers' compensating wage and benefit payments and post-injury payments should equal the full costs of occupational disease. In the case where labor markets are perfect, no post-injury compensation need be paid.

If a manufacturer provides risk information to exposed workers, the workers will demand extra wages as compensation for previously unrecognized risks. New precautions will be taken by employers as long as employers' savings from reduced hazard wages are greater than additional costs of precautions. Thus efficient care will be taken. If employers are informed but workers are not, employers will take precautions to reduce future liabilities. As a result the employers' costs of using the hazardous substance, and thus the costs of their products will increase so demand for them will decline. If the increased costs equal the full social costs of occupational illness, efficient care will have been taken.

It can be shown that a profit-maximizing manufacturer will provide risk information if the resulting decline in disease costs net of prevention costs is greater than the costs of providing the information. If it is efficient not to provide the information, the manufacturer will face liability for the health costs of occupational disease. The resulting increase in the price of the hazardous product will lead to the alternate efficient level of care, given that it is not efficient to provide information. See Brown (1973), Shavell (1980), and Polinsky (1980), for related discussions.

Other Sources of Hazard Information
We recognize that there are sources other than the manufacturer for information about hazards. The toxicity of asbestos, for example, was established in the medical literature and was beginning to enter public awareness by the mid-1960s.

Consider the case of a worker who was exposed to asbestos for ten years and then developed asbestosis. During the first five years of exposure the employer was not informed by the manufacturer of the hazards of asbestos, but during the latter five years the employer became aware of the dangers through other information channels. At what point do we hold the employer responsible for acting on independent sources of information? If the duty to warn is an efficient due care standard, as we have argued, then this mixed case is formally equivalent to the "successive joint torts" case described by Landes and Posner (1980). An efficient liability arrangement enables plaintiffs to sue for total damages either the manufacturer or both the manufacturer and the employer. In the latter case the employer can only be held responsible for the incremental damages caused by the last time period of exposure, in this case the last five years.

Incentives to Generate Information
Of course in reality the process of gathering and disseminating hazard information is far more complicated than presented in this simple model. First, information on the toxicity of a substance involves a more complex situation than that suggested by a dichotomous variable. After an initial warning about a potential hazard, probably on the basis of clinical diagnoses, the process of demonstrating the hazard is both time- and energy-

intensive. At this point information will be incomplete. The issue must be addressed: Should the liability system be used to provide incentives to collect information? If lack of information can be used as a defense, the incentives clearly bias manufacturers and employers away from collecting information.

If we believe that the liability system should promote the development of information, the second critical question becomes, Who can generate additional information at least cost? In general, it can be argued that both manufacturer and employer have important roles in the process. In the downstream workers' risk case discussed here, however, the employers are construction subcontractors, who tend to have small companies with a transient work force. We suggest that the process of generating information will be carried out more cost-effectively by highly concentrated manufacturers than by small employers with transient workers. Though we consider information generation to be an important issue, we will not address it directly in the rest of the chapter.

Probabilistic Damages
For many diseases with long latency periods, uncertainty about individual causation is not simply caused by the difficulties of collecting exposure information or of doing toxicological and epidemiological studies. Even with good population information, only probabilistic statements about causation can be made for individuals. For example, the lung cancer of an asbestos worker cannot be shown to be caused by asbestos exposure if the worker also smokes or is exposed to other hazardous substances. The likelihood that the lung cancer is related to asbestos exposure is determined in part by the duration and intensity of asbestos exposure.

In the context of multiple causation, an efficient liability system would require payment by each of the defendants equal to the product of the value of harm times the share of disease attributable to the defendant's actions. In this way defendants' liability payments would reflect the expected harm attributable to them (Landes and Posner 1984; Shavell 1984).

Asbestos Product Liability Law and Workers' Compensation
Legal Principles

Legal Principles of Product Liability
Third-party product liability suits against asbestos manufacturers are generally filed under the theory of negligence or strict liability in tort. The grounds for suit are that asbestos is a defective product because the

manufacturers failed in their duty to warn employers of the dangers of working with asbestos and did not provide adequate safety instructions for its use. Most jurisdictions require constructive knowledge by the manufacturer of the dangers of asbestos, although some hold the manufacturer liable for all injuries even if the firm had no knowledge of the dangers of asbestos at the time of worker exposure (see *Beshada* v. *Johns-Manville Products Corp.* 1982). The successful product liability plaintiff is awarded damages intended to reflect both purely financial losses as well as pain and suffering. In some cases punitive damages have also been awarded. For a more detailed discussion, see Burns et al. (1983).

Legal Principles of Workers' Compensation
Workers' compensation was established on a no-fault principle, effectively making employers strictly liable for all injuries and illnesses that arise "out of and in the course of employment." Workers' compensation laws require employers to pay for all medical and rehabilitation costs and for two-thirds of all lost wages, up to a statutory ceiling, generally tied to some fraction of the state average weekly wage. No payments are made for pain and suffering or punitive damages. In general, worker negligence is not a defense. However, a small number of states explicitly allow apportionment of causation between occupational exposure and cigarette smoking, a comparative negligence approach. Employers covered by workers' compensation are generally protected from workers attempting to recover damages at tort against them for occupational injuries or illnesses.

Comparison of Legal Principles with Theoretical Norms

Allocation of Liability between Manufacturers and Employers We argued previously that the employer should be indemnified by the manufacturer only when there is a failure to warn. Furthermore, independent of the manufacturers' failure to warn, indemnification should not be allowed if the employer knew, or should have known, of the dangers during the exposure period and negligently exposed workers as a result. The design of the current liability system could provide the manufacturer with reasonable incentives to disclose information about the hazards associated with asbestos and, to a lesser extent, to gather information from available sources. The system does not appear to provide strong incentives for manufacturers to develop information.

The major problem in the allocation of liability, however, appears to rest with workers' compensation. Though it is a strict liability system, in all but three states the employer (directly, or indirectly through the insurer) is entitled to indemnity for workers' compensation payments from product liability awards or settlements (Larson 1984). Whenever the manufacturer has failed in its duty to warn, in principle, the employer is free of liability independent of the employer's knowledge of the hazards. Thus the system may not provide incentives to employers to gather information; furthermore it may not provide incentives for employers to use information unless they receive hazard warnings from the manufacturers.

Level of Compensation We argued that to provide adequate deterrence incentives, the liable parties should bear the full social costs of disease. For liable manufacturers the product liability system should impose the full social costs of asbestos-associated diseases. For liable employers the sum of compensating wage differentials, workers' compensation payments and legal costs should also equal these costs.

Product liability awards may come close to or exceed the full cost of disease in some cases, when pain and suffering and punitive damages are levied.

Workers' compensation is explicitly designed to cover less than full earnings losses. First, statutory limits for indemnity payments are typically set at two-thirds of lost wages, subject to a generally restrictive ceiling. Second, workers' compensation payments for death or long-term disability are not usually adjusted for lost prospective increases in earnings over the worker's career. In addition there is no adjustment for lost benefits, such as retirement contributions or medical insurance. And, as noted earlier, there is no compensation for pain and suffering or for losses associated with foregone life experiences independent of value generated by earnings losses.

The level of compensation also will be affected by the treatment of probabilistic causation. The primary criterion for determining causality in product liability is that a "preponderance of evidence" indicates that the particular defect in question was the cause of injury. If the decision about causation in each specific case is dichotomous and based on this rule, incentives to take care will not generally be optimal (Landes and Posner 1984; Shavell 1984).

Worker Moral Hazard The structure of workers' compensation appears to discourage potential moral hazard problems: though the payment scheme is based on strict liability, it contains substantial risk-sharing. Whether the possibility of moral hazard justifies the extent of risk-sharing in the policy design is unclear. When workers have not been warned of the risks of asbestos, contributory negligence under workers' compensation would not affect worker care. Where workers are warned of the risks of asbestos, employers who can monitor worker safety behavior should be able to use hiring and payment policies to achieve optimal worker care. Since product liability payments are, in principle, only available when workers have not been warned of health risks, moral hazard should not be a problem in this area either.

Incentives for Preventing Occupation Disease: Policy Implementation

We now turn to available data on compensating wage differentials, on asbestos workers' compensation, and on product liability payments and compare these payments with the norms described earlier.

As we mentioned earlier, efficient incentives will be created when manufacturers are liable for the full cost of asbestos-caused harm, unless they have warned their purchasers of the hazards. Once the purchasers have been informed, they should become liable for the asbestos-related damages generated after they were informed. To impose the efficient deterrence incentives on employers requires that the sum of workers' compensation and compensating wage differentials equals the full costs of asbestos-related disease.

Substantial evidence exists that manufacturers were aware of asbestos hazards long before 1964.[1] After the publication of Selikoff's 1964 article on asbestos insulators' mortality, information about the relationship between asbestos and disease became widely publicized. We suggest that 1964 be considered a turning point: before that time manufacturers should be fully liable; after that time manufacturers and employers should be jointly liable for the incremental costs of asbestos-related disease.

In the following discussion we determine the proportions of damages associated with occupational disease borne by employers and by manufacturers. First, we discuss the measures of damages associated with asbestos-related disease employed in the analysis. Then, we present data on the performance of the product liability system for asbestos insulators and calculate the share of damages borne by manufacturers. Finally, we present estimates of compensating wage differentials and on the performance of the workers' compensation system for asbestos insulators, and we calculate the share of damages borne by employers.

Table 10.2 Estimates of present discounted value of losses due to asbestos-related deaths of insulators, 1967–1976

Wage and household production losses	$.21 \times 10^6$
Estimated average losses of asbestos workers[a]	
Deaths prior to expected retirement, $N = 568$	$.24 \times 10^6$
Deaths after expected retirement, $N = 77$	0
Total deaths, $N = 645$	$.21 \times 10^6$
"Value of life" estimates of losses	1.5×10^6
Estimate employed in calculations: Viscusi (1983), minimum estimate (1982 $)	1.5×10^6
Range of estimates in literature (1982 $)[b]	
Thaler and Rosen (1975)	$.39 \times 10^6 - $.75 \times 10^6$
Viscusi (1983)	$1.5 \times 10^6 - 4.2×10^6
R. Smith (1976)	3.3×10^6
Olson (1981)	7.1×10^6

Note: In 1982 dollars. Rounded to nearest thousand. Discount rate employed throughout is aftertax rate of return on U.S. Treasury Bonds in order to be consistent with Johnson and Heler methodology for earnings losses.
a. Source: Johnson and Heler (1983).
b. Estimates summarized in Violette and Chestnut (1983).

Unless stated otherwise, the data source used in this section is a sample of AWU members identified to have died from asbestos-related causes during 1967 to 1976. The determination of the asbestos association of their death was part of a long-term project documenting the causes of mortality among members of the union. The data on the risks of asbestos exposure appearing in table 10.1 are from this population. After the mortality study was completed, Irving J. Selikoff and his associates collected extensive information about the occupational disease compensation experience of their survivors (Selikoff 1983).

Damages Associated with Asbestos-Related Deaths

As noted earlier, the social cost of disease in a workplace is the amount the workers, if fully informed, would require to accept those risky jobs relative to safe, but otherwise equivalent, jobs. In our calculations we will use two proxies for losses. The first measure, value of lost wages and household services estimated from the asbestos workers sample, is hypothesized to underestimate losses substantially. The second, the estimated "value of a statistical life," taken from among the lower estimates in the compensating wage differential literature, may also be an underestimate. Table 10.2 provides information about both measures.

Lost Wages and Household Services Johnson and Heler (1983) calculated the present discounted value in 1982 of the loss of wages and household services for asbestos-associated deaths in the insulation workers' sample. We will refer to this partial measure of losses as earnings loss (EL). This damage estimate does not include medical care costs, lost fringe benefits, pain and suffering, or compensation for risk-bearing. For their discount rate Johnson and Heler chose the aftertax rate of return on U.S. Treasury bonds. The mean EL per asbestos-associated death was $214,000 in 1982 dollars, with a mean of $244,000 for the 568 individuals who died prior to their expected retirement age and zero for the 77 insulators who died after regular retirement (see table 10.2).

Compensating Wage Differentials As observed earlier, market estimates of compensating wage differentials for workplace injuries can provide a better measure of these disease costs than the earnings loss measure. However, estimates of compensating wage differentials vary considerably with the characteristics of the samples and with measurement error and specification bias in estimation. Table 10.2 displays some estimates spanning the range reported in the literature. On the low end, Thaler and Rosen estimated a wage premium of $390,000 to $750,000 per statistical life lost. On the high end, Olson estimated a value of $7,100,000. Other estimates include $1.5 to $4.2 million (Viscusi 1983) and $3.3 million (Smith 1976). Estimates of wage differentials for unionized workers are substantially higher: $8 million (Viscusi 1983), and $17 to $18 million (Olson 1981). All figures are reported in 1982 dollars. To be conservative, we have chosen Viscusi's lowest estimate, $1.5 million, as our measure of the "value of a statistical life," which we refer to as VL.

Estimated Losses Borne by Manufacturers
Table 10.3 presents data on product liability filing rates and payments to those who filed. Sixteen percent of all the insulators or their survivors filed product liability suits. The filing rates increased dramatically through time, however. Whereas only 3 percent of deaths during 1967–68 resulted in suits, 32 percent of deaths in 1975–76 generated suits. This reflects the impact of higher payment levels and growing knowledge about asbestos disease in the 1970s.

For those deaths in which a product liability action was brought, the mean present discounted value of payments (with 1982 as the base year) was $89,000. Along with the filing rate, the payment level increased dramatically through time. For asbestos workers who died in 1967–68, mean

Table 10.3 Product liability payments to asbestos insulators, by date of workers' death

	1967–68	1969–70	1971–72	1973–74	1975–76	1967–76
Percent filing suit	3	7	9	22	32	16
Mean present discounted value of lifetime payments to survivors who filed (base year = 1982)	$29,000	$31,000	$78,000	$83,000	$110,000	$89,000

Note: Numbers are rounded to nearest thousand. Sample of 995 AWU Members identified to have died of asbestos-related diseases, surveyed by Mt. Sinai Environmental Sciences Laboratory (see Selikoff 1983). Calculations by authors. Percent filing suits variable calculated for subsample ($N = 754$) with available information. Data were available to calculate value of payments variable for 88 of 101 individuals known to have filed suits resolved by end of period. An additional 19 suits were filed but not resolved as of 1983.

compensation was $29,000; deaths in 1975–76 resulted in compensation averaging $110,000.[2] The reasons for the increase in mean payments include changes in the law that improved plaintiffs' probability of success, growing expertise in the plaintiffs' bar in pursuing these cases, and the accumulation of evidence to support plaintiffs' factual contentions.

Manufacturers pay legal costs as well for these claims, and total payments, including legal costs, provide incentives to inform workers of risks of exposure to asbestos. Kakalik et al. (1984) estimated that legal expenses for asbestos product liability suits were 58 percent of payments to plaintiffs, based on data from a larger and more diverse sample of asbestos suits resolved in 1980 to 1982. Using this estimate, we calculate that the mean cost borne by manufacturers per product liability action filed for death in 1975–76 was $174,000.

With this information, we can calculate the ratio of manufacturers' payments to asbestos-related health costs, starting first with the earnings loss measure. For asbestos-associated deaths in 1975–76 for which suits were filed, the ratio of total costs borne by manufacturers to earnings losses was 81 percent (see row 1A, table 10.4). When we take into account the statistical correction for expected deaths from the targeted diseases, the share of earnings losses borne by manufacturers for this special group increases to 100 percent (see row 1B, table 10.4). Once we take into account the filing rate, the cost shares borne by manufacturers fall dramatically. Row 2A of table 10.4 illustrates the cost share of EL borne by manufacturers for all asbestos-associated deaths: Total costs borne by manufacturers for 1975–76 deaths represent 26 percent of EL. After the statistical correction, manufacturers bear 32 percent of EL (see row 2B of table 10.4).

Table 10.4 Share of losses associated with asbestos-related deaths borne by manufacturers (loss measure 1: lost wages and household services)

Samples of asbestos-related death cases[a]	Date of death of worker					
	1967–68	1969–70	1971–72	1973–74	1975–76	1967–76
1. A. Product liability claimants only	0.21	0.19	0.58	0.61	0.81	0.66
B. Claimants only, with correction for expected deaths[b]	0.26	0.29	0.71	0.75	1.00	0.81
2. A. All deaths	0.01	0.01	0.05	0.14	0.26	0.11
B. All deaths with correction for expected deaths[b]	0.01	0.01	0.06	0.17	0.32	0.13

Source: Derived from tables 10.2 and 10.3. Original data from Selikoff et al. (1983). Calculations by the authors.
Note: Dependent variable = (Product liability compensation plus legal defense costs) ÷ (Earnings losses associated with asbestos-related deaths). Our measure of "earnings losses" accounts for the value of lost wages and household services associated with the deaths. Both the cost and the loss measures are reported as present discounted values of the streams as of 1982.
a. I. J. Selikoff and Associates of Mt. Sinai Environmental Sciences Laboratory made the determination as to whether a death was asbestos related by examining medical records and sometimes by autopsy.
b. The statistical correction subtracts from the denominator losses associated with the expected cancer deaths based on population disease rates for the demographic group.

Table 10.5 Share of losses associated with asbestos-related deaths borne by manufacturers (loss measure 2: "value-of-life" estimate of losses)

Samples of asbestos-related death cases[a]	Date of death of worker					
	1967–68	1969–70	1971–72	1973–74	1975–76	1967–76
1. A. Product liability claimants only	0.03	0.03	0.08	0.09	0.12	0.09
B. Claimants only, with correction for expected deaths[b]	0.04	0.04	0.10	0.11	0.14	0.12
2. A. All deaths	0.00	0.00	0.01	0.02	0.04	0.01
B. All deaths with correction for expected deaths[b]	0.00	0.00	0.01	0.02	0.05	0.02

Source: Derived from tables 10.2 and 10.3. Original data from Selikoff et al. (1983). Calculations by the authors.
Note: Dependent variable = (Product liability compensation plus legal defense costs) ÷ (Value-of-life losses associated with asbestos-related deaths).
a. I. J. Selikoff and Associates of Mt. Sinai Environmental Sciences Laboratory made the determination as to whether a death was asbestos related by examining medical records and sometimes by autopsy.
b. The statistical correction subtracts from the denominator losses associated with the expected cancer deaths based on population disease rates for the demographic group.

Finally, when we employ the second estimate of losses, the "value of a statistical life" (VL), to calculate the share of costs borne by manufacturers, the shares drop further. In table 10.5 the share borne by manufacturers of asbestos-associated losses from deaths in 1975–76 for which suits were filed is 12 percent, or 14 percent with the statistical correction. For all deaths in 1975–76, the shares are 4 and 5 percent, respectively.

Estimated Losses Borne by Employers

Compensating Wage Differentials Barth (1983) estimates compensating wage differentials for members of the AWU. Because of lack of data, he does not estimate the conventional wage determination model. His alternative methodology is to estimate divergences from pattern bargaining within the building trade unions across the last four decades. The analysis focuses on the relationship between asbestos insulators and bricklayers, a trade of comparable skill level but without the high exposures to asbestos of the insulators and related mechanical trades. Regression results suggest that the compensating wage differential reached a level of approximately 4.5 percent of insulators' wages by 1971, which was maintained through 1977. Assuming that in 1977 an asbestos worker's gross wage level was $10.44 and that he would work 2,000 hours per year for thirty more years, Barth reports that the present discounted value of the stream of wage differentials, discounted at 6 percent is $8,259. This amount appears very small for an occupational group in which approximately 44 percent of the deaths in the 1967–76 period are due to asbestos-related diseases.

We cannot attribute such a small effect to complete lack of knowledge about asbestos risks. The AWU members were the subjects of the watershed 1964 Selikoff study; in the late 1960s, the union was heavily involved in a joint effort with Johns-Manville and Selikoff at Mt. Sinai to develop safer products and work practices. Most workers would have been at least partially aware of the hazards of asbestos.

Rather, we speculate that the explanation is related to the labor market power of the AWU and the resulting lack of comparable opportunities for asbestos insulation workers. Experienced labor arbitrators for the construction trades suggest that the skill level required is comparable to that of laborers, though the installers' wages generally carry a 15 to 30 percent premium over the laborers.[3] The continuing supply of individuals applying and waiting ("on permit") for membership throughout the 1960s and 1970s is consistent with this interpretation.[4]

Table 10.6 Workers' compensation death payments to asbestos insulators, by date of workers' death

	1967–68	1969–70	1971–72	1973–74	1975–76	1967–76
Precent of survivors filing claims	24	35	40	37	41	36
Mean present discounted value of lifetime payments to survivors who filed (base year = 1982)[a]	$49,000	$54,000	$35,000	$36,000	$41,000	$42,000

Note: Numbers are rounded to nearest thousand. Sample of 995 AWU Members identified to have died of asbestos-related diseases, surveyed by Mt. Sinai Environmental Sciences Laboratory. See Selikoff (1983). Calculations by authors. Percent filing claims variable calculated for subsample ($N = 748$) with available information. Data were available to calculate value of claims variable for 200 of 247 claims filed and resolved by 1983. An additional 26 claims were filed but not resolved by that time or were of unknown status.

a. These numbers do not take into account the reduction in employed payments when workers compensation claims are indemnified by manufacturers paying liability damages for the same individual.

Table 10.7 Share of losses associated with asbestos-related deaths borne by employers (loss measure 1: lost wages and household services)

Samples of asbestos-related death cases[a]	Date of death of worker					
	1967–68	1969–70	1971–72	1973–74	1975–76	1967–76
1. A. Workers compensation claimants only	0.26	0.29	0.19	0.19	0.22	0.22
B. Claimants only, with correction for expected deaths[b]	0.32	0.35	0.23	0.24	0.27	0.28
2. A. All deaths	0.08	0.12	0.09	0.09	0.11	0.10
B. All deaths with correction for expected deaths[b]	0.10	0.15	0.11	0.11	0.14	0.12

Source: Derived from tables 10.2 and 10.5. Original data from Selikoff et al. (1983). Calculations by the authors.

Note: Dependent variable = (Workers compensation costs plus legal defense costs) ÷ (Earnings losses associated with asbestos-related deaths). Our measure of "earnings losses" accounts for the value of lost wages and household services associated with the deaths. Both the cost and the loss measures are reported as present discounted values of the streams as of 1982. These cost numbers do not take into account the reduction in employer payments when workers compensation claims are indemnified by manufacturers paying liability damages for the same individual.

a. I. J. Selikoff and Associates of Mt. Sinai Environmental Sciences Laboratory made the determination as to whether a death was asbestos related by examining medical records and sometimes by autopsy.

b. The statistical correction subtracts from the denominator losses associated with the expected cancer deaths based on population disease rates for the demographic group.

Table 10.8 Share of losses associated with asbestos-related deaths borne by employers (loss measure 2: "value-of-life" estimate of losses)

Samples of asbestos-related death cases[a]	Date of death of worker					
	1967–68	1969–70	1971–72	1973–74	1975–76	1967–76
1. A. Workers compensation claimants only	0.04	0.05	0.03	0.03	0.04	0.04
B. Claimants only, with correction for expected deaths[b]	0.05	0.06	0.04	0.04	0.05	0.05
2. A. All deaths	0.01	0.02	0.02	0.01	0.02	0.02
B. All deaths with correction for expected deaths[b]	0.02	0.03	0.02	0.02	0.02	0.02

Source: Derived from tables 10.2 and 10.5. Original data from Selikoff et al. (1983). Calculations by the authors.
Note: Dependent variable = (Workers compensation costs plus legal defense costs) ÷ (Value-of-life losses associated with asbestos-related deaths). These cost numbers do not take into account the reduction in employer payments when workers compensation claims are indemnified by manufacturers paying liability damages for the same individual.
a. I. J. Selikoff and Associates of Mt. Sinai Environmental Sciences Laboratory made the determination as to whether a death was asbestos related by examining medical records and sometimes by autopsy.
b. The statistical correction subtracts from the denominator losses associated with the expected cancer deaths based on population disease rates for the demographic group.

Workers' Compensation Claims Table 10.6 presents data on filing rates and claim values for workers' compensation. We can see that 36 percent of the survivors filed workers' compensation claims, whose mean present discounted value of payments was $42,000. No obvious time trend can be discerned in either the filing rate or in the payment levels.

Data from a group of 89 workers' compensation death claims filed by asbestos factory workers between 1979 and 1985 indicate that mean legal expenses were 14 percent of death benefit payments.[5] Based on this estimate, legal plus indemnity payments for workers' compensation claims in the asbestos insulators' group averaged $48,000.

Table 10.7 indicates that between 1967 and 1976 workers' compensation imposed 22 percent of EL on employers for asbestos-associated deaths for which claims were filed, or 28 percent with the statistical correction. For all asbestos deaths, however, the figures are 10 and 12 percent respectively. Furthermore these figures are overestimates: if a tort award or settlement occurred, the employer/insurer was usually eligible for indemnification for workers' compensation payments made for the individual involved.

The average share of social costs borne by employers, estimated by VL, was 5 percent for all claims filed for asbestos-associated deaths (row 1B, table 10.8 and 2 percent for all deaths (row 2B, table 10.8).

Two observations are noteworthy. First, the share of losses borne by employers is extremely low, even for asbestos deaths in which claims were filed. Second, the ratio of employers' payments to health costs apparently did not increase after 1964, even though after 1964 employers should bear at least partial responsibility for asbestos-related disease costs. (If a worker died in 1975 after thirty years of exposure, two-thirds of the exposures would have occurred prior to 1964, one-third after 1964.) These estimates of losses borne by employers do not include estimates of compensating wage differentials, although the preceding discussion suggests the omission would have a relatively small effect on the estimates.

Extrapolation to the Current Period

The rate at which liability suits are filed has continued to increase dramatically. It appears that AWU members have historically filed at a higher rate than other exposed occupation groups, and so it is not appropriate to apply the overall rate of increase directly to this sample. The value of claims also has continued to increase. Kakalik et al. (1984) estimate that the value rose 5 percent annually between 1980 and 1982.[6]

Let us assume that currently all workers who die of asbestos-related disease receive payments that are an overestimate of the true compensation rate, and that their suits are valued at the rate for workers who died in 1976, which is an underestimate of claim value. In this way manufacturers would bear 100 percent of the earnings loss statistically attributable to asbestos disease, (row 1B, table 10.4), or 14 percent of the full social costs, (row 1B, table 10.5).

We observe no time trend in the workers' compensation figures. Consequently our best estimate of current performance of the workers' compensation system is that employers are bearing less than 12 percent of the earnings loss of the deaths statistically attributable to asbestos and less than 2 percent of the full economic losses, based on our VL measure. As noted earlier, we do not have a comparable estimate of costs imposed through compensating wage differentials, but the Barth analysis suggests that the effect is small.

Before generalizing from these numbers, it is important to note that this group is likely to have an unusually high propensity to file claims relative to other occupational disease victims. The relationship between occupational asbestos exposure and disease in asbestos insulation workers is widely recognized to be very strong. Furthermore asbestos insulation workers are probably the best informed group of workers regarding asbestos disease. Consequently we expect that the product liability and workers' compensation systems generally perform less effectively for other occupational groups.

Level of Incentives Imposed by the Labor Market and Liability Systems

Product liability claim costs borne by manufacturers and their insurers dramatically increased during the 1970s, after the strict liability principle was established. For asbestos insulators' deaths in 1975–76, total compensation and legal defense costs borne by manufacturers represented 32 percent of the estimated earnings losses and 5 percent of economic losses, based on our VL measure.

The experience of the Manville Corporation suggests that the filing rate has continued to increase into the 1980s: In 1982 Manville stopped the accumulation of suits by filing for protection under the Chapter 11 of the bankruptcy code, because new suits had doubled every year since 1975.[7] Even if the filing rate were 100 percent among all individuals Selikoff identified to have died from asbestos-related disease, manufacturers would be paying 100 percent of estimated earnings losses, or 14 percent of social costs, measured by VL multiplied by the correction for expected deaths.

The Barth study (1983) suggests that by 1971, asbestos insulators were earning only a 4.5 percent compensating wage differential, which subsequently remained flat through 1977. For the early years of the sample we attributed the lack of differential to limited information; for the later years of the analysis the explanation may be that the workers were receiving such substantial rents in the occupation that much of the compensating differential was absorbed by the rents. It is important to emphasize that these results are only suggestive: the data are not available to estimate a more complete wage determination model that would control for changing factors in the market.

Employers have been paying workers' compensation claims for asbestos-related disease in substantial numbers since the 1960's, though the filing rate for claims leveled off for deaths occurring after 1969. Surprisingly the share of costs borne by employers is low even for deaths in the latter part of the asbestos insulators death cohort, when employers should have been at least partially informed about asbestos hazards. The value per insulator claim did not increase for deaths occurring between 1967 and 1976. In our sample, total workers' compensation and legal defense costs represent 12 percent of the estimated earnings losses, and 2 percent of the estimated social costs associated with excess mortality from asbestos-related disease. Excluding the estimated compensating wage differentials in the calculation of total payments by employers underestimates employers costs in the later years. On the other hand, including payments subsequently indemnified by manufacturers paying product liability damages to the same individual overestimates the costs borne by employers.

Conclusions

Currently the workers' compensation and product liability systems provide inadequate incentives for the control of occupational disease. Our results, however, suggest that product liability compensation in the asbestos case may provide substantial incentives for manufacturers to warn of future hazards. The filing rate has increased, and the aggregate level of payments has approached the level of earnings losses incurred by the families of individuals who died of asbestos-related disease, but manufacturers are not bearing full social costs.

Our data clearly reveal that workers' compensation provides extremely low incentives for control of asbestos hazards. It is often assumed that strategies for improving worker information would lead to substantial compensating wage differentials for workers with high occupational disease risks. Barth's (1983) estimates of compensating wage differentials for asbestos insulators, a well-informed occupational group, are not encouraging; we speculate the explanation is a lack of comparable job opportunities for the insulators. Our results suggest that workers' compensation and compensating wage differentials should be supplemented with additional interventions to reduce the social costs of asbestos-related disease to the efficient level.

In addition to low payments of manufacturers and employers relative to losses, several other factors limit the deterrence role of product liability and workers' compensation: moral hazard as a result of insurance coverage, limited assets and bankruptcy protection, and the impact of disease latency on managerial incentives (Shavell 1984; Eads and Reuter 1983).

Many firms purchase workers' compensation and general liability insurance policies. Because insurance spreads the losses from occupational diseases, it may lower the incentives of manufacturers, employers, and workers to reduce risks.

Another factor that may limit the impact of the liability system on incentives is the level of assets of the manufacturer. If the manufacturer's ability to pay is less than the potential liability, then incentives to inform workers of hazards will be reduced. Three asbestos manufacturers, Manville, Amatex, and UNARCO, have already filed for protection under Chapter 11 and others may follow.

Finally, we confront a fundamental assumption in our analysis of post-damage compensation schemes: managers today take into account compensation costs to be incurred in ten to thirty years. Uncertainty about future liability is not in itself a bar to assessing this liability. However, providing appropriate incentives and determining managerial responsibility may pose substantial problems. If it is impossible to predict future liability accurately, then basing managerial incentives on such outcomes will inappropriately cause these managers to bear responsibility for uncontrollable events. Indeed, Eads and Reuter found that no firms in their sample held individual managers responsible for design decisions later found faulty.

Even if firms were to hold managers responsible for decisions that increased liability for health risk, long delays between exposure and effect would severely limit the impact of such a policy. It may be very difficult to reconstruct decisions that were made ten or more years in the past. Furthermore the manager responsible for the decisions may well be employed by another firm or retired when liability costs begin to appear. In such a case it would be impossible to apply sanctions.

Notes

1. See U.S. Congress, Education and Labor Committee (1978); and U.S. Congress, Committee on the Judiciary (1980).

2. Information on dates of filing or resolution is not available. We expect that filing would generally occur within two years after death. Payment is assumed to occur five years after death.

3. The union may have been more successful in expressing its interests in safer workplaces through its work with Selikoff and Johns-Manville (Hirschman's "voice" mechanism) than through the labor price mechanism ("exit").

4. Personal communication with Jack Keene of the Asbestos Workers Union, January 1986.

5. Personal communication to the authors.

6. The average compensation per claim in the Kakalik et al. (1984) sample was $60,000. This amount is lower than what we observe for the asbestos insulators, substantially due to differences in the claim populations. Recalculating Kakalik's numbers for the disease mix observed in the AWU sample and discounting has data in the same manner as ours, the average compensation is $79,000, which is close to the $89,000 from the sample we analyze.

7. Johns-Manville 10-K Reports to the SEC, 1970–1984.

References

Arnould, R. J., and Nichols, L. M. 1983. "Wage-Risk Premiums and Workers' Compensation: A Refinement of Estimates of Compensating Wage Differentials." *Journal of Political Economy 91*:332–340.

Arrow, K. J. 1963. "Uncertainty and the Welfare Economics of Medical Care." *American Economic Review 53*:941–973.

Baram, M. S. 1984. "The Right to Know and the Duty to Disclose Hazard Information." *American Journal of Public Health 74*:385–388.

Barth, P. S., and Hunt, H. A. 1980. *Workers' Compensation and Work-Related Illnesses.* Cambridge: MIT Press.

Barth, P. S. 1983. "Economic Analysis of Asbestos-Associated Disease." In Irving J. Selikoff, eds., *Disability Compensation for Asbestos-Associated Disease in the United States.* New York: Mount Sinai School of Medicine. Beshada v. *Johns-Manville Products Corp.* 1982. 90 NJ 191, 447 A.2d 539.

Boden, L. I., and Jones, C. A. 1985. "Filing for Compensation of Asbestos-Related Disease." Unpublished manuscript. Boston University School of Public Health.

Bouhuys, A., Schoenberg, J. B., Beck, G. J., Schilling, R. S. F. 1977. "Epidemiology of Chronic Lung Disease in a Cotton Mill Community." *Lung 54*:167–186.

Bridbord, K., Decoufle, P., Fraumeni, J. F., Hoel, D. G., Hoover, R. N., Rall, D. P., Saffiotti, U., Schneiderman, M. A., Upton, A. C. 1978. "Estimates of the Fraction of Cancer in the United States Related to Occupational Factors." Report of the U.S. Dept. of Health, Education, and Welfare. Washington, D.C.

Brown, J. P. 1973. "Toward an Economic theory of Liability." *Journal of Legal Studies 2*:323–350.

Burns, J. P., Cassady, G. E., Cole, K. B., Dodson, T. R., Holladay, P. E., Ney, P. C., Parobek, D. T., Payne, K., Sanders, D. B., Simmons, L. D. 1983. "Special Project—An Analysis of the Legal, Social, and Political Issues Raised by Asbestos Litigation." *Vanderbilt Law Review 36*:573–846.

Doll, R., and Peto, R. 1981. "The Causes of Cancer." *Journal of the National Cancer Institute 66*:1191–1308.

Eads, G., and Reuter, P. 1983. "Designing Safer Products." Santa Monica: The Rand Corporation.

Enterline, P. E. 1981. "Proportion of Cancer Due to Exposure to Asbestos." Paper presented to Conference on Quantification of Occupational Cancer, Cold Spring Harbor Laboratory.

Epstein, R. A. 1984. "The Legal and Insurance Dynamics of Mass Tort Litigation." *Journal of Legal Studies 13*:475–506.

Green, J. 1976. "On the Optimal Structure of Liability Rules." *Bell Journal of Economics*, 553–574.

Gould, J. P. 1973. "The Economics of Legal Conflicts." *Journal of Legal Studies 2*:279–300.

Hammond, E. C., Selikoff, I. J., and Seidman, H. 1979. "Asbestos Exposure, Cigarette Smoking, and Death Rates." *Annals of the New York Academy of Sciences 330*:473–490.

Hogan, M. D., and Hoel, D. G. 1981. "Estimated Risk Associated with Occupational Asbestos Exposure." *Risk Analysis 1*:67–76.

Johns-Manville 10-K Reports to the SEC, 1970–1984.

Johnson, W. G., and Heler, E. 1983. "The Costs of Asbestos-Associated Disease and Death." *Milbank Memorial Fund Quarterly* 61:177–194.

Kakalik J. S., et al. 1984. "Costs of Asbestos Litigation." Rand Corporation, R-304200ICJ.

Landes, W. A., and Posner, R. A. 1984. "Tort Law as a Regulatory Regime for Catastrophic Personal Injuries." *Journal of Legal Studies* 13:417–434.

Landes, W. A., and Posner, R. A. 1980. "Joint and Multiple Tortfeasors: An Economic Analysis." *Journal of Legal Studies* 9:517–576.

Larson, A. 1984. *Workmen's Compensation for Occupational Injury and Death.* New York: Matthew Bender.

Olson, C. A. 1981. "An Analysis of Wage Differentials Received by Workers on Dangerous Jobs." *Journal of Human Resources* 16:167–185.

Pauly, M. 1968. "The Economics of Moral Hazard: Comment." *American Economic Review* 58:531–537.

Polinsky, A. M. 1980. "Strict Liability vs. Negligence in a Market Setting." *American Economic Review* 70:363–367.

Schwartz, A. 1986. "Products Liability, Corporate Structure and Bankruptcy: Toxic Substances and the Remote Risk Relationship." *Journal of Law and Economics*, forthcoming.

Selikoff, I. J., Churg, J., and Hammond, E. C. 1964. "Asbestos Exposure and Neoplasia." *Journal of American Medical Association* 188:22.

Selikoff, I. J., Hammond, E. C., and Churg, J. 1968. "Asbestos Exposure, Smoking, and Neoplasia." *Journal of American Medical Association* 204:106–112.

Selikoff, I. J. 1983. *Disability Compensation for Asbestos-Associated Disease in the United States.* New York: Mt. Sinai School of Medicine.

Shavell, S. 1979. "Risk Sharing and Incentives in the Principal and Agent Relationship." *Bell Journal of Economics* 55:55–73.

Shavell, S. 1980. "Strict Liability vs. Negligence." *Journal of Legal Studies* 9:1–25.

Shavell, S. 1983. "A Model of the Optimal Use of Liability and Regulation." *Rand Journal of Economics* 15:271–280.

Shavell, S. 1984. "Liability for Harm vs. Regulation of Safety." *Journal of Legal Studies* 13:357–374.

Shavell, S. 1985. "Uncertainty over Causation and the Determination of Civil Liability." *Journal of Law and Economics* 28:587–609.

Shavell, S. 1980. "Strict Liability vs. Negligence." *Journal of Legal Studies* 9:1–25.

Sindell v. *Abbott Laboratories.* 1980. 20 CAL3d 588, 607 P.2d 924.

Smith, R. S. 1976. *The Occupational Safety and Health Act*, Washington D.C.: American Enterprise Institute for Public Policy Research.

Smith R. S. 1979. "Compensating Wage Differentials and Public Policy: A Review." *Industrial and Labor Relations Review* 32:339–352.

Spence, M. 1977. "Consumer Misperceptions, Product Failure and Producer Liability." *Review of Economic Studies*, 561–572.

Thaler, R., and Rosen, S. 1975. "Labor Market Valuations of Life and Limb." In N. E. Terleckyj, ed., *Household Production and Consumptions.* New York: Columbia University Press.

U.S. Congress, House of Representatives, Committee on Education and Labor. 1978. "Asbestos-Related Occupational Diseases." Hearings before a subcommittee of the House of Committee of Education and Labor. 95th Cong., 2nd session.

U.S. Congress, House of Representatives, Committee on the Judiciary. 1980. "Corporate Criminal Liability." Hearings before a subcommittee of the House Committee on the Judiciary on H.R. 4973. 96th Cong., 1st and 2nd sessions.

U.S. Department of Labor. 1980. *An Interim Report to Congress on Occupational Diseases.* Washington, D.C.

Violette, D. M., and Chestnut, L. 1983. "Valuing Reductions in Risks: A Review of the Empirical Estimates." Report prepared for U.S. Environmental Protection Agency. Energy and Resource Consultants, Inc. Boulder, Colo.

Viscusi, W. K. 1980. "Imperfect Job Risk Information and Optimal Workers' Compensation Benefits." *Journal of Public Economics 14*: 319–337.

Viscusi, W. K. 1983. *Employment Hazards: An Investigation of Market Performance.* Cambridge: Harvard University Press.

Walker, A. M. 1982. "Projections of Asbestos-Related Disease," 1980–2009." Epidemiology Resources Inc. Chestnut Hill, Mass.

11

Industrywide Regulation and the Formation of Reputations: A Laboratory Analysis

Andrew F. Daughety and Robert Forsythe

When industries are deregulated, it is generally presumed that technology and demand will determine the new equilibrium; what is past is (at most) prologue. In this chapter we examine how industrywide regulation provides incentives for regulated firms to develop reputations for cooperation that persist into a deregulated environment.

Industrywide regulation, wherein prices are set with regard to an industrywide aggregate performance measure, has been (and still is) widely used. Examples include trucking, the airlines, natural gas production, insurance, portions of the dairy industry, World War II industry price controls, taxicabs, and (in the near future) hospital cost reimbursement by Medicare. These examples have the common characteristic of being industries composed of a number of firms of different sizes yet subject as a group to regulatory control via an aggregate performance measure, such as the ratio of total industry costs over total industry revenues. Industrywide regulation has typically evolved in the past when the decision to regulate an industry recognized the cost of case-by-case review and opted instead to have the industry, as a whole, meet a regulatory criterion. This form of regulation provides strong incentives for firms to engage in noncompetitive behavior, resulting in high prices and an inefficient distribution of firms in the industry affected (see Daughety 1984). Most of the industries that have been the subject of recent regulatory change were previously regulated in this manner. Moreover the apparent administrative advantage of using such a procedure when regulating a collection of firms augurs its use in the future.

An important attribute of many regulated, multifirm industries has been the general ability of firms to communicate, cooperate, and coordinate. Indeed, this form of regulation presupposes some form of coordination of firms' decisions. Often this has been institutionalized through organized interest groups. For example, rate bureaus for railroads, trucks, and (in many states) insurance companies have provided a means by which firms could act in unison to provide price proposals to regulators. The Reed-Bulwinkle Act of 1948 specifically recognized such entities and provided for exemption from antitrust statutes on the theory that the firms involved were already subject to government scrutiny.

This aspect of industrywide regulation has significant implications for the regulated equilibria achieved and for the equilibria that occur after a regulatory reduction or a deregulation. We focus on these issues in this chapter. Specifically, we have conducted experiments involving homogeneous product duopolies, wherein each subject knows the industry demand function and its own cost function and is rewarded with the profits made from choosing an output level. In a previous study (Daughety and Forsythe 1985a) experiments involved sellers making independent production decisions for a number of periods in an unregulated environment, followed by a sequence of periods wherein the two sellers' decisions were subject to industrywide regulation. In that set of experiments two results emerged. First, sellers almost never engaged in cooperative behavior in the unregulated phase (to be precise, the collusive outcome occurred in only one out of thirty-two experiments). Second, although sellers typically did not converge to a readily characterized equilibrium in the unregulated phase, convergence was swift under regulation and almost always to a constrained Cournot or Stackelberg solution. Moreover many of the regulated equilibria reflected cooperation and coordination, such as alternating between Stackelberg solutions. It should be further noted that no communication was permitted in the unregulated phase, but communication was permitted (and coordination required) in the regulated phase.

In this chapter we describe a second set of experiments involving regulated and deregulated duopolies and entry (triopolies). First, we reverse the order of the previous duopoly experiments: subjects encounter a sequence of market periods under regulation where communication is permitted and then face a sequence of unregulated periods in which communication is prohibited. We find that in many of the experiments a new phenomenon has emerged: the general attributes of the cooperative strategies that subjects employ during regulation carry over into the "deregulated" phase, even though the subjects can no longer discuss or coordinate actions. Moreover the cooperative solutions played tend to maximize joint profits and resemble an extended version of the "tit-for-tat" structure analyzed in the Prisoner's Dilemma (see Axelrod 1984 and Kreps, Milgrom, Roberts, and Wilson 1982 for a discussion of this strategy in the infinite and finite repeated Prisoner's Dilemma game, respectively). The emergence of this equilibrium in the unregulated phase is somewhat surprising since, in some of the experiments where such equilibria occur, no announcement of the deregulation was made ahead of time, and thus there was no opportunity for firms to plan for the unregulated environment while they are still able to communicate. Furthermore the outputs and profits that the cooperative strategies achieve are significantly different from those available under regulation (they involve output pairs that were infeasible under regulation).

To analyze this reputation effect further, we have examined environments where there are (1) a deregulation announcement during the regulated phase, (2) entry during the deregulated phase, and (3) limited knowledge of the nature of the entrant by the incumbents. Our basic finding is that industrywide regulation not only provides firms with the ability and incentives to cooperate (thereby providing quick convergence and price stability when compared with the preregulated activity) but also encourages the development of reputations for cooperation—something that can be costly to try to develop in a competitive environment—and that these reputations persist into the deregulated environment.

Free entry after deregulation should reduce the value of a reputation for cooperation since cooperative equilibria are (presumably) harder to achieve. Surprisingly entry appears to have only a very moderate effect: equilibria involving collusion or Stackelberg leadership occur, and the unregulated triopoly industry output is indistinguishable from the unregulated duopoly industry output for firms never regulated (the unregulated portion of the experiments reported in Daughety and Forsythe 1985a).

One would also expect announcements of impending regulatory change to affect the formation of reputations. This of course cuts both ways. Announcement of an impending deregulation should encourage joint planning for the future and provide incentives to demonstrate cooperative play while still regulated. Alternatively, an announcement that deregulation will be accompanied by free entry may encourage noncooperative behavior in anticipation that cooperative behavior is unlikely to be individually rational. We find that subjects use the remaining regulated periods after the announcement to plan their future actions, taking particular advantage of periods of deregulated activity before entry to act collusively but also planning strategies to respond to the announced entry.

There are two methodological issues that can be raised. First, why study duopolies and triopolies? After all, most of the previously mentioned industry examples, which were subject to industrywide regulation, are composed of many firms. Although this is true in aggregate, the individual markets in which these firms compete usually involve only a few firms (e.g., airlines; see Bailey, Graham, and Kaplan 1984, table 4.3). Thus the duopoly and triopoly cases are quite relevant.

Second, in what sense are we studying regulation when we conduct laboratory markets? In other words, what is the role of laboratory techniques (see Plott 1982; Smith 1982) in the analysis of regulation and regulatory change? To begin, we wish to emphasize that it is *not* the purpose of such techniques to "simulate" a regulatory regime; we did not ask subjects to "behave as if" they were members of a regulated industry. Rather, we specifically designed the laboratory markets to test a basic attribute of a regulatory process: the requirement for decision-making entities to meet some aggregate performance criterion.

It is worth contrasting such a methodology with a more standard technique such as econometric analysis of industry data. The latter procedure aims to provide *external validity* to the analysis by using the "right variables" in the "right model" so as to describe the industry in question (which is itself a naturally occurring experiment). What is necessarily incomplete in such models, however, is a notion of *internal validity*: surrogates for the "right variables" are used, aggregation of decisions (outputs, inputs, etc.) occurs, and approximations are employed. Experimental techniques place us at the other end of the spectrum. Properly employed, they provide analyses with high internal validity by taking the essential attributes of a theoretical model and implementing them in a controlled laboratory setting. Put another way, both experimental and econometric procedures involve data. The former provides substantial control over the error term in an analysis of a stripped-down version of a theory. Under these conditions there is a strong linkage between theory and the data generated. In the case of econometric estimation greater external validity of the analysis is achieved at the cost of weaker linkage to theory.

The Laboratory Markets

Each laboratory market was conducted for twenty-five to thirty market periods. During the first ten market periods (phase I), each industry was conducted as a regulated duopoly. Beginning in period 11, phase II began and the industry was deregulated. In markets without entry the sellers in this unregulated duopoly continued to make individual production decisions for fifteen additional periods. In markets were entry took place the unregulated duopoly continued for five periods before the third seller entered the industry, and after entry (phase III) the sellers in this unregulated triopoly continued to make production decisions for fifteen additional periods. This design was chosen to examine the effects of deregulation and any subsequent effect of entry on incumbent seller's behavior.

As in most previous studies of duopoly and triopoly behavior,[1] the markets we conducted employed a completely passive demand side during all market periods. To operationalize this passive demand, sellers were told their industry's demand curve, and after they had made their production decisions, they received the price that cleared the market given their industry's total output.

The experimental procedures were those that have become standard in the literature. Subjects in the same industry were seated in different rooms and given instruction sets for the regulated phase of the experiment. The experimenter read the instructions aloud and answered questions. The instruction sets (reproduced in appendix B) included a market demand schedule, the subject's own cost schedule, and a profits table. Each subject was given no information about the cost schedule of the other seller in the industry. The profits table gave the subject's own profit as a function of all sellers' individual production decisions. Although this could be calculated directly by each subject from the market demand and cost schedules, this table was provided to reduce the computational burden.

During phase I of each market the regulatory constraint used was modeled after the operating ratio constraint.[2] With this constraint sellers in each industry had to reach an agreement on how to share the market; feasible market-sharing agreements were limited to those where the total industry cost had to be at least some prespecified fraction (which we denote as α) of total industry revenues. To assist subjects, profits corresponding to regulatory infeasible output levels were printed in red on their profit tables.

Each market period in phase I was divided into two parts. In the first part of a market period, subjects were given ten minutes to reach a regulatory feasible agreement, that is, a pair of outputs that would result in the ratio of total costs over total revenue being greater than the prespecified fraction α (the operating ratio restriction). To accomplish this, subjects were permitted to communicate via written messages. They were not permitted to offer bribes or communicate any quantitative information from these cost schedules or profit tables. Other than that, they were allowed to communicate freely about all aspects of the market. When a subject wanted to send a message, he/she gave it to an assistant, who recorded the time it was sent and delivered it to the other subject in the same industry. If an agreement was not reached within the allotted time, the subjects were given a price ceiling of 0 when entering the second part of the market year. If a feasible agreement was made, the subjects were given a price ceiling equal to the market-clearing price corresponding to the industry's output agreement.

During the second part of a market period in phase I, sellers could no longer communicate and were required to make their actual production decisions. The market price they received for their output was the minimum of the price ceiling and the market-clearing price corresponding to the industry's actual production. Subjects earned zero profits at any time that their actual production levels did not satisfy the operating ratio restriction.[3]

In all experiments in which deregulation was announced, the announcement was read to sellers prior to the beginning of period 6, informing them that deregulation would take place in period 11. In experiments where entry took place, this announcement also informed incumbents that an entrant would appear in period 16. In those environments in which the entrant's type was unknown to incumbents, they were told in this announcement that there was an equally likely chance that the entrant would be of the same type (i.e., have the same cost schedule) as either seller 1 or seller 2. In environments where the type of the entrant was known by incumbents, they were told in the announcement which type the entrant would be (i.e., which incumbent had the same cost schedule as the entrant). Finally, this announcement was also read to entrants during their instructional period; incumbents knew that the entrants would receive this announcement, entrants knew that incumbents knew, and so forth, in order to make this announcement common knowledge to all industry participants.

When phase II of the experiment was implemented, the subjects were given new instruction sets (see appendix B). Their new profits tables contained the same numerical entries as the old ones but there was no longer a region printed in red (since there no longer were regulatory infeasible outputs). During each market year in phases II and III sellers wrote down their individual production decisions and handed them to an assistant. The production decisions for the sellers in each industry were totaled (by industry), and the market-clearing price for each industry was determined. The assistants then recorded this price on each seller's profit sheet. At the end of the experiment each subject's profit calculations were checked, and each was paid individually and out of sight of all other subjects.

Finally, in experiments without (with) entry, subjects were not told when phase II (phase III) would end. They were told only that they would continue to make unregulated decisions "for a large number of periods." In experiments with entry, entrants were told that the incumbents had been regulated during the first ten periods and had also participated in five unregulated periods. Entrants were told the individual production decisions made by the incumbents during these five periods (periods 11 to 15). After entry occurred, all sellers were told the individual production decision of each seller in the industry.

The subjects in the experiments were male and female students at the University of Iowa. None of them (other than the entrants) had ever participated in any previous oligopoly experiments. Subjects in the same industry never had any visual or verbal contact with each other throughout the experiment. Since several experiments were often run simultaneously, subjects in different experiments (industries) shared the same room. In experiments with entry, entrants were taken from the pool that had previously participated in the regulated duopoly experiments reported in Daughety and Forsythe (1985a). Through this previous experience entrants were familiar with the general attributes of the environment that the incumbents had been participating in during the first fifteen market periods.

The currency use in the experiments was called "francs." To obtain substantial differences in the level of each seller's profits for each of the theoretical predictions considered here, the cost of using dollars directly would have been prohibitive. The use of francs overcomes this difficulty. Value for francs was established by application of induced value theory (Smith 1976; Plott 1979). This artificial currency has been used in market experiments in Friedman (1967) and Forsythe, Palfrey, and Plott (1982). Thus payoffs for a given experiment are of the form bz, where b is the exchange rate of francs into dollars and z is the total francs earned by a subject during the experiment.

The parameter sets and environments that we studied are given in table 11.1. We use the following mnemonic. The first letter in the experiment number identifies the functional form of the cost function in that experiment. These are

L = both firms' cost functions were linear,
Q = both firms' cost functions were quadratic.

The second letter in the experiment number indicates whether or not deregulation (phase II) was announced. An N indicates that sellers were not told during the regulation phase (phase I) that, beginning in period 11, deregulation would occur. An A indicates that an announcement was made to all sellers prior to the beginning of period 6 that their industry would no longer be regulated after period 10.

The third letter in the experiment number indicates whether or not there was entry after deregulation and, if there was, whether or not incumbents knew the type of the entering seller. N indicates that no entry occurred, a U indicates that entry occurred but the type of the entering seller was unknown to the incumbent sellers, and a K indicates that the type of the

Table 11.1 Experimental parameters

Experiment number	Number of periods in			Market demand	Seller type	Cost function	Exchange rate	Regulatory parameters
	Phase I	Phase II	Phase III					
LNN-1-8	10	15	0	$p = 33 - X$	1	$3x_1 + 4$	0.02	
LAN-1-8	10	15	0					
LAU1-1-4	10	5	15					0.65
LAU2-1-4	10	5	15		2	$x_2 + 40$	0.02	
LAK1-1-4	10	5	15					
LAK2-1-4	10	5	15					
QNN-1-4	10	15	0	$p = 950 - 25X$	1	$10x_1^2 + 30x_1 + 40$	0.0005	0.90
					2	$10x_2^2 + 30x_2 + 40$	0.0005	

entering seller was known by all subjects. In experiments with entry there is a fourth character (number) which identifies the entrants' type. Finally, the number to the right of the hyphen gives the number of the experiment that was run under the corresponding environment.

The regulatory parameter for the industry (α) is also given in table 11.1 for each experiment. Based on this parameter, the operating ratio restriction required that output be chosen so that the sum of both sellers' total costs was no less than α of the sum of both sellers' total revenue. The basis for the choice of α was to (1) enforce integrality of equilibria, (2) provide, to the greatest degree possible, separation of equilibrium predictions, and (3) ensure the existence of output vectors other than the predicted equilibria, where both sellers could earn positive profits. The rates at which subjects could convert francs into dollars is also given table 11.1. Although these exchange rates may seem small at first, they were sufficiently high to make dollar payoffs and the value of each decision comparable to other experiments that have been successfully completed. For example, the average amount earned by the incumbents was about $30 for three hours of participation, whereas entrants earned approximately $12 on average for one hour of their time.

Duopoly and Triopoly Equilibrium Models

The experiments we conducted involve two different environments—regulation and postregulation—and two industry "sizes": a duopoly and a triopoly. Here we briefly describe the equilibrium concepts to be used to predict behavior of unregulated duopolies and triopolies and regulated duopolies.

Unregulated Oligopoly Equilibria

Consider an n firm industry with firm i ($i = 1, \ldots, n$) producing output x_i of a homogeneous product. Industry demand is represented by the (downward sloping) inverse demand function $p(\cdot)$, which depends only on aggregate output $X = \sum_i x_i$. Firm i faces a cost function denoted as $c_i(\cdot)$ which is monotonically nondecreasing. Thus profits for firm i, denoted $\pi^i(\mathbf{x})$, where $\mathbf{x} \in R_+^n$, are $\pi^i(\mathbf{x}) = p(X)x_i - c_i(x_i)$ for $i = 1, \ldots, n$. In what follows let $\mathbf{x}_{)i(}$ be the $(n-1)$ vector derived from $\mathbf{x}$ by deleting the ith element (i.e., x_i).

Various industry structures are of course possible. To capture the main possibilities of interest, we will consider three models: Cournot, Stackelberg, and collusive (e.g., see Friedman 1977 for a review of these equilibrium concepts).[4] Our goal is to provide point predictions of equilibria that can be used to examine and interpret the experiments.

Cournot Equilibrium In the Cournot model firm i chooses x_i, given $\mathbf{x}_{)i(}$, so as to maximize its profits, $\pi^i(\mathbf{x})$. Under suitable conditions on π^i (e.g., strict concavity of π^i in x_i) we can express this optimal response to $\mathbf{x}_{)i(}$ as a reaction function (or best response function) ϕ_i, that is, $x_i = \phi_i(\mathbf{x}_{)i(})$. A Cournot equilibrium (C) is a vector $\mathbf{x}^C \in R_+^n$ such that $x_i^C = \phi_i(\mathbf{x}_{)i(}^C)$, $i = 1, \ldots, n$.

Stackelberg Equilibrium A Stackelberg equilibrium involves one (or more) firms—called leader(s)—choosing best responses to the *reaction functions* of those firms—called followers—choosing best responses to output. If firm i is the leader[5], it solves the following problem:

$$\max_{x_i} \pi^i(\mathbf{x}) \tag{1}$$
$$\text{s.t.} \quad x_j = \phi_j(\mathbf{x}_{)j(}), \quad j = 1, \ldots, n, j \neq i.$$

Note that the only "free" variable is x_i. Once it is chosen, the rest of the variables are determined via the constraints in (1). Thus a single leader Stackelberg equilibrium, with firm i as leader (Si) is a vector $\mathbf{x}^{Si} \in R_+^n$ such that $x_j^{Si} = \phi_j(\mathbf{x}_{)j(}^{Si})$, for $j \neq i$, and i's profits are maximized.

As an example of Cournot and Stackelberg equilibria, let us consider the cost and demand functions for the duopolies in phase II of experiments LNN-1-8. The Cournot equilibria occur at $\mathbf{x} = (9, 11), (10, 11)$, and $(9, 12)$; the nonuniqueness is due to the integrality requirements of the experiment. The Stackelberg equilibrium with seller 1 as leader (S1) is $\mathbf{x} = (15, 8)$, while $S2$ is at $(6, 17)$.

Collusive Equilibrium The collusive outcome is the third concept we will consider. Since there are no procedures for creating binding contracts in the experiments, the collusive outcome must come about from noncooperative play on the part of the subjects. Moreover, as is clear from the discussion in the previous section, side payments are prohibited in the markets we examined, and thus not all collusive solutions (e.g., for one seller to produce its monopoly output during all periods while the other seller always produces zero) are sensible. A third difficulty arises from the presence of sellers with asymmetric cost functions, as is true in the experiments using the linear parameter sets (see table 11.1). The traditional definition of the collusive solution as the vector of equal outputs that maximizes joint profits (thereby providing each firm half the monopoly profits) is not applicable here since the sellers are not identical.

We resolve these difficulties in the following manner. First, consider the use of "alternating strategies" in a repeated game setting. An example of an alternating strategy is one wherein each firm produces its monopoly output for one period and produces zero for $n - 1$ periods, with outputs sequenced so that no two firms produce in the same period. Thus for the duopoly case a pair of alternating strategies involving monopoly outputs for the linear parameter sets for phase II is $(15, 0)$ for seller 1 and $(0, 16)$ for seller 2, meaning seller 1 produces 15 units of output in one period, while seller 2 produces zero, and then produces zero in the other period while seller 2 produces 16.

Let us use the alternating monopoly strategy to define the set of collusive outcomes.[6] Let $\bar{\pi}^i$ be the average per period profit for firm i if it is engaged in playing a T-period alternating monopoly strategy. Thus, for example, $\bar{\pi}^1 = 108.5$ and $\bar{\pi}^2 = 88$ for the duopoly case considered earlier. Then the T vectors $\mathbf{x}^1, \ldots, \mathbf{x}^T$ provide a T-period collusive solution, if they solve the following problem:

$$\max_{\mathbf{x}^1, \ldots, \mathbf{x}^T} \sum_{t=1}^{T} \sum_{i=1}^{n} \pi^i(\mathbf{x}^t)$$

$$\text{s.t.} \quad \frac{1}{T} \sum_{t=1}^{T} \pi^i(\mathbf{x}^t) \geq \bar{\pi}^i, \quad i = 1, \ldots, n. \tag{2}$$

In other words, the T vectors maximize joint profits over the T periods and ensure for each firm the average profit of the reference collusive strategy (the alternating monopoly strategy). It is clear from the formulation of (2) that all the T-period collusive solutions are undominated.

In the case of the linear parameter sets, the 2-period collusive solution for the duopoly is to alternate between $(15, 0)$ and $(0, 16)$; the alternating monopoly strategies provide the only collusive solution (there is no 1-period collusive solution). In the triopoly experiment the result depends on the nature of the third seller. When the third firm is a type 1 seller (experiments LAU1-1-4 and LAK1-1-4), there are forty-eight 3-period collusive solutions. When the third firm is a type 2 seller (experiments LAU2-1-4 and LAK2-1-4), there are fifty-one 3-period collusive solutions.

In the case of the quadratic parameter set the alternating monopoly strategies of $(13, 0), (0, 13)$ are dominated by another pair of alternating strategies, namely $(8, 7)$ and $(7, 8)$. This is because of the strict convexity of the cost function. It is also interesting to observe that this latter pair of strategies dominates the 1-period traditional collusive solution of (8, 8).

Regulated Duopoly Equilibria

We now provide predictions for Cournot, Stackelberg, and collusive equilibria for a two-firm industry subject to industrywide regulation. As discussed in the previous section, regulation was imposed on the industries we examined via the operating ratio (OR) constraint, which requires that total industry cost be at least some prespecified fraction, α, of total industry revenues. This constraint will be written as

$$F(x_1, x_2, \alpha) = c_1(x_1) + c_2(x_2) - \alpha p(x_1 + x_2) \cdot (x_1 + x_2) \geq 0.$$

The constraint must be met by the industry when it makes a proposal to the regulator. For the parameter sets that we will consider in this chapter, the OR constraint acts to restrict both feasible outputs and prices (this need not be true; see Daughety and Forsythe 1985a).

A simple summary of the regulatory scenario used in the phase I portion of the experiments is the following:

1. The firms come to an agreement as to how to share the market ($\mathbf{x} \in R_+^2$) and what price to propose ($\bar{p} = p(x_1 + x_2)$), subject to the regulatory constraint. The firms now provide the regulator with the proposal $(\mathbf{x}, \bar{p})$.

2. The regulated price acts as a price ceiling; all firms use the ceiling price to guide their output decisions.

In the Cournot model each firm knows industry demand and its own cost function. During the agreement phase firms propose output levels to produce. Since they know that the regulatory restriction must be met, they each pick their output level so as to maximize their profit, subject to the regulatory constraint and given the level of output the other firm is choosing. Thus a regulated Cournot model (RC) is as follows:

$$\underset{x_i}{\text{Max}}\, p(X)x_i - c_i(x_i) \tag{3}$$

s.t. $F(x_1, x_2, \alpha) \geq 0.$

Figure 11.1 illustrates the regulated Cournot equilibria for the linear parameter sets. In the figure line AD is the unregulated Cournot reaction function for firm 1, and line CF is the unregulated Cournot reaction function for firm 2. Curve BE is the relevant portion of the operating ratio constraint. The regulated reaction function for firm 1 is $AHGE$, and the

Industrywide Regulation and the Formation of Reputations 359

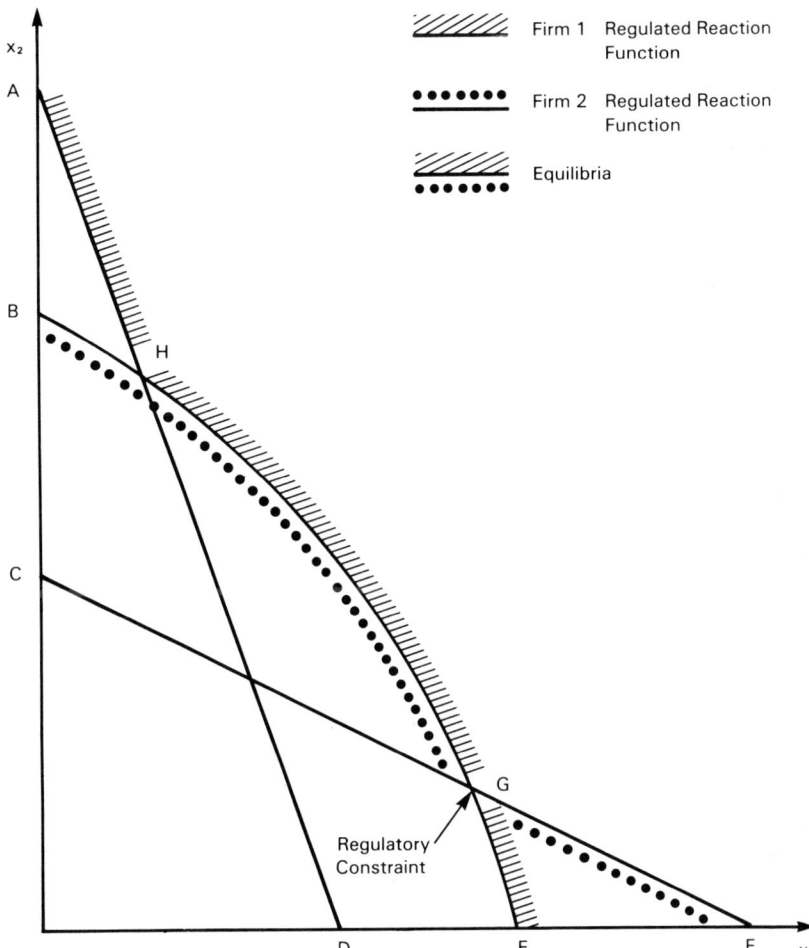

Figure 11.1 Regulated equilibria

regulated reaction function for firm 2 is FGHB. The area of overlap (GH) is the set of regulated Cournot equilibria.

The second model, the regulated Stackelberg model, involves a leader and a follower, with the follower taking the price ceiling and the leader's output as given while the leader takes the follower's reaction function as given; the leader, say, firm i, chooses the price ceiling and its output so as to maximize its profit. The leader does this subject to the regulatory restriction and the follower's regulated reaction function ψ_j which is the solution to the follower's problem, which we denote as f_j:

$$\text{Max}_{x_j} p(X)x_j - c_j(x_j)$$

$$\text{s.t.} \quad p(x_i + x_j) \leq \bar{p}, \tag{4}$$

where x_i and $\bar{p}$ are given (see Daughety 1984 for details). Problem f_j is solved by the follower in step two of the regulatory scenario. Knowing this, at step one (the agreement phase) the leader solves the following problem:

$$\text{Max}_{\bar{p}, x_i} p(X)x_i - c_i(x_i)$$

$$\text{s.t.} \quad F(x_1, x_2, \alpha) \geq 0 \tag{5}$$

$$x_j = \psi_j(x_i, \bar{p}).$$

In figure 11.1 points G and H are regulated Stackelberg equilibria for firms 1 and 2, respectively. For example, in the linear parameter sets, the regulated Stackelberg equilibrium with seller 1 as leader is $\mathbf{x} = (18, 9)$, while that for seller 2 is $\mathbf{x} = (10, 18)$.

Finally, we extend the T-period collusive solution in a natural way to provide the T-period regulated collusive solution, namely the vectors $\mathbf{x}^1, \ldots, \mathbf{x}^T$ that solve the following problem:

$$\max_{\mathbf{x}^1, \ldots, \mathbf{x}^T} \sum_{t=1}^{T} \sum_{i=1}^{n} \pi^i(\mathbf{x}^t)$$

$$\text{s.t.} \quad \frac{1}{T} \sum_{t=1}^{T} \pi^i(\mathbf{x}^t) \geq \bar{\pi}^i, \quad i = 1, \ldots, n, \tag{6}$$

$$F(\mathbf{x}^t, \alpha) \geq 0, \quad t = 1, \ldots, T,$$

where, for example, $\bar{\pi}^i$ is the average profit for firm i associated with the alternating regulated Stackelberg strategy. (In the linear set, $\bar{\pi}^1 = (\pi^1(18, 9) + \pi^1(10, 18))/2$.) In both the linear and quadratic parameter sets, the alternating regulated Stackelberg strategy is the 2-period collusive solution under regulation.

Model Predictions

Table 11.2 summarizes the foregoing equilibria by providing equilibrium predictions by parameter set. For all of the regulated equilibria, it is assumed that both the production agreements and actual production decisions satisfy the regulation. After the industry was deregulated, the same four equilibria were computed for these phase II production decisions and are also presented in table 11.2. Finally, in those experiments where a third seller entered in period 16, there is an additional Stackelberg outcome included among the predictions.

It should be noted that all of the collusive equilibrium solutions entail a stragegy where sellers alternate between two (three) industry output vectors when there are two (three) firms in the industry. For example, in the linear parameters sets, the collusive equilibrium strategies require that sellers alternate monopoly production levels when there is only one seller of each type in the industry. Further, when there are three sellers in the industry with, say, two sellers of type 1, collusive equilibrium strategies not only entail all three sellers alternating the monopoly position but also include all other production vectors where the two sellers of type 1 jointly produce their monopoly output in two of the three periods, and the third seller is the monopolist in the third period.

Results

The entire time series of production decisions in each experiment is shown in appendix A as figures 11.A1 through 11.A9 for all seven parameter sets that were examined. Thus, for example, figures 11.A1 and 11.A2 display the data from the eight experiments using linear cost functions where deregulation was not announced and there was no entry (LNN-1-8). Similarly figure 11.A6 displays the data for the four experiments using linear cost functions, with a type 1 entrant appearing in period 16 where deregulation was announced but the type of entrant was not (LAU1-1-4).

In what follows, we analyze each phase of the experiments. For both the regulated phase (phase I) and unregulated duopoly phase (phase II) of each experiment we perform a classification of the observed outcomes. In these instances the data are sufficiently regular so that statistical analysis seems unwarranted. Unfortunately the phase III data on unregulated industry performance after entry is considerably less regular, and therefore we

Table 11.2 Model predictions

Parameter set	Phase	Cournot	Stackelberg 1 (firm 1: leader)	Stackelberg 2 (firm 2: leader)	Stackelberg 3 (firm 3: leader)	Joint
All linear	I	(18, 9) and $x_1 + x_2 = 28$, $10 \leq x_1 \leq 17$, $11 \leq x_2 \leq 18$	(18, 9)	(10, 18)	na	Alternate between (18, 9) and (10, 18)
	II	(9, 11), (10, 11), (9, 12)	(15, 8)	(6, 17)	na	Alternate between (15, 0) and (0, 16)
LAU1 LAK1	III	(7, 9, 7), (6, 9, 8), (8, 9, 6), (7, 8, 8), (8, 8, 7), (7, 10, 6), (6, 10, 7)	(12, 7, 5)	(4, 17, 4)	(5, 7, 12)	Alternate among $(0, 16, 0)$, $(x, 0, 15 - x)$, and $(15 - x, 0, x)$
LAU2 LAK2	III	(7, 8, 8), (6, 9, 8), (6, 8, 9)	(13, 6, 6)	(4, 15, 6)	(4, 6, 15)	Alternate among $(15, 0, 0)$, $(0, x, 16 - x)$, and $(0, 16 - x, x)$
All quadratic parameter sets	I	(14, 16), (15, 15), (16, 14)	(3, 24)	(24, 3)	na	Alternate between (24, 3) and (3, 24)
	II	(10, 10)	(13, 8)	(8, 13)	na	1-period: (8, 8) 2-period: alternate between (8, 7) and (7, 8)

perform a statistical analysis to measure the effect of entry on total industry output and surplus.

Regulated Phase (Phase I)

As in our previous study where industrywide regulation was imposed after fifteen periods of unregulated activity, the behavior observed during this phase was very stable. Although there is some variation due to cheating on agreements and misunderstandings, 87.5 percent (315 out of 360) of all regulatory periods resulted in actual production decisions that coincided with those agreed on. (In our previous study the rate of congruence between agreed on and actual levels was 87.6 percent.) Further, from period 4 onward, 94.0 percent of all agreed upon levels were actually produced. Even when there appears to be a large variation in the strategies being played (e.g., LNN-3, 5, 6 and QNN-2; see figures 11.A2 and 11.A3, respectively), this is an explicit strategy pursued by the market participants to take turns, alternating between two sets of industry outputs.

We present a classification of regulated outcomes in table 11.3. This classification is based on the last several periods observed in each experiment. As can be seen there, 27.8 percent (10 out of 36) of the outcomes were at or near the collusive prediction, whereas 69.4 percent (25 out of 36) were at the Cournot prediction. In only one experiment, LAU1-1, were we unable to classify the outcome since the sellers failed to produce the amount they had agreed on in any of the ten periods.

The outcomes that are classified as near the collusive prediction are all ones in which the sellers alternated between different output vectors at or near the Stackelberg perdictions. In most of these cases, one or both sellers produced more than his Stackelberg leader output when it was his turn. For example, sellers in QNN-2 alternated between (1, 25) and (25, 1) while the predicted alternation is between (3, 24) and (24, 3). In this case, however, sellers average profits differed by $.00125 per period from the average profits per period achievable at the collusive outcome. Although these outcomes differ from the collusive prediction, they exhibit the alternating strategies required for successful collusion. Sellers seem to have a difficult time locating the exact strategies to alternate between. This is perhaps due to the fact that the sellers had incomplete information about each other's profits and were not permitted to communicate this information.

The results in these experiments can be contrasted with the outcomes observed in six other regulated duopoly experiments previously reported in Daughety and Forsythe (1985a). These experiments used the same linear

Table 11.3 Classification of regulated outcomes

Experiment	Cournot	Stackelberg	Collusive Exact	Collusive Near	Alternating strategies	Comments
LNN-1	X					
LNN-2	X					
LNN-3				X	X	Alternated between (26, 3) and (3, 26)
LNN-4	X				X	
LNN-5			X		X	
LNN-6				X	X	Alternated between (26, 0) and (2, 27)
LNN-7	X				X	
LNN-8	X				X	Alternated between (13, 15) and (10, 18)
QNN-1	X	X			X	Alternated Stackelberg and Cournot
QNN-2				X	X	Alternated between (1, 25) and (25, 1) but same profits as exact collusive
QNN-3	X					
QNN-4	X					
LAN-1	X					
LAN-2				X	X	
LAN-3	X				X	
LAN-4			X		X	
LAN-5						Produced equal Cournot output in in last period since there was not two periods left to continue alternating
LAN-6	X			X	X	Alternated between (4, 25) and (19, 8)
LAN-7	X					
LAN-8	X					

				Alternating Stackelberg and Cournot		Failed to produce agreed on levels in all ten periods
LAU1-1						
LAU1-2	X					X
LAU1-3	X					
LAU1-4						X
LAU2-1		X				
LAU2-2	X					X
LAU2-3	X					X
LAU2-4	X					X
LAK1-1		X				X
LAK1-2	X					
LAK1-3	X					X
LAK1-4	X		X			X X
LAK2-1	X					
LAK2-2	X					
LAK2-3	X					
LAK2-4	X					

Industrywide Regulation and the Formation of Reputations

parameter set as in the markets reported here; the major difference between these two sets of experiments is that in the previous experiments industrywide regulation was imposed on the duopoly after fifteen periods of unregulated activity. After five periods under regulation, five of these six experiments settled at the equal output Cournot equilibrium. In the only exception, sellers alternated between the Cournot equilibria of $(x_1, x_2) =$ (13, 15) and (15, 13). Only in this latter case can it be hypothesized that sellers are building some reputation capital with respect to pursuing alternating strategies. Since this alternating strategy yields the same average profits as the equal output Cournot equilibrium, it is riskier to the seller who is producing the low output in a given period since he does this in return for the promise of being the high output seller in the succeeding period.

For the experiments we focus on here, wherein industrywide regulation is imposed in the first ten market periods, 61.1 percent (22 out of 36) of the regulated duopolies engaged in some form of explicit alternation (see table 11.3) during the last five periods of regulation. Further many of the regulated duopolies pursued alternating strategies that led to an industry output of twenty-eight units in each period. Since sellers could have earned the same average profits by each producing fourteen units every period, we hypothesize that this is due to sellers engaging in building their reputation capital.

Deregulated Phase without Entry (Phase II)

To analyze the effect of deregulation on duopoly behavior, we have classified the observed phase II outcomes of each experiment in table 11.4. If during phase I (when communication was permitted) sellers made an agreement concerning output levels in phase II, we have summarized the output agreement in the last column of the table.

In those experiments in which deregulation was not announced, five of the twelve unregulated duopolies (LNN-1, 6, QNN-1, 3, 4) produced at or near the collusive prediction. Experiment LNN-1 is particularly interesting. The two sellers had played some alternating strategies during the regulated phase, and upon deregulation seller 2 initially produced zero units of output. This was an attempt by seller 2 to signal seller 1 to take turns and employ an alternating monopoly strategy in this phase. In the second unregulated period, seller 2 produced his monopoly output, but seller 1 continued to produce ten units. Finally, in the fourth unregulated period seller 1 produced zero units, thereby signaling his acceptance of

Industrywide Regulation and the Formation of Reputations 367

Table 11.4 Classification of deregulation (phase II) outcome

Experiment	Cournot Exact	Cournot Near	Stackelberg Exact	Stackelberg Near	Collusive Exact	Collusive Near	??	Comments	Agreement made during phase I for phase II
LNN-1					X				
LNN-2				X					
LNN-3				X					
LNN-4	X								
LNN-5		X							
LNN-6		X				X		Between Cournot and collusive predictions	
LNN-7		X							
LNN-8		X							
QNN-1						X			Considered potential deregulation, agreed to alternate monopoly positions should that event occur
QNN-2							X	Industry output less than collusive but individual productions not classifiable	
QNN-3		X				X		Between Cournot and collusive predictions	
QNN-4					X				
LAN-1						X			Alternate (14, 1) and (1, 16)
LAN-2						X			Alternate (13, 4) and (3, 15)
LAN-3		X							(8, 12)
LAN-4						X			To each produce 8 or 9
LAN-5						X			Alternate (14, 3) and (3, 14)
LAN-6						X			(8, 8)
LAN-7						X			Alternate (8, 9) and (9, 8)
LAN-8	X								(9, 12)

Table 11.4 (Continued)

Experiment	Cournot		Stackelberg		Collusive		??	Comments	Agreement made during phase I for phase II
	Exact	Near	Exact	Near	Exact	Near			
LAU1-1							X		(10, 8)
LAU1-2						X			(8, 8)
LAU1-3	X								(9, 11)
LAU1-4		X							To each produce between 4 and 10
LAU2-1						X			(8, 8)
LAU2-2						X			(8, 9)
LAU2-3						X			(8, 8)
LAU2-4						X			To each produce 8 or 9
LAK-1						X			(8, 8)
LAK1-2						X			(8, 8)
LAK1-3						X			(8, 8)
LAK1-4		X							To produce "in the general vicinity of (10, 10)"
LAK2-1						X			Alternate (0, 16) and (16, 0) twice and produce (10, 10) in period 15
LAK2-2						X			(8, 8)
LAK2-3							X	Between Cournot and collusive predictions	To each produce between 4 and 10
LAK2-4						X			Alternate (5, 12) and (12, 5)

seller 2's previous offer. For the remainder of the experiment these two sellers continued to play the alternating monopoly strategy which is the collusive prediction.

To the extent that industrywide regulation provides firms with the ability and incentives to cooperate, the reputations for cooperation that evolve seem to manifest themselves in the improved ability to forecast each other's decision after deregulation occurred. To provide some evidence on this, we have reproduced the unregulated periods from the thirteen experiments, L1-13 of Daughety and Forsythe (1985a), in figure 11.2. Again, recall that these experiments involved unregulated activity preceding regulation, where sellers were unaware of the impending regulation phase. These unregulated duopoly experiments provide a startling contrast to the deregulated duopoly (phase II) experiments presented in figures 11.A1 through 11.A9. In particular, sellers' production decisions seem not to converge to a recognizable equilibrium in the unregulated experiments L1-13. On the other hand, the decisions made in the deregulated environments exhibit more characterizable behavior. In particular, when deregulation was not announced, 75 percent (9 out of 12) of the markets seemed to exhibit Cournot, Stackelberg, or collusive equilibrium behavior, and over all experiments the deregulated duopoly outcome was easily classified in 88.9 percent (32 out of 36) of the experiments.

As reported in our earlier study, the Cournot output seemed to be the best predictor of the strategies chosen by individual sellers in unregulated duopolies L1-13. However, sellers seemed to have had a "planning problem" in accurately forecasting their opponent's output and reacting to it. Although industrywide regulation and the ability to communicate seems to allow sellers to overcome this problem, the current experiments indicate that this improved ability for sellers' to forecast and/or coordinate their decisions seems to carry over into the deregulated phase.

On the other hand, in those environments in which deregulation is announced, the degree of cooperation is quite remarkable. Although sellers sometimes failed to make agreements during phase I to produce at or near the collusive equilibrium, they always came to some form of an agreement for phase II. In only two cases did sellers ever deviate from the agreed on strategy. In LAU2-1 seller 2 cheated on the agreement to produce 8 in the last period prior to entry (period 15) and instead chose his best response strategy of producing 12. Sellers in LAU1-1 had agreed to produce (10, 8) for all five deregulatory periods prior to entry but instead produced (10, 12), (1, 11), (11, 8), (10, 11), and (9, 10). These are the same sellers who

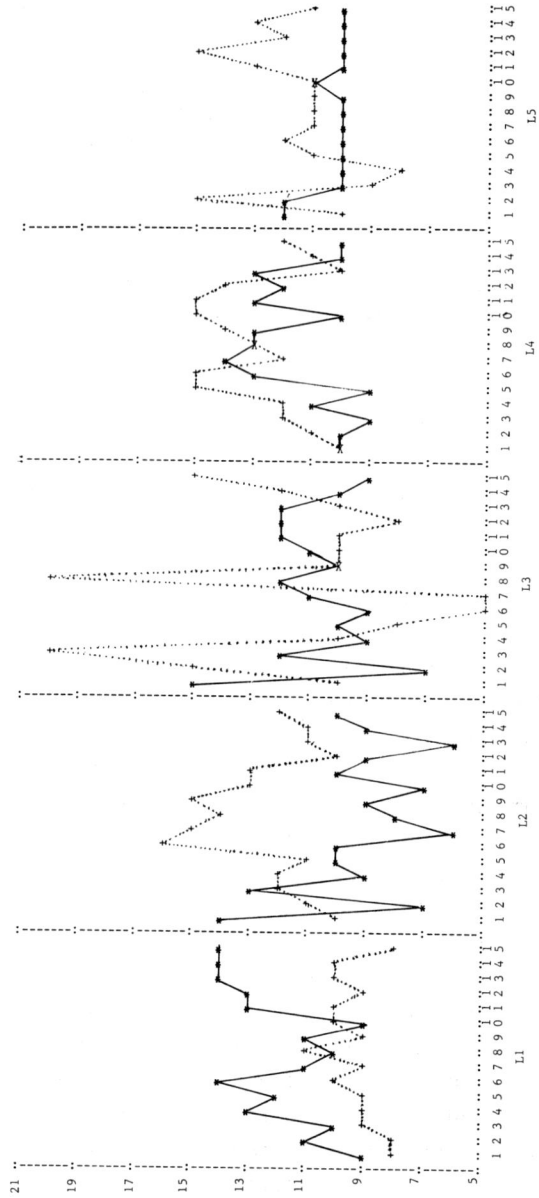

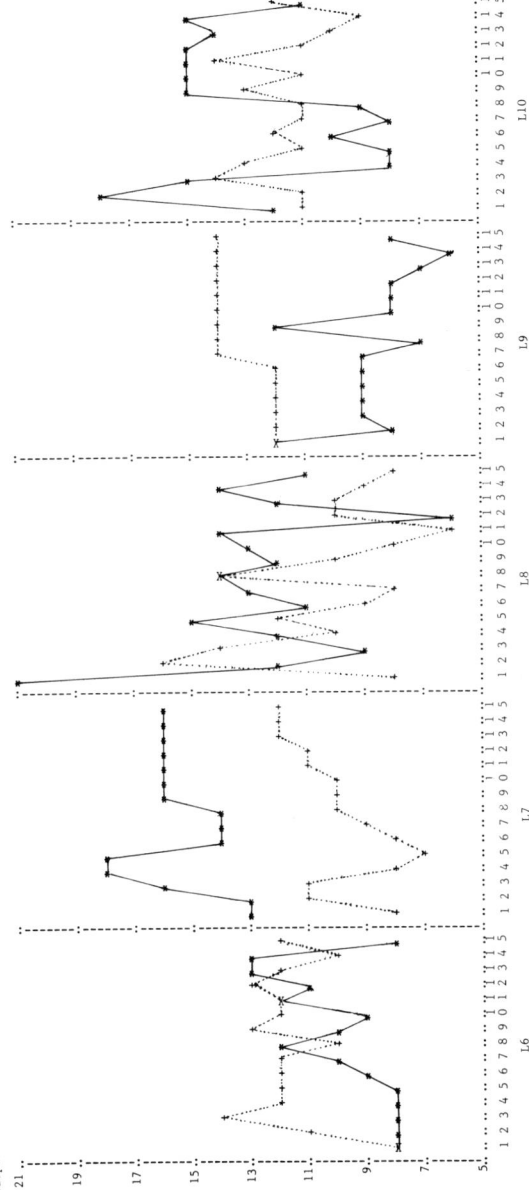

Figure 11.2 Experiments L1-13 (unregulated): firm 1 (Solid line); firm 2 (dotted line). Source: Daughety and Forsythe (1985a).

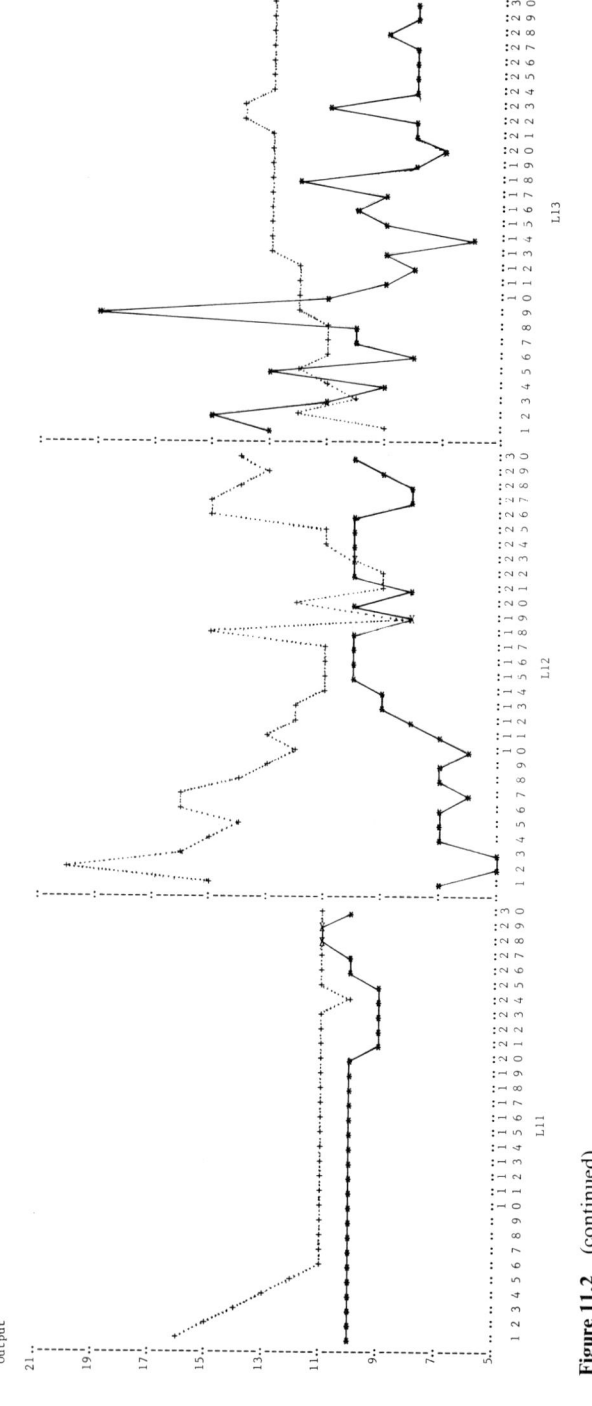

Figure 11.2 (continued)

consistently failed to adhere to their agreements in all ten periods under regulation (see table 11.3). Thus their failure to establish reputation capital in phase I carried over into the deregulation phase. Aside from these two defections, the cooperative behavior seems very stable. Sellers seem to find cooperative behavior to be individually rational even when there is an announcement that deregulation will be accompanied by entry.

Finally, in 70.8 percent (17 out of 24) of the experiments where deregulation was announced, the exact or near collusive prediction was observed in phase II. Many of these outcomes are not at the exact collusive prediction since sellers frequently made minor perturbations on that strategy. For example, in experiment LAN-5 seller 2 was determined to not make negative profits in any period, and thus the agreement to alternate between (14, 3) and (3, 14) was made. Similarly sellers frequently opted for producing (8, 8) instead of alternating since they seemed to realize that they each have individual incentives to defect from any agreement, and this strategy is less risky.

We have not attempted to correlate the behavior of duopolists who chose alternating strategies during phase I with those who operated at or near the collusive outcome during phase II. In particular, eight pairs of duopolists who had not chosen alternating strategies while regulated chose to produce at or near the collusive solution after deregulation when this deregulation had been announced. In many of these latter cases sellers explicitly chose to produce at the equal output Cournot solution under regulation in order "to concentrate on what we should do starting in period 11."

Finally, it is important to observe a significant parallel between the phase II outcomes and some of the earlier literature on oligopoly experiments, namely Friedman (1963). In those early experiments Friedman found that after extensive use of highly experienced subjects involving many periods of activity, duopoly pairs converged to collusive equilibria. By contrast, in our experiments we used inexperienced subjects and observed collusive behavior after a very few number of periods. The difference of course is the phase I activity which involved[7] (1) communication[8] (2) the incentive to cooperate on planned activity levels, and (3) the ability for each subject to penalize the other for violations of planned activity levels. Thus phase I accomplished what would otherwise take many periods of subject interaction: subjects learn how to predict each other's behavior, and they develop reputations for how they will behave. In other words, the important experience gained is learning about the other subject's behavior, and how one's own behavior influences the other's behavior.

Deregulated Phase after Entry (Phase III)

As is evident in figures 11.A6 through 11.A9 sellers' production decisions become increasingly variable when entry occurred.[9] Due to this variability we will not present a classification table as we did for both phase I and phase II outcomes, but instead we will discuss the behavior we observed. Although incumbent firms frequently discussed strategies they could employ, there was no alternative adopted in a majority of cases. In three of the regulated duopolies, LAU1-1, LAU2-4, and LAK2-4, sellers were unable to suggest a feasible strategy and decided to "see what the third seller does and wing it." In twelve of the remaining thirteen cases sellers reached a production agreement during the regulatory phase which they adhered to for period 16 or longer. The lone exception, LAU2-1, is the duopoly where seller 2 defected from the collusive arrangement in period 15 and chose his best response strategy. In retaliation seller 1 played his best response to their postentry agreement during period 16.

In general, incumbent sellers reduced their period 16 production decisions below their previous levels. In fourteen of the sixteen experiments conducted, neither incumbent increased his output in period 16 from his period 15 levels. Of the remaining two experiments, one (LAU2-1) is where seller 2 had defected from the previous collusive agreement in period 15, and although they had agreed to cut back their production in period 16, seller 1 retaliated instead. In the other exception, LAK2-4, sellers had not come to any agreement as to what to do after entry, and their joint output increased by one unit after entry. Thus we have no evidence of incumbent sellers "playing tough" to cause the entrant to incur losses after period 16. Instead, they consistently reduced their output levels to make room for the entrant into the industry.

During four of the regulated duopolies (LAU2-3, LAK1-2, LAK1-3, and LAK2-1), the incumbent sellers discussed a near-collusive equilibrium for the triopoly. This called for all three sellers to produce 5 units of output apiece. With these decisions the average profits of type 1 sellers are exactly the same as they would be at the exact collusive equilibrium, whereas average profits for type 2 sellers are $.0067 per period lower. In all four of these cases, the incumbent sellers were concerned with how to communicate their strategy to the entrant. In LAK1-3 and LAU2-3 both incumbents produced in accordance with their agreement in period 16. After observing the entrant's production decision, one of the incumbents chose to deviate from the agreement and produced his best response output to the other two sellers' previous decisions. This defection caused the previous agreement to collapse.

In LAK1-2 sellers were successful in achieving the near collusive equilibrium after entry. During phase I the incumbent sellers suggested that "somehow we have to get seller 3's production down after period 16" and agreed to do this by keeping production as low as possible (between 3 and 5 units). After entering, seller 3 played a crucial role in enforcing the collusive outcome. By periods 20 and 21 the two incumbents had increased their outputs up to 5 and 6, respectively, and to halt this, seller 3 varied his production from 4 to 10 units of output in period 22. In response to this, seller 2 dropped his production level backed to 5 units for the next two periods as did seller 3. In period 25, however, seller 2 again raised his output level to 6 units and in period 26, seller 3 responded to this by producing 9 units. After that, all three sellers continued producing at the near collusive equilibrium of 5 units each for the remaining four periods.

Finally, in experiment LAK2-4, sellers 1 and 2 agreed to produce 4 and 6 units apiece in period 16. The sellers adhered to this agreement in period 16, but in periods 17 and 18, seller 1 produced zero units. This was an attempt by seller 1 to signal the other two sellers to take turns and employ an alternating monopoly output strategy. After taking his "turn" in period 19, this seller again produced zero units in periods 20 and 21. When seller 1 again took his "turn" in period 22, the other two sellers continued to produce positive amounts. At this point seller 1 abandoned this alternating strategy.

In all but one of the markets conducted, the effect of entry was to increase output relative to the preentry periods (phase II). The exception occurred in LAK1-2 (the tripoly that achieved the near-collusive outcome). Further, with this same exception, the effect of entry was to increase the total surplus (i.e., sum of consumers' plus producers' surplus) that was realized.

Entry does seem effective, in general, for impeding the cooperation between incumbent sellers. On the other hand, an analysis of the full impact of regulation leads one to ask whether or not the deregulation outcomes are at least as desirable as would have occurred if regulation had never been imposed. As our analysis of phase II outcomes clearly shows, the deregulated duopoly industries achieved inferior outcomes to the duopoly outcomes we observed prior to regulation in our previous study. We next perform a comparison of the postentry outcomes with our earlier preregulation observations. In table 11.5, we present the average of the industry output over the last two periods (periods 14 and 15) for all preregulation experiments (L1-13) and over the last two periods (periods 29 and 30) for all sixteen postentry experiments. The critical probability that the means of

Table 11.5 Industry output and total surplus (average of last two market periods)

Preregulation			Postentry		
Experiment	Industry output	Total surplus	Experiment	Industry output	Total surplus
L1	22.5	399.00	LAU-1	20.5	384.75
L2	21.0	388.00	LAU1-2	23.0	337.75
L3	23.0	408.00	LAU1-3[a]	24.0	315.75
L4	21.5	392.75	LAU1-4[a]	23.0	393.50
L5	22.0	397.50	LAU2-1	25.5	390.75
L6	21.5	390.75	LAU2-2[a]	22.0	366.00
L7	28.0	428.00	LAU2-3[a]	31.5	390.00
L8	21.0	365.50	LAU2-4	24.0	382.00
L9	21.0	393.00	LAK1-1	22.5	389.75
L10	23.5	405.75	LAK1-2[a]	15.0	299.50
L11	20.0	378.00	LAK1-3[a]	21.5	369.75
L12	20.5	382.75	LAK1-4	25.0	404.00
L13	20.5	385.75	LAK2-1[a]	24.5	384.75
			LAK2-2[a]	19.5	337.75
			LAK2-3	18.5	315.75
			LAK2-4[a]	30.5	400.00
Averages			**Averages**		
all preregulation	22.0	393.44	All LAU1 and LAK1	21.81	361.84
			All LAU2 and LAK2	24.50	370.88
			All postentry	23.16	366.36

a. Exhibited same behavior under regulation as L1-6.

these two sets of experiments are equal is 0.3886. Since each set of experiments was conducted under different conditions, we identified the entry experiments where, under regulation, the incumbent firms made the same production decisions over the final three periods as the regulated duopolists had done in Daughety and Forsythe (1985a). Thus we identified those entry experiments where sellers produced 14 units each or alternated between $(x_1, x_2) = (15, 13)$ and $(13, 15)$. These nine experiments are identified by an asterisk in table 11.5. The critical probability that the mean of this subset is the same as that for experiments L1-13 is 0.4673. Thus from an industry output perspective the effect of entry after deregulation only restores the industry to the same level of production it had been operating at prior to ever being regulated. This holds true even controlling for industries who exhibited identical behavior under regulation.

The average industry output measure used earlier coincides with measures of consumer surplus since the latter is a monotonic transformation of the former. We further examined the data to see if their was any significant

Appendix A

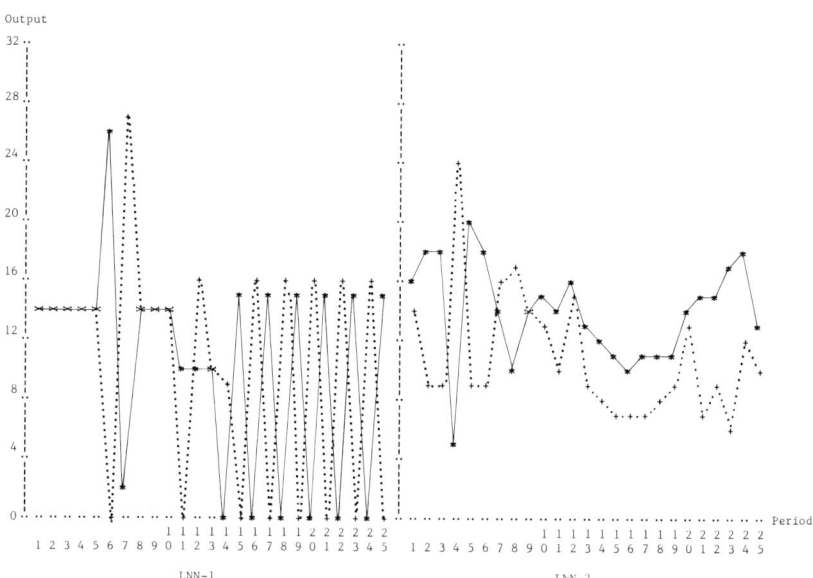

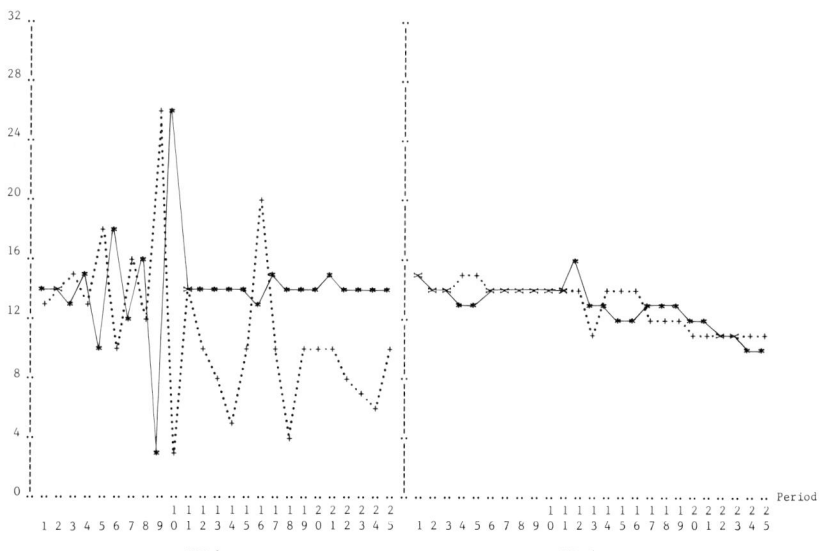

Figure 11.A1 Experiments LNN–1–4: subject 1 (solid line); subject 2 (dotted line)

Kaplan, and Sibley 1983; Bailey, Graham, and Kaplan 1985; Call and Keeler 1985). This has been interpreted, to varying degrees, as a failure of the contestable markets hypothesis (see Baumol, Panzar, and Willig 1982). Our results suggest that in-place reputation capital also contributes to explaining why deregulated airline prices are not equal to cost. In particular, the experimental results suggest that if firms that were previously regulated have developed stocks of reputation capital, then those markets mainly comprised of newly certified carriers should have fares closer to costs than those markets dominated by previously regulated carriers.

This also is suggestive of an implication for antitrust policy in the case of collusive arrangements among unregulated firms, namely that once firms "learn" about each other, remedies beyond criminal penalties and fines may be necessary to avoid future collusive behavior.[12] What remedies are necessary is unclear, but one possibility suggested by our laboratory market experiments is encouraging sufficient entry in the industry so as to "dilute" the existing reputation capital developed by the previously colluding firms. It is important to reemphasize, however, that the focus of the experiments is on a particular regulatory mechanism, and its anticompetitive properties, not the generaly oligopoly situation.

When industries are deregulated, the past is more than prologue: the reputation capital formed under regulation is available for use by the deregulated firm. Use of such capital (e.g., restricting output) is the method of investment to counter depreciation. Moreover its use (independent of whether or not the users are successful in achieving a collusive solution) affects the deregulated industry equilibrium, even with entry. Thus the welfare costs of regulation persist well past its demise, with a potentially permanent distortion in industry conduct and performance its legacy.

proposals in rate bureau meetings. In the experiments production in the "red region" was used (rarely, but clearly) as a form of retaliation for cheating on the agreements formed under regulation. This resulted in both sellers making zero profits, and an unmistakable statement by one seller to the other about his willingness to retaliate.

Thus regulation lowers the "cost" of cooperation (and raises the cost of noncooperation). Consistent with this, we observed extensive use of 1-period collusive strategies and of alternating monopoly (or near-monopoly) strategies. Do we see alternating strategies in nonlaboratory settings? Clearly not directly:[11] few stockholders are prepared to accept a promise from management of great profits next year if it shuts down all its plants this year! It is important to remember that such a strategy (employed by the subjects in a laboratory setting) is a reflection of the available set of strategies, and its use does not indicate lack of external validity so much as it indicates internal validity: subjects find means to maximize individual returns. The important point is that such strategies provide two returns to the users: increased profits relative to many other noncooperative strategies and continued investment in the reputation capital necessary to support future profits from collusion. Such strategies are risky to introduce and pursue in a competitive environment; regulation facilitates their introduction and development. Thus regulation reduces the initial investment costs in reputation capital.

The development of a stock of reputation capital means that the "flow of capital services" is still available upon deregulation. Does entry overcome this reputation effect? The answer from the experiments is yes and no. Yes, the unregulated triopoly industry output is higher than the unregulated duopoly industry output within the same experiment. No, the unregulated triopoly industry output is not higher than the industry output for the unregulated duopolies studied in our previous paper. Since the main difference is that the current experiments involve a regulation phase preceding the unregulated activity, it is reasonable to attribute this effect to the regulation (and, in particular, to the reputation capital).

The insights gained from the laboratory experiments reported here provides a new interpretation of some of the recent studies of airline competition. Early studies of the airline industry under regulation indicated the great disparity between unregulated intrastate airline fares and regulated interstate airline fares (see Jordan 1970; Keeler 1972; and MacAvoy and Snow 1977). Recent studies of fares since deregulation have found some improvement but generally find that fares are still above cost and that airline markets are still imperfectly competitive (see Graham, differences in the total surplus achieved in the postentry experiments versus the preregulation experiments.[10] The total surplus of each observation is also reported in table 11.5. We tested the difference in the average total surplus between the preregulation experiments and the following three sets of postentry experiments: all postentry experiments, postentry experiments with type 1 entrants, and postentry experiments with type 2 entrants. The critical probabilities in these three cases are 0.0143, 0.0851, and 0.0655, respectively. At best, the entrants are barely able to cover their fixed costs relative to preregulation allocations. This is especially revealing since all the postentry average surplus values are below the average surplus value for the preregulation experiments.

We also examined the effect of the type of entrant and whether that type were known or unknown by the incumbents prior to entry. Due in a large part to the small number of observations of each treatment, we were unable to identify any significant differences between these treatments.

Conclusions

The experimental results reported here, in conjunction with those reported in our previous paper, indicate that not only does regulation influence the formation, structure, and efficiency of equilibria during the regulatory epoch, it affects the formation, structure, and efficiency of equilibria after deregulation too. This assertion reflects the two main results of the experiments presented in this chapter. First, regulation provides a low cost opportunity for sellers to learn cooperation and to develop a reputation capital that supports collusive solutions in a noncooperative setting. Second, although entry reduced the ability of sellers to achieve collusive solutions, a net reputation effect was clearly discernable: in welfare terms, the unregulated triopoly was, on average, worse than duopolies never subjected to regulation. We consider each of these results in turn.

As indicated at the beginning of this chapter, industrywide regulation has often involved some sort of institutionalized means for coordination and communication among firms, such as a rate bureau. Our method for handling this in the laboratory was to allow messages between sellers in the industry. Moreover in each setting the form of regulation provides a means for the industry to reward cooperation and penalize renegades. In a naturally occurring setting these options include logrolling (or withholding of support) on price proposals in bureau meetings and filing of actions/complaints before commissions. It is noteworthy that as late as 1983 regulated motor carriers could interfere with (i.e., vote on) single-line rate

Industrywide Regulation and the Formation of Reputations 381

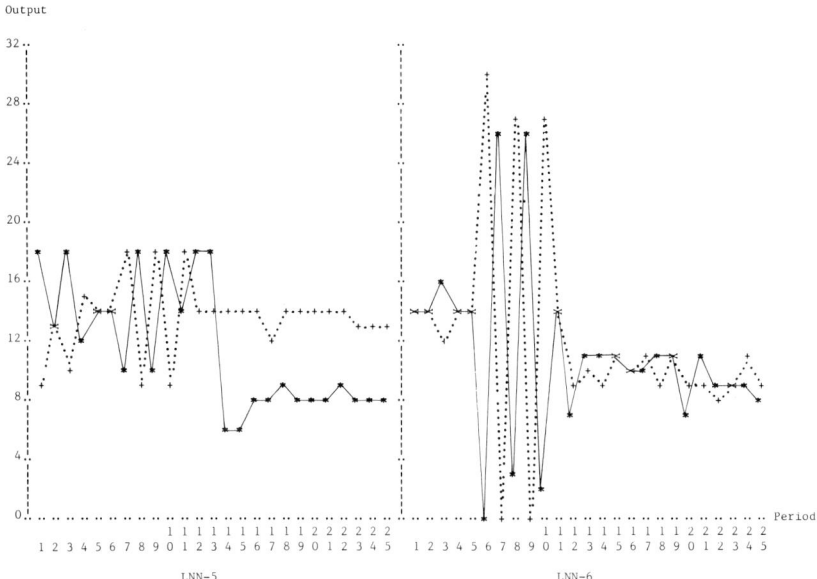

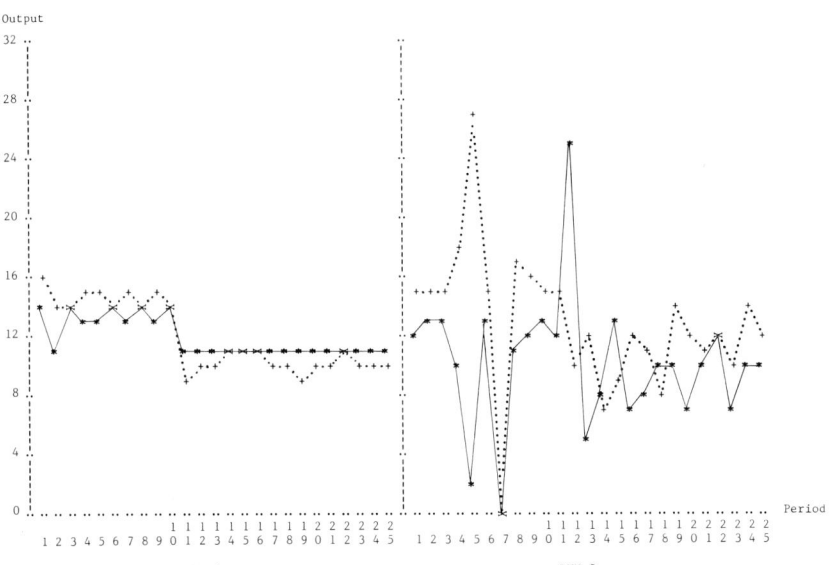

Figure 11.A2 Experiments LNN–5–8: subject 1 (solid line); subject 2 (dotted line)

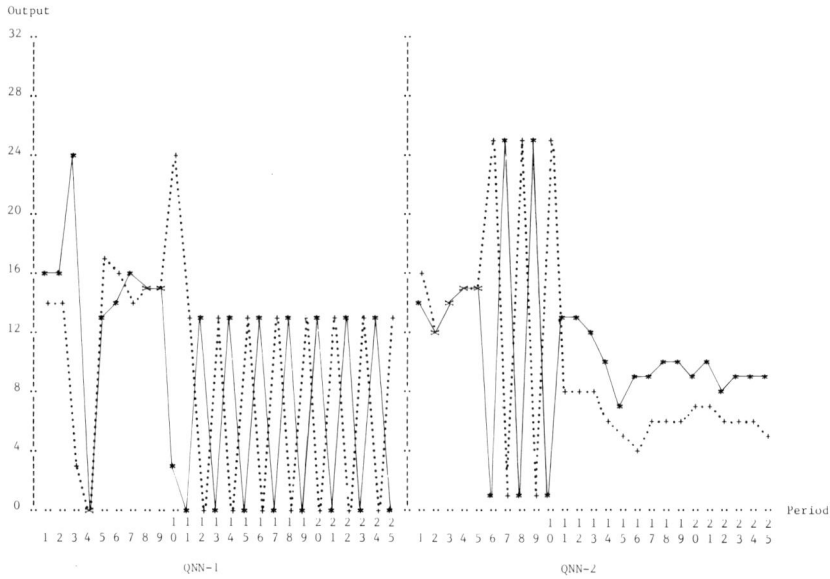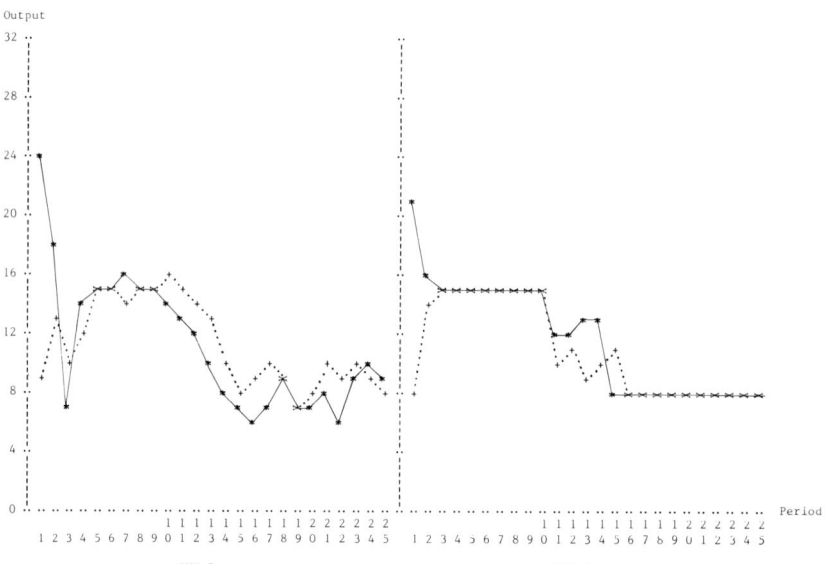

Figure 11.A3 Experiments QNN–1–4: subject 1 (solid line); subject 2 (dotted line)

Industrywide Regulation and the Formation of Reputations 383

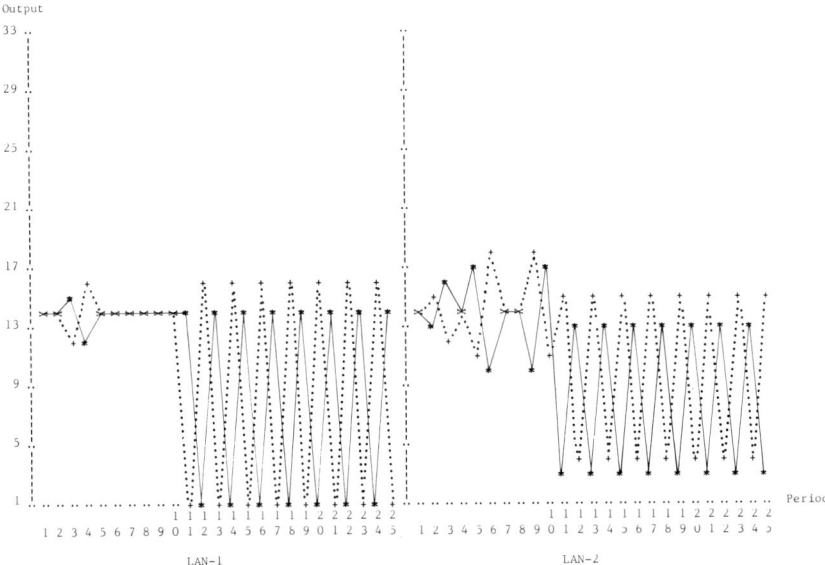

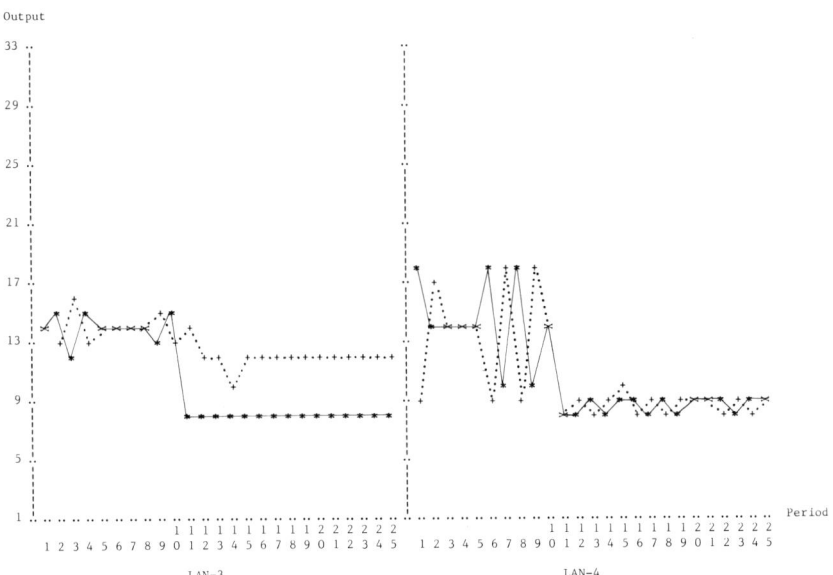

Figure 11.A4 Experiments LAN–1–4: subject 1 (solid line); subject 2 (dotted line)

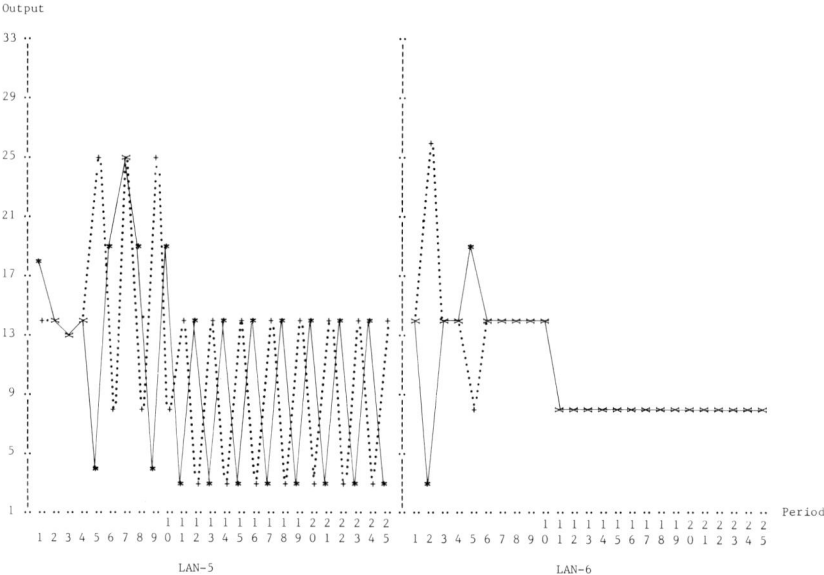
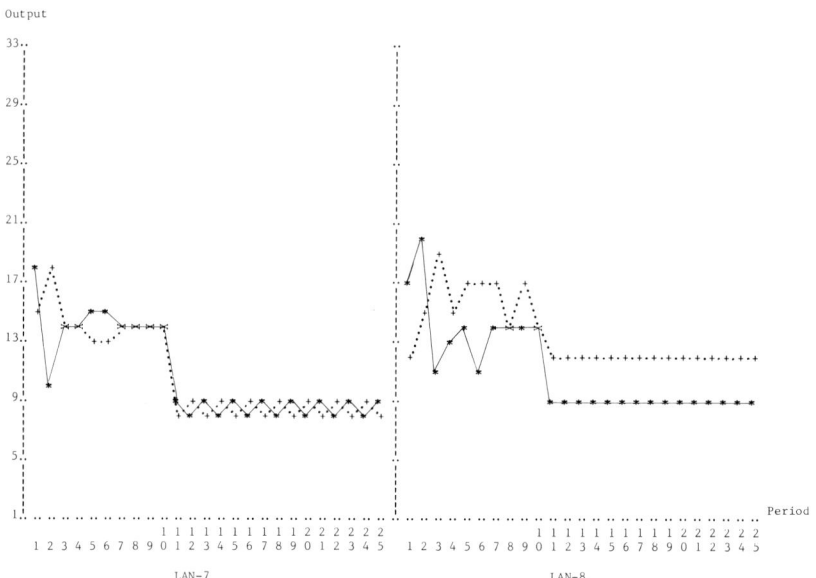

Figure 11.A5 Experiments LAN–5–8: subject 1 (solid line); subject 2 (dotted line)

Industrywide Regulation and the Formation of Reputations 385

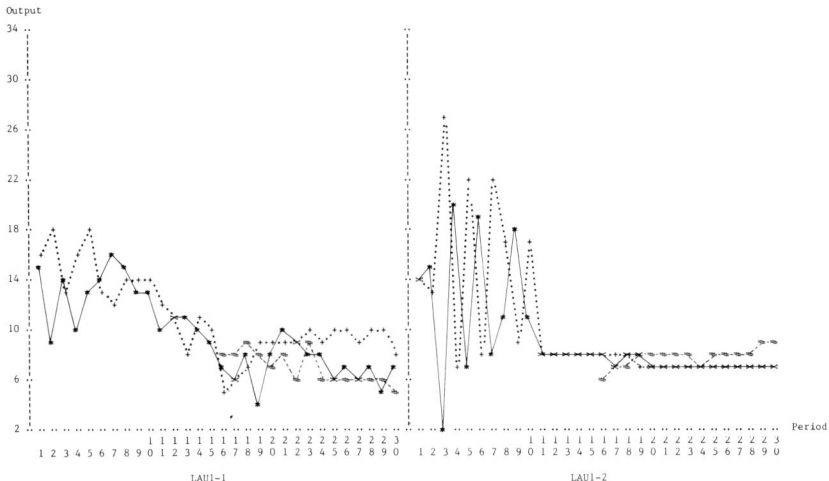

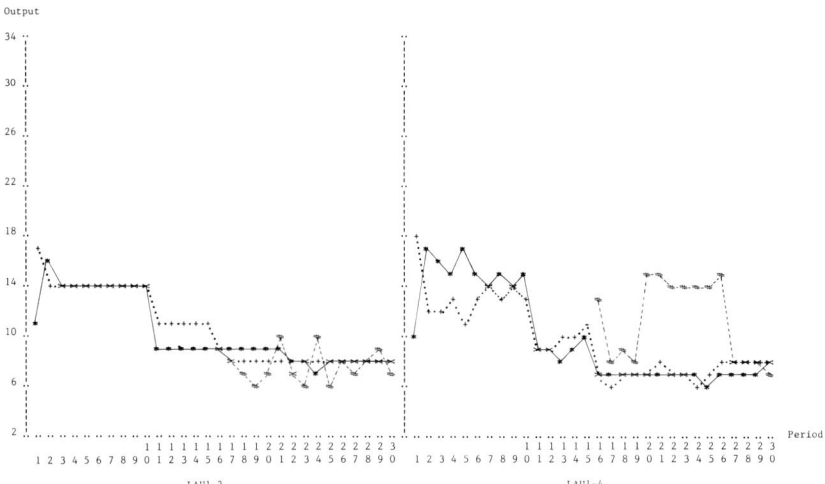

Figure 11.A6 Experiments LAU1–1–4: subject 1 (solid line); subject 2 (dotted line); subject 3 (dashed line)

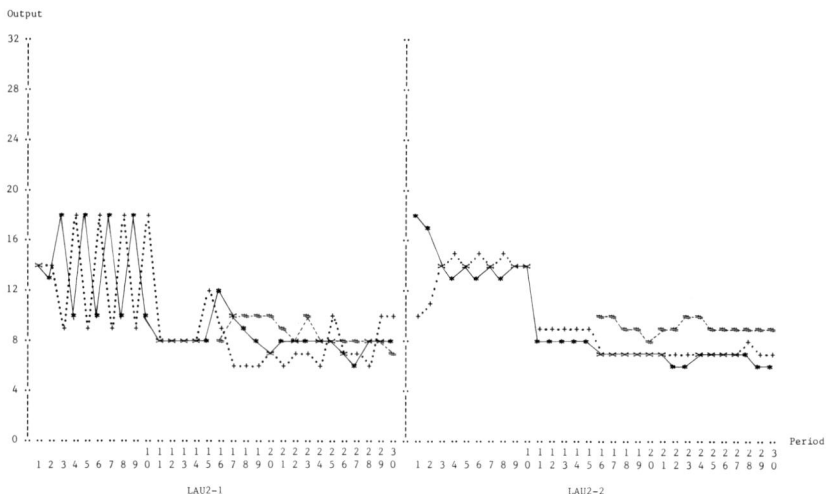
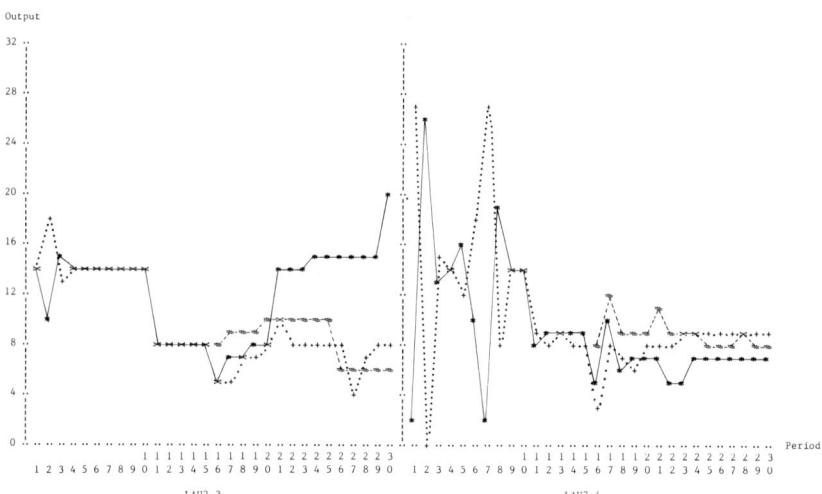

Figure 11.A7 Experiments LAU2–1–4: subject 1 (solid line); subject 2 (dotted line); subject 3 (dashed line)

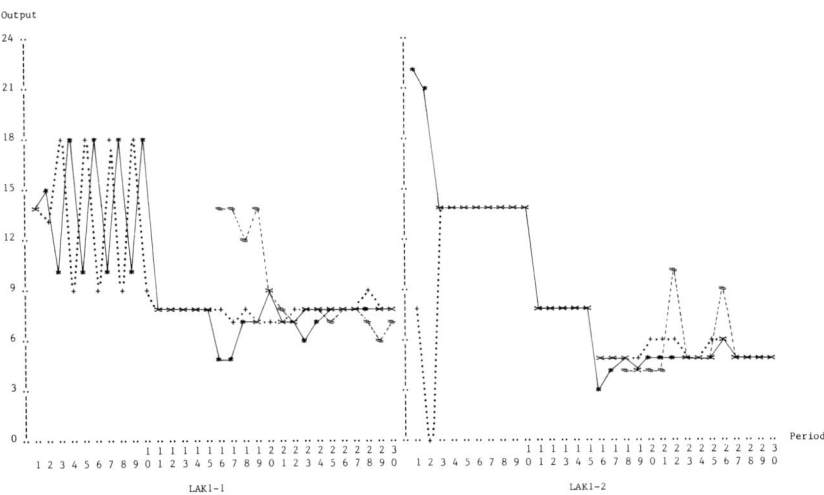

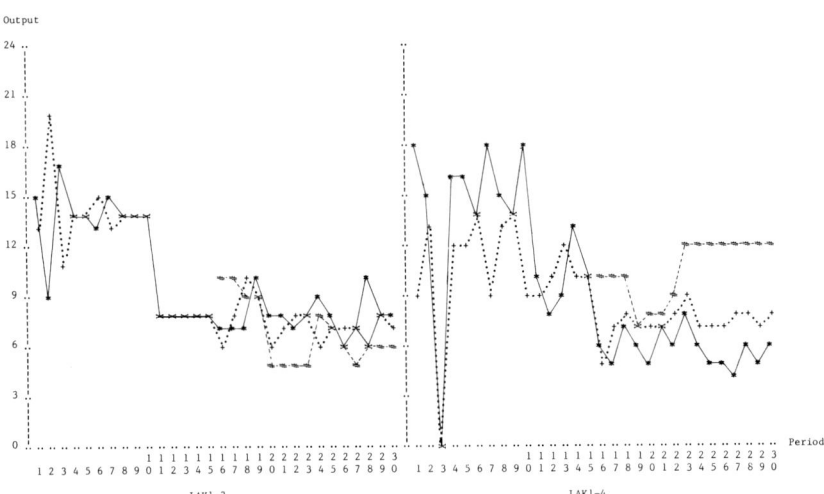

Figure 11.A8 Experiments LAK1–1–4: subject 1 (solid line); subject 2 (dotted line); subject 3 (dashed line)

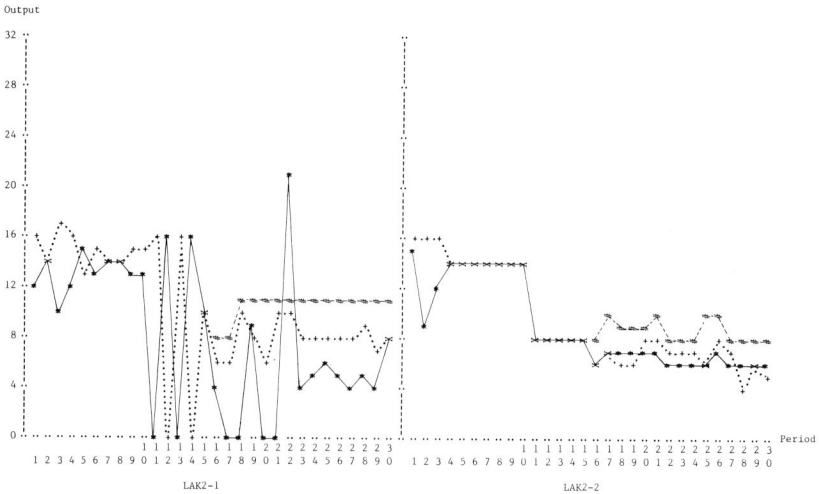
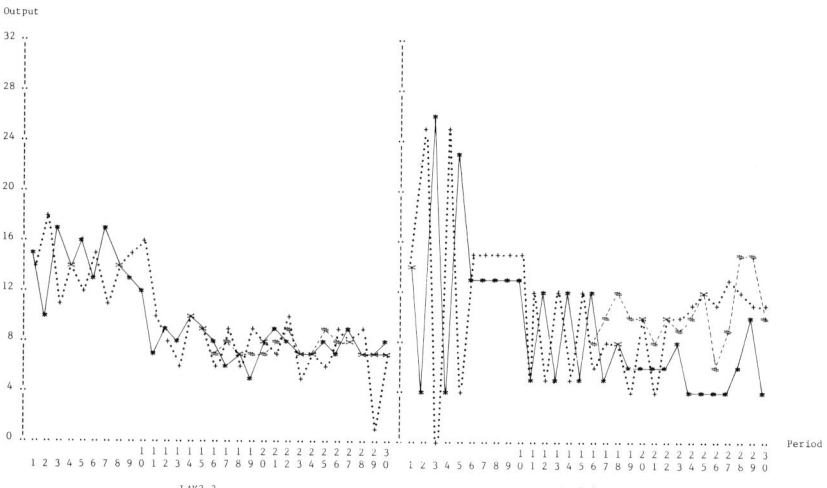

Figure 11.A9 Experiments LAK2-1-4: subject 1 (solid line); subject 2 (dotted line); subject 3 (dashed line)

Appendix B

Seller No. _____

Industry _____

INSTRUCTIONS

General

This is an experiment in the economics of market decision making. The instructions are simple, and if you follow them carefully and make good decisions, you might earn a considerable amount of money, which will be paid to you in cash.

In this experiment we are going to simulate a market in which you will be producers and sellers in different industries for a sequence of market years. There are _____ other producers and sellers in your industry who are in another room. All producers in the same industry produce a product that is identical in all respects to the products produced by other sellers.

The type of currency used in this market is francs. All trading and earnings will be in terms of francs. Each franc is worth _____ dollars to you. Do not reveal this number to anyone. Notice that the more francs you earn, the more dollars you earn.

Attached to these instructions you will find two sheets. The first is labeled the market demand schedule. This schedule determines the price you receive for each unit of output which the industry produces. Each seller in the same market has the same market demand schedule.

The second sheet is your cost schedule. This schedule gives the costs you incur for producing different possible quantities. This information is for your own private use. Do not reveal this information to anyone since other sellers in your industry do not necessarily have the same cost schedule.

Market Organization

In each market year the market for your output will be organized in two parts. First, you will be able to send messages to the other producer in your industry, and you will also receive messages from the other producer. The purpose of these communications is to come to a preliminary agreement as to what amounts each of you will produce and what price is to be charged. This price will serve as a *price ceiling* on the amount you may receive for each unit of your output.

To assist you in reaching an agreement, you have been given a profits table. This table specifies your potential total profit for the market year for each pair of outputs you produce. On this table there is a region that has been printed in red which indicates pairs of output that you may *not* agree to produce. Thus you must settle on your individual production levels in the region of the table that is printed in black. Since this table has been computed using your cost schedule, this information is for your own private use. Do not reveal this information to anyone.

When sending messages you are free to communicate whatever you wish as long as you stay within the confines of the rules: you cannot offer bribes or make physical threats (threats not to honor the agreement *are* permissible), and you cannot reveal the detailed quantitative information from your cost schedules or profit tables. Other than these specific items, you can communicate fully about all aspects of the market. In particular, you may indicate whether your profits are positive or negative or whether they are "too high" or "too low." Once you have come to an agreement as to what each of you will produce, submit this proposal to the experimenter who will verify that your proposal is not in the red region of your profits table.

Once a successful proposal has been made, the total industry output that was proposed determines a price ceiling on what you will receive for your output. This is the price that you find on your market demand schedule corresponding to the industry's planned output. The industry's planned output is the sum of seller 1's planned output and seller 2's planned output. If you fail to submit a feasible proposal within 10 minutes, your price ceiling will be 0.

In this part of the market year you can no longer communicate with each other. You must come to your own decision regarding how much output you will actually produce. Once you have come to a decision, you will submit your actual output to the experimenter who will total them to determine actual industry output. Again, using the market demand schedule, the price at which you could sell each unit of your output is determined. If this price is less than the price ceiling, you will receive this new price for each unit of output you produced. If this new price is greater than the price ceiling, you will receive the price ceiling for each unit of output you produced. Your actual profit for the market year may then be calculated.

If your actual production decision places you in the black region of your profits table, the entries in your profits table need not be accurate since there is a price ceiling on what you may receive. To know what you will receive, you will need to use the market demand schedule and your cost schedule.

Your profits from sales are computed as follows: for every unit you choose to produce, you will receive the difference between your sales revenue and your cost. For example, if you were to sell two units at 100 francs each, total revenue would be 200 francs. Suppose your cost schedule indicated that the cost of producing two units was 190 francs. Your total profits from sales would then be $200 - 190 = 10$ francs for the market year. If you sold these two units for less than 190, you would incur a loss. Obviously these figures are illustrative only and should not be assumed to apply to the actual sellers in this experiment.

Your profits in each market year will be added together, and any losses you might incur will be subtracted. Your total profits will be accumulated over several market years, and the total amount will be paid to you after the experiment. The decisions made by producers in industries other than yours *will have no effect* on your profits.

Trading and Recording Rules
In your folder you will find an ample supply of three types of forms. The first is labeled "Production Decision." When you make your actual production

decision, write down the amount you have decided on and pass the form to the experimenter.

The second type of form is labeled "Message Form." On this form you may write any message you desire, so long as it is within the rules discussed above. When you have a message to send to the other producer in your industry, simply hand it to the experimenter, and he will deliver it for you. When you wish to make a formal proposal, fill in the bottom line of your message form which says, "I propose that seller 1 produces ____ units and seller 2 produces ____ units." Once a formal proposal has been made no other proposals can be submitted until it is either accepted or rejected by the other seller. To do this, the seller who has not made the proposal must check either the square marked "accept" or the square marked "reject" following the proposal. If a proposal is accepted, the sellers in the industry may proceed to the second part of the market year. If a proposal is rejected, the sellers in the industry should continue to communicate with each other until a proposal is agreed on or the time limit is exceeded.

The third sheet (labeled "Profit Sheet") will be used to determine how much you earn. On line (1) of that sheet record your actual production decision, and on line (4) record your cost of producing your output. After all sellers have submitted their production decisions to the experimenter, the price that you will receive for each unit of output will be determined according to the rules given above. After the experimenter announces the price, record it on line (2). On line (3) you can determine your total revenue by multiplying lines (1) and (2) together. Your profits from sales for the market year, line (5), are determined by subtracting your costs, line (4), from your revenue, line (3). This profit is yours to keep.

Do not be alarmed if your total profit in some market year is negative. This will sometimes happen and is not necessarily your fault. If however, you accumulate losses in excess of ____ francs during the course of the experiment, we will shut down your industry at that point. At the end of the experiment, add up your total profit in francs from each market year. Multiply your total profit by ____. This will tell you how many dollars you have earned. The experimenter will pay you this amount of money. You are free to make as much profit as you can.

Seller No. _____

Industry _____

INSTRUCTIONS
PHASE II

General
A price ceiling will no longer be imposed on the output of your industry. Due to this, however, you can no longer communicate with the other producers in your industry.

Market Organization
In each market year you must come to your own decision regarding how much output you will actually produce. To assist you in making your production decisions, you have been given a new profits table. This table is exactly the same as the one you were previously using with the exception that there is no longer a region printed in red.

Once you have come to a decision, you will submit your actual output to the experimenter who will add up the amounts produced by all producers in your industry to determine actual industry output. Again, using the market demand schedule, the price at which you could sell each unit of your output is determined. You will receive this price for each unit of output you produced. Your actual profit for the market year may then be calculated. The decisions made by producers in industries other than yours *will have again no effect* on your profits.

Trading and Recording Rules
In your folder you will find an ample supply of two types of forms. The first is labeled "Production Decision." When you make your actual production decision, write down the amount you have decided on and pass the form to the experimenter.

The second sheet (labeled "Profit Sheet") will be used to determine how much you earn. On line (1) of that sheet record your actual production decision, and on line (4) record your cost of producing your output. After all sellers have submitted their production decisions to the experimenter, the price that you will receive for each unit of output will be determined according to the rules given above. After the experimenter announces the price, record it on line (2). On line (3) you can determine your total revenue by multiplying (1) and (2) together. Your profits from sales for the market year, line (5), are determined by subtracting your costs, line (4), from your revenue, line (3). This profit is yours to keep.

Do not be alarmed if your total profit in some market year is negative. This will sometimes happen and is not necessarily your fault. If, however, you accumulate losses in the excess of ____ francs during the course of the experiment, we will terminate the experiment at that point. At the end of the experiment add up your total profit in francs from each market year. Multiply your total profit by ____. This will tell you how many dollars you have earned. The experimenter will pay you this amount of money. You are free to make as much profit as you can.

Seller No: _____

Industry _____

INSTRUCTIONS
(To Entrants)

General

This is an experiment in the economics of market decision making. The instructions are simple, and if you follow them carefully and make good decisions, you might earn a considerable amount of money, which will be paid to you in cash.

In this experiment we are going to simulate a market in which you will be producers and sellers in different industries for a sequence of market years. There are ____ other producers and sellers in your industry who are in another room. All producers in the same industry produce a product that is identical in all respects to the products produced by other sellers.

The type of currency used in this market is francs. All trading and earnings will be in terms of francs. Each franc is worth ____ dollars to you. Do not reveal this number to anyone. Notice that the more francs you earn, the more dollars you earn.

Attached to these instructions you will find two sheets. The first is labeled the market demand schedule. This schedule determines the price you receive for each unit of output that the industry produces. Each seller in the same market has the same market demand schedule.

The second sheet is your cost schedule. This schedule gives the costs you incur for producing different possible quantities. This information is for your own private use. Do not reveal this information to anyone since other sellers in your industry do not necessarily have the same cost schedule.

Market Organization

The market for your output is organized in a similar fashion to the experiment in which you previously participated. However, the other two producers in your industry will have completed 15 market periods prior to your entering the industry. Over these 15 periods the market has been organized in the following way:

1. During the first 10 period they were free to communicate with each other about which pairs of output they would produce. (Recall that during this part of the market there were certain pairs of outputs, given by a red region of the profits table, which you could *not* agree to produce.)

2. At the end of period 5, they were given the following announcement:

ANNOUNCEMENT

Beginning in period 11, a price ceiling will no longer be imposed on the output of your industry and all output combinations will be possible. At that time, however, you will no longer be able to communicate with the other producers in your industry. When the price ceiling is removed, you will only make an actual production decision in each market period. The profits you can earn are given in your profits table. All numbers currently in red will become black, and thus even if your actual production decision places you in the region of your table that is presently red, you will earn the amount listed there.

Beginning in period 16, there will be a third seller in your industry. You will not be able to communicate with this third seller prior to his entry into your industry. The new seller will have a cost schedule that is the same as either yours or the other seller in your industry. In other words, there is a 50-50 chance that he will have the same cost schedule as you, and if not, he will have the same cost schedule as the other producer in your industry. After this new seller enters your industry, your profit table will stay the same with the exception that the column/row currently labeled "Output Decision By Seller Number ___" will be relabeled "Total Output Produced by Other Sellers."

(This announcement will be given to the new seller in your industry when he or she arrives.)

3. Before beginning period 16, we will tell you the production decisions that the other two sellers in your industry have made during periods 11 through 15.

In each market year you must come to your own decision regarding how much output you will actually produce. To assist you in making your production decisions, you have been given a profits table. This table specifies your total profit for the market year, given your output and the output of the rest of your industry. Since this table has been computed using your cost schedule, this information is for your own private use. Do not reveal this information to anyone.

Once you have come to a decision you will submit your actual output to the experimenter who will add up the amounts produced by all producers in your industry to determine actual industry output. Using the market demand schedule, the price at which you could sell each unit of your output is determined. You will receive this price for each unit of output you produced. Your actual profit for the market year may then be calculated. The decisions made by producers in industries other than yours *will have again no effect on* your profits.

Trading and Recording Rules
In your folder you will find an ample supply of two types of forms. The first is labeled "Production Decision." When you make your actual production decision, write down the amount you have decided on and pass the form to the experimenter.

The second sheet (labeled "Profit Sheet") will be used to determine how much you earn. On line (1) of that sheet record your actual production decision, and on line (4) record your cost of producing your output. After all sellers have submitted their production decisions to the experimenter, the price that you will receive for each unit of output will be determined according to the rules given above. After the experimenter announces the price, record it on line (2). On line (3) you can determine your total revenue by multiplying lines (1) and (2) together. Your profits from sales for the market year, line (5), are determined by subtracting your costs, line (4), from your revenue, line (3). This profit is yours to keep.

Do not be alarmed if your total profit in some market year is negative. This will sometimes happen and is not necessarily your fault. If, however, you accumulate losses in the excess of ____ francs during the course of the experiment, we will terminate the experiment at that point. At the end of the experiment add up your total profit in francs from each market year. Multiply your total profit by ____. This will tell you how many dollars you have earned. The experimenter will pay you this amount of money. You are free to make as much profit as you can.

Notes

This research has been supported by NSF Grant SES-8218684. We thank James Friedman, Ted Keeler, and participants in the NSF/CMU Conference for suggestions, and Lisa Armstrong, Cynthia Carlson, Myra Hart, Sri Vaidyanathan, William Vigdor, and David Waldron for their assistance in conducting the experiments.

1. See, for example, Fouraker and Siegel (1963), Friedman (1963, 1967), or Holt (1985).

2. This is one of the types of constraints used in regulating the industries mentioned in the previous section; the other is the average cost constraint which requires the average of the average costs of firms in the industry be a specified fraction of the price charged. For a discussion of these two forms of industrywide regulation, see Daughety (1984).

3. Perhaps a more realistic penalty procedure would be to penalize firms in the current market year for past transgressions by adjusting the regulatory parameter. Unfortunately this would involve a dynamic game that would be too difficult to implement in a laboratory environment. Instead, industries were informed that if their individual decisions on actual output level generated an output vector that violated the constraint they would earn zero profits for the market year. This penalty is sufficient to ensure that no firm prefers to operate at these levels, thereby presumably leading firms to produce at a regulatory feasible outcome. As a secondary note, the complexity of representing the regulatory-infeasible output region restricted us from conducting regulated triopoly markets, which would have required a three-dimensional representation.

4. One might also consider perfect competition, but given the declining average costs of the linear parameter sets described in table 11.1, marginal cost pricing will not be an equilibrium.

5. A multiple leader model can be solved by having the leaders take the followers' reaction functions as given and then playing Cournot among themselves (see Daughety 1985; Sherali 1984). An alternative procedure for handling multiple leaders is to further subdivide the leaders into leaders and followers, thereby embedding Stackelberg games within Stackelberg games. We do not pursue this here.

6. Alternating strategies lead to an extended version of the Prisoner's Dilemma. As a repeated game (see Kreps et al. 1982 or Axelrod 1984) the collusive solution can be achieved through an extended version of the tit-for-tat strategy (see Daughety and Forsythe 1985b).

7. Other differences include (1) Friedman's experiments involve prices (not quantities) and (2) his subjects knew all payoffs. An aspect in common was that subjects did not know, a priori, the behavioral type of player they faced each time (in terms of their willingness to cooperate).

8. In Friedman (1967) messages are allowed.

9. Some of the outcomes are very close to equilibrium predictions, however. In particular, the final period outcomes in LAU1-2, LAU1-3, LAU1-4, LAU2-1, LAU2-2, LAU2-4, and LAK1-1 coincide or are very close (i.e., sellers' profits are each within $.03 per period) to the Cournot equilibrium predictions. Also LAK1-2 seems to have converged very near to the collusive equilibrium prediction. Experiment LAK1-4 is close to the S3 equilibrium prediction. It is also worth observing that LAK2-4 is close to a multiple-leader solution, with firm 1 as follower (see note 5).

10. In most laboratory studies an efficiency measure is used where the total surplus achieved is divided by the maximum possible surplus (see Plott and Smith 1978). Here, however, the maximum possible surplus changes after entry since the entrant must pay fixed costs. Thus we report only the total surplus of each observation. If the total surplus increases due to entry, then entry has been beneficial since the surplus more than covers the entrant's fixed costs.

11. The "Phases of the Moon" conspiracy was an alternating strategy. Furthermore "live and let live" equilibria (wherein firms in multiple markets are leaders in some markets and followers in other markets, thereby trading-off leadership and followership roles with each other) appear to occur, and thus the alternation is spatial rather than temporal.

12. This observation was suggested by Roger Noll and an anonymous referee.

References

Axelrod, R. 1984. *The Evolution of Cooperation*. New York: Basic Books.

Bailey, E. E., Graham, D. R., and Kaplan, D. P. 1984. *Deregulating the Airlines: An Economic Analysis*. Cambridge, Mass: MIT Press.

Baumol, W. J., Panzar, J. C., and Willig, R. D. 1982. *Contestable Markets and the Theory of Industry Structure*. New York: Harcourt Brace Jovanovich.

Call, G. D., and Keeler, T. E. 1985. "Airline Deregulation, Fares, and Market Behavior: Some Empirical Evidence." In A. Daughety, ed., *Analytical Studies in Transport Economics*. New York: Cambridge University Press.

Daughety, A. F. 1984. "Regulation and Industrial Organization." *Journal of Political Economy* 92:932–953.

Daughety, A. F. 1985. "Endogenous Information and Industrial Organization." University of Iowa Working Paper 84-34a.

Daughety, A. F., and Forsythe, R. 1985a. "Regulatory-Induced Industrial Organization: A Laboratory Investigation." University of Iowa Working Paper 85-31.

Daughety, A. F., and Forsythe, R. 1985b. "Regulation and the Formation of Reputations: A Laboratory Analysis." University of Iowa Working Paper 85-32.

Forsythe, R., Palfrey, T. R., and Plott, C. R. 1982. "Asset Valuation in an Experimental Market," *Econometrica* 50:537–567.

Fouraker, L. E., and Siegel, S. 1963. *Bargaining Behavior*. New York: McGraw-Hill.

Friedman, J. W. 1963. "Individual Behavior in Oligopolistic Markets: An Experimental Study." *Yale Economic Essays* 3:359–417.

Friedman, J. W. 1967. "An Experimental Study of Cooperative Duopoly." *Econometrica* 35:379–397.

Friedman, J. W. 1977. *Oligopoly and the Theory of Games*. Amsterdam: North Holland.

Graham, D. R., Kaplan, D. P., and Sibley, D. S. 1983. "Efficiency and Competition in the Airline Industry." *Bell Journal of Economics* 14:118–138.

Holt, C. A., 1985, "An Experimental Test of the Consistent Conjectures Hypothesis." *American Economic Review* 75:314–325.

Jordan, W. 1970. *Airline Regulation in America*. Baltimore: John Hopkins University Press.

Keller, T. 1972. "Airline Regulation and Market Performance." *Bell Journal of Economics* 3:399–424.

Kreps, D., Milgrom, P., Roberts, D. J., and Wilson, R. 1982. "Rational Cooperation in the Finitely Repeated Prisoner's Dilemma." *Journal of Economic Theory* 27:245–252.

MacAvoy, P. W., and Snow, J. W. 1977. *Regulation of Passenger Fares and Competition among the Airlines*. Washington, D.C.: American Enterprise Institute.

Plott, C. R. 1979. "The Application of Laboratory Experimental Methods to Public Choice." In C. S. Russell, ed., *Collective Decision Making: Applications from Public Choice Theory*. Washington, D.C.: Resources for the Future.

Plott, C. R., and Smith, V. L. 1978. "An Experimental Examination of Two Exchange Institutions." *Review of Economic Studies 45*: 133–153.

Sherali, H. D. 1984. "A Multiple Leader Stackelberg Model and Analysis." *Operations Research 32*: 390–404.

Smith, V. L. 1976. "Experimental Economics: Induced Value Theory." *American Economic Review 66*: 274–279.

Index

Administrative Procedure Act, 55
Adverse selection problem, 22, 23, 25, 28
Agency action
 Congressional monitoring of, 87–88
 and constituent groups, 88
 judicial review of, 45–68
 and policymaking, 55–67
Agricultural marketing boards, and induced voting behavior, 255–280
Agricultural price supports, 136–137
Airline deregulation, 142, 285–315, 378–379
 cost-function analysis of efficiency effects of, 285–315
 total factor productivity study of, 296–300
Alternating strategies, 357
Alternative economic policies, ordering of, 153–186
Americans for Democratic Action, 99, 101
Antitrust policy, 137–140, 378
Arrow-Debreu model, 11–12
Arrow's impossibility theorem, 173
Asbestos, and occupational disease, 321–343
Atomic Energy Commission, 230, 231
Auctions, as means of control, 13–14, 16, 20
Auditing, 24–25
Austen-Smith, D., 82
Automobile industry regulation, 56–59, 62–63
Averch-Johnson model, 4, 27

Bailey, E., 285
Bankruptcy constraints, 23, 342
Bargaining problems, 5
Baron, D., 22, 24, 27
Barten, A. P., 158
Barth, P. S., 337, 341, 342
Baumol, W. J., 191–192, 198–200, 202, 212
Bayesian probability, 237–238, 240
Beck, N., 99
Becker, G. S., 74, 78, 79, 80, 86
Behavioral effects of regulation, 347–379
Belgium, air carrier agreement with, 293
Bensel, R. F., 119
Bergson, A., 153
Bergstrom, T. C., 264

Bernhardt, M. D., 95
Bertrand-Nash assumption, 191–192, 201–205, 207, 210–212
Besanko, D., 24
Bigham, T. C., 105
Boden, L. I., 321–343
Brenner, M. A., 285
Breyer, S. G., 45–68
Brock, W. A., 200–201
Browne, S. D., 285
Bureau of Alcohol, Tobacco and Firearms, 48

Canada, airline regulation in, 287, 288, 291
Cartels
 agricultural marketing, 255–280
 in political decision making, 78–80
Cave, J., 255–280
Caves, D. W., 285–315
Chile, airline deregulation in, 287, 288
Christensen, L. R., 285–315
Civil Aeronautics Board, 288, 306
Clean Air Act of 1970, 133–134
Clodius, R. L., 260, 261
Coal Mine Health and Safety Act of 1969, 321
Coase theorem, 5
Collusive equilibrium, 356–358, 360–361, 369
Commitment, limited, 31–32
Comparative performance, 29–31
Competition, imperfect, 4, 378
Congruence property, 274
Consumer behavior, econometric model of, 154–163
Consumer groups, 60–61, 79, 136
Consumers' surplus, 199, 376, 377
Contestable markets hypothesis, 191–212
Control, government
 auctions as means of, 13–14, 16, 20
 hierarchy of, 6–11
 importance of, 11–12
 indirect control, 4, 5
 locus of, 14–17
 under nationalization, 8, 12
 under regulation, 8

Control, government (cont.)
  reasons for, 4–6
  residual control, 11
Cooperation, and industrywide regulation, 347–379
Core and periphery industrialized regions, 118–144
Cost-function analysis, of airline deregulation, 285–315
Cournot equilibrium, 356, 358, 360, 366, 369
Cournot quantity game, 264–265
Coursey, D., 191–192, 194–200, 202–203, 212
Courts. *See* Judicial review; Product liability litigation

Dalton, H., 175
Daughety, A. F., 347–379
Debtors, effect of government control on, 7–8
Demand functions, 153–154
Demand side model of regulation, 7
Demski, J., 29, 30
Denzau, A., 90
Department of Agriculture, 279
Department of Energy, 165
Department of Health and Human Services, 53
Department of Labor, 322
Department of Transportation, 56
Deregulation. *See also* Airline deregulation
  airline industry, 142, 285–315, 378–379
  and interest groups, 80
  and reputation formation, 349, 366–379
  railroad industry, 142
  trucking industry, 142
Diewert, W. E., 297
Dixit, A., 201
Downs, A., 82
Duopoly experiments, 194, 196, 198, 348–379
Dynamic General Equilibrium Model, 165, 166, 183

Eads, G., 343
Eckert, R., 89
Econometric model, of aggregate consumer behavior, 154–163
Economic interests, and regulatory structure, 89–99
Electric Power Research Institute, 228

Energy conservation programs, 134
Entry barriers, 197–200
Environmental Protection Agency, 52, 85, 97, 227, 230, 240
Environmental regulation, 5, 6, 133, 227
Equitable marketing opportunity, 257
Expenditure function, 154, 157, 160, 176, 177
Externalities, 5

Federal Communications Commission, 62
Federal Highway Administration, 63–64
Federal Power Commission, 62
Federal Trade Commission, 86, 90, 91
Fenno, R., 101
Finsinger, J., 29
Fiorina, M., 82–84, 89, 100
First-best outcome, 22–24, 29
Forsythe, R., 347–379
Foster, J. R., 285
Free rider problem, 8, 260, 264
Friedman, J. W., 353, 373
Friendly, Henry, 46, 48

Gas industry regulation, 132–133
  general equilibrium analysis of, 153–186
General equilibrium analysis, 14
  of natural gas price regulation, 153–186
Geographically distributive policies, 103–106
Geographic influences, on regulation, 118–144
Germany, air carrier agreement with, 293
Graham, D. R., 285
Greenwald, B., 4

Hammond, E. C., 324
Hammond, P. J., 171, 174
Harrison, G. W., 191–212
Heler, E., 334
Heston, R., 296, 308
History of regulation, 118–144
Holmstrom, B., 27
Household welfare function, 154
Hudson, E. A., 165

Incentive problem, 24
Information
  biased, 60
  dissemination of, 327–329
  imperfect, 4–7, 13, 16–18, 23–24, 28–29

perfect, 4
private, 22–25
probabilistic, 238
and regulatory behavior, 3–33
toxicity and exposure information, 325–329, 337, 340
and unobservable actions, 22
Ingberman, D., 82, 95
Institutional structure, 6–11, 81
Insurance coverage, and occupational disease litigation, 342
Insurance industry regulation, 4–5, 347
Interest groups, 80, 82
  cartel interests, 78–80
  constituent interests, 93–106
  consumer groups, 60, 61, 79
  support groups, 101–104
International Air Competition Act of 1979, 291
International Air Transport Association, 293, 294
International Civil Aviation Organization, 286, 294, 295, 306, 307, 308
Interstate Commerce Commission, 105
Isaac, R. M., 191–192, 194–200, 202–203, 212
Israel, air carrier agreement with, 293

Johnson, W. G., 334
Jones, C. A., 321–343
Jorgenson, D. W., 153–186, 307
Joskow, P. L., 89
Judicial review
  deferential attitude, 47, 49, 51, 52, 54, 55, 56
  independent attitude, 47, 48, 56
  of legal interpretations, 46–55, 65
  of policy decisions, 55–67

Kahn, A., 288
Kakalik, J. S., 335
Kalt, J. P., 93, 95, 99, 102, 103
Kaplan, D. P., 285
Kau, J. B., 99
Ketcham, J., 203
Klevorick, A., 73
Knieps, G., 201
Kramer, G. H., 73
Kravis, I. B., 296, 308
Krehbiel, K., 98–99

Laffont, J., 22, 24, 25
Land-use planning, 134
Landes, W. A., 328
Lau, L. J., 154
Legal interpretations by agencies, 46–55, 65
Legal issues, in occupational disease litigation, 329–332
Legislatures
  and constituent's interests, 93–106
  delegation of regulatory authority by, 83–84
  direct legislation by, 83–84
  dominance model of, 87–88
  geographically distributive policies of, 103–106
  ideological voting in, 94–99, 101–102, 103, 106–107
  models of, 81–108
  periodicity in activity of, 118
  pivots in, 90–93
  policy choice by, 85–86
  roll call voting, 94, 95, 98–100, 103, 105
Likelihood functions, 238
Linhart, P., 29
Loeb, M., 13, 23, 30, 191
Loury, G., 264
Luke, M., 197, 198, 199, 200, 203

Mackay, R., 90
Magat, W., 13, 23, 30, 191
Market allocation schemes, 259, 260
Marketing cartels, agricultural, 255–280
McCubbins, M., 85
McKee, M. J., 191–192, 194–197, 201–204, 212
Meyer, J. R., 285–286
Moe, T. M., 91–92, 99
Money metric individual welfare, 163–171
Money metric social welfare, 178–186
Moral hazard problem, 22–25, 29, 331–332, 342
Moran, M., 86, 90–91, 99, 105
Morrison, S. A., 287
Multiple regulators, 32
Myerson, R., 22

Nalebuff, B., 29, 30, 31
National Commission on Food Marketing, 261

National Highway Traffic Safety Administration, 56–59, 60, 62–63
National Labor Relations Board, 47, 51, 91, 107
Nationalization, 4, 5
 control hierarchy under, 8, 12
 similarity to nonnationalized firms, 8, 10
Netherlands, air carrier agreement with, 293
New Deal legislation, 122, 125–128, 143
New Zealand, airline deregulation in, 287, 288
Nuclear power regulation, 33
 licensing process, 231
 retrofit of existing plants, 228, 231
 risk analysis in safety decisions, 227–251
 uncertainty in risk assessment and management, 241–250
Nuclear Regulatory Commission, 227–228, 230–231, 237, 240–241, 247, 250

Occupational disease, 321–343
Occupational Safety and Health Act of 1970, 322
Occupational Safety and Health Administration, 96, 106–107, 137, 230
Oil industry regulation, 132–133
Olson, C. a., 334
Ordering of alternative economic policies, 153–186
Oster, C. V., Jr., 285–286

Palfrey, T. R., 353
Panzar, J. C., 191–192, 198–200, 202, 212
Pareto efficiency, 4, 12, 17, 153, 171, 173
Partial equilibrium analysis, 14–15
Paté-Cornell, M. E., 227–251
Peltzman, S., 74, 78–79, 93, 99, 101–102
Phillips, S., 90
Plott, C. R., 277, 278, 353
Policy decisions
 by agencies, 55–67
 by legislatures, 85–86
 judicial review of, 55–67
 research into policy formation, 73–108
Political Action Committees, 94, 95
Political economy. *See also* Legislatures; Voting models
 alliances behind regulation movement, 117–144
 core and periphery economies, 118–144

policy formation research, 73–108
 price theory of, 75
Political models, 81
Political parties, 77–78, 100, 118–119, 125–126, 131, 140, 143–144
Political power function, 79
Political representation, localism of, 118–119, 122, 126, 131, 140, 143–144
Pollak, R. A., 154, 176
Polyani, K., 117
Poole, K. T., 94, 95, 99, 100, 103, 104
Posner, R. A., 78, 328
Pricing
 Laspeyre's index, 29
 monopoly pricing, 14, 16, 17
Principal-agent model, 6–11, 19, 32, 88, 239
Prisoner's Dilemma game, 348
Probabilistic risk analysis, 228–251
Producer allotment schemes, 259, 262, 271–273, 276
Producers' surplus, 199
Product liability litigation, 322, 329–343
Profit maximization, and agricultural marketing cartels, 261, 275
Protectionism, 122, 125, 140–141
Public utility regulation, 4, 89, 125

Radner, R., 29
Railroad industry regulation, 142, 347
Railroad Retirement Board, 53
Ramsey prices, 14, 16
Rate setting bureaus, 347, 377
Reaction functions of firms, 356
Reciprocal Trade Agreements Act, 122, 125
Regulation, 4, 5, 7, 45, 75. *See also* Environmental regulation; Public utility regulation; Nuclear power regulation
Regulator-firm interaction, 18–32
Regulatory structure
 and economic behavior, 89
 and economic interests, 89–99
 and legislators' preferences, 82–85, 90
Rent extraction, 22, 25
 from established firms, 17–18
Reputation formation, 347–379
Reuter, P., 343
Riordan, M., 24, 30
Risk analysis
 in nuclear safety decisions, 227–251
 uncertainty in, 241–250
Risk aversion, 23, 29

Rivers, D., 98–99
Roberts, M. J., 105
Robson, J., 288
Romer, T., 73–108
Rosen, S., 334
Rosenthal, H., 73–108
Roy, R., 155
Rutstrom, E. E., 191, 192, 194, 203

Salant, Stephen W., 255–280
Samuelson, P. A., 153, 154
Sanders, E., 117–144
Sappington, D., 3–33
Scaling property, 274
Scheinkman, J. A., 201
Securities and Exchange Commission, 86
Self-selection, 25–26
Selikoff, I. J., 323, 332, 337
Sen, A. K., 171
Shareholders, control exercised by, 7, 11
Shephard, W. G., 201
Shepsle, K., 86, 90
Sibley, D., 28
Sinden, F., 29
Slesnick, D. T., 153–186
Smith, V. L., 191–192, 194–200, 202–203, 212
Social expenditure function, 176, 177
Social Security Board, 49–50
Social welfare function, 153, 157, 171–178
  money measures of, 178–186
Soviet incentive problem, 28
Spence, M., 200, 202, 264
Stackelberg equilibrium, 19, 356, 360, 363, 369
Stigler, G., 73–75, 77–78, 89, 198
Stiglitz, J., 3–33
Stoker, T. M., 154
Strip-mining regulation, 96–99, 102–104
Subsidies, 5, 13, 15, 23, 30, 80
Summers, A., 296, 308
Sunk costs, 197–200

Taggart, R., 27
Taxation, 5
  optimal, 14, 16–17
Taxicab markets, 89
Thaler, R., 334
Thayer, F. C., 285
Tirole, J., 22, 24, 25

Total factor productivity study, of airline deregulation, 296–300
Trading areas, 119
Tretheway, M. W., 285–315
Triopoly experiments, 355–379
Trucking industry regulation, 63–64, 142, 347, 377–378

Uncertainty, in risk assessment and management, 241–250
United Kingdom, air carrier agreements with, 293
Utility function, 154, 157, 158

Varian, H. R., 264
Viscusi, W. K., 334
Vogelsang, I., 29, 201
Volume, administrative committees restricting, 255–280
von Wiezsacker, C. C., 199
Voting behavior, of agricultural marketing boards, 255–280
Voting models, 77
  average characteristics models, 99–101, 103
  Congressional dominance model, 87–88
  constituent interest models, 93–106
  geographic redistribution in, 103–106
  ideological voting models, 81, 94–99, 101–102, 103, 106–107
  multidimensional voting, 86, 90
  pivotal decision makers, 90–93
  support group models, 101–104
  undimensional models, 81, 94–99, 101–102, 103, 106–107

Wage and price controls, 96, 134
Wage differentials, and workplace hazards, 325, 331, 332, 334, 337, 340, 341
Wallerstein, I., 118
Weingast, B. R., 86, 88, 90–91, 99, 105
Welfare
  comparisons, 153, 154, 163–171
  economics, 4
  individual, 154, 174
  money metric, 163–171
William, A. W., 203
Willig, R. D., 191, 192, 198, 199, 200, 202, 212
Windle, R. J., 285–315

Winston, C., 287
Workers' compensation, 330–331, 339–340

Zecher, R., 90
Zellner, A., 302
Zupan, A. M., 93, 95, 99, 102–103